Alex Fynn has advised both Arsenal and Spurs on advertising, the Football League on television contracts and the Football Association on commercial matters. He feels he is entitled to be called a football 'expert', as he was once selected for Queen's Park Rangers' Juniors. Unfortunately they were playing Watford at Vicarage Road, the dog track flooded, and the game was cancelled. He lives in north London with his wife and two daughters.

Lynton Guest is probably the only football writer who has had a No. 1 hit, when he played keyboards for The Love Affair on 'Everlasting Love'. He has always been passionately interested in sport and played football for Leicestershire as a schoolboy. Following an illness, he was forced to give up music and is now an established writer on sport. He is a regular contributor to the *Sunday Telegraph* and compiles the annual *Sunday Telegraph* 'Top 40 European Football Clubs'.

Alex Fynn and Lynton Guest also collaborated on *The Secret Life of Football*, an acclaimed critique of the English game.

Heroes and Villains

THE *INSIDE* STORY OF THE 1990–91 SEASON AT
ARSENAL AND TOTTENHAM HOTSPUR

ALEX FYNN AND LYNTON GUEST

PENGUIN BOOKS

For Bennett Fynn (Benvenuto Finelli)
and Amelia B. Maxwell

PENGUIN BOOKS

Published by the Penguin Group
Penguin Books Ltd, 27 Wrights Lane, London W8 5TZ, England
Penguin Books USA Inc., 375 Hudson Street, New York, New York 10014, USA
Penguin Books Australia Ltd, Ringwood, Victoria, Australia
Penguin Books Canada Ltd, 10 Alcorn Avenue, Toronto, Ontario, Canada M4V 3B2
Penguin Books (NZ) Ltd, 182–190 Wairau Road, Auckland 10, New Zealand

Penguin Books Ltd, Registered Offices: Harmondsworth, Middlesex, England

First published 1991
1 3 5 7 9 10 8 6 4 2

Printed in England by Clays Ltd, St Ives plc
Filmset in 10/12 Monophoto Baskerville

Contents

Acknowledgements

In addition to those directly featured in the book we would like to thank Tim 'Rixy' Bates, Chris Belt, Amanda Clark, Tom Clarke, Mark Delaney and friends, Richard 'the boy done' Duguid, Martin Duke, Patricia Felix, Gary Frankel, Mel Goldberg, John Harris, Pam Kemmey, Mark King, Joe Macgregor, Jonathan Martin, Steve Mono, Dermot Pereira, Derek Peter, Tony Reiff, Mike Roffey, Daniel, David and Paul Stern, and Mark Sutton.

Special thanks are due to Irving Benjamin, Graham Betts, David Dein, Darren Epstein, Cliff Findlay, George Graham, Morris Keston, Alban Lloyd, Denis Roach, Terry Venables, Tony Lacey, who has perfected the role of publishing *libero*, the football correspondents of the national, daily and Sunday Press, the *London Evening Standard, London Talkback Radio*, the late lamented *Talking Sport, Capital Gold*, and the Arsenal and Spurs fanzines, especially the *Gooner, Gunflash, One-nil Down Two-one Up, My Eyes Have Seen the Glory, Off the Shelf* and the *Spur*.

Acknowledgement is gratefully given to Times Newspapers Ltd for permission to reproduce plates 1–5, 9, 11–23 and 25, to Stuart Clarke for plates 6–8 and 24, and to Mark Leech for plate 10.

1

The Right to Dream

The unpredictable summer of 1990 was ushered in amid doom and despondency throughout English football, a mood that seemed to fit perfectly the dull June weather. Violence had disfigured the closing matches of the previous season, and the nation waited with bated breath, sustained by hysterical campaigns on the part of Government and media, for the barbarian onslaught to devastate Italy during the forthcoming World Cup. The one consolation for the gloom merchants was that the England team was probably not good enough to get into the second round of the competition, so the worst of the trouble would be confined to the first-phase games in Sardinia. This Mediterranean island, usually the idyllic haunt of well-heeled Italians and up-market European tourists, was now donning the look of a medieval fortress-town about to undergo a lengthy siege. Moreover, the prospects for a return to European competitions by English clubs were, it was generally agreed, about zero, while the Taylor Report which followed the Hillsborough disaster was forcing clubs towards the most radical and costly changes in spectator accommodation for a hundred years, an eventuality for which many were totally unprepared. Then suddenly, as the temperature began to rise, the whole world was turned upside down.

The first promising signs came with an announcement from the Football Trust that finance would be released to help clubs pay for the implementation of the Taylor Report. This, along with a reduction in the Government's pools levy, at least made the task facing cash-starved Football League clubs a little less daunting. These developments were followed by more good news as the expected bloodbath in Sardinia did not materialize. In fact the tournament passed off without any major incidents of violence, despite the best efforts of some of the British press. Then, wonder of wonders, the England team, after a hesitant start, began to make progress and was only unluckily deprived of a place in the final by the lottery of a penalty shoot-out. The achievement captivated the nation, with half the population, over 25 million people, watching the semi-final against West Germany on television. It was the third-highest TV rating of all time and the biggest ever audience for a sporting event. For perhaps the first time since the Blitz, London's evening rush-hour failed to take place, and the normally congested West End streets were eerily deserted by seven o'clock.

Football was once again in tune with the culture from which it sprang. Moreover, the vehicle of the renaissance had not been one of the great League clubs, but the national team. In those few short weeks the game revealed in its premier tournament just why it is the greatest game in the world and why it has always been the national game in Britain. Everywhere, prospects were discussed, argued over and debated, as each succeeding England match became an event, a common denominator for millions of people. Winning the fair-play award was also important, a symbol of sporting behaviour that had the power to help restore pride in the game at home, even among politicians. For so long in the past the British were associated with the concept of fair play, a heritage which has made the experience of recent years so catastrophic for the country which gave football to the world.

Hundreds of thousands, many of them born-again fans, made the pilgrimage to Luton to hail the return of Robson's heroes. Even the Minister for Sport, Colin Moynihan, announced a dramatic shift in his position. Moynihan had spent the previous three years advocating continued isolation from European competitions, and only two weeks before had described over 200 of his fellow citizens who were thrown out of Italy without being charged with any offences as the 'effluent tendency' of football supporters. The Government, the Minister now declared, fully supported the reintegration of English clubs into Europe.

The transformation in the fortunes of English football was under way. UEFA voted for a return by two clubs, while the knock-on effect of England's success began to be felt throughout the domestic game, as season-ticket sales and the value of sponsorship deals rose. If any proof were needed to support the contention that success for the national team stimulates success at every other level of the game, *Italia 90* provided it in abundance.

In the north London district of Highbury, the streets surrounding Arsenal's famous old stadium were usually rather sleepy places at this time of year, but summer 1990 saw the residents' traditional respite from the hustle and bustle that sweeps the area during the football season rudely shattered by the comings and goings of builders and their vehicles. Like every other First and Second Division club, Arsenal were beginning to carry out the recommendations of the Taylor Report, by installing more seats, thus reducing the capacity of the ground to 47,000 for the coming season. The new accent on safety procedures also made it necessary to allocate extra turnstiles and exits to visiting supporters, although the overall number of places for away fans was cut. In addition, work was being carried out on a new media centre, a first-aid complex and an access route to the pitch for emergency vehicles. The South Stand terracing was reduced and the stadium comprised 18,000 seats, 29,000 standing places and fifty-three executive boxes.

At White Hart Lane, it was business as usual. Perhaps it is the location of the Spurs stadium on a busy main road, perhaps the fact that a public company trades all year round and is no respecter of such unbusinesslike concepts as seasons, but the ground always gives the impression of being at the centre of things, even during the close season. The reason for the air of importance is that while the football club may be the jewel in the crown of Tottenham Hotspur plc, Spurs is no longer just a football club. It is a sports and leisurewear business, a travel company and a computerized ticket operator. It publishes books and sells videos through its own outlets and by mail order, and it has even endorsed its own credit card.

There was little evidence of construction work at White Hart Lane during the 1990 summer, since changes to the stadium had been taking place since the late 1970s, when the decision had been taken to construct the new West Stand, an event that almost left the club bankrupt and led to the takeover by Irving Scholar in 1983. Major refurbishment of the East Stand had cut ground capacity in 1989–90 (although it added thirty-six executive boxes, which, when added to the seventy-two in the West Stand, made Tottenham's the highest total in the League), but the architects' plans had to be changed at the last minute to retain the famous Shelf as a standing area after a campaign by supporters. Now the Taylor Report and its requirement for all-seat stadia meant that the Shelf would eventually have to go. Still, at least White Hart Lane already had a better than average seat-to-standing ratio, and for the new season capacity was set at 35,000, of which half would be seated.

The air of unreality generated by events during and following the World Cup seemed to permeate everything. Arsenal were League Champions in 1988–89 with a team largely based on home-grown talent, at least eight of whom could reasonably have expected to be in with a chance of inclusion in Bobby Robson's final selection for the World Cup. In the event, Alan Smith, David Rocastle, Nigel Winterburn, Brian Marwood, Michael Thomas, Tony Adams, Paul Davis and Lee Dixon, who had all been in the England squad at various stages of the qualifying competition, did not make the plane to Italy. The only Arsenal player who did was one who had never kicked a ball for the club, David Seaman, the third-choice England goalkeeper transferred from Queen's Park Rangers shortly before the start of the tournament. Spurs meanwhile, who had not won anything since the UEFA Cup in 1984, had two players in the England team. Gary Lineker was an automatic first choice, while Paul Gascoigne emerged as one of the stars of the tournament and, in Franz Beckenbauer's words, 'became the major influence on the [England] side'.

Transfer arrivals also suffered from the wind of change blowing through the English game. Spurs' usual policy was to buy players before the start of the season to excite the fans and improve the team. Chairman Irving Scholar once explained the difference between the two north London clubs, saying, 'Arsenal will spend £1 million on a solid, safe defender, while we will spend £1½ million on an exciting, erratic attacker.' At the Annual General Meeting in December 1989, however, it was made clear that Spurs' finances had suffered a downturn and no money would be available for new players until all ground improvements were completed. This turn of events resulted in some friction between Scholar and manager Terry Venables, which was not surprising given that Spurs had not long before sold Chris Waddle to Marseille for over £4 million. Venables had wanted to make an offer to Glasgow Rangers for Terry Butcher but was told that there was no possibility of Spurs paying the kind of fee the England international would command, nor would another large addition to the wages bill be sanctioned. So only two signings were completed in the close season, both low-key deals involving players who were not likely to claim an immediate first-team place. Tottenham paid Dundee £30,000 for John Hendry, a 20-year-old centre forward, while Justin Edinburgh, a left back, arrived from Southend for £150,000. Financial constraints were never allowed to be forgotten, though, as even the low-budget Edinburgh transaction almost never took place. The player had been on loan to Spurs during the 1989–90 season and Venables wanted to make the move permanent. The board procrastinated, however, and a positive decision was only forthcoming when Plymouth Argyle made an offer for the defender. For Spurs to be outbid by Plymouth for a promising youngster would have been ignominy indeed. The transfer that caused the most interest concerned a departure, as John Polsten left the club. It was not the player who aroused the passions of the Spurs faithful but the club to which he had been sold. Yet another Spurs 'reject' was about to head along the M11 to Norwich, the ex-Spurs academy in East Anglia, which has made a speciality of turning players supposedly not good enough to wear the white shirt into outstanding First Division performers.

Arsenal, the bastion of good housekeeping, the club that rarely spends ostentatiously, contrarily splashed out £3.6 million on three players. In addition to David Seaman, George Graham bought Andy Linighan from Norwich and Swedish international Anders Limpar from the Italian club Cremonese. The outlay was only partially offset by the sales of John Lukic, Kevin Richardson and Martin Hayes for a total of £2.4 million. Still, some things never change. While most supporters would agree that it was a lack of goals that characterized the post-Championship malaise in

1989–90, Arsenal, invariably true to their history and bearing out Irving Scholar's analysis, spent the majority of the cash on two defenders.

There were also changes in the coaching staff at Highbury for the new season, following the departure of assistant manager Theo Foley to Northampton Town after four years as Graham's number two. Foley's position was filled by the promotion of Stewart Houston, the ex-Manchester United defender who had guided the Arsenal reserve team to the Combination title, while George Armstrong, a contemporary of George Graham in the 1971 double side, returned to the club as reserve team coach.

Having no Arsenal players in the England squad hurt the club's vice-chairman, David Dein, deeply. Nevertheless, he made a point of going to all of England's World Cup games up to the semi-final. Few would have travelled in similar style. Dein arrived in Cagliari Bay on board his yacht, *Take it Easy*, which he had sailed across the Mediterranean from Antibes in the South of France. By contrast, Irving Scholar could only find the time to attend the semi-final and final. Their differing experiences had one thing in common, though. Both of them realized the importance of what they had witnessed to their own clubs. It was now more vital than ever to get their respective teams back into Europe. Furthermore, it had become increasingly obvious that the future well-being of English football was bound up with the success of the national team.

Back home in England, as searing heat pushed up temperatures to record levels, the decision-makers of English football almost managed to undo all the good that the World Cup had achieved. It would be tempting to put the collective madness down to the abnormal sunshine. Unfortunately, the Football League has often distinguished itself by its propensity to make absurd decisions in the face of what, to the vast majority of football supporters, is obvious logic. On this occasion the League chairmen sat down to consider a proposal from Ken Bates of Chelsea to increase the number of clubs in the First Division from twenty to twenty-two.

The move was opposed by the Football Association, in the person of its chief executive Graham Kelly, and by the newly appointed England manager Graham Taylor. However, in the run up to the meeting it was clear that there was going to be a big majority in favour of expansion. Seeing the way the situation was developing, Irving Scholar did not attend the gathering. David Dein not only went to the meeting, he made a strong plea to keep the status quo, which itself had only been established for three years. Dein appreciated the rationale behind the proposal, to bring cash-hungry First Division clubs two more home games per season, raising revenue accordingly. Arsenal would benefit more than most from the extra matches, but in Dein's view it was a short-term, short-sighted benefit. It went against the trend in the rest of Europe, would not raise the overall quality of First Division football and was incompatible with the interests of the national team. Quality not quantity was the cornerstone of his position. 'We [the League chairmen],' he argued, 'have openly defied a request from the FA and are basically going against a new England manager, which I think is morally wrong.' Despite Dein's efforts, the Bates line won the day and the League decided to increase the First Division by two, with only Arsenal, Spurs and Manchester United voting against the motion.

At Highbury and White Hart Lane the new season brought particular challenges. After two and a half years in the manager's job at Spurs, Terry Venables had now to produce the goods; perhaps it would be his last chance. Similarly, players like Gascoigne and Lineker, in whom the club had shown its faith by rejecting reported approaches from Juventus and Torino, had, as Venables remarked, 'to do for Spurs what they have done for England'. For Arsenal, 1989–90 could justifiably be viewed as a year of reaction to the Championship-winning season, as several key players lost form at the same time. The 1990–91 season would reveal whether that title triumph was a diverting one-off, or whether the club really possessed the ability and the strength in depth to challenge Liverpool's dominance of English football. The former would be a confirmation of George Graham's greatest fear. 'I don't want to be a one-season wonder,' he said. 'I would hate to be that.'

The fruits of England's performances in Italy began to be tasted when season-ticket purchases shot up by 20 per cent at both clubs. Spurs took over £3 million in advance sales and, a month before the season started, announced a sell-out for the first home game against Manchester City. The ever-ambitious Irving Scholar mounted a radio advertising campaign in an attempt to exploit the favourable marketing conditions and sustain the same level of interest in subsequent matches. With the excitement generated by the World Cup, a good start to the new season would almost certainly see Spurs playing to capacity crowds up to Christmas. Suddenly, 1990–91 took on an almost mystical significance. The history books were consulted and it was confirmed that in 1900–1901 Spurs had won the Cup. The feat was repeated in 1920–21, 1960–61 and 1980–81. League titles had come in 1950–51 and 1960–61, which was also the season of the double, and the League Cup was won in 1970–71. Could it be that 1990–91 was going to be the year of the cockerel?

The scene was set then, for the beginning of a season of real import for both of these famous clubs. Arsenal and Spurs. The emotions stirred by the two names will be recognized, not only in London, but in any football city where local rivalries are far more intense affairs than those thrown up in the mundane world of unrelenting League matches against changing opposition. But first came the warm-up games. For Spurs, there was a generally successful tour to Ireland, Norway and Scotland, during which Paul Gascoigne made headlines for being booked twice and substituted once. He was also responsible, according to local reports, for a crowd of over 18,000 turning up to see a 1–1 draw at Hearts. Arsenal's rehearsal consisted primarily of participation in the Makita pre-season tournament at Wembley, which featured matches against Aston Villa and Sampdoria. After brushing Villa aside 2–0 with a spectacular goal from Anders Limpar and a second-half piece of opportunism from Kevin Campbell, Arsenal were defeated 1–0 in the final by the Italians. Despite the loss of the Makita trophy, which the club had held since its inception in 1988, George Graham saw the games as an opportunity to integrate his new signings. Taking comfort from the team's overall performance, he said: 'We have played against one of the sides that won a European competition [Sampdoria were holders of the Cup-Winners' Cup] and hit the woodwork three times.' In a domestic context, Arsenal's display promised much.

A note of poignancy was clearly in the air at Wembley with the realization that League runners-up Aston Villa, beaten so comprehensively, would be one of the two English teams to play in Europe. For both Arsenal and Spurs the goal is the same. They must get back into European competitions. Only this, they believe, will allow them to produce teams that can take on the best in the world. For David Dein and the rest of the Arsenal board, ever mindful of the club's traditions, it would help them towards their goal of restoring the reputation of Arsenal to what it had once been and to what they regard as its rightful place, that of the most famous football club in the world. For Irving Scholar and Tottenham Hotspur plc, Europe would bring with it the chance of corporate expansion and increased revenue. Of course, if the UEFA decision had been made twelve months earlier, Arsenal would have been playing in the European Cup, but, like others, their chance had gone. Spurs, meanwhile, could never imagine a better time for the team, promising in recent years but always ultimately disappointing, to realize its potential and return to the European stage.

Any true supporter of either club, however, already knew that the really big game in the early months of the new season would come on 1 September. The Football League fixture computer, which often reveals a perversity that would not shame its human masters, threw up the north London derby earlier than usual. No matter what the temperature by then, Highbury would that day be one of the hottest spots in Europe.

2

The Gascoigne Factor

It was a moment of supreme bliss for all England supporters. For over twenty years the most creative players the country had produced were either under-used or unable to transfer the skills they displayed for their clubs to the international arena. In their opening match of the 1990 World Cup Finals in Italy, an uninspired performance against Jack Charlton's Irish team did not bode well for England's chances against the more accomplished Dutch side, which contained the European Footballer of the Year, Marco Van Basten, and his two colleagues at Milan, Ruud Gullit and Frank Rijkaard. But just before half-time, Paul Gascoigne received the ball near the Dutch goal-line on the left side of their penalty area. Sweeper Ronald Koeman moved across from the centre of defence to block off the route goalward, while a forward, tackling back, harried Gascoigne from behind. There seemed no danger to the Dutch goal. Gascoigne, however, had other ideas. A perfect flick back left the two Dutchmen bemused, Gascoigne turned into the space created by Koeman's absence and delivered a wickedly hit low cross that Gary Lineker failed to reach by the narrowest of margins. It was the kind of exquisite manoeuvre of which Johan Cruyff himself would have been proud, and it signalled at last the emergence of an England midfield player who could actually deliver the goods at the highest level.

When Gazza ran on to the pitch of a sold-out White Hart Lane for the first match of the 1990–91 season, he was arguably the world's most famous Englishman, a status secured by the very public shedding of tears on an unforgettable night in Turin when England dramatically went out of the World Cup. Few sportsmen in Britain have experienced the kind of media and public attention that Gascoigne now commanded, perhaps only George Best and Ian Botham in the last generation. There had been many pretenders to the superstar crown, two of them surprisingly bought by Arsenal. Charlie Nicholas had arrived in 1983 from Celtic to the kind of publicity Gascoigne was now receiving, and supporters with long memories still feel embarrassed at the mention of Peter Marinello's name. These two, like so many others, proved incapable of living up to their advance billing. It could have turned out the same for Gascoigne. But, quite apart from his unique talent, he was the beneficiary, first, of the kind of fortune that eluded his predecessors, then, of the misfortunes of others, notably the England captain Bryan Robson. When Bobby Robson first picked Gascoigne to play for England, the player received the kind of media hype that had accompanied the selection of many gifted players in the past. Glenn Hoddle was given his first chance by Ron Greenwood in a European Championship qualifying match at Wembley against Bulgaria in 1979, and his inclusion in the team followed precisely the sort of press campaign that attended Gascoigne's call-up. Hoddle scored a brilliant volleyed goal on his début but was not chosen to play in the next three England matches. 'I'm convinced,' wrote Hoddle in his book, *Spurred to Success*, 'that [had I been retained] I would have justified my place. Not only that but my entire career might have been completely different.' Greenwood said Hoddle had to learn that football was full of ups and downs and the manager never considered building his team around Hoddle's extravagant talents. Hoddle maintained that this attitude, which continued into Bobby Robson's era, affected his confidence at international level, and, despite the fifty-three caps which the Spurs midfielder won, he felt that England had never really seen the best of him.

This mental block in accommodating potentially great players, including Peter Osgood, Tony Currie, Stan Bowles, Charlie George and Frank Worthington, could so easily have afflicted Gascoigne. Indeed, after coming on as a substitute against Albania in a World Cup qualifying tie he clearly left the England manager in a state of shock. 'We need two balls,' Robson said, 'one for him, one for the team . . . at one time I thought he was going to play in the front row of F Stand, because he played all over the pitch except the position I told him to play in. But we do have a precocious talent.'

The manager must have quickly regained his equilibrium, as he was sufficiently emboldened to start Gascoigne for only the second time in eight appearances three months before *Italia 90* in a game against Czechoslovakia. Robson was rewarded by a scintillating performance. The new star of the England team set up three goals and scored one in a 4–2 victory.

'Gascoigne passed the test tonight,' said Robson. 'If he repeats that sort of display I can trust him.' Later, Gazza himself saw the performance as his greatest display. 'When people say to me the game against Holland or against West Germany was my best,' he said, 'I will not have any of it. Without doubt, it was the game against the Czechs – because it got me to Italy.'

His stunning contribution in that game did indeed ensure his selection in Robson's squad of twenty-two for the World Cup. However, it was by no means certain that he would be in the starting line-up for the first-round matches. The England manager still sounded cautious whenever Gascoigne's name was mentioned, and on the eve of the tournament he claimed that the player was something of a luxury, who could only be effective if he had the steadying influence of Bryan Robson next to him to keep the team's shape if Gazza had a rush of blood. It could have been four years before, and he could have been talking about Glenn Hoddle.

To be fair to Bobby Robson, when the crunch came he was prepared to stick by the man he had previously seen as wayward and irresponsible. This was in marked contrast to the way, like Greenwood before him, he rarely felt able to put his faith in Hoddle. Indeed Robson once said to Hoddle, 'You are the most skilful footballer in England, but there's no place for you in my team.' The circumstances of his change of heart over Gascoigne, though, were entirely out of the manager's control. Just as in Mexico in 1986, injury to Bryan Robson put him out of the World Cup, and, also as in Mexico, the unhappy turn of events for the captain coincided with a dramatic improvement in England's performances. With doubts continuing about the fitness of Steve Hodge and Neil Webb, and with Steve McMahon finding the step up to the highest level difficult, Gascoigne seized his chance.

When the moment of truth arrived, the very traits which had previously attracted criticism ensured that Gascoigne would be equal to the task. A common description of the Geordie on his arrival in London was that although talented, he was also arrogant, money-orientated and underachieving – just like the club that had bought him. For the late Jackie Milburn, perhaps the most popular player to have played for Newcastle, Gazza's show in Italy would have been entirely predictable. 'I think it's about thirty-five years since I've seen a kid as good as . . . this lad,' Wor Jackie enthused in 1988, 'and I just cannot believe the skills on him. He's got everything, everything. Two and a half years ago I wrote after I saw him in the youth team, "this fellow's the next England captain". There's no holding him. He's the best in the world. Honestly, the best in the world.' Unlike so many creative players, including England team-mate John Barnes, Gascoigne's arrogant side gave him the confidence to turn it on when it really mattered, just like George Best could.

Perhaps the best example of this came in the 118th minute of the second-round game against Belgium. Gascoigne received the ball on the edge of his own penalty area looking so tired that all he could manage was a pass back to goalkeeper Shilton. Having given everything over ninety minutes and extra time, both teams now looked to have settled for a penalty shoot-out. The Belgian players around Gascoigne were momentarily lulled into a false sense of security. Suddenly, he turned and surged out of defence on a storming run that took him into the opposing half, where the Belgians were happy to bring him down and regroup before the free kick was taken. It was this free kick, delivered with precision by Gascoigne, that led to David Platt's strike that put the game beyond the reach of Scifo and company. The Belgians had been not so much outplayed as outwitted.

It was incidents such as this that cemented Gascoigne's growing worldwide reputation as a player. The inch-perfect free kick, struck in a typical flat arc, which landed on Mark Wright's head for the winner against Egypt; conceding a penalty against Cameroon yet having the presence of mind to surge forward and help win one back with a superb ball to Gary Lineker; the overall display against West Germany, particularly after he had recovered from the shock of being booked – all led to accolades from around the world. Gascoigne appeared in numerous 'World Elevens', including those of the most important football magazines in Germany and Spain, *Der Kicker* and *Don Balon* respectively. Franz Beckenbauer remarked, 'I like him very much. If I were the president of a club, Paul Gascoigne would be one of the first I would buy.' Bobby Robson's successor as England manager, Graham Taylor, was in no doubt about Gascoigne's impact on *Italia 90*. 'Without being accused of bias or patriotism,' he said, 'I think Paul Gascoigne has to be seen as the discovery of the tournament. A lot of the opposition . . . are full of admiration for him. He has this tremendous ability to go past people with very quick feet, very quick surges as well, which open up things for other people. [This is] coupled with the ability to put [in] some telling through-passes from the centre of the midfield. And it is particularly important when you have people with the pace of Gary Lineker that you have someone who can see these runs and measure passes through for them.'

The Spanish newspaper *El Pais*, commenting on Gazza's selection in its 'Best Team' feature, said, 'Paul Gascoigne, the English midfielder, was the player with most character. His displays on the pitch were contagious. He covered more kilometres than anyone and still had enough energy left not to lose his smile.' This perceptive analysis touches on a point which, until then, had been neglected by Gazza-watchers in England. For years, various managers from Alf Ramsey down had been suspicious of the gifted individual. It had become a cliché that such players did not contribute to the team in terms of work-rate and could not be relied upon when the going got tough. Such opinions became so ingrained, few noticed that, alongside the mesmeric skills, Gascoigne is also a tireless work-horse, always prepared to try to win the ball as well as use it, even when things are not going well. Unfortunately, this enthusiasm has also led him to commit fouls, argue with referees and retaliate against opponents, which all too often have led to avoidable bookings.

Accident, then, rather than design, had presented Gascoigne with his opportunity. The jinx to Bryan Robson meant that Bobby Robson had to restructure his team for the second World

Cup running. The luxury had become a necessity and Gascoigne's antics were set to endear him to the world. The joking, the obvious enjoyment, the rapport with the fans (he looks like one of them and but for an accident of ability would probably be one of them), let alone the rest of his repertoire, fooled opponents and turned a footballer into a star, a larger-than-life figure who now transcended the sport that spawned him. Back home, the inevitable bandwagon began to roll.

Offers from Italian football were expected to follow Gascoigne's World Cup performances. Gianni Agnelli, president of Juventus, had shown interest when he described the player as 'a dog of war with a face like a child'. Terry Venables immediately announced that, as far as he was concerned, any sale of Gascoigne would be a matter for resignation. He told reporters, 'While I am manager at White Hart Lane there is no way Gazza will be allowed to leave.' Venables could be forgiven his outburst since he made clear how he had received hate-mail after having spent £2 million of Spurs' money to buy Gascoigne in July 1988. The manager also recanted the words he used when selling Chris Waddle to Marseille. 'I said at the time that every player has his price. But Gazza . . . has changed my mind.' Now, according to Venables, even a world-record bid could not tempt him to part with his star performer.

While speculation mounted in England, however, Agnelli was having second thoughts. The Juve boss toyed with the idea of paying a reputed £500,000 for an option on Gascoigne's services should Tottenham decide to sell in the future, but soon abandoned it on the advice of his staff. Gascoigne, they reasoned, was far too volatile to make the grade in the Italian League. The conclusion was that Italian opponents would goad him mercilessly until he snapped. Gazza wouldn't last a game in Italy, they said, and, anyway, he would find it difficult to accept the rigorous methods used to prepare players for matches there. Moreover, they guessed that he could not survive without frequent visits back home to the North-East and his old drinking mates. Gary Lineker underlined the point when he described Gascoigne as a player for 'home consumption'. Despite Agnelli's view, European interest in Gascoigne's availability continued and Bobby Robson spoke wistfully of buying the player for his new employers at PSV Eindhoven, though he realized he would have to 'sell the club' to fund the purchase. Waxing ever more lyrical, Robson claimed, 'Gazza is the finest player to emerge under me in eight years.' Bryan Robson spoke in similar vein, saying, 'All through my years I have never met a player as skilful as Paul Gascoigne.' Considering Robson played alongside Glenn Hoddle, Kevin Keegan and Trevor Brooking during his England career, this was praise indeed.

In fact, Venables need not have worried, at least in the short term. No firm offer had yet been made for Gascoigne, but, even if a bid had been received, Irving Scholar, despite the club's financial problems, fully realized that selling Gascoigne was simply not an option at this stage. Not only would he be crucified by fans and media, but Gascoigne represented, along with Gary Lineker, Spurs' best chance to win a trophy, fulfil the ambition to get back into Europe and turn the club's finances around. Scholar even went so far as to take advice on how he could help with plans for the marketing of Gascoigne, which was the only way he could hope to match the kind of money on offer abroad. In addition, staying in England, at any rate for a couple of years, might actually be in Gazza's best financial interests. In Italy, he would be one of a number of stars, Italians such as Baggio and Schillaci and imports like Martin Vasquez and Lothar Matthäus, and there was still the ominous presence of Diego Maradona in Naples. In England, Gascoigne was unique and would have the lucrative marketing field more or less to himself.

From the moment he appeared on the open-top bus that took the returning England squad through the packed streets of Luton, in false breasts and stomach, Gascoigne was front-page news virtually every day. Jimmy Greaves referred to each of the nation's popular newspapers in turn as the 'Daily Gazza'. In the world of the tabloids, anything goes when a star is discovered, and Gascoigne began to feel the kind of pressure their attentions can bring when news of his love-life was splashed across the front pages. However, Gazza had signed up exclusively with the *Sun* for a reported £120,000 (a deal negotiated by editor Kelvin Mackenzie himself), so he could hardly complain if other sections of the popular press tried to keep up with the *Sun*'s scoop. In fact, it is a measure of Gascoigne's success that the *Sun*'s arch rival, the *Daily Mirror*, along with the rest of the press, actually found positive stories, and did not attempt to detract from the legend in any way.

The commercial exploitation of the Gazza name now went into overdrive, organized by his advisers, Len Lazarus, an accountant, and a lawyer, Mel Stein. A boot and clothes deal, videos, a recording contract, a poster magazine, an autobiography, a Christmas calendar, a computer game and the obligatory T-shirt were just a few of the activities revealed as part of the Gazza merchandising plan. The diminutive name itself – Gazza – was also to be registered as a trademark. All this meant that during the 1990–91 season, Gascoigne could expect to gross up to £1 million from sources other than football, and that would be only the beginning. It is not a huge amount when compared to the incomes of Nick Faldo, Boris Becker or Diego Maradona, but for a British footballer it is a figure never bettered, even by that most prolific of earners, Kevin Keegan. Despite the hype, Lazarus and Stein went out of their way to emphasize that they were not simply in the business of milking the Gascoigne name for all it was worth.

'We are only proceeding with these deals where we are satisfied with the companies plus the quality and image of the product, to protect Gazza's good character,' Lazarus commented. 'We have said no to a number of offers because we are not happy with the quality. We want to be sure that if somebody buys a Gazza-endorsed article they will be happy with it.' For his part, Gascoigne made it plain he did not think that money would override other considerations, like those visits to his native North-East. Displaying image-consciousness for perhaps the first time, he declared, 'I know I could earn loads more by agreeing to do extra personal appearances or taking on more contracts but that's not for me. Playing football is my whole life and after that it's about relaxation and going fishing.'

Another fisherman, Jack Charlton, was in no doubt about Gascoigne's elevation to the realm of the gods. Charlton was in charge at Newcastle when Gazza was first offered professional terms, at the age of seventeen. Now manager of the Republic of

Ireland, he was uncharacteristically fulsome in his appraisal of Gascoigne's new status. 'There's no going back,' he declared. 'A megastar had been created. It's frightening how much pressure is going to be put on the lad now – on and off the field ... But Gazza can live with being a megastar. He has that special thing that separates the great players from the very good ones.'

After the World Cup performances and the media build-up, the pressure on Gascoigne to be at the top of his form in the first game of the new season was, as Jack Charlton predicted, mounting. In club terms, was he really a new George Best or would he prove to be more of a Peter Marinello? The player himself seemed to have managed to put any self-doubt he may have had behind him, and felt he had answered his critics in Italy. Yet some of the things the detractors had said obviously hurt. Gazza told readers of the *Sun*: 'It's not that long ago that people like Tommy Smith [the former Liverpool defender] were saying that I was the joke of the First Division. He said I would be better off in a circus than playing football. Well who's the embarrassment now – Tommy Smith or myself?'

During the pre-season games, crowds flocked to see Gazza everywhere, and White Hart Lane was full to the rafters for the season's first League encounter against Manchester City. Outside the ground, tickets were being touted at three times their face value. Spurs' fans were not to be disappointed. Apart from a dazzling goal which sealed the 3–1 win, Gascoigne managed to combine skilful football and entertainment for the crowd in about equal measure. The two sides of the Gazza character came together when he brought the ball out of defence, beating two players in the process, laughing and gesticulating, beside himself with glee at what he had just done.

The match gave Spurs a perfect beginning to the new season. Gascoigne's contribution was in many ways overshadowed by Gary Lineker, who scored the first two goals, showing his appetite for life in the English First Division was undiminished. Deficiencies in defence were punished only once, by the head of ex-Arsenal player Niall Quinn. The defensive limitations made it all the more difficult to understand the sale of John Polsten to Norwich, but it could not be denied that Spurs had provided what the crowd wanted: excitement, goals, and a winning start. The worldwide interest in the game can be seen from the fact that the Football League, which produces a weekly television programme of League action for sale overseas, overturned its usual policy of concentrating on the Champions for the first show of the new season and featured the Spurs–Manchester City clash as its main game.

None the less, doubts about the team's ability to lift the championship for the first time since 1961 remained. George Best never had the chance to perform on the global stage that the World Cup has now become, but he reigned supreme in European Cup matches, making his international reputation with match-winning displays on opponents' grounds, particularly at Benfica, where he destroyed the Portuguese team almost singlehanded in a 5–1 victory for Manchester United in the quarter-final of the 1966 European Cup. Best was just nineteen. He was voted European Footballer of the Year in 1968. But he also produced the goods week in, week out, on First Division grounds in this country, as United won the League twice in three years. To be considered in the same breath, Gazza must do the same. It should be remembered, however, that Best had Bobby Charlton and Denis Law around him, not to mention Nobby Stiles, Brian Kidd and Pat Crerand. Apart from Gary Lineker, there was little evidence in the game against Manchester City that Spurs possessed players even approaching the class of these illustrious names.

George Best himself had a few harsh words to say about the comparison. 'There are plenty of reasons why he [Gascoigne] won't last,' Best predicted. 'The main one, sad to say, is that he's just not good enough. Forget the hype, he's light years away from being the best player on earth. He's not even world-class, not by the biggest stretch of the imagination. He's been set up as a false idol. He's being hailed as a superstar because there aren't any, there's a void. There's more to the making of a superstar than a couple of fair games in an abysmal World Cup . . . I survived [for ten years at the top] because I was the best . . . twenty years ago he would have been another average midfield player.'

Observer columnist Hugh McIlvanney took up the argument,

writing, 'it is worth remembering that the pop cult that grew around George Best in the sixties was a far more organic, less contrived process, rooted as it was in a ratio of magnificent performances to adulation that Gascoigne cannot approach ... no footballer bred in these islands in my lifetime has come close to rivalling Best's incredible amalgam of gifts.'

The Gazza promotional machine was not at all affected by such scepticism. Gazza was a star, the World Cup had proved it, and the nation couldn't get enough of him. Even Arsenal supporters had to revise their opinions of the player. 'Gazza,' according to an editorial in *Gunflash*, the Arsenal supporters' magazine, 'has now become a completely different person to my red and white eyes. He came of age in the Holland match and I heard myself saying "this bloke ain't a bad player".' Learned articles were produced to explain the phenomenon, one by a Research Fellow at Caius College, Cambridge, comparing Gazza with the great athletes of ancient Greece. Charles Nevin, writing in the *Guardian*, saw Gascoigne's popularity among teenage girls as stemming from the lack of suitable pop-star role models. 'There is an interregnum,' he intoned, 'an inter-hype, a vacuum. You can only do so much with mutant turtles.'

With the spotlight almost exclusively on Gascoigne and Spurs, Arsenal's opening day fixture in the humbler surroundings of Plough Lane, SW19, seemed to merit little consideration from outsiders. Coolly and efficiently, Arsenal put away three goals in the second half without reply. Although the scorers were Paul Merson, Alan Smith and Perry Groves, the inspiration behind the win was the midfield performance of Paul Davis. Davis, once described by Bobby Robson as a possible successor to Bryan Robson, was only now emerging from a two-season nightmare, during which he made only twenty-three first-team appearances. At twenty-eight, Davis's long-term international prospects were probably slim, but the game against Wimbledon showed that he was far from a spent force, and Arsenal with an in-form Paul Davis would pose a threat to anyone harbouring title aspirations.

It is ironic that George Graham, having apparently cornered the market in six-foot central defenders, had come up with a team that seemed capable once again of scoring goals. If League tables were produced on the first day of the season in England, as they are in many other countries, including France and Italy, Arsenal would have been top on goal difference. For both clubs though, Liverpool's 3–1 win at Sheffield United was a timely reminder, if one were needed, that the real threat remained 200 miles to the north.

3

Thanks for Nothing

The depth of feeling for football manifests itself perfectly in a local derby. European Cups and domestic Leagues may be won, relegation may threaten, or the match itself may be of little consequence to any of these, but on Derby Day, all of that is forgotten and for ninety minutes of glorious intensity, nothing in the world could be more vital.

At 7.30 p.m., on Wednesday 29 August, fifteen minutes before the scheduled start of Arsenal's first home game of the season, summer seemed to be coming to an abrupt end as Highbury was engulfed in a rainstorm that would last for a large part of the match. The downpour was most keenly felt around the six ticket windows, which are open to the elements and were that night besieged by many hundreds of supporters. There were no orderly queues, rather a seething mass of bodies, at first attempting to steer a course vaguely in the direction of the sale-points, then forced to take evasive action against the unexpected cloudburst. The faithful were not trying to gain entry into that night's game against Luton, but were desperate to get their hands on the few remaining tickets on offer for the encounter to come on Saturday, against their old adversaries from the other end of the Seven Sisters Road.

For the clubs, and particularly the managers, it was, or should have been, an entirely different matter. When the passion gets through to the players, the form book can be thrown away. If both clubs were serious in their European ambitions, then the derby had to be approached as just another game, since long-term objectives were more important than the ephemeral delights of being north London's premier team until the next clash. For George Graham, the priority was to open the League campaign at Highbury with a win against Luton.

The visitors that night had obviously not studied their role as sacrificial lambs, as they proceeded to dominate the early minutes, and even had the audacity to steal the lead through a stooping header at the near post by Lars Elstrup. The spectre of defeat brought a hitherto subdued Arsenal to life, and as Limpar and Rocastle began to make serious inroads into the Luton defence, goals from Paul Merson and Michael Thomas turned potential disaster into a victory tinged with more than a little relief. 'They gave us a very hard game,' George Graham admitted afterwards, 'it was a bit of a struggle at times.' It had not been a totally convincing performance, although Paul Davis once again looked to have that extra bit of class, and it is a truism in football that the ability to win games when not playing well is the mark of champions. Somehow, Graham had turned logic on its head. It was now quite clear to anyone that if you want to cure a goal famine, buy a couple of defenders. Two games, two wins, five goals for, one against. Who could possibly complain about that?

Twenty-four hours before the Arsenal–Luton match, Spurs faced what an objective reader of the fixture list would have concluded was the first of two difficult away games. Terry Venables' strategy was to secure victory at home against Manchester City, then avoid defeat away. Sunderland were an unknown quantity, the unexpected beneficiaries of Swindon's harsh demotion to Division Two for financial irregularities. One thing was certain though – bringing points back from Roker Park was never easy, and if the Sunderland team were lifted by a crowd of 31,000 fanatical supporters, anything could happen. To come away with a draw, then, was creditable, and, if it had to be a draw, Spurs could take some pleasure from the fact that the game ended 0–0. After all, criticism following the Manchester City match centred on defensive inadequacies, so a shut-out was no mean feat, particularly in view of the way Marco Gabbiadini dominated play in the first half for the Wearsiders. However, in the second half Spurs began to improve and should have ended up winning comfortably.

No matter how plausible the strategy, no one, neither committed professional nor mercenary director, neither dedicated supporter nor interested outsider, could fail to be affected by the widespread anticipation for the impending derby game. It was something special. Terry Venables was in no mood to pull his punches when talking about the significance of the match to Londoners.

'Players are aware it's a huge game for the supporters,' he said. 'They feel for the supporters a lot more than people realize. They want to do it for them. We've had the thin end of the wedge for the last several years and we beat Arsenal last year, which pleased our supporters. It's a bit special really. We both want to win badly – personally and obviously for the club and the fans. Everything is red raw for it. The atmosphere is different. I think you could take Wembley for this game and perhaps we might fill it. It gave us tremendous satisfaction to finish third [last season], with Arsenal fourth, I feel so strongly about it because it is important to our fans. They love it when we are top dogs in the area. This has got all the makings of a cracking match and we can't wait to get stuck in.'

Arsenal's build up to the game was interrupted by the news that Colin Pates, who had only been at the club since January following his £450,000 move from Charlton and had made just two first-team appearances, had asked for a transfer. Pates' request was the third received by George Graham over the summer. Both Brian Marwood and Perry Groves, who, like Pates, were not automatic choices for the starting line-up, had expressed their desire to leave. Groves told the press, 'I want to get away. I don't want my career to stagnate. I feel I can go somewhere else to find first-team soccer.' There was also a rift between the manager and David O'Leary, the club record-holder with over 500 League appearances to his name. After his World Cup exertions, O'Leary had defied Graham and taken an extra few days' holiday with his family. He was fined and left behind as the club went on its pre-season tour of Sweden. When confronted by the discontented players' demands, Graham talked tough. 'No one goes unless I want them to,' was his response. 'When you put your name to a long-term contract you're not signing for the first team – you're signing for the club and you'll honour the deals. All big clubs have good players out of the team. If people want us to be successful they'll have to put up with a big squad and the problems it brings.' With the manager's admonishment ringing in their ears, Marwood and Pates were summarily dispatched to join O'Leary in the reserves.

While many applauded Graham's strong line, the fact that Groves remained in the first-team squad, albeit in his perennial role of substitute, suggested that discipline took second place to pragmatism. The arrival of Anders Limpar, the re-emergence of Paul Davis and the purchase of Andy Linighan (who could also get no further than the substitutes' bench) meant that, unless injury or severe loss of form intervened, Marwood, Pates and O'Leary were surplus to normal first-team requirements and could be safely purged with a spell in the second team. Goal-scoring, however, was another matter, and as long as Graham did not believe that Kevin Campbell was ready for an extended run, Groves was urgently needed. The manager was beginning to suffer from his own ambition. Wanting a squad with the depth of Liverpool's is no bad thing, but it is obviously not enough simply to buy good players. The art of man-management in a situation like this is almost as crucial as the ability to judge a player's skills, and keeping first-team squad members content with reserve foot-ball, when in many other First Division clubs they would be playing in the senior side, is as important as any managerial quality at a big club. This perspective is often overlooked when Liverpool's success is analysed, but the Merseyside club must be doing something right, as disaffection on the scale witnessed at Highbury is unknown at Anfield. There, internationals can be dropped but they rarely react by asking for a transfer. Indeed, Peter Beardsley, Ray Houghton, Jan Molby and Ronny Rosenthal, all of whom are current internationals, were left out of the first team in the opening two weeks of the season. And even expensive players frequently have to serve long apprenticeships at Liverpool before being given the chance to show what they can do.

One other odd aspect of the affair at Arsenal was the very public way it was conducted. None of the parties involved seemed to mind the row being widely reported in the media. Arsenal, the club with the solid, sound reputation, the place where discretion and caution are woven into the fabric, were gaining a new name, for washing their dirty linen in public. This latest bust-up followed in the wake of earlier, more disturbing behaviour, when drink-related excesses by Paul Merson at the Supporters' Club Dinner, and Kevin Richardson and Steve Bould while the team was touring in Singapore, led to disciplinary action against the players concerned. All this suggested that Graham's management style is as abrasive and autocratic to those at the receiving end as it is confident and successful to the fans.

The days before the big game were thus filled with pressure for both sides, but this does not in itself explain why the match, generally agreed to be both frenetic and sterile, should prove so disappointing. Spurs obviously took more satisfaction from the 0–0 scoreline than Arsenal – they had not won at Highbury for five seasons – and if Venables' plan had been to reach the second home game against Derby unbeaten, it could hardly have been more efficiently carried out. The manner and shape of the perform-ance, though, left much to be desired.

In what many, including George Graham, were to excuse as a typical north London derby, the Spurs defence came under constant and relentless pressure, with their midfield totally over-run. The speed of Arsenal's game left no time for the creative skills of Gascoigne and Nayim, and it took the scrapping qualities of Paul Allen to provide what little relief came Spurs' way. Gazza tried, but looked increasingly subdued and was pulled off with two minutes to go. After the game, Venables, in a pointed reference to the player's off-the-pitch activities, claimed Gascoigne had not been sleeping well of late. 'Paul looked very, very tired,' he said. 'He was tired even before the game.' Perhaps it was just not Gazza's day. From the moment the referee refused his request to change the ball at the beginning of the game (a diversion that Gascoigne has employed quite often, for instance in the previous match against Sunderland), nothing seemed to go right, not even after he actually managed to switch the match-ball behind the referee's back.

For all Arsenal's attacking verve and territorial supremacy, they rarely managed to break through the defensive barrier presented by Gary Mabbutt and Steve Sedgley. This new-found stability was at least one positive outcome of the match for Spurs, though the confidence it should have brought failed to spread to

26

the rest of the team. The success of Spurs' rearguard action can be seen in the fact that Arsenal's first shot on target did not arrive until the eighty-seventh minute. If this seems bad, Spurs failed to produce a goal-bound effort for the whole of the ninety minutes. Paul Merson, after his success against Wimbledon and Luton, began promisingly enough but faded in the second half, as he is sometimes prone to do, and was eventually replaced by Perry Groves. The match showed clearly that, despite the five-goal start, Arsenal still needed a partner for Alan Smith to fully capitalize on good approach play. Ironically, Smith's ideal co-striker, a player with whom he had enjoyed a prolific goal-scoring partnership at Leicester, was, in the person of Gary Lineker, ploughing a similarly lonely furrow up front for the opposition. And if Spurs, despite the strength of their performance in defence, still looked to need a third central defender alongside Mabbutt and Sedgley – a commanding organizer at the back – he was sitting on the Arsenal bench. Once again Andy Linighan had not made the team.

As in the previous games, Paul Davis was Arsenal's outstanding player, with Anders Limpar not far behind. Davis's performance seemed all the better for the below-par display by Gazza. It was one more step in Davis's rehabilitation, and Arsenal must take credit for persevering with the player through his difficult period, when many clubs would have looked to offload him at the earliest opportunity. There was never any doubt about Davis's skill, but now his performances were revealing a hitherto unknown side to his character – the temperament to come back when his career could so easily have slid further towards oblivion. Commenting on Davis's decline, George Graham said, 'He was one of our most influential players when I first came to the club. He was outstanding. He was on the verge of the England set-up.' Davis justified his manager's faith by once more bringing a touch of class to the midfield battle. 'It is very difficult to get high-class skill when the game is so tight and competitive,' Graham said later, 'but Davis proved you can do it.' The comparison with Gascoigne was exemplified in the fifty-fifth minute when, after beating his opposite number, Davis played a smart one-two with Limpar, only to be pushed off the ball by Howells. Referee Joe Worrall, however, ignored the resultant claims for a penalty.

Davis's road back from the nine-match suspension he received for punching Southampton's Glenn Cockerill in the face two years before had been interrupted by constant injury problems, so the club sent him to play in Sweden for the second-division team Eskilton. 'It was difficult,' said Davis, 'because they were a struggling side, but it was good for both of us in the end.' Davis made seven appearances for the Swedes during the summer, which according to Graham had the beneficial effect that was required. 'He gained a lot of strength,' was the manager's opinion, '[he] got a lot of his touch back.' Things were at last beginning to work out well again for Davis. In the quiet backwater of the small Swedish town, away from the pressures and the big-city media hype, he was able to concentrate on his game and become ready once again to exhibit the talent that first made his name. His manager now felt able to give him a full vote of confidence. 'I think he's back to his best again,' he said. 'He looks like the Paul Davis of old.' Davis himself was more cautious, saying, 'I am not back to my best form yet. After being out for so long it takes more than a few games to get back to where you were before . . . this year is very important because it's the first time in two years I've actually started a season fully fit.'

Paradoxically, of the two goalkeepers in the derby game, David Seaman had the more difficult chores, although the total number of shots on target by both teams could be counted on the fingers of one hand. Seaman, who was conscious of the need to impress those who questioned the wisdom of selling John Lukic, was singled out for special praise by Graham. 'He kept his concentration very well,' Graham said in his post-match comments. 'He's actually making saves look very easy. I'd rather have that than see a goalkeeper diving all over the place. I was very impressed by him.' It seemed to be the consensus that Seaman had settled in well and was displaying a command in his penalty area that would have surprised supporters of Queen's Park Rangers. It was important that the signing of the new keeper was viewed as a success, particularly given the fact that many considered the treatment of Lukic, who was a particular favourite of the fans, not to have been of the highest order. It was abundantly clear that Arsenal were chasing Seaman for a year before the signing actually took place, since stories concerning Graham's interest in the QPR man appeared regularly in the press.

All in all, the derby game was an anti-climax that failed dismally to fulfil the expectations that had been whipped-up by the pre-match publicity. The press was virtually unanimous in its condemnation. It did not make good television viewing either, and provided a poor start to London Weekend Television's new Sunday-afternoon highlights programme. Perhaps worse, it was hardly the stuff to consolidate the new passion for football that had been a consequence of *Italia 90*. The Spurs manager was a little more sanguine. Venables described the encounter as 'a very hyped-up sort of a game, without a lot of space. For me,' he continued, 'the encouraging aspect at Highbury was that it proved to be the type of match that in the past we would have lost 0–1. I was quite satisfied with the result even if we can play better.'

Although all 47,000 tickets had been sold before the match, the crowd was officially put at 40,009. The missing 7,000 might well have incurred wrath from a number of quarters given the arrangements made by both clubs for spectators. When the summer changes had been completed at Highbury, accommodation for visiting supporters had been cut. For the derby game, Spurs' usual ticket allocation of 11,000 was cut to just 5,500. Imaginatively, Tottenham decided to relay the game to a giant TV screen at Wembley Arena, but in the event the idea proved to be a complete disaster. The Arena, which was originally built as a swimming pool for the 1948 Olympic Games, is not the most salubrious of venues at the best of times and on this occasion the Wembley machine had surpassed itself in finding new ways to mistreat its customers. The price of parking was prohibitively set at five pounds (the amount Wembley charges for an international fixture), there was no reduction for children attending the event, and a cup of Coke cost £1.30. Even at the ludicrously high price of £5 a ticket, Spurs needed to attract 2,000 people to make a profit, a testament to the exorbitant cost of staging anything at Wembley. On the day, only about 500 turned up, of which 90 per cent were Spurs fans. The atmosphere quickly degenerated into an intimidating mixture of insults and boorish behaviour, and some parents who had taken their children left early. While praising the initiative of Spurs, the club must also be criticized for their choice of venue. No pre-match entertainment was provided and the television picture was poor. Spurs, in the moment of their innovation, had slipped into the thinking of old-style football administrators – just put the match on and people will turn up. Unfortunately, the lesson was costly, and the club didn't make money on the enterprise.

The ugly scenes at Wembley had their counterpart at Highbury. There was no trouble at the game, no violence or anything like that. But the bad language and demeanour of a number of aggressive spectators was a reminder that the blight on English football had not been entirely lifted by the events of the summer. The offensive verbal onslaught was not heard so much in the standing areas. It was from the seats that the rancour emanated. What was perhaps worse was that although the hurling of insults is against the law, neither the police nor the stewards took any action. Football in England will never be able to capitalize on its new-found place in the hearts and minds of the public as long as these outbursts are not tackled. The eradication of this unaccept-able face of football – in which racial taunting is paramount – cannot be effected unless it is recognized and faced by those whose job it is to administer the game at club level. Alongside such a recognition, prompt action against offenders to show supporters that this issue is of the gravest concern would be a simple yet symbolically important way of beginning to put the matter right. To be fair, the offensive language at Highbury was confined to a tiny minority, and there was little intimidation of opposing fans (though perhaps a little more tolerance could have been shown to the standing Spurs supporters, instead of the request which boomed from the PA system: 'Will the supporters in the South Bank,' the voice implored, 'please stop jumping up and down – it's against ground regulations'). On the other hand, when compared to the lingering malaise at some other clubs, the behaviour at Arsenal was moderate and good-natured.

In the days after the game there was inevitable speculation concerning the substitution of Paul Gascoigne and the comments by his manager. Then, in an uncharacteristic public statement, Irving Scholar declared that certain reporters were 'hounding' the player, and were 'camped outside his house, trying to find some dirt'. The deterioration in conduct was, according to the Spurs chairman, the reason why Gascoigne looked so jaded against Arsenal, and he intended to complain to the Press Complaints Commission. Such intrusions by the media were supposed to have been outlawed in a code of conduct agreed by Fleet Street editors some months before, but it must surely count against Gazza's advisers that they did not foresee the two-edged nature of the tabloid sword. Gascoigne had been paid a large sum by the *Sun*, and those who live by this particular sword, must be prepared to die by it. It also seemed somewhat inconsistent for Gazza to appear on the Terry Wogan show saying that he now wanted to be left alone. None the less, Irving Scholar had a point. The hounding of heroes until they eventually fall has become almost a national pastime, fuelled by the relentless battles of a circulation war in which everyone is fair game. While there is bound to be interest in the type of lurid story the tabloid press were likely to be looking for, the real fans would, of course, read it, but they wouldn't be unduly concerned with it, whatever the revelation. For those whose lives revolved around their football club, what a player did on the pitch was all that really mattered.

4

Whose Game is it Anyway?

Football fans can be categorized in many ways. Some would argue that a division lies between the standing and seated spectator, or perhaps between season-ticket holder and pay-on-the-day visitor. Recently added to these traditional customers has been the privileged corporate client. In fact, there is a much simpler, yet more fundamental, distinction: those who mainly go to home matches, limiting their away trips to local derbies, and those who try to see all their team's games, home and away. One of those who travels extensively recounted how his ultimate dream was fulfilled when Arsenal won the League title at Anfield in 1989.

'It was the best day of my life, full stop,' he said. 'The atmosphere, the emotions, and beating them, and going there and singing at them for ninety minutes, and for them to be cocky one minute and the next minute flattened. That was it, that was like ... I tell you, you can't describe that feeling, it's goose-pimples, it's everything. I saw three or four thousand blokes crying their eyes out, it was too much in the end.'

This does not mean that one group of fans is more committed than the other. There may be many reasons why a supporter is unable to go to opponents' grounds on a regular basis – the cost, for instance, or the desire to avoid the kind of inhospitable reception that is the away fan's lot in all the football towns of England these days. Since the Heysel disaster, football supporters have been perceived by the general public as at best a nuisance, at worst mindless thugs. The clubs have belatedly begun to recognize their responsibilities towards the paying customer, though it took the deaths of ninety-five people at Hillsborough to finally drive the point home. If the ambition of big clubs like Arsenal and Spurs to compete in Europe is to be realized, supporters must be allowed to play their full part, and their role should be a crucial element in the future of football. A realistic picture of the current state of relations among rival supporters and the attitudes of clubs towards them can best be gauged by examining the experiences of travelling fans.

The Arsenal away supporters have come to look forward to their trips to Merseyside. This is, of course, due mostly to memories of that dramatic night at Anfield which saw the League Championship return to London for the first time in almost twenty years. Beyond that, a number of Londoners have developed friendships with supporters in Liverpool, particularly those of Everton. It is not surprising that this affinity exists. Everton, though their fans would not like the description, could be called the 'Arsenal of the North'. Both clubs are solid and family-run, almost part of the establishment; both have rich footballing traditions; and they are the longest-serving members of the First Division. When Arsenal won at Everton in the Championship season, the home crowd gave the Gunners a standing ovation.

As Arsenal fans contemplated the early fixtures of the season, the away match at Goodison seemed difficult. Few, however, could have predicted the dreadful start that Everton suffered – no points from three games – so by the time the coaches and cars set off from London, victory was a distinct possibility. However, Everton's vulnerability did not appear to have got through to the Arsenal team, as a lacklustre though competent defensive performance earned a point in a 1–1 draw. Groves followed up a Limpar shot that Southall could only parry to give the Londoners the lead, but that was about the only worthwhile attack Arsenal put together in the game. Although they lost Alan Smith to an ankle injury early on, that mishap alone cannot account for the fact that they managed to produce only one shot on goal during the entire first half. After the game, George Graham offered a more prosaic explanation. 'This is always a hard place to come to,' he said. Everton's equalizer must have given Graham cause for concern. Once again a header at the near-post, this time by Newell, had exposed Arsenal's tall defenders in the air. The travelling support saw things differently. 'We murdered them 1–1,' was a typical comment.

During the game the Arsenal section behind the Everton goal made fun of Neville Southall, who had given a very public display of his discontent at not being allowed a transfer with a sit-down protest in the goalmouth before the start of the second half of Everton's previous home game against Leeds. 'We chanted "sit down Southall, sit down",' one Arsenal fan said later. 'And he did do a little sit down for us so we applauded him.' As the majority of Arsenal fans headed down the M6, a few stayed behind in Liverpool for the weekend, to be looked after by their scouse mates. The hospitality on offer soon became legendary as stories of pubs and clubs staying open way past normal closing times, just for the Arsenal boys, filtered back to London. 'One Everton fan put up ten of us in his house,' recalled an enthusiastic participant in the revelry. Here was a camaraderie rarely glimpsed outside the world of the committed football supporter, and an aspect of the game seldom examined by the media.

Like many supporters, the Arsenal fans like to 'wear the colours' (home or away shirts – one aficionado has a combination of both – shorts and socks optional). This is often seen as provocative, but the Liverpool experience showed it could equally be a simple expression of identification, with their own team certainly, but also with the game as a whole.

'The only time I didn't wear the colours,' one diehard traveller explained, 'was at Glasgow Rangers, because we were told it would cause a hassle, but there was no hassle. They were absolutely brilliant. They took us into the pub and got us out of our face, bought us drinks all night. That's what football is all about, but the press won't let you believe that is football.'

Unfortunately, the Everton trip was not entirely characterized by goodwill to all men. The one discordant note was struck by the racist abuse directed at Michael Thomas, David Rocastle and Paul Davis. Being nearest the touchline, Rocastle was the recipient of the worst of the cat-calls ('shoot, shoot, shoot the nigger'). After the game, as he was getting on to the coach, one Everton fan shouted to Rocastle to come and play for the Merseysiders. 'I can't do that, I might get shot,' he replied. Similar outbursts followed in subsequent games at Goodison, causing the Everton board to say they were 'totally ashamed' at what the black players had to endure and that they would be 'taking all possible steps to stamp out this problem'. Whether 'all possible steps' will include a black player on the books at Everton, which is known as an all-white club, remains to be seen. While welcoming the directors' response to the abuse, Paul Davis stated a truth which all clubs know but to which they turn a blind eye, namely, that the taunting of black players was a running sore. 'You get so used to it you don't even mention it. But it has been going on at Goodison, and a few other places are bad, like Leeds . . . you have to put a coating round yourself and not let it affect you, because that's the idea, to put you off your game.' This stoicism does not mitigate the foulness of the abuse black players still have to bear in the Football League. Before Davis joined Arsenal, Brendan Batson was the only black player to achieve regular first-team status at Highbury, so Davis was very much a pioneer. He remembers how, in the early days, 'one or two of the players thought I had a chip on my shoulder'. Davis made it clear he did not like the sort of comments he was forced to endure. 'I didn't think it was the right way to treat a fellow professional,' he said. While times may have changed in the dressing room, the Goodison experience shows that many on the terraces remain stuck in a time warp.

By 2 p.m. the following Saturday, the North Bank was filling up rapidly. The visit of Chelsea would be a good test of the optimism expressed after *Italia 90* that crowd behaviour had improved. The reputation of the Chelsea fans needs no elaboration here, yet the baiting between the two sets of supporters was generally good-natured and humorous. Amazingly, a couple of Chelsea loyalists, decked out completely in blue, were spotted in the North Bank. They experienced no problems, in fact the opposite – they were welcomed like long-lost brothers. Another Chelsea fan was accorded hospitality in the Supporters' Club, with no hint of trouble. Before the game, players, officials and crowd were asked to observe a minute's silence in memory of David Longhurst, the 25-year-old York City striker who had tragically collapsed and died on the field the previous week. Such a tribute might well have been shamelessly interrupted in past years but now there was indeed an eerie silence, broken only by some momentary agitation at the Clock End. No doubt the way the game went added to the generally good mood of the Arsenal fans, but the Chelsea contingent remained well behaved as well, even when their team went 4–0 behind.

Chelsea manager Bobby Campbell adopted a safety-first policy towards the match, stringing five across the midfield and leaving Kerry Dixon alone up front. The suspension of Dennis Wise and an injury to Graeme Le Saux hardly merited such a negative approach, and Chelsea paid the price when sustained Arsenal attacking play early in the second half saw the Blues' defence collapse. Anders Limpar was the star of the show, running at defenders, involved in all the goals and scoring the first himself. The performance drew the description from George Graham that Limpar was 'a spasmodic player, but one we'll be looking to to supply that little bit of magic to unlock games.' There was also a quick, powerful throw-out by David Seaman, delivered with pin-point accuracy into the path of David Rocastle on the halfway line. Seaman's speed of thought turned defence into immediate attack and led to Arsenal's third goal. On the debit side, Seaman was once again beaten by a header at the near-post, this time by Wilson. Incredibly, Chelsea only started to play when they were 4–0 down, but during that time they missed a penalty and saw Seaman make a number of crucial saves. The introduction of Andy Linighan as substitute when the score was 4–0 was an unhappy affair, as the player and the defence looked distinctly shaky and ill at ease after he came on. Still, the 4–1 victory was more than enough to be going on with, and the North Bankers left as they had arrived, in the highest of spirits.

The rapport between supporters and players is a feature of football clubs everywhere, and Arsenal fans, like all others, have always had their favourites. If anything, the interplay goes deeper at Highbury than at other clubs, with the belief that a player is or is not an 'Arsenal Person'. More problematic has been the lack of communication between fans and the officials of the clubs they support. Any recent improvement in atmosphere and behaviour is due more to the actions of supporters themselves than directors. The Taylor Report provided the first official stamp of approval and seemed to open the door to a new era, although so far no ordinary fan has been invited into the inner sanctum.

An incident on Arsenal's pre-season tour of Sweden is instructive. One of the fans who made the trip outlined what happened. 'We made the effort to put over the fact that we were there just for a good time. In one of the games we sang "we love Sweden". We did the conga on the pitch at another game. It all got them on our side. And you know those games they have – the athletics meeting at Bislet where the crowd claps in time – they were doing that when we went round. [Afterwards] David Rocastle came up to us and said, "that was a great conga lads. I wish I could have joined in but you know what the gaffer is like."' The same supporters tried to get a lift on the team coach when they became stranded in a small town after one match. 'I know what you're going to ask,' said George Graham when they approached him. 'I'm sorry but the answer is no. Only players and officials go on the coach.'

With space at a premium at Highbury, both on the terraces and at the old Clock End, where the deficiency was compounded by exposure to the elements, Arsenal faced problems in their plans for redevelopment. There ought to be no conflict, vice-chairman David Dein reasoned, between seeking to increase the potential of the upmarket customer and improvements for the traditional supporter who may well prefer to stand. So when the Clock End rebuilding was conceived, it contained provision for the covering of the terrace, paid for by advance income from the executive boxes housed above. Since the Clock End is the traditional place for away supporters at Highbury, the Arsenal scheme was unique in upgrading facilities for opposing fans, although numbers had to be reduced in the process. 'I love the way it looks with the boxes on top. When I think of how it used to look . . .' was a particularly emphatic opinion from one North Bank fan. The development of the new 'World of Arsenal' shop underneath the arches at Finsbury Park station is another example of a facility providing increased income to the club while at the same time giving a better service to the fans. The existing shop at the ground was totally inadequate to cope with the demand for Arsenal products. Moreover, all this expansion at Arsenal is strictly related to the football club; there has been no diversification into the kind of non-football business that has taken place at Spurs.

Welcome though the Arsenal approach may be, it does not mean that the club can be complacent. According to fans, catering and toilet facilities in the ground still leave much to be desired. It seems incredible that football clubs are unable to make simple improvements which would cost little, particularly in the quality of food on sale to the average spectator. While a club may not be able to control what goes on outside the ground, inside is another matter. If British Rail and motorway-service stations can transform their catering, why can't football clubs? Another bone of contention at Arsenal is the accommodation for the Supporters' Club. Although not the direct responsibility of the football club, the Gunners' most dedicated followers could surely be housed in premises more in keeping with the rest of the Highbury image, rather than in the cramped conditions which they are at present forced to suffer. For most fans, recognition by the club is the common aspiration, and the official supporters' club is as near as the vast majority ever get to that dream. 'The Supporters' Club at Arsenal is completely self-sufficient,' said one. 'But all the major northern teams have big social clubs open all week. Highbury is shut from 6 o'clock on Saturday until the next home game, maybe on Tuesday night.' The contrast between facilities was shown clearly at Everton, where the Supporters' Club occupies a three-storey building next to the ground, housing bars, television, snooker table, etc. The club is a focal point for daily gatherings and is in a different class to the Arsenal fans' headquarters. For all that, Arsenal supporters are more fortunate than their Spurs counterparts, who have been forced by the club to leave their premises in Tottenham High Road and whose very existence is threatened by the Spurs membership scheme, which has encroached on away travel opportunities, one of the main reasons why supporters' clubs were formed in the first place.

Any club wishing to establish itself in Europe must take on board the UEFA directives on ground standards which, along with the recommendations of the Taylor Report, mean that standing will soon become a thing of the past. The way clubs deal with the enforced changes could well determine their future viability, if not their very existence. Supporters, whose attendance rituals will be most undermined by all this, are far more conscious of the implications of such matters than most directors realize, and it might prove an interesting extension to Arsenal's more sympathetic approach to fans if they could be incorporated into some consultative process, or at least if market research were carried out so that clubs can determine what supporters want and evaluate whether they have the ability to provide it.

The conjunction of a relatively enlightened administration and an increasingly articulate stance on the part of the fans has ensured that Highbury, even when visited by the former bad boys of the Fulham Road, is without doubt a friendly place to be on a Saturday afternoon. With mixed feelings, one North Bank regular explained the changing circumstances. 'There really is a family atmosphere at Arsenal,' he said. 'Daft as it seems, I'd prefer to say Arsenal is a right hard bloody football club but the fact is, Arsenal is a really nice family club where people go to watch football and respect football and love it.' Could it be that finally the fashion for violence was passing, that a new trend was emerging among English football fans, just as committed, but with a more human face? Or is such a positive opinion nothing more than premature wish-fulfilment?

Of course, supporters who watch Gazza every week are bound to produce an infectious atmosphere. Spurs have been known to suffer from crowd trouble over the years, but in 1990 there wasn't much likelihood of threatening behaviour, when even opposing fans seemed to appreciate Gascoigne's trickery. His first-ever League hat-trick in the 3–0 defeat of Derby at an ecstatic White Hart Lane included two goals direct from free kicks, one to Shilton's left, the other to his right, which he described as 'unstoppable'. Rarely in his long and distinguished career can England's premier goalkeeper have been left so bemused. Gazza's remarkable performance brought tributes from both camps. Arthur Cox, who was his manager at Newcastle, explained, 'I have known him since he was thirteen and it's nice to see the lad grow up the way he has. He's always been dominant, but it's brilliant to see an English lad play like that, though not against my team.' For Terry Venables, Gascoigne was simply 'exceptional'. So the road-show was set to move on, but the Spurs fans' next trip posed an entirely different prospect to the new friendliness encountered elsewhere. As the story of the link between Irving Scholar and Robert Maxwell began to unfold in the press, Spurs supporters were about to rediscover the delights, after an eight-year absence, of a visit to Leeds United.

Many English clubs have experienced severe hooligan problems over the years, and Leeds were one among several with a particularly vicious reputation. The majority of clubs, however, have taken firm steps to eradicate the problem, over and above more intensive policing. Millwall supporters have been transformed through the community initiative pioneered at The Den, while even Chelsea's support has moderated itself following Ken Bates' programme to secure the future of the club at an improved Stamford Bridge. What remains is a passionate but now less violent rivalry. Leeds fans, however, appear determined to preserve an atmosphere of intimidation and impending violence wherever they venture, and no stadium in England has become more chilling to enter than Elland Road.

These are the people who started a fire on the terraces at Bradford just weeks after the horrific inferno that claimed fifty-three lives; who were responsible for a disturbance that resulted in the death of a fan at Birmingham; who, as recently as May 1990, wreaked havoc along the Dorset beaches and inflicted their own brand of rioting and looting on the unsuspecting inhabitants of Bournemouth, turning a normally peaceful bank-holiday weekend into a nightmare. At home in Yorkshire the potential for causing havoc was equally evident. Indeed, the club's promotion season was characterized by stories of the intimidating atmosphere at Elland Road. Things had got so bad that after the Bournemouth incident the FA, fearful of jeopardizing the return of English clubs to Europe, issued a unprecedented warning that Leeds' very existence was now at stake. If crowd trouble at home or away continued, the FA would be prepared to remove the club's affiliation, thus rendering it unable to play. It was certainly a tough position for the FA to adopt, although it remains to be seen whether the governing body has the will to carry out its threat. And what will happen if Leeds qualify for Europe? Perhaps the FA believes that the sword of Damocles hanging over the club will be enough and that the ultimate sanction will not have to be used.

Despite the protestations of the Leeds directors, they had done little over the years to address some of the deep-rooted problems at the club. For example, where other clubs intervened in varying degrees to try to rid football of racist or obscene verbal outbursts, at Leeds the sore festered. The only racial overtones at Highbury occur when Spurs are playing there, and the Arsenal fans chant 'Yiddos'. This, however, is more in the nature of banter than hostility, and the term has become a nickname embraced by the Spurs supporters themselves. Its complete absurdity was shown when Mitchell Thomas arrived on the pitch as Spurs' substitute in the derby game. The sight of a black player being greeted with the 'Yiddo' chant was surreal. Arsenal supporters know full well that their club probably has as many Jewish fans as Spurs. Indeed, both Spurs and Arsenal took identical advertisements in the *Jewish Chronicle* to wish their Jewish fans a happy new year. Elland Road, on the other hand, is now known for its constant and offensive racist taunts, an irony considering that the first black player to make the grade in England in modern times was Albert Johansson, whose dazzling sorties up the wing enraptured the Leeds public in the 1960s. Moreover, the current chairman, Leslie Silver, is Jewish, as was his predecessor, Manny Cousins. More recently, Yorkshire sport and racism have frequently been seen as willing collaborators. The Yorkshire County Cricket Club, for instance, has attracted widespread criticism for failing to recruit youngsters from the county's ethnic minorities, and Viv Richards left the field in a match against Yorkshire after being called a 'black bastard', allegedly by a member. While developments at other places pass them by, many Leeds fans cling to a twisted mutation of the 'blunt Yorkshireman' tradition, manifested in overt hostility in what can only be described as an environment of hate. It should come as no surprise to discover that the National Front magazine *The Flag* sells more copies outside Elland Road than most other football grounds.

The match itself seems incidental to the problems experienced by the Spurs travelling fans. Some were urinated upon from a higher tier of seats; others were attacked inside and outside the ground, while effective stewarding and security were noticeable by their absence. Indeed, some of the St John Ambulance people seemed intent on drumming up business by joining the anti-Spurs chants.

'I went with my son, who's seventeen years old,' said one Spurs fan. 'He was even scared before we left, he was dead worried in case I said any words outside the ground. I just laughed. I said "Don't be stupid". We got seats in the main stand. In front there was a line of eight hard guys swearing the whole time. We didn't say a word the whole game, we never let out we were Tottenham supporters. When the first Spurs goal went in some Tottenham supporters stood up. One guy deliberately and intentionally pissed over one of them. The fellows down the front shouted "Go on – hit them, hit them". There were no police anywhere. When Leeds went down the other end and scored an equalizer (which was disallowed) we stood up and cheered because we daren't not. That was how stupid it was. Then, when Spurs got the second, these blokes were looking around saying, "Where are those cockney —?" The other fellow we were with said "Come on, let's go – this isn't football", so we left. I've never left a match before the end before. We were pleased to get out of there, it was the most horrible experience, I've never been in the midst of such hatred.'

The hostility was not only directed at Spurs and their fans, it was more general than that. The minute's silence for David Longhurst was constantly interrupted, for instance. Another travelling Spurs supporter told a similar story. 'The St John Ambulance lot who were on the left of us in the gangway were singing "We are Leeds" throughout the game. There were guys wearing T-shirts which said: "Bournemouth May 1990 – Leeds United Invasion". There were other people wearing T-shirts stating: "Don't send British troops to the Gulf – Send Leeds United Supporters". I've been going to football for thirty years, I've seen football in South America and Russia, and I've been to all ninety-two League grounds – there was more hatred and violence within two minutes of being at Leeds than in two weeks of watching the World Cup in Italy. Inside the ground, outside the ground, it was just pure hatred. I said to my friend, "If Spurs score, whatever you do, don't stand up." Tottenham scored. We sat down. When the Leeds goal went in we stood up and clapped. The goal was disallowed – it was bedlam. Then Spurs scored again. As the ball went in the net I said, "Let's get out of here". And we left. I saw fifty-eight minutes, if you can call it football.'

The Spurs fans were happy to contrast their experiences at Elland Road with those at the derby game at Highbury. 'I've grown up with Arsenal supporters at school,' said one. 'There wasn't the animosity. I sat in the West Stand. There was only one guy at the front . . . standing up and shouting. I didn't feel at all intimidated.' Another was more stark in his comparison, saying, 'Arsenal were angels compared to them [Leeds]. The great rivalry [between Arsenal and Spurs] has always been there, will always be there, and I'm pleased it is there because that's what makes the game. But at Leeds you could feel it in the air. We ended up sitting in the car park listening to the last half-hour of the game on the radio.'

These stories are by no means unique. A seasoned Arsenal travelling supporter looked forward to his team's visit to Elland Road at the end of September and at the same time commented on the troubles encountered by the Spurs supporters. He said, 'It's normal for Leeds. It's typical of them and always has been. Those in the know don't go in the seats because the seats aren't segregated and the Leeds fans know they're not segregated, so therefore the Leeds people who want to have a fight and want to do things against other people go in the seats. It's not like other grounds where the general public and normal people go in the seats – animals go in the seats at Leeds. That's where they go because they know they can start causing trouble. There's seven or eight of us, fully grown blokes going up there and none of us are going to go in the seats.'

For the record, Spurs won the match 2–0, with goals from Howells and Lineker. Leeds' manager, Howard Wilkinson, said Spurs were 'the best side we have played [this season] by a long way . . . they know that First Division football is not just about painting pretty pictures . . . it was welcome-to-the-First-Division day. When they couldn't play as they wanted they played for mistakes, and when those mistakes came along they took their opportunities and it was goodnight Vienna.' While Terry Venables couldn't have known what was happening off the field, he recognized how difficult it is to play at Elland Road when he said, 'I don't expect many teams will go to Leeds and win 2–0, but Spurs deserved that victory, not only because we were the better team, but because the players maintained total concentration on a very difficult job.'

With Arsenal second in the table and Spurs third, attention turned to the next day's televised match between Liverpool and Manchester United. Peter Beardsley's hat-trick in a 4–0 victory took away what little gloss was left of the weekend for Spurs' supporters, while everyone else groaned again at the sight of another Liverpool triumph which left them top of the First Division with five straight wins.

The real legacy of that weekend, however, is that no matter how much is done by the majority of clubs, no matter how far the supporters themselves are prepared to work for an improvement to their image, if the madness that engulfs Leeds is at all sympto-matic of other clubs, life for the true fan will become intolerable. With the abandonment of the national membership scheme and its detested ID cards, the stigma that all fans are potential troublemakers was removed. In its place is a professed openness on the part of the football authorities to improve the status of the game's paying customers. However, actions speak louder than words. If the Leeds match is anything to go by, measures are urgently required to stamp out the worst aspects of crowd beha-viour. Supporters turn a game into a spectacle. Their voice needs to be heard, now more urgently than ever, but as long as the intimidation and violence persist, even at one club, that prospect is remote. The major clubs with their large support also have a responsibility. Improvement of basic amenities, for instance, is an ongoing necessity. As the Taylor Report pointed out, if this is not addressed, 'crowd conduct becomes degraded and other misbeha-viour seems less out of place.'

For all Spurs fans, whether or not they had travelled to Leeds, there was more bad news. The revelations concerning Robert Maxwell's involvement in the club were causing concern in a number of quarters, including the Spurs boardroom, the Stock Exchange and the Football League, which was no stranger to battles with the proprietor of the *Daily Mirror*. Suddenly, the club was looking extremely shaky. So far the problems had not affected the team, but that could not continue indefinitely. And what was Terry Venables to make of it all? The situation was more like a story from one of his 'Hazell' detective books than real life, yet his obligation was to carry on as if nothing were wrong. As he pondered the future, he must have thought that compared to the goings on at Spurs, Barcelona politics had been like a boy-scout jamboree.

5

El Tel, Son of Fred

Langan's Brasserie, described by *The Good Food Guide* as probably London's finest restaurant of the 1980s, is not the place to visit for a quiet, discreet meal. It has often been the subject of press reports, usually concerning the outrageous exploits of one of its proprietors, Peter Langan, who was killed in a fire at his home which he started himself after an argument with his estranged wife. Another part-owner is the actor Michael Caine, who, together with the excellent reputation of the food and service, helped attract a clientele of the rich and famous. It is hardly possible to make the short walk from Green Park or the Ritz Hotel to the restaurant's location on Stratton Street without running the gauntlet of the world's paparazzi, all eager for a chance to catch the customers momentarily off their guard.

Once, such a rendezvous would have been the exclusive domain of film stars, businessmen and the denizens of Mayfair, not the sort of place where you would expect to find two old professional footballers out of Dagenham and Glasgow. But times change. It is unlikely that Bertie Mee or Bill Nicholson ever made a habit of visiting such chic eating-houses, yet the venue was entirely in keeping with the modern image of football and no one turned a hair when, on 20 September 1990, two old friends, Terry Venables and George Graham, sat down for one of their regular meals together.

In football terms, there was much to be optimistic about for both men. Arsenal and Spurs had made unbeaten starts to the season and each was in a good position to take advantage of any slip-up by Liverpool. Moreover, the prospect of their clubs doing well in the same season highlighted the rivalry for managers and supporters alike. Since 1972, apart from 1987, when the two teams finished in the top six, Arsenal won the Littlewoods Cup (knocking out Spurs in the semi-final) and Tottenham reached the FA Cup Final, the usual pattern of the seventies and eighties had been that when Arsenal were winning things Spurs were generally out of contention, and when Spurs were collecting silverware Arsenal were usually nowhere. If the two rivals, together with Crystal Palace, could keep up their early promise, the passion for football in the capital would be electrifying.

While there was little to cloud this vision for George Graham, the Spurs manager was unable to share completely in the optimism. At the moment when Spurs were enjoying an unusually good start to the season, the euphoria had been shattered by the news that the club's finances were in such a parlous state that Irving Scholar had been conducting secret negotiations with Robert Maxwell to secure an injection of £13 million. It had also become clear that without such a rescue package, Spurs were on the verge of collapse. Venables had known for some time that no money was available for players, and that building work and the failure of other companies in the plc group were draining the resources of the football club, but the true extent of the financial problems had come as a shock as much to the manager as it had to the fans and certain members of the Tottenham Hotspur board. While Graham could leave Langan's safe in the knowledge that he didn't have to worry about the stability of Arsenal, the most profitable club in the entire Football League, he did permit himself a moment of sympathy for his old friend. After all, Graham had himself experienced football's perilous financial climate at Millwall and was only too well aware of his good fortune in being manager of a club where such things never intruded on to the playing side.

Two days after the lunch at Langan's, Spurs faced Crystal Palace at White Hart Lane. The talk around the ground was less to do with the team's prospects or the merits of Steve Coppell's beaten Cup-finalists than with the story of Robert Maxwell's involvement. Many supporters wondered whether the upheavals in the boardroom would affect the team on the pitch. In a niggling match Spurs conceded only their second goal of the season when Palace captain Geoff Thomas struck a seventy-ninth minute equalizer to Paul Gascoigne's first-half free kick, which was cheekily taken while the opposition goalkeeper, Nigel Martyn, was still lining up his wall. It was the first point dropped at home by Spurs since they were beaten by Palace in March, and the result ended a run of seven consecutive home victories. None the less, for a team supposedly suffering from defensive inadequacies, Spurs' parsimony at the back was beginning to spread confidence throughout the side and provide a new experience for the club's supporters. 'We are proud of our defensive record,' observed captain Gary Mabbutt. 'Tottenham sides are not always regarded as having the safest defences, so we want to work on that side of our game.'

The wrangles behind the scenes did not seem to have affected morale, and the team and coaching staff could take full credit for a professional performance. While Terry Venables was confirming that he had been asked to discuss a new contract, his players went public in their backing for the manager. Mabbutt, speaking on behalf of the playing staff, said, 'It would be crazy to spoil things now and break up our partnership. I think it would make good sense to allow him to finish the job. Terry is technically the best manager I have played under, and his knowledge in Europe has helped us. If we get into Europe then that knowledge could be put to good use.'

Arsenal, meanwhile, had a difficult-looking trip to Nottingham Forest. Brian Clough's team had not started too well, though there were signs that this was merely an early-season blip. In the event the Gunners gave, in the words of George Graham, their 'worst performance of the season', yet still managed to win the game 2–0. 'The way we performed in defence at times, it was amazing that we kept a clean sheet,' Graham continued. 'There were a lot of below-par performances in our team today. Organization and professionalism got us through.' What Graham meant was that Arsenal soaked up pressure for most of the match and scored with the two opportunities that came their way: first after half an hour, when the ball fortuitously reached David Rocastle in the penalty area, where he had the skill to beat a defender before putting the ball beyond Crossley in the Forest goal; and again in the eighty-fourth minute, when Alan Smith beat Des Walker on the left and crossed for Anders Limpar to supply the finish. Many were surprised at the ease with which Walker was beaten in that incident, but it has become a feature of Smith's play that on occasion he will drift out wide, generally to the left. If the central defender follows, as is often the case, he is forced into playing like a full back, while a considerable gap can open up through the middle of the defence which others can exploit. Limpar, displaying a refreshing if naïve frankness, ascribed his goal and the win to good fortune, saying, 'It was very lucky. I shot and the goalkeeper made a big mistake. We were very lucky to win. This is the baddest [*sic*] we have performed. They could have shot [*sic*] three goals.' Although Liverpool won yet again to remain the bookies' favourites at odds of 11–4 on, the weekend's results meant that both Arsenal and Spurs remained the likeliest challengers.

When Irving Scholar flew to Miami in October 1987 to woo Terry Venables following the departure of David Pleat, one of his greatest assets was the sound financial basis of the Spurs set-up. Venables was promised money to strengthen the team and the guarantee that he would be taking over a rejuvenated and high-profile club that was geared to achieve success. The Spurs chairman's powers of persuasion obviously had the desired effect on the man who had just been ousted from Barcelona (and who was, in his own words, 'determined to have the rest of the season off'), and Venables arrived at White Hart Lane as the messiah – the saviour who would at last bring the club a League title after a gap of more than a quarter of a century. For Scholar, the new manager was the perfect choice, and his appointment was one of the chairman's few decisions to meet with the immediate approval of the Spurs faithful.

Born in Dagenham, Essex, in 1943, Terry Venables has retained the notional identity of a Londoner, a common-enough trait for those whose families had moved out of the East End and north London into the overspill towns of Hertfordshire and Essex. Today he can truthfully claim to be the same person, unlike another Dagenham boy whose studied speech and behaviour now betray no trace of his working-class upbringing. Again, unlike Sir Alf Ramsey, the image of the cheeky cockney would follow Terry

Venables throughout a football life based exclusively in the capital until the move to Barcelona in 1984. His early football prowess suggested a glittering career lay ahead, and to this day Venables remains the only English footballer who played for his country at every level, from schoolboy to the full England team. But somehow he never quite attained the level of greatness those early days promised.

In the late 1950s, few clubs were producing exciting talent from youth policies. Outstanding exceptions in the North were Burnley and Manchester United. The latter, with a team based on 'Busby's Babes', rarely went into the transfer market until after the Munich air crash. In the South, Ted Drake produced a string of youngsters for Chelsea who became known as 'Drake's Ducklings', a process that was to be carried on by his successor, Tommy Docherty. Venables came through these ranks, along with the likes of Jimmy Greaves, Bobby Tambling and John Hollins. He became the youngest captain in the First Division, and won his two England caps by the time he was twenty-one. After breaking a curfew to spend a night enjoying the pleasures of Blackpool, eight of the Chelsea team, including Venables and George Graham, were sent back to London in disgrace. After this incident relations with Docherty were never the same and it precipitated the break-up of the team before its full potential could be realized. Graham was sold to Arsenal, and the final rift came after Chelsea lost in the 1966 FA Cup semi-final, with Venables quickly offloaded to Spurs before the season was out.

The move across London somehow brought Venables' career to a standstill. At Chelsea he had emerged as a leader, cajoling a team of young talent to performances that should have been beyond them. At Spurs, he was treading in the bootsteps of Danny Blanchflower and John White, and many of the players who had won the double in 1961 were still at the club, including Dave Mackay. This was a hard act to follow and Venables never really found either his true role or his best form with Spurs. There was success of course, particularly the FA Cup win of 1967, when Venables lined up at Wembley against his old club, Chelsea. On the international front, the two games in which

Venables played ended in draws, against Belgium and Holland. After these performances, Alf Ramsey's search for players to conform to his idea of how the national side should play was never again to include the Spurs player. It would be fair to say that Venables was probably picked too young and definitely discarded too early. As England approached the 1966 World Cup, the emergence of Alan Ball and Martin Peters put paid to any lingering hopes he may have entertained of an international comeback, although he was included in the initial World Cup squad of forty.

After playing over 100 games for Spurs, Venables moved to QPR in 1969, where he spent three years in the Second Division. Revelling in the role given him, Venables found Loftus Road more conducive to his talents than White Hart Lane, so much so that Stan Bowles described him as 'the most skilful player I've played with'.

Venables' final cross-town journey as a player took him south of the river to Crystal Palace and the Third Division. He only played fourteen games for Palace, as the manager, Malcolm Allison, told him he was finished as a player and should concentrate on coaching. Although he initially found the decision hard to take after a career which spanned 500 games, the heady days at Selhurst Park saw Venables flourish as a coach. When Allison left in 1976, chairman Reg Bloye offered the manager's job to Venables, which he accepted. Before the contract was signed, Arsenal chairman Dennis Hill-Wood and secretary Ken Friar invited him to a meeting at the Park Lane Hotel. They asked Venables about his views on the game, then, after going for a walk for ten minutes to discuss matters among themselves, returned and offered Venables the vacant manager's job at Highbury. Venables was flattered and admired Hill-Wood's courage in going for someone with no managerial experience, but he turned the offer down. 'I was incredibly impressed,' he recalled later, 'how they came up with me. I couldn't get over it. I still can't to this day.' There were two reasons for Venables' rejection of the Arsenal post. First, he had given his word to Reg Bloye that he would take the Palace job, but also he felt he was not ready for the task required at Highbury. 'I thought I might be overreaching myself at that stage,' he said. He believed that if he found success in the lower divisions, such a position would come around again. So it was Palace that acquired the young coach's services.

One of the new manager's first buys was a midfield player who had reached the heights but whose career was now in the doldrums. From Portsmouth, where the team had just been relegated to Division Three, arrived none other than George Graham. A disastrous season on the south coast, coupled with injury problems, had resulted in his football future apparently heading towards oblivion, But Graham, bringing experience to a young side, played twenty-three games for Palace that season. More importantly, he was influential in helping his new club to promotion to the Second Division. Terry Venables' managerial career, which would prove to be far more successful than his playing career had ever been, was set to take off.

The record since then speaks for itself. In 1978–9 Crystal Palace won promotion to the First Division. The Second Division Championship was clinched on an incredible Friday night at Selhurst Park, when Palace beat Burnley in front of a 52,000 crowd. The first season in the top flight saw them finish a respectable thirteenth, but cracks were beginning to appear in the relationship between Venables and Bloye as the manager insisted that his team were a couple of players short of a trophy-winning side. Palace were simply not geared up for life in the First Division. Money was not available for improving the team and the board began to resent the bonuses they were having to pay. They never anticipated the success he brought them, nor the increase in profile that accompanied a manager like Venables, who had interests outside the game. Since his days at QPR he had been involved in writing. With Gordon Williams he was co-author of *They Used to Play on Grass*, a futuristic football novel which presaged Loftus Road having the League's first artificial pitch, and the 'Hazell' books, which were made into a television series starring Nicholas Ball. While at Palace, Venables cultivated a talent for communication through work as a television pundit, a national platform which caused further rumblings of discontent behind the scenes at Selhurst Park.

The following season started well, and Palace topped the table early on, but as a slow decline set in, Bloye sounded out the availability of Howard Kendall, who was player-manager at Blackburn Rovers. Venables found out about it and resigned.

As the post-Venables Palace began the slide that was to take them back into the Third Division, the man who created the 'team of the eighties' accepted the manager's job at Second Division Queen's Park Rangers. A remarkable run of success over the following three years saw Venables rewarded with a director-ship, a most unusual event in English football (the FA had only just allowed paid directors). To Rangers chairman Jim Gregory, Venables was like a son, and there was an understanding between the two that in time Venables would run the football club, while Gregory administered the stadium at Loftus Road. Never had an English manager formally wielded so much power and control. Many years later, when debate about the ownership of football clubs had finally opened up, Venables spoke about the period. 'People were sceptical at the time,' he said, 'but events now are suggesting that it was a visionary concept and could be the future for our football.'

On the pitch, the success story continued. In 1981–2 QPR reached the Cup Final, where they put on a tenacious display built around offside tactics which Spurs, including Hoddle and Ardiles, did not have the wit to counter. The uninspiring 1–1 draw was followed by an even worse replay, won eventually by Tottenham with a single goal from a Hoddle penalty. Some time before, Morris Keston, a legendary Spurs fan and friend of Venables, had asked the QPR manager if he could have a seat on the bench if he ever managed a side to a Wembley final. When QPR were set to play Spurs, Keston reminded Venables of their chat. Venables enquired whether Keston would stand up and cheer if Spurs scored. 'Of course,' Keston replied. 'Well you can't have it then,' said Venables, although the thought of his friend applauding a Spurs goal from the QPR bench appealed to his sense of humour.

The next year, Venables' side was promoted, winning the Second Division by a ten-point margin, and the season after that QPR qualified for the UEFA Cup, the first time the club had made it into a European competition since the great days of Stan Bowles and company in the 1970s. At the end of that season the team had set a new First Division record for the lowest number of goals conceded, twenty-four.

The end of the 1983–4 campaign saw Venables at the pinnacle of his success in England. He managed a team which looked capable of mounting a serious challenge for the title, a season in Europe was to come, and he was set to take over completely at QPR. But he was, in his own opinion, still a couple of players short of a title-winning team, which is how he justified QPR's increasing use of the offside game. Speculation mounted that he might be tempted away from the niche he had carved for himself in west London. Then came an offer that no ambitious manager could resist.

The job of coach at Barcelona presented unique opportunities and challenges. For one thing, the salary was quadruple anything paid by even the top English clubs. There could never be any worries over lack of finances to buy and keep players either. But Barcelona was a restless giant, a club that could regularly attract 120,000 fanatical spectators who felt fully justified, as did the media, in condemning failure on the football field in the most vehement of terms. Coaches did not last long in this environment. Moreover, the club had not won the Spanish League since the time of Johan Cruyff in 1974 and had never won the European Cup. Anyone who could deliver these trophies would surely be hailed as a hero for the rest of his days. So when Jose Luis Nunez, Barcelona's president, decided that Venables was his man, there was only ever going to be one outcome.

The choice of the Barcelona president was a bombshell in Spain. Bernd Schuster, the wayward German midfield star of the team, asked whether the president had picked the new coach up from the beach. When Venables sold Maradona and replaced him with Steve Archibald the amazement was complete, but the magic touch had not deserted the Dagenham boy. Venables looked at the quality of Spanish football and decided that, while most teams boasted excellent individuals with good technique, they would be vulnerable to the English style of teamwork. The system Venables developed to effect his theory did not bring immediate plaudits. Once again the offside game was employed (though not as much as it was at QPR), and Venables deliberately sought to suppress individuality in order to create a team. Before the season began, he took his new charges away to Andorra for two weeks. Here, the new coach introduced his tactics, based on what was later dubbed the pressing game.

Early on in the season the Catalans went to the Bernabeu and beat the mighty Real Madrid 3–0. El Tel was on his way. Gradually, with an abundance of goals from the ex-Spur Archibald, Barcelona wore down rather than outplayed the opposition, including Real, and Venables brought the city its first championship for eleven years. At a party to celebrate the success, the players revealed that when Venables introduced the pressing game they thought he was crazy but knuckled down to the task as good professionals should. After the win against Real they began to change their minds, thinking there might be something in the new tactics after all. It was this style of play that was later refined, honed and perfected by Arrigo Sacchi, coach of AC Milan. Milan, with the Dutch contingent of Gullit, Rijkaard and Van Basten, not only won the European Cup two years running but finally helped rid the Italian game of some of its traditional defensive attitudes. Under the *catenaccio* (or defensive sweeper) system, tight marking had been all; now, with a perfected pressing game, good defence was compatible with attacking play. While it may be overstating the case to say that the pressing game was invented by Venables (the Dutch World Cup team of 1974, for instance, played a similar pattern defensively), there can be no doubt that its development owed much to his success in Spain.

In 1985–6, Venables took Barca to the European Cup Final, where the team, the hottest favourites for years, froze and lost to Steaua Bucharest on penalties in one of the most disappointing finals of recent times. Later, Venables ruefully remarked that he was 'one penalty away' from immortality. In Spain, however, the dividing line between immortality and ignominy is exceedingly fine. After buying Gary Lineker from Everton but finishing runners-up to Real Madrid (although Barca won the Cup), Venables was under pressure (it was at this time he turned down a second approach from Arsenal), and following a poor start to the 1987–8 season, he was dismissed. It was a harsh judgement on a coach who had won the League in his first season and finished second in the next two, as well as reaching the European Cup Final.

Throughout his time as a coach and manager, Terry Venables built a reputation as one of the finest tacticians in the game. Moreover, he seemed to inspire both respect and loyalty from those players that came under his wing. He coached the England Under-21 side for a short time, and in the squad was the young Glenn Hoddle. Hoddle was in no doubt about Venables' ability, commenting that he learnt more from Terry Venables in two days with the Under-21s than in two years at Spurs. Steve Wicks, who played for Venables at QPR, pointed to the manager's style in handling players, saying, 'He always liked to be one of the lads and you could always enjoy a laugh and a joke with him, but when you went to see him on a one-to-one situation you had butterflies in your stomach.'

For some years Venables seemed to be a serious candidate for the full England job, and indeed when he joined Spurs a clause was put in his contract to allow for this possibility. It was always unlikely, though, that Venables would become manager of the national team. Later, he reflected on what he now believes was always a lost cause. 'I'm not their [the FA's] sort of guy,' he said. 'I prefer to stay as I am and not make those fake changes.' After Bobby Robson's resignation he didn't even make the short-list, which consisted of Graham Taylor, who got the job, Howard Kendall, and the surprise third man, Joe Royle. The Football Association, perhaps overly concerned with image, saw Venables as a wide-boy who would not bring dignity to the post. This was a partisan interpretation of Venables' character. The record shows that when necessary, Venables' principles were not found wanting. He turned down the chance to manage Arsenal, for instance, on the first occasion because he had given his word to the chairman of Crystal Palace and the second time because, as he saw it, there was a failure to comply 'with certain things on which we had agreed'. These are two instances among many when Venables has acted in a manner that belies the image. Furthermore, rarely will a player be found who has a bad word to say about him. Unlike many managers, it is unlikely that Venables will ever have to suffer the type of press revelations from former players that are so common in the tabloids. Even those like Clive Allen, who Venables transferred three times, don't have a go at him. His sensitive treatment of players was confirmed by his long-time colleague Allan Harris, his assistant manager at QPR and Barcelona, who paid this compliment: 'He doesn't rule the players with a rod of iron, because he loves all the banter, but he knows the game as well as anyone I've ever met and he's always dead straight with the players. That's why they all respect and love him so much.'

The return to Spurs as manager, however, seemed to present Venables with similar problems to those he had encountered over twenty years before as a player. David Pleat had been a popular manager, who had departed because of difficulties in his personal life rather than anything to do with football. There are Spurs fans who argue that Pleat left a good team behind which Venables failed to build upon, and it is certainly true that Pleat was innovative enough to bring the five-man midfield, which had been a feature of the 1984 European Championships in France, to England and Spurs. Others, including Venables himself, saw the Pleat legacy rather differently. In Venables' words, the club was akin to a 'sinking ship' when he took over. Like the side Venables joined in the sixties, Pleat's team was ageing and out of sorts. There was a feeling of complacency engendered by long contracts, and the hunger to get over that last obstacle and actually win something appeared to be missing. Clive Allen and Steve Hodge had lost form, while the best of Ardiles was in the past, which left a yawning gap in midfield. Then Richard Gough went back to Scotland for personal reasons, robbing Venables of the rock on which he had hoped to build the Spurs defence. Few would disagree that to this day Gough has not been adequately replaced in the Spurs team. Ray Clemence and Danny Thomas never played again, and Glenn Hoddle had reached the end of his time at Tottenham. The loss of Hoddle entailed a change in the entire playing system, since his gifts and playing style were unique. Subsequently, Venables admitted that he did not 'look at the picture closely enough'. There was, he explained, 'a lot of work to be done'. Looking back on this period, Doug Livermore, who had served under Peter Shreeves and David Pleat before stepping up to replace Allan Harris as assistant manager, recalled that 'the playing staff wasn't as strong as a lot of people outside the club thought, plus everybody was expecting him [Venables] to change it overnight. It was a major rebuilding job. It does take time.'

Perhaps Venables took longer than he realized to get Barcelona out of his system and didn't give himself enough time to become reacquainted with the British transfer market before raiding it. Whatever the reason, it looked as if Spurs and Venables were a mixture that simply did not gel. In response to the setbacks Venables became more determined than ever to succeed, and, when the roof fell in on the finances, the backs-against-the-wall approach actually seemed to improve Spurs' performances, making the finish to the 1989–90 season and the start of the new one the manager's best period since his arrival. This turn of events was exemplified in Spurs' defensive displays, which were now actually looking rather assured.

When he became manager of Spurs, Venables encountered a totally different regime from the one he had left behind at Queen's Park Rangers. Instead of full control, he now found that many areas of the club's operations were off limits. This was due to a number of factors. The obligations of a publicly quoted company meant that the board of directors were much more interventionist than would usually be the case. In addition, the establishment of ancillary companies ensured that the matrix of financial relationships which characterized the various parts of the Tottenham empire was outside the control of the football club manager. Finally, the personality of Irving Scholar would not allow him to refrain from giving his opinion on playing matters, and gradually the chairman became more and more involved in team affairs through his control of the purse strings.

There is a story that when Venables first arrived at White Hart Lane he announced to Scholar that the team would have to learn to utilize the offside game if it was to be successful. Scholar quickly informed the new manager that the fans at Tottenham would never abide such a style of play. As his predecessor, David

Pleat, could have told him, 'Anybody who manages that club has to play in a certain way, with good passing, preferably with one or two individualistic characters in the team. Any other way is not acceptable.'

The offside plan was thus modified by a system in which Terry Fenwick played as sweeper, which was not particularly successful. Although Scholar made large sums of money available to buy players, particularly young players for the future, there seemed little evidence that Venables' transfer policy was geared to an overall plan. Even the signing of Paul Gascoigne produced widespread criticism, but at this stage the manager could not complain that the board were not backing his judgement with cash. Scholar continued to offer his opinions of the team every time he met Venables, but then Scholar is like that with everybody. The situation became more serious, however, when Chris Waddle was sold to Marseille for £4.25 million in the summer of 1989.

Before the Waddle sale, Venables had splashed out £3.5 million on Gascoigne and Lineker, and Spurs fans came forward in great numbers to purchase season tickets to watch what promised to be an exciting, attacking side. The sudden sale of Waddle not only baffled them, given the expenditure on the new arrivals, it appeared as if Spurs had taken their money under false pretences. Having swallowed the loss of Waddle, Venables believed that the majority of the money from Marseille would be made available to him to buy more players. However, after laying out £1.4 million on Sedgley and Van Den Hauwe – a trifling amount for a club with serious title aspirations – the board called a halt to the spending. It was all the more galling for Venables because the dire financial position had not been caused by anything the football team had done; indeed the football operations were, at the time, in profit.

The manager still believed that Scholar would find a way for him to strengthen the department he thought was most in need of reinforcement – the defence. An earlier approach to Manchester United for Paul McGrath had foundered because the player's wife did not want to move to London, and Venables had been forced to continue his search elsewhere. Having been told that Terry Butcher was too expensive, Venables eventually set his sights on Mark Wright of Derby, but Scholar refused to sanction the signing. Following the World Cup, the manager toyed with the idea of offering Gary Lineker to Derby in exchange for Wright and Dean Saunders, but the deal never got off the ground as there was no chance of Spurs raising the cash adjustment that would be required. Even the Justin Edinburgh signing from Southend was a long, drawn-out headache.

With stories of Spurs' financial plight becoming more prevalent and allegations of boardroom rows surfacing in the press, the team's morale and determination seemed, paradoxically, to increase. Much of this can be attributed to Venables, who became used to boardroom politics and intrigue at Barcelona. Allan Harris explained how what happened there would stand the Spurs manager in good stead. 'Nothing could shock Terry now after what we went through at Barcelona,' he said. 'Terry's experience in Spain will help him now and he won't take any notice. As ever, he will just keep his mind on football and make sure he keeps the team in the right frame of mind.'

By the time Robert Maxwell's interest had become public knowledge, Venables had decided, as Allan Harris predicted, to put the team first.

'Ever since we got paid directors and the City became involved with football clubs, we have been heading rapidly for the day when the English manager is reduced to the Continental coach,' he explained. 'I'm supposed to be the whizz-kid boss with business acumen as well as the football brain, but I have no alternative at the moment but to concentrate all my energies solely on the team. Psychologically, it is vital to separate the dressing room from the boardroom ... I have spelled it out to them [the players] that as long as they are being paid in full – and there is no danger of that not happening – the business affairs of the club are none of their concern.'

He was not averse to giving his thoughts on the disputes raging at Spurs, however, saying, 'I'm past worrying about who is supposed to own the club. I'll wait and see what develops. But I have to be aware of the possibility that if Maxwell were at Spurs there might be funds available for new players. At the moment I couldn't lay out a fiver on a World Cup star.'

He also recognized that there was a downside to the situation. 'The role of manager in the English League is being diminished by amateur directors who want to play at professional football,' he ventured. 'If we get Maxwell as well as Scholar then we all move one step down towards the bootroom, myself included.' Given Venables' nature, it is not surprising that, as the problems at Spurs became more acute, he began to wonder whether he might be able to do something about them himself.

With all the turmoil at White Hart Lane, it was surprising that Spurs had started the new season in such good form. Venables had managed to make a virtue out of necessity, instilling a sense of considerable pride in the fact that the team's defensive record was the best in the First Division, although many were convinced it could not last. None could deny, however, that Mabbutt, Van Den Hauwe and Sedgley, and the overseas contingent of Thorstvedt and Bergsson, had somehow stemmed the flow of goals which had plagued the side since the departure of Richard Gough. A new role for David Howells, who was now playing in front of the back four, was achieved smoothly and with great success as it allowed Gascoigne, Nayim and, on occasion, Howells himself more licence to go forward, a change which reaped a rich harvest as Gazza began to score a hatful of goals. In a reference to the lack of pre-season transfer activity, Venables said, 'I think the supporters were expecting the club to sign someone – so was I. To be fair to the club they've always done that. At the moment it's just not possible. Everyone is working very hard to turn the situation round. They [the directors] could have cashed in after the World Cup but they never wavered. Through all that will come better times and we will entertain people by playing attractive football.'

With a candour rare in a football manager he attempted to put the situation firmly in perspective, saying, 'I personally don't think . . . I've achieved anything at the moment. All I know and all I've always said is that if you can keep improving every year that's as much as you can do. I feel we have an improvement without a doubt. I think we've got a side now that's full of optimism, not only from the club but from the supporters. We've got an excitement now. People want to watch us home and away, and you can't guarantee winning the competitions because there are so many other big, strong clubs. To create the sort of excitement we've created I think is something we are pleased with.'

This new-found attitude was shown to great effect in Spurs' Rumbelows League Cup tie against Fourth Division Hartlepool in the week after the draw against Crystal Palace. Spurs had been humiliated by lower-division teams in cup competitions in recent seasons (FA Cup defeats against Port Vale and Bradford, for instance), but, with Gazza leading the way by scoring four times, Spurs wrapped up the first leg with a comfortable 5–0 victory. As expected, Lineker got the other goal.

The visit of Aston Villa to White Hart Lane would finally prove the point to any doubters. In a game during which Spurs were outplayed for long periods, Venables reorganized his tactics and the team took the match 2–1, having conceded the lead to a David Platt goal after thirty-three minutes. The match saw the introduction of Paul Walsh for the second half, and it was his pass that put Paul Allen in for the winning goal. When Lineker grabbed the equalizer on the stroke of half-time, David Howells went down injured and swallowed his tongue. Such an occurrence could easily have proved fatal, but thankfully Howells made a complete recovery once he had been carried off to the dressing room. After the Villa game Spurs were third in the table and still unbeaten, having conceded only three goals in seven League games. 'We have had some difficult matches and I think it's been an outstanding start to the season,' commented Venables. In a reference to Liverpool, who had just recorded their seventh straight win, the Spurs manager added, 'It's just a bit disappointing when you look at the table and see the leaders six points ahead.'

Arsenal also got through the first leg of their Rumbelows Cup tie with a win in Macclesfield against Third Division Chester. Although the home team missed a few first-half chances and often looked good, it always seemed as if the Gunners were doing just enough, and a goal from Paul Merson on the hour made sure they would go back to Highbury with the lead. On the following Saturday came the trip to the Leeds cauldron, a match that lent weight, ironically, to Irving Scholar's view on how the game should be played. Leeds possessed creative midfielders in Gordon Strachan and Gary McAllister, which made it all the more baffling that the team played continually for offside, a tactic which had nearly cost them goals in a number of games and was now about to cost them two points.

Any supporter knows that playing the offside game is a risky business at best. With the pace of modern football the margin of error has continually been reduced, and it is only a matter of time before a referee or linesman makes a mistake or gives the benefit of any doubt to the attacking side. And since the offside tactic stifles play and annoys fans, it always seems to be poetic justice when the trap fails and the defence is left in tatters.

For the first forty minutes of the game at Elland Road, Arsenal looked as though they might lose for the first time. Leeds took the lead with an early goal by Lee Chapman, a failure in his Arsenal days but resurrected by Howard Wilkinson, first at Sheffield Wednesday and then at Leeds after he was discarded by Brian Clough. Thereafter, Leeds threatened Arsenal continually, with little by way of reply. Then Limpar received the ball in a blatantly offside position from which he went on to score. To the fury of the Leeds fans, referee John Lloyd allowed the goal to stand, having decided that David Batty had actually taken the ball off David Rocastle's toe and played it towards Limpar, who would, in that circumstance, be onside. Such a precise interpretation of the law was entirely lost on the Leeds fans, who were unaware of what actually happened. They, of course, saw to it that the temperature was turned up for the second half. The incident affected both teams, with Leeds rocked back by the decision and Arsenal rejuvenated. In one of Arsenal's best moves of the season, Limpar put them 2–1 ahead. Dixon, deep in his own half, relieved himself of the attentions of Batty with an overhead kick, then raced thirty yards along the right wing before hitting a diagonal pass to Merson on the left. Merson turned the ball inside and Limpar swept it home first time. Perfect. The home fans didn't like it and the intimidating atmosphere intensified. In the eighty-fourth minute McAllister went down in the box and the referee awarded Leeds a dubious penalty, which Strachan converted to leave the game at 2–2. George Graham was philosophical enough to observe that the two crucial decisions represented the 'profit and loss of the referee's judgement'.

Once again both north London clubs had shown that they were contenders. Equally, Liverpool were setting the standards against which each would inevitably be judged. George Graham ran a smooth operation, where everything was ordered and in its place, and the manager knew exactly what was going on. Terry Venables, by contrast, had somehow forged a team from the adversity that was now his lot. At the start of the season he had bemoaned the lack of cash, saying in his now famous lament, 'I need the money, I'm one player short.' At that time Venables, who was the first to admit that he had not achieved what he hoped at White Hart Lane, was in a weak bargaining position. Seven games into what was already proving to be a traumatic season, he was suddenly the old Terry Venables. The cheeky cockney was actually revelling in the troubles and his team finally looked capable of delivering the goods. Now he could sit down with his chairman in a position of strength. And rather than take the manager to task for his criticism, Scholar was more concerned to quell rumours of a rift by opening negotiations on a new contract.

But no matter what Venables did, he could not dispel fears that the massive problems facing Irving Scholar were about to encroach on the field of play. In such a situation, any manager would be hard pushed to maintain the momentum of the team. No matter what Venables may have learned at Barcelona, there was nothing in his experience to prepare him for the possibility of his employers going out of business. That such a famous club should have been brought once again to the brink of bankruptcy is a catastrophe that requires some explanation.

6

Irving's Lament

At 5.10 p.m. on Friday 19 October 1990, the Panel of the Committee on Quotations to the International Stock Exchange, which can best be described as the City equivalent of an FA disciplinary hearing, suspended dealing in the shares of Tottenham Hotspur plc, the parent company of the football club. The reason given for the action was that there was 'insufficient public information ... available for determining the current value of these securities', because factors that were likely to affect the share price had been concealed. The club that had made history in 1983 by becoming the first British football club to go public, a move seen by many at the time as a model for the future, had reached the point of collapse, its financial affairs in disarray, its board of directors in open confrontation with each other. The significance of the intervention by the Stock Exchange was that it underlined the fact that the directors had not only failed to establish a sound financial basis for the club but had compounded that failure by excessive secrecy. How could it have happened that the euphoria and profits of past years had evaporated to the point where the club could not afford to pay the final instalment of Gary Lineker's transfer fee? And since little detail of the causes of the company's true financial plight had been revealed, what would be the future of the club and those who had led it into the brave new world of corporate finance, particularly chairman Irving Scholar, when the full facts became public knowledge?

Since the sale of Chris Waddle to Marseille in June 1989, it was widely known that Spurs' finances were not as buoyant as had been thought. Few, however, could have known that Scholar had been worried about the overall health of the company for at least a year before the Waddle sale and a full two years before the details of the disastrous state of the club's financial affairs began to be revealed in the press, in September 1990.

All the signs were there that history was repeating itself. Back on 12 December 1981, Scholar and a group of like-minded, wealthy Spurs fans travelled to an away game against Leeds. Although the team, FA Cup holders, was performing well, the cost of rebuilding the West Stand had spiralled out of control and the club faced a loan-repayment schedule it could not possibly meet. The mismanagement of the building work seriously weakened the credibility of the board of directors led by Arthur Richardson, and after talking through the problems with his friends on the trip to Leeds, Scholar became convinced that Spurs were headed for bankruptcy unless someone like himself intervened. When his offers of free professional assistance were rejected, he decided to attempt a takeover bid.

That Irving Scholar succeeded at all, let alone at the modest cost of £600,000, surprised even himself. Indeed, he hadn't made any arrangements to move back to England from tax exile in Monaco, which precluded him from taking a formal role at White Hart Lane for almost a year, although there was never any doubt about who was pulling the strings. It was Scholar's belief that Tottenham was a big club on the field but a small one off it, meaning that it had never cashed in on its commercial potential, a situation he was determined to change. In fact, Spurs had always been the most conservative of clubs commercially, White Hart Lane being one of the last League grounds, as recently as 1972, to allow perimeter advertising. Under the new regime, debts left by the old administration were to be wiped out by a public flotation, while diversification into other areas was designed to provide a steady stream of profits to fund the football club. Although this plan can hardly be faulted for its objectives, it suffered from two crucial flaws. The first was that since the flotation left no significant cash reserves once the debt began to be repaid, there was little margin for error in the diversification process. In other words, while cash was not immediately necessary, if just one of the new businesses failed to perform as budgeted, or if some sudden unforeseen expenditure became necessary, Spurs could be in trouble. Thus the flotation itself, a visionary concept which should have provided the solid base necessary to achieve Scholar's ambitions, in fact contributed to the precarious nature of the club's finances. The flotation was seen at White Hart Lane as the first stage of a longer-term plan. It was envisaged that, at some point in the future, a rights issue of new shares would be effected. The trouble with this was that it assumed financial conditions would remain the same and that the parent company would retain its value. In fact, when the board decided to go ahead with the rights issue in 1987 as Tottenham Hotspur plc was about to purchase a ladies' fashion company called Martex, the stock market collapse in October intervened and the rights issue had to be shelved.

The second flaw in the Scholar plan was the personality of the chairman himself. While there can be no question about Irving Scholar's commitment to the club, he had to have total control. This unwillingness to delegate, coupled with an effusive and often bombastic manner, meant that cooperation was only sought on his terms. As the club captain he inherited, Steve Perryman, said: 'He's a Spurs fanatic and wants the best for the club. Sometimes I would say he's a little misguided in how to get it but nobody can say he's not got the best interests of Tottenham at heart.' Scholar's methods, however, alienated so many factions that when he needed wholehearted support, it was unlikely to be forthcoming.

The first person to question Scholar's intentions was manager Keith Burkenshaw, who resigned after taking the team to a UEFA Cup triumph in 1984 with the now famous comment that 'there used to be a football club over there'. Burkenshaw had wanted to retain the power over club affairs that managers had come to expect. Under the new regime, which was now part of a public company, this was impossible. Burkenshaw was replaced by his number two, Peter Shreeves, whose inexperience facilitated Scholar's desire to take a more active role in matters such as the buying and selling of players. Previously, this had been entirely in the hands of the manager but was now often handled by the chairman personally. Such changes in the role of the manager became more common in the 1980s as football's financial problems increased, but as a pioneer in this field, Scholar felt the wrath of a conservative football establishment.

More importantly, it did not take Irving Scholar long to gain the displeasure of the supporters. The share flotation had been over-subscribed, indicating the mood of optimism it had engendered, but the raising of admission prices to the highest in London, the sale of assets such as the Cheshunt training ground, the continued marginalization of the Supporters' Club (which had always had an uneasy relationship with the football club), along with the institution of a membership scheme seen by many as little more than a money-making venture, and the use of the programme as a mail-order catalogue (the price of a child's home shirt in 1990 was £17.99), led increasing numbers of fans to view the administration as more interested in corporate profits than football. But the issue which really whipped up opposition against Scholar was the proposed rebuilding of the East Stand, which included a contentious plan to replace the famous Shelf standing area with executive boxes and seats.

In principle, the decision to rebuild the East Stand was surely correct. Economically, the case was clear. The West Stand provided income, but since it was mostly occupied by season-ticket holders and executive boxes, its contribution to cash flow at important times was negligible. In practice, however, everything that could go wrong did go wrong, and the rebuilding turned into a disaster that eventually reached monstrous proportions. No consultations were carried out with supporters over the details of the proposed changes. Moreover, the way the architects' plans were presented to Haringey Council led supporters to think that the club might be attempting to manipulate the procedures in order to conceal what was going on. As this view became more widespread, the development began to turn into a public-relations catastrophe of the highest order. It seems incredible that anyone at the club could believe they could push the plans through without the public noticing or objecting. Surely Irving Scholar must have realized that there would be widespread opposition, particularly over the abolition of the Shelf, which he himself called 'the best standing view in London'.

The incident says much about Scholar's style of management. Ironically, he had not originally been in favour of rebuilding and had to be convinced of the need for it by Paul Bobroff, chairman of the parent company, Tottenham Hotspur plc. But once he had decided that White Hart Lane should be at the forefront of the move away from standing spectators, Scholar sought to implement the decision as soon as possible without being encumbered by the opinions of anyone else. Scholar also took personal control of the project, identifying himself with it and refusing until the last moment to acknowledge the fans' right to have their say. Despite having invested so much of his credibility in the new stand's success, Scholar failed to appear personally at planning meetings of Haringey Council to defend his decisions, preferring instead to send the club secretary, Peter Barnes. This public reticence did not extend to the more elegant surroundings of the Palace of Westminster, where Scholar, while refusing to listen to his own supporters on the Shelf issue, was quite prepared to lecture the House of Lords on the iniquities of the Government's proposed membership scheme. His willingness to go public on major issues, invariably to great effect – he spearheaded the move to break the BBC/ITV cartel, which he regards as his 'best business deal' – was never carried over to dealings in his personal fiefdom, which is what the football club had effectively become.

After the Taylor Report into the Hillsborough disaster, Irving Scholar could justifiably claim that he was right to seek an all-seat East Stand, but by then the damage, to both the image and the finances of the club, had been done. It was not as if the original Scholar plan merely provided seating for fans who previously stood: it increased the space for the corporate customer to the highest in the League (thirty-six new boxes to add to the seventy-two in the West Stand). Moreover, the lack of regard for the fans' views and the way the planning application was carried out rankled with Spurs' supporters and led to the creation of a pressure group, Left on the Shelf. Eventually, when Scholar was forced by the resistance campaign to include a reduced area for standing spectators, the delay and the substantial architectural alterations proved extremely costly. When the stand finally opened for business, the project had more than doubled in cost to over £10 million.

Another consequence of providing more facilities for the corporate customer was that White Hart Lane's capacity was reduced. When it eventually becomes an all-seat ground, it will hold no more than 25,000, the smallest ground of the big five English clubs. There is a plan which would ultimately see capacity rise to 35,000 but, like the rights issue, it is dependent on factors outside the control of the club. The contraction goes against developments elsewhere in Europe, where capacities are actually increasing. It would surely be impossible for Tottenham Hotspur to compete with the really big clubs of Europe playing in a stadium holding only 25,000 or even 35,000 people. When Spurs are doing well, they could expect to pull crowds of 40–50,000 on a regular basis. To plan for such a low number of paying customers always seemed at odds with the professed ambition of the club to be counted among the biggest in Europe. The only way it made sense was if there was a long-term view that the future lay in a new stadium elsewhere or if Wembley were used for big games. But if that was the case, why spend so much money turning a great sporting arena like White Hart Lane into a miniature version of San Siro?

Two other problems affected the rebuilding of the East Stand, the financing of the work and relations with the building contractors, Wimpey. Allied to both of these was the significant cost overrun. Whereas Arsenal's rebuilding of the Clock End was largely paid for before any work started, through a ten-year lease scheme, the Tottenham development was financed through loans, the same erroneous strategy employed for the construction of the West Stand by the previous administration. The significance of these arrangements lies in the fact that the terms of the loans did not protect the club against either rising costs or time-delays. They were, in fact, fixed-term loans from the Midland Bank and meant that the club's overdraft could be called in at any moment.

No one at Tottenham was unduly concerned about the nature of the deal they had struck with Midland. Tony Berry, the chairman of Blue Arrow, a high-profile company which at the time was a byword for success, had just joined the Tottenham board, and it was felt that his connections in the City, combined with a bullish stock market, would ensure that money could easily be raised as and when it was needed. It was not long before both of these misplaced beliefs were shattered. The worldwide stock market crash of 1987 put paid to hopes of easy money, while in 1988 Tony Berry was removed from the chairmanship of Blue Arrow amid allegations that loans he had made on the company's behalf, some to Tottenham Hotspur, had not been authorized by the board. Berry had been an occupant of one of White Hart Lane's executive boxes who bought his way on to the board via the purchase of 400,000 new shares. He later bought a further 400,000 shares from Paul Bobroff and remained a Spurs director throughout the club's troubles. Once sacked from Blue Arrow, however, his access to funds in the City on behalf of Spurs was somewhat curtailed. The business that Berry did introduce, despite Irving Scholar's reservation that it was just too far removed from football, turned out to be spectacularly unsuccessful. In 1987, the plc bought Martex and Stumps, two women's fashion companies. 'If we hadn't done this,' Scholar said somewhat ruefully at a later date, 'we would be millions better off.' According to one insider, the actual figure was over £5 million.

Meanwhile, throughout the time when building work was taking place, deadlines were not met and there was an ongoing debate over the quality and cost of the work. Things got so bad that the first home game of the 1989–90 season against Coventry had to be postponed as the new stand had not been completed, a turn of events the club blamed on Wimpey. (The Football League docked Spurs two points for failing to fulfil a fixture on the due date, which were only recovered through legal action.) Scholar withheld payment to Wimpey, which led to a long legal dispute. The East Stand, which had caused so much controversy and been so expensive, had one last sting in its tail. The receipts for the first home game in 1989–90 were not recouped until the following April, by which time the club's finances had badly deteriorated, and attendances at the three home games following the Coventry postponement were substantially reduced, because the delay in opening the new facility had drastically cut ground capacity. The cost to the club in lost income during this crucial period was approximately half a million pounds.

It could be argued that the real moment when Spurs' financial health was compromised occurred at Anfield on 26 May 1989, when Michael Thomas's goal won the title for Arsenal. Had anyone other than their arch-rivals lifted the championship, Irving Scholar might just have resisted the pleas of his manager that he was a couple of players short of a trophy-winning team. As it was, Scholar sanctioned the outlay of £1.5 million on Gary Lineker and Mohammed Ali Amar (Nayim) from Barcelona. It was a classic example of Scholar's ambition for the club. He couldn't say no to the opportunity, perhaps because he put on-field activities first. The expenditure could possibly have been afforded even with the mounting problems of rebuilding the East Stand, although this is debatable as interest rates had started to climb, but within a month the chairman's worst fears were confirmed when the trading losses of subsidiary companies suddenly reached overwhelming proportions.

When Spurs first went public, a central plank in the strategy was that the holding company, Tottenham Hotspur plc, would diversify into business areas not directly related to football. Profits from these activities would provide the football club with sound finances for years to come. When fears were raised about the effect on the team if these new ventures failed, they were calmed with assurances from Irving Scholar that since each area would consist of a separate company, the extraneous activities would never encroach upon team matters. The concept for this type of operation is simple. The renown of a big football club like Tottenham Hotspur has what is known as a 'halo-effect' on any product or service associated with it. Thus, in theory, sales of the product or service are enhanced by the spin-off from publicity gained by the football club. A key component of such a strategy, however, is that when a new area of business is contemplated which is not related to football, then the operation should be franchised out to experts. This means a certain loss of control, with a concomitant reduction in a share of any profits. But any negative factors are balanced by the likelihood that a business will be more efficiently run by people with an intimate knowledge of the relevant industry than when managed by outsiders. Irving Scholar saw any dilution of profits as contrary to his principle of maximizing the income potential of the Spurs name. In addition, Scholar's reluctance to delegate, which saw him assume as much control as possible over everything, meant that the full benefits of expert management would probably be lost. Someone who has worked with the Spurs chairman said of him, 'He has this great gift of self-delusion. He believes he delegates and only gets involved when he is needed. Then when things go wrong it's nothing to do with him.'

Most of the subsidiary companies did not perform particularly well, but this fact had been buried in the minutiae of the accounts. So when the parent company turned in a profit of almost £1 million in 1987–8, it was mainly due to a profit on football operations and the sale of assets, especially the Cheshunt training ground, which brought in £4.5 million. Neither a computer-ticket operation, Synchro Systems Ltd, nor the Hummel sportswear franchise, had made large profits, but both companies deteriorated dramatically during the summer of 1989. The worst figures came from Hummel, which required a huge cash injection to survive. Where a sober analyst might have cut his losses, the plc made the crucial decision to support the Hummel franchise with football-club money, at a cost of over £3 million. Scholar had always believed in his publicly stated position that the function of subsidiaries was to fund the football club. Paul Bobroff, on the other hand, thought that profits from the football club should be used to bolster ailing parts of the empire. As Tottenham was now a quoted company, its prime responsibility was to shareholders rather than to one specific area of operations; thus there was some force behind Bobroff's argument, and Scholar, fatally, allowed himself to be persuaded. The situation led to a stormy board meeting during which Scholar clashed with his erstwhile friend. Bobroff thought he commanded enough support to get rid of Scholar, but the attempted coup failed. Finding that the other major shareholder, Tony Berry, was backing Scholar, Bobroff resigned and put his 10 per cent stake in the club up for sale, only to be reinstated within a week at the insistence of the company's merchant bankers and following the realization by Scholar and Berry that they could not buy Bobroff's shares without having to make a similar bid to all shareholders, in accordance with Stock Exchange regulations.

The problems with Hummel were too deep-rooted to be solved

with a cash injection and a new bout of enthusiasm from Irving Scholar. The mail-order side of the business hardly got off the ground and retail sales were slow in a highly competitive market. Poor distribution, and the fact that the margin for retailers was fixed by Spurs/Hummel at a percentage that was way below the accepted industry norm, inevitably resulted in destocking and a dramatic dip in sales. Other clubs, including Coventry City, Sunderland and Aston Villa, which had agreed to use the Hummel kit, pulled out as agreements were broken. Coventry's managing director, George Curtis, remarked, 'They could not supply us in the time-scale we wanted. There was a case when we could not get stock in time for Christmas.' Sunderland's commercial manager, Alec King, confirmed the bleak picture when he said, 'The distribution was pretty poor. There was always some excuse.'

As the summer of 1989 drew to a close and the new season beckoned, Scholar realized that even with the money from season tickets and boxholders, there was not enough coming in and expenditure on the East Stand was out of control. Suddenly, he was offered salvation from an unlikely source. It was the first of a number of unusual events that gave Scholar hope that he could rectify the situation. On the morning of the press conference to announce Gary Lineker's transfer from Barcelona, Scholar received a telephone call from France. On the other end of the line was a Yugoslav soccer agent called Barin, who was known to Scholar through his involvement in transfer negotiations concerning Glenn Hoddle and Paris St Germain (which did not materialize), and Clive Allen and Bordeaux (which did). On behalf of Marseille, Barin made an offer of £2.5 million for Chris Waddle. By the end of the conversation the amount he was bidding went up to £3 million. Scholar spoke to Terry Venables, who was at first opposed to the idea, but once the chairman had explained that the offer was too good to turn down for a player of Waddle's age, and that the sale could release funds for the purchase of players, Venables' opposition dissolved. He asked Scholar if he would attempt to get the French to increase their offer, and to look into the possibility of doing an 'Ian Rush' type deal, whereby Spurs would retain Waddle for the forthcoming season, as Liverpool had been able to do when Rush was sold to Juventus. With his manager's blessing, Scholar could now express some interest in the bid, and Barin came to London, accompanied by Bernard Tapie, the multi-millionaire businessman and French Deputy (MP), who is president of Marseille. Still Scholar was reluctant to sell, but as the price went up to £4.25 million, he felt honour-bound to give Waddle the option of taking what he described as a 'once in a lifetime opportunity for a player of twenty-nine'. After sleeping on the offer, Waddle decided to accept. The disappointment felt by Scholar and Venables at losing the player was mitigated by thoughts of how the squad could be strengthened. However, the ailing plc took most of the money, reneging on the understanding that it would all go to Venables. By way of explanation to Scholar, Bobroff told him that he didn't think the fee received for Waddle would be anything like as high as £4.25 million. It was one more nail in the coffin of the Scholar–Bobroff axis. Although the sale of Waddle alienated supporters, it was justified on the basis of the player's age and the large fee. However, there can be no doubt that Waddle was transferred because without the sale Spurs could well have faced the spectre of receivership and possible bankruptcy.

The Marseille cash bought Scholar time, but the situation remained on a knife-edge. When *Italia 90* started, Hummel, Martex and Stumps were plainly no longer going concerns, while the ticketing operation, Synchro Systems, which had staggered along for a year on the back of a contract to print tickets for the World Cup, experienced major technical problems. Something went wrong with the computerized mailing system at the beginning of the 1990–91 season, and a number of clubs, including Crystal Palace, which had contracted to Synchro, were left with irate season-ticket holders whose tickets had not arrived by the start of the season. Another injection of cash was needed, now more urgently than ever, first to write off the losses involved in the retail fiascos and second to service the debt to the Midland Bank, which had reached £10 million and was rising. There were distinct signs that the bank was getting nervous. Realizing that he could not possibly sell Gascoigne and Lineker and survive, Scholar found another potential saviour, one with whom he had dealt briefly when they were on the Football League's Television Committee in 1984. In early July, when he came back from the World Cup, Irving Scholar called Robert Maxwell.

By the time Scholar and Maxwell sat down to talk in the *Daily Mirror* building on 25 July, the Spurs chairman had come up with some concrete, if last-ditch, proposals. The only way new money could be raised was to go back to the idea of a rights issue, which entailed the creation of new shares in the holding company, Tottenham Hotspur plc. However, in the harsh economic climate of 1990, there was little prospect of City investment. Therefore, the plan called for Robert Maxwell personally to underwrite the rights issue, in effect guaranteeing to buy up any unsold shares at a fixed price of £1.30, substantially above the going rate. The shares would first be offered to existing shareholders on a one-for-one basis, but since the major shareholders, particularly Scholar, would give 'certain assurances' to the effect that they would not take up the whole of the offer, Maxwell would be left owning at least 26 per cent of the holding company (and possibly as much as 50 per cent if nobody bought the new shares) at a cost of £13.2 million, which would wipe out the debt to Midland and provide funds for new players. Maxwell asked Scholar two questions. Will you sell your shares? Will you stay to run the club? When Scholar answered 'no' and 'yes' respectively, Maxwell replied, 'it's a deal. I'll do it.' Yet again, Irving Scholar looked to have come up with the lifeline he so desperately needed.

For Robert Maxwell, this was the chance to get involved with a major football club for which he had been waiting for some years. Maxwell always claimed that his initial involvement in the game with Oxford was undertaken because he could not turn down a request for help. 'If I were a woman I'd always be pregnant,' he joked, 'because I can never say no.' Once involved, Maxwell found the great game gave him a platform that even his enormous wealth and media ownership could not provide. Frustrated in his desire for change by the arcane structure of the Football League, it did not take Maxwell long to criticize the Management Committee at every possible opportunity. However, he also realized that unless he had the power of a big club behind him, his excursions into football were always likely to end in disappointment. Having pulled out of a deal to buy Manchester United in 1984 when Martin Edwards raised the price overnight from £10 million to £15 million, Maxwell concentrated on clubs like Derby, potentially a First Division outfit but debt-ridden and with an apathetic public, and those in towns where he already had business interests, such as Oxford, Reading and Watford. The offer presented by Irving Scholar gave him the opportunity to strike back at those who had thwarted his ambitions. It also provided him with the chance to become involved with the big clubs of Europe should a European Superleague be established. It certainly had nothing to do with any love of Spurs as a club. Maxwell's allegiance, if any can be discerned, belongs to Arsenal. When he had made his bid for Manchester United in 1984 he said, 'I am an original Arsenal supporter going back to the 1930s. When I came out of the army in 1947 I was among thousands queueing to pay half a crown at Highbury.'

Maxwell agreed to Scholar's deal on the condition that his involvement remain secret. He also explained that he wanted no role in the management of Spurs. This declaration was obviously designed to allow Irving Scholar to continue in his management capacity and to placate any fears among the rest of the directors and the supporters once the deal became public knowledge. But of course it was, in reality, a mere gesture. Irving Scholar might well have been one of the few people involved in football whom Maxwell liked and respected and with whom he could deal: Scholar had, after all, supported Maxwell in his bid to raise the price of television rights for League football, which led to the blackout of 1985 when football disappeared from domestic screens for the first half of the season. But if the financial performance of the company continued to deteriorate, then Maxwell, a self-confessed 'hands-on' manager, could well be 'forced' to step into the breach to save the day, rather as a 'reluctant' Silvio Berlusconi took over AC Milan.

Although the general state of Spurs' finances gave the greatest cause for concern, there was an even more pressing problem for Irving Scholar. When Spurs bought Lineker and Nayim from Barcelona it was agreed that the transfer fee was to be paid in instalments. The day of the meeting with Maxwell was just six days before the deadline for the final payment of £850,000, but the money was just not available. There was no chance of getting the cash from the Midland Bank, which was busy swallowing up virtually all the season-ticket payments not needed to cover immediate costs. Scholar had used his own money when cash crises had loomed in the past – he had loaned the club £350,000 and had not cashed his £120,000 dividend cheque – but what was needed now was beyond his resources. Talks had been proceeding with the sportswear manufacturer Umbro, about a new kit-sponsorship deal, but the contract had not yet been finalized. Money had also been made available in the past by Tony Berry, but this source dried up when Berry was removed from Blue Arrow. So Scholar asked Maxwell to loan his own business, The Holborn Property Company, £1.1 million, which Holborn would then re-loan to Spurs to see the club over its immediate crisis by paying Barcelona the outstanding monies for Lineker and Nayim. The rest of the money was to be used to make payments on the East Stand. Incredibly, Maxwell agreed and once again the Spurs chairman had somehow managed to stave off insistent creditors – at least for the time being. Scholar put up the property in King's Road, Chelsea, to guarantee the amount, and since the re-loan to the football club was to come from Holborn, Maxwell's involvement could remain secret. Maxwell made the money available through a private company, Headington Investments, and the two men agreed to meet again after Scholar had put the share package to his directors.

On 1 August a board meeting of sorts took place. This meeting was attended by only two members of the board, Scholar, who had a direct interest in the Maxwell loan, and Derek Peter, the financial director. Nevertheless, the meeting authorized the loan deal on behalf of Tottenham Hotspur plc. Two days later, Irving Scholar put the rights-issue negotiations and the loan deal to most of the remaining members of the board but did not disclose the name of the mystery benefactor. The chairman of the parent company, Paul Bobroff, was not present, but the other directors, Frank Sinclair, Tony Berry and Douglas Alexiou, gave Scholar and Peter the authority to continue negotiations on the rights issue, provided that the cost of the new shares was above the listed price of £1. Much of the later criticism of Scholar centred on these meetings. The idea that directors of a public company could be involved in negotiations about a rights issue and a substantial loan without either the chairman present or the shareholders informed is viewed with distaste by the Stock Exchange, since such measures could create a false market in the shares. In Scholar's defence, he insists that when the purchase of Gary Lineker was agreed, the plc board gave him the freedom to underwrite the deal until money became available again.

Although Paul Bobroff was chairman of the plc, the power really belonged to Scholar, as it was Scholar, chairman of the football club but only a director of the holding company despite being the main shareholder, who made all the important day-to-day decisions. Bobroff, an old City hand and head of Markheath Securities, was nevertheless a major shareholder and had been hounding Scholar for months with his view that the football club should do more to help the ailing parent. When he was eventually informed of the proposed deal with Maxwell, he felt that Scholar had prevaricated for too long and had now come up with a desperate plan. Perhaps Scholar was naïve in thinking that Bobroff would accept the deal quietly. In fact, Bobroff did all he could to slow down, then stall, any possibility of it going through.

Most of the 10,000 small shareholders were Spurs supporters and had been treated as such by the club, that is, with little or no consultation, throughout the period since the flotation. Keeping the negotiations secret was simply the normal way football clubs went about these things. Public ownership should have forced the board to inform and consult, but no such process ever took place, and the shareholders/supporters, who were used to poor treatment, never really complained. Maxwell, by contrast, had played it by the book, and, since the deal involved a private company which he owns, he was under no obligation to inform anybody of what he was doing.

On 6 August Maxwell, Scholar and Derek Peter met to finalize arrangements for the rights issue. Although the basic agreement was concluded at that meeting, it soon became clear that under new rules passed by the Football League after Maxwell tried to buy Watford, when he still owned Derby and Oxford and had a stake in Reading, the would-be patron of Spurs would have to offload his other football interests if he wanted the deal with Scholar to proceed. On 23 August the agreement was postponed until such time as Maxwell disposed of his holdings in the other clubs, most particularly Derby County. By the end of the month, Derek Peter had resigned for reasons unconnected with immediate events. On 1 September, having failed to secure a management buy-out at Derby, Maxwell put the club, which had cost him £850,000, up for sale at £8 million. The reason he gave was the paucity of response to his efforts on the part of the Derby public. 'Nothing illustrates the lack of support better than last Saturday's 12,000 turn-out,' he announced. 'It was lamentable. The non-support is the reason for me saying enough is enough. They must realize I don't have a licence to print £50 notes.' More enigmatically, Maxwell also maintained that any money he received from the sale of Derby would be 'reinvested in football'.

Although Maxwell may have believed that he could quickly sell Derby at the asking price of £8 million, anyone with any knowledge of the state of the football market realized that buyers would hardly be queueing up at the door. This setback did nothing for Scholar's peace of mind, but there seemed little he could do. Meanwhile, he was likely to come under increasing pressure to reveal the name of the backer and the reason for the delay. All these considerations were removed on Sunday 9 September, ironically the day after the Gascoigne hat-trick against Derby County, when the Scholar–Maxwell deal was revealed in the *Sunday Times*, a full day before a 'world exclusive' appeared in Maxwell's own paper, the *Daily Mirror*. Someone had not been entirely discreet about the identity of Scholar's investor. At this stage only Scholar, Derek Peter and Maxwell himself knew the full scope of the share issue, although it is possible that Scholar also briefed one or more of the other directors privately. When the deal stalled because of Maxwell's need to sell Derby, details of the rights-issue talks, but not the loan, were leaked.

In the days that followed the *Sunday Times* story, all hell broke loose. Paul Bobroff expressed surprise and anger when Maxwell's involvement became known, claiming he knew nothing about the deal until he read it in the press. The Football League were next into the fray on Monday when a spokesman somewhat pompously told the press: 'We brought in the . . . rule [about multiple ownership of clubs] after Maxwell tried to buy Watford. There is nothing we can do to stop any deal for Tottenham, but he must release the majority of his other shares. These rules also apply to relatives, so having his son, Kevin, at Oxford would make no difference. And although it is speculation at the moment, what is being proposed at Spurs is of significant interest and all parties must understand the implications. We will keep a close eye on the situation. I know Maxwell is proposing to sell Derby, but that alone is not enough. He has a great interest in Oxford and nearly 30 per cent of Reading. The bulk of that must go.' The chief of the players' union, the PFA, Gordon Taylor, said, 'I don't want to see football clubs being used as Monopoly pieces for big City moguls.'

Another effect of the newspaper story was that it pushed up the price of Spurs' shares to £1.11. Guy Libby, whose Abingdon Management consortium controlled 6 per cent of shares, criticized the way the board had gone about things, saying, 'As in the past, we are waiting for more official facts from the Tottenham plc board. The awful thing is the lack of hard information.' Libby's concern centred on the fact that the value of Spurs' shares under his control would fall if the deal went through as reported, since Maxwell was not obliged to bid for existing stock. As the Spurs board met to discuss the situation, a statement was promised for later in the day, but none materialized as Scholar and Bobroff clashed over what had happened. The same day the Quotations Panel formally told Spurs' financial advisers, Barclays de Zoete Wedd, to furnish full information to themselves and shareholders as soon as possible.

Whatever credit is due to Irving Scholar for doing everything he could to save Spurs, it is diminished because, first, the problems were largely of his own making, and second, his obsession with secrecy led him to carry the burden of the club's problems for two years. The idea of a rights issue had long been in the background, but no one outside Spurs knew anything about it, so when it was finally revealed in the press it came as a great shock to everyone. No doubt the involvement of Robert Maxwell would have provoked a furore in its own right, but this could have been tempered if the rights-issue project had been explained to supporters and shareholders from the beginning. Disclosure from an early date may also have prevented official action by the Stock Exchange. As it was, the newspaper stories started a bandwagon process that would become impossible to stop.

No statement was forthcoming until three days later, when details of the £1.1 million loan from Maxwell were given to the Stock Exchange and the press. The Football League expressed disquiet at the news and mounted an investigation to determine whether the loan had breached League rules. A separate enquiry was launched by the Stock Exchange into the negotiations with Maxwell, while the Spurs board promised to send a circular explaining the background to the situation 'as soon as practicable'. In legal terms, the loan from Maxwell should have been put to a meeting of shareholders for their approval. After this information was released, the share price slipped back to £1, the same as when it was first floated seven years before (a substantial loss in real terms).

Another board meeting took place on Friday 14 September, during which Scholar privately told Bobroff to resign, as Maxwell had indicated that the deal would be called off if the Tottenham board continued its internecine warfare. 'I'm flashing the yellow card at those involved in squabbles,' Maxwell remarked to the press. Bobroff opposed Maxwell's involvement on the grounds that the true value of Spurs was far higher than the notional amount conferred on the club by the rights issue, and that money could be found elsewhere. Bobroff flatly refused to resign, so Scholar put forward a motion of no confidence in the chairman, which was passed by four votes to one. Although he was ousted as chairman, Bobroff could not be sacked from the board except by a shareholders' vote. He refused to resign his directorship and vowed to fight on 'to safeguard shareholders' interests'. Scholar announced that he would ask an extraordinary general meeting to vote Bobroff off the board. The next day, Tottenham's financial advisers, Barclays de Zoete Wedd, and its broker, de Zoete & Bevan, resigned in protest at the sacking of Bobroff and the fact that they had not been informed of the Maxwell deal.

Two days after the board meeting that saw the end of Bobroff (it was 'blood on the walls' according to one source), Robert Maxwell told David Frost on TV-am that he was now prepared to resume talks on the Tottenham deal.

'I have agreed, if they end this unseemly squabbling between Mr Bobroff and Mr Scholar, if they are a united board, that if they wish to recommence those discussions as to whether I might help them get away a rights issue, I would be happy to help them,' he said. 'Plans can go ahead tomorrow or the day after. Spurs need to have professional advisers and must comply with the rules governing a public company and proceed in a proper manner.'

Never one to pass up an opportunity for a sideswipe at the Football League, Maxwell went on to criticize severely the statements coming from Lytham St Annes. 'Football's mismanagement committee are shooting off their mouths, investigating this . . . looking at that,' he blasted. 'Yet here is a game totally mismanaged and virtually destroyed by their incompetence. The League have been saying they are going to write to Spurs asking for details, but I've checked this morning with the chairman of Spurs whether they have written, and nothing. They have been making all sorts of innuendoes . . . it is disgraceful.'

When Frost pressed him about who would control Tottenham if the deal went through, Maxwell replied, 'I would not like to end up with any [shares]. I have agreed to help out and if everything is agreed we will proceed with a rights issue. Twenty-five per cent is the maximum I would end up with if nobody else took a share.'

For the next two weeks the now irrevocably split Spurs board wrangled over the text of the promised circular. At the same time, new lawyers and financial consultants had to be found. Legal advisers, Ashurst Morris Crisp, were appointed by the board to produce a detailed report on the affair for the Stock Exchange. This was pushed through by Paul Bobroff as a means of establishing the probity of directors' conduct. There was no doubt to whom he was referring. The eventual report set back Spurs at least another £50,000, a rather costly way to wash dirty linen in public. More importantly, while the wrangles continued, the board was hamstrung for several weeks, creating an impasse that continued long after the report was eventually issued.

On 26 September a group of Spurs fans met at the University of London Union in Malet Street to discuss the situation. Stuart Mutler, co-editor of the *Spur* fanzine, gave the reason for the gathering when he said, 'I don't think there is anything we can actually do, but the meeting will give supporters an opportunity to get up and express our feelings. I think a lot of supporters are frustrated because they haven't been able to make their views known.'

The thrust of the meeting became clear when Ed Horton, the editor of the Oxford United fanzine, warned that Maxwell 'never gets involved with anything for more than a few years . . . he will use Tottenham Hotspur and then when it has served his purpose he will take as much money as he can out of it and he will put it down.' There was a realization that, in Horton's words, 'we don't have much power as football supporters, but we do have the power to be like terriers at the ankles of people who run football.' Maxwell had to be deterred and Scholar controlled. A working party was born, its purpose to see whether a body of shareholders could be formed that would supply valid opposition when the extraordinary general meeting was convened.

The same night, Robert Maxwell appeared on BBC television's *Question Time*. A resourceful questioner asked the panel: 'If it is wrong for one person to own more than one football club, why is it right for them to own more than one newspaper?' Robert Maxwell, having defended his right to multiple press ownership, went on to speak about his talks with Spurs. 'The *Sunday Times* article was correct,' he said, 'but I insisted that I wanted no part of the management of Spurs.' By the end of the week, new financial advisers, Brown Shipley, were appointed, paving the way for a resumption of the talks with Maxwell, who, it now emerged, might be able to place his other footballing interests in trust in order to avoid the League rule prohibiting multiple ownership. It seemed that whatever new regulations the League brought in to stop him, Maxwell would find an ingenious way round them.

On 3 October, the long-running dispute with Wimpey reached

the high court. It should have taken place months earlier, but another extraordinary piece of good fortune occurred for Irving Scholar, when, on the day of the original hearing, the judge was taken ill and the case adjourned. When it did reach court, Spurs lost the action and were ordered to pay £750,000 to the aggrieved construction company. Magnanimously, Wimpey agreed to Spurs' request for time to find the money. Meanwhile, as speculation mounted in the media over the possible contents of the Ashurst Morris Crisp report, which had already overrun the deadline set by the Stock Exchange, the League began pressing for answers to its questions regarding the Maxwell loan. Irving Scholar, realizing that little could be achieved in discussions while Paul Bobroff was present, decided to take a break in Monaco to recharge his batteries, leaving Brown Shipley and Ashurst Morris Crisp to hold the fort.

Amid all the attention that the boardroom fight was receiving, the country's most exciting football team had all but been forgotten. The 0–0 draw against QPR at a blustery Loftus Road was a much better match than the scoreline suggests, with both teams missing good chances. Although Gascoigne received a booking for dissent by testing referee Pierce's patience once too often (and if Mabbutt had not intervened after the final whistle he could have got a red card), Terry Venables was again happy that his team had kept yet another clean sheet away from home. The draw left Spurs in third place, behind Liverpool, who beat Derby to record an eighth successive win, and Arsenal, who defeated Norwich with two first-half goals from Paul Davis, the first a flick from a delicate Paul Merson through-ball, the second the result of a four-man move involving Siggi Jonsson, Nigel Winterburn and Anders Limpar.

More good news came Terry Venables' way when Paul Stewart scored his first goals of the season in the second leg of the Rumbelows Cup tie against Hartlepool. Admittedly, the opposition was modest and there was no pressure because of the 5–0 lead from the first leg, but still the performance was a professional one, and Stewart's goals should have done wonders for his confidence.

But it was as if football, the reason why everyone is so interested in Spurs in the first place, was merely a diversion from the goings-on in the boardroom. Two days after the Hartlepool game the Football League's Management Committee discussed a letter received from Ashurst Morris Crisp in explanation of the Maxwell loan and issued a statement saying, 'The Management Committee did not consider the loan to be a breach of League regulations as presently written.' The following day the full Ashurst Morris Crisp report into the affair was passed to the Stock Exchange. With the Saturday matches postponed because of England's European Championship game against Poland, and few statements coming from the involved parties, the vacuum was filled by speculation concerning the report's conclusions, most focusing on criticisms of Irving Scholar's role. One report suggested that Scholar might even be forced to resign. Neither the Spurs board nor the Stock Exchange made any official comment, and as the silence was maintained into the following week it was clear something was not right. In fact, the Spurs board was busy producing circulars for shareholders which the Stock Exchange was equally busy rejecting. When a final draft was again thrown out at 4 p.m. on 19 October, the Exchange decided to suspend trading in Spurs' shares. In a statement put out later that evening, the Exchange indicated that new information had been presented to it which influenced its decision. Part of this information was the news that a deal with Umbro had finally been clinched. It was to be the biggest kit sponsorship in English football, worth £4 million over four years, with a down payment of £1.1 million, exactly the amount of the Maxwell loan. The Exchange also indicated that trading in the shares could not resume until the circular had been agreed and sent out.

Irving Scholar arrived back from France in time for the home game against Sheffield United on 20 October. Somehow it had all gone horribly wrong, though Scholar himself felt that if he kept a cool head and managed to push through the Maxwell deal he would be vindicated. He would also be rid of Paul Bobroff. The formation of Spurs into a public company with thousands of supporters as small shareholders should have led to democracy and consultation. Instead it led to secrecy and financial collapse, as Irving Scholar continued to run Spurs as if it were a private company. David Murray, chairman of Glasgow Rangers, a club that more than most has cashed in on its commercial potential, said that football clubs should stick to football business, and that any club going for outside profits was 'taking its eye off the ball'. 'Supporters want one thing,' he continued, 'and that is to see the team win on a Saturday.'

A similar lesson could have been learned closer to home. At Highbury, the club has stuck religiously to football in its expansion plans. It has produced profits and a Championship-winning team. It has also managed to stay out of debt when carrying out stadium improvements. The most inexplicable part of the Spurs saga is the way Irving Scholar, who knew better than anyone how building work leads to financial problems, got into such a mess over the East Stand development. The only credible explanation lies in the character and style of Scholar's management. He had a vision of Spurs that saw outside interests providing finance to create a dream-team to rival the great Spurs sides that all football fans of his generation remembered with affection. But once he had decided to redevelop the East Stand, he sought to implement the scheme without heeding any words of restraint or delegating any responsibility to those with more objective judgements. The same style was applied to the running of the subsidiary operations and the rights-issue negotiations. Spurs could have gone under on a number of occasions in the preceding twelve months, but each time fate dealt Scholar unexpected largesse. They were cruel twists though, for they only postponed the final collapse. Now Scholar's future in football lay in the hands of Robert Maxwell.

There were many who questioned the need for Maxwell. One of them was David Dein, who warned Scholar that Maxwell may not be a silent partner. He may have been so at Derby, but his investment there was £850,000; at Tottenham it would be more than £13 million. Anyway, in his own words, Maxwell was an OAP and his children were primed to take over. While recognizing the relevance of these assertions, Scholar felt that the personal relationship between himself and Maxwell transcended them. He believed that he could control Maxwell. That this could prove to be a naïve position was illustrated by journalist

Hunter Davies, who remarked, 'They [the Spurs board] think they can take the money from him and keep him on the sidelines, but of course the minute that happens they'll be gobbled up and we'll never hear from them again.'

Jeff Randall, City editor of the *Sunday Times*, who broke the story in the first place, agreed, saying, 'The idea of Robert Maxwell as a passive partner is a contradiction in terms.' For Scholar there was still the comfort of lying third in the table and being unbeaten. But look who was second. Arsenal had retained their own unbeaten start to the season with the win against Norwich and followed that up by thrashing Chester 5–0 in the Rumbelows Cup, a victory achieved without Anders Limpar, who went AWOL to be with the Swedish international squad. Perry Groves got a rare chance to start a game and seized his opportunity by scoring the first two goals. In the match against Norwich, it was noticeable that Arsenal were using physical tactics to curb Robert Fleck's effectiveness, and Fleck was eventually forced to limp off the pitch. Although some superb play made the incidents which led to Fleck's departure pale in the memory, events were about to bring the subject of the Arsenal approach to football to the forefront of national and international attention.

7

Gunning for Glory

The day after shares in Tottenham Hotspur were suspended, Arsenal resumed centre-stage with a visit to Old Trafford. The Football League's highest crowd of the season so far – over 47,000 – testified to the glamorous nature of the match, as did the fact that it was to be televised around the world. Manchester United, despite inconsistent League form, had progressed to the second round of the European Cup-Winners' Cup, which had once again brought to the club the kind of international profile that all those connected with Arsenal craved. With Arsenal second in the table and unbeaten, everything was set up for a high-class game of football.

Instead, the match will be remembered for an eighteen-second incident midway through the second half, when fighting broke out among the players after a clash between Anders Limpar and United full back Dennis Irwin. Nigel Winterburn arrived on the scene with a high, scything tackle and the bomb went off. Irwin had been involved in a feud with Limpar for most of the match, characterized by a series of niggling fouls by both sides. Many observers were later of the opinion that the referee, Keith Hackett, should have clamped down earlier. Gordon Taylor, the head of the PFA, who was watching the game, said, 'I felt Keith Hackett didn't see two incidents happen together and that other players were starting to get involved.'

The England manager, Graham Taylor, made a similar point when watching a replay of the fracas on television: 'Where was the starting point at Old Trafford?' he asked. 'I saw the view the camera gave me. I saw what the camera showed as the starting point but in my view the camera didn't go back far enough into the game.'

As many as three players from each team could have been sent off. Brian McClair and Dennis Irwin of United aimed blatant kicks at opponents in the mêlée and Paul Ince dived head first into Anders Limpar. On the Arsenal side, in addition to Winterburn, Paul Davis pushed a United man in the face, while Limpar took his cue from Davis and did likewise. In the event, referee Hackett failed to see exactly what had happened and merely showed Winterburn and Limpar the yellow card.

The fact that Arsenal preserved their unbeaten record by winning the game 1–0 with a goal from Limpar, who caught United goalkeeper Les Sealey off-guard by deftly shooting for the near post when a centre was expected, was drowned in the furore that followed the brawl. On any other Saturday, the result from Carrow Road, where Norwich had halted Liverpool's 100 per cent record with a 1–1 draw, would have made all the headlines, but after the incident at Old Trafford there was only ever going to be one story. Radio and press were unanimous in their criticism of both teams, and with television broadcasting pictures of the imbroglio to sixty-four countries it was only a matter of time before the FA charged the two clubs with bringing the game into disrepute. As Keith Hackett could not report on what he had not seen, the FA would have to resort to trial by television. This did not augur well for Arsenal, since it was video evidence that got Paul Davis suspended for nine games in 1988.

Arsenal were likely to bear the brunt of any FA punishment, because the club had been involved in a similar incident in a match against Norwich the previous November, for which they were fined £20,000 and warned about their future conduct. It was this case that changed the FA view of player discipline. A circular was sent to all clubs warning them that they would now be responsible for the behaviour of their players. Moreover, the Arsenal team had developed something of a reputation for bad or churlish behaviour on the field, particularly when things seemed to be going against them. Six weeks after the Norwich game, for instance, four players were fined £1,000 each by the club for surrounding the referee after a game against Aston Villa to complain that Villa's winning goal was offside. Chairman Peter Hill-Wood said of the Villa incident, 'It was very silly and totally unacceptable. It was undignified and it was not Arsenal.' Such incidents undermined the aura of discipline and professionalism created by George Graham, but a number of other incidents had occurred that lent support to the view that problems of discipline at Highbury went deeper than the occasional flare-up in the heat of battle.

A previous game against Manchester United in January 1987 had ended with six bookings and David Rocastle sent off. A year later, George Graham was fined £250 by the FA for insulting remarks made to a referee. Six months after that came the Paul Davis–Glenn Cockerill clash, and 1989 was marred by the Norwich and Aston Villa incidents. Furthermore, in the week of the Manchester trouble, a number of officials attending a referees' seminar criticized the Arsenal team for continually disputing decisions. Apart from the occurrences on the pitch, there had also been disturbing disciplinary lapses off it – rowdy behaviour at the Supporters' Club dinner in 1989, for instance, after which Paul Merson and Steve Bould were fined; and a late-night drinking spree in Singapore, which led to four players being sent home early.

The disputes and disagreements that go on at all clubs have been, in Arsenal's case, magnified by the willingness of all and sundry to talk to the media, often with unforeseen consequences. In the weeks before the game against Manchester United, a number of these negative elements – a headstrong player, poor communication between manager and player, and the involvement of the press – combined to produce an eminently avoidable confrontation between George Graham and Anders Limpar over the latter's desire to represent his country.

Limpar was scheduled to turn out for Sweden against the newly united Germany, a particularly important match, as the Swedes are the hosts of the 1992 European Championships and therefore have only friendlies by way of preparation. However, George Graham refused him permission to go because of injury. Limpar flew to Stockholm anyway, citing a clause in his contract that gave him the right to a second medical opinion. In Sweden, he was declared fit and Graham was accused of claiming a false injury to a player who was required for international duty. Not unnaturally, Graham reacted badly to the slur.

'What people don't know is that he needed four days' treatment after our game against Leeds . . . and was also on antibiotics for a heavy cold,' exclaimed the irate manager. 'I am not a medical man, it was not my decision alone that he shouldn't go to Sweden. I took him off before the end against Norwich to avoid any risk of further aggravating the hamstring because we had already taken a gamble on playing him. Our doctor, John Crane, who is also the England doctor, gave Anders a medical after the match and judged that he wasn't fit enough to play in an international a few days later. I can't be accused of keeping him back for Arsenal's needs. He wouldn't have played against Chester in the Rumbelows Cup.'

The strain of the public argument, and the disciplinary measures that the press assured him were awaiting his return to Highbury, clearly got to Limpar, who injured a calf muscle in training and pulled out of the international at the last minute. Swedish coach Nisse Anderson, said, 'He was never allowed to concentrate on the match. Perhaps this was his real problem, his mind was not on training.' Anderson also recognized the value of his star players to the foreign clubs for which most of them play, saying, 'I can understand George Graham. Limpar is also their best player and all the fans in England want to see him. George did his best to protect him.'

The day after the Sweden–Germany game, Limpar met three Swedish journalists in his Stockholm hotel. The interview concentrated on the injury and how upset Limpar was at the way things had turned out. It was a straightforward, non-controversial encounter, and two of the reporters, Arne Norlin of *Aftonbladet* and Conny Hetting of *Idag*, filed their copy along these lines. The third reporter present, Peter Kadhammar, from the biggest Swedish tabloid, *Expressen*, did not use the formal part of the interview in his story, but instead concentrated on comments Limpar made after the notebooks were put away, when the player believed he was speaking off the record. The remarks, taken completely out of context, were published in *Expressen* on Friday and were picked up by the *Sun*, which made them appear even more controversial in its Saturday edition. The main thrust of Limpar's reported outburst concerned George Graham's management style. 'The talk is about money all the time,' he said. 'Nobody is worried about me and I am suffering. Mr Graham is never satisfied and wants control over everything you say . . . In Italy you couldn't eat bananas and ice-cream. In England they don't care about what you eat – only what you say. George Graham is always shouting at everyone . . . Mr Graham and Michael [Thomas] had a terrible row. They stood up and were shouting at each other. Michael was going to the toilet. Mr Graham told him to get back. Michael said, "Can't you even go to the toilet at this club now?"'

Luckily for all concerned, Norlin and Hetting sent a fax to George Graham condemning Kadhammar's use of Limpar's words and explaining how the story had come about. By way of redressing the balance, the two reporters emphasized that Limpar had 'several times . . . said he admired your way of managing the team and he gave examples from his experiences in Italy as a player'. This at least ensured that Limpar's return to the fold was not followed by any disciplinary action.

The whole sorry mess seemed to stem from two factors that should have been foreseen. First, there was a failure to recognize the extent of the passion felt by Limpar to play for his country. Limpar had played all his football on the Continent, where the game's culture is permeated with the ethos that the national team comes before any club commitments. Second, there was a lack of meaningful communication between player and manager. When Limpar went through twenty-four hours of soul-searching before deciding to fly off to Sweden, it never occurred to him to talk things over with George Graham. The way they eventually communicated their thoughts to each other was through the press. Compare this with the experience of another Swedish player, Roland Nilsson, who plays for Sheffield Wednesday. Nilsson explained, 'Ron [Atkinson] tried to pull me out of the match, but he is the type of manager you can sit down and talk with, he will listen to players. I wanted to play for Sweden and Wednesday this week, but I knew it was impossible. He said if I wanted to go then there was no problem.'

The Limpar incident showed clearly that Graham, having at last bought a star, could hardly expect him to become an 'Arsenal type' overnight. Limpar obviously needed special handling, which did not, in this instance, seem to be forthcoming.

After it was announced that the FA would be charging both Arsenal and Manchester United with bringing the game into disrepute, the comment and condemnation became even more extreme. Rene Eberle of UEFA said, 'The best solution is to deduct points, because the clubs will laugh off any fine.' They would certainly not smile if Patrick Barclay, at the time the football correspondent of the *Independent*, had his way. He called for the clubs to be fined £1 million, a solution described as 'absurd' by his counterpart at the *Sunday Times*, Brian Glanville. While it was often stated that both clubs would have to take strong internal action to pre-empt the FA from issuing a Draconian punishment, there was little analysis of why the Arsenal team in particular should be so prone to confrontations of this sort.

As a contact sport, football is always liable to produce explosive situations from time to time. On the same day as the United–Arsenal game, the *Manchester Evening News* reported the following incident from the match between Derby and Manchester City. 'Then a flashpoint situation saw Heath and Wright trading punches as players from both sides rushed in to separate the pair, with even County boss Arthur Cox sprinting from his touchline seat to assist. The outcome was a yellow card for Heath.' There have also been 'mean teams', like the Leeds of the sixties and seventies, who used gamesmanship like Terry Venables used the offside game.

However, the approach at Arsenal had seen the side become almost predisposed to reacting badly at real or imagined injustices on the pitch. And there were endless headlines concerning unrest and indiscipline behind the scenes. Many, like Emlyn Hughes, blamed Graham. Hughes offered the explanation that the manager had 'lost control of the club'. Hughes went on, 'Whether he has mislaid his sense of values in his drive for success and perfection I do not know, but from what I have heard he has lost respect ... Perhaps George, the Great Dictator, the man the players call Colonel Ghadaffi, has overstepped the limit in his guidelines to discipline.'

To find the real roots of Arsenal's propensity for trouble, though, it is necessary to look beyond the most visible targets. In fact the seeds were sown far away from the pressure-cooker atmosphere of First Division football, in matches watched by a handful of spectators.

On the Saturday before the Manchester United–Arsenal clash, the First Division programme had been cancelled because of England's forthcoming European Championship qualifier against Poland at Wembley. Yet there were two games between Arsenal and Spurs that day. In the afternoon, a testimonial for Graham Rix was played at Highbury, which Spurs won 5–2 with the help of a hat-trick from Paul Stewart. Although the match featured most of the current first-team squads, together with famous old boys like Liam Brady and Rix himself, a better insight into the collective psychology of both clubs was to be found earlier, in a country setting far from the crowds of London, in a football game where the participants were unknown, except to their families and the most ardent of fans.

Beyond the M25 in Hertfordshire, unobtrusive amid its rural surroundings, the Arsenal training ground at London Colney is barely noticeable from the road. There is no sign to reveal its location, which is a sports ground belonging to the University of London. But behind the unprepossessing façade are modern technical facilities that single the place out as the training ground of a professional football club. Here, on the morning of 13 October, Arsenal met Spurs in a youth game in the First Division of the South-East Counties League.

The crowd of 150 or so were, in the main, Arsenal supporters as might be expected. Pat Rice was, of course, present in his capacity as youth-team coach, but so were George Graham and the rest of the coaching staff, including Stewart Houston and George Armstrong, as well as a number of more senior players. One of these was David O'Leary, who had been banned from playing in the Rix testimonial by his international manager, Jack Charlton. Also in attendance, as usual, was vice-chairman David Dein, who professed his love for a 'double header' (the juniors in the morning and the first team in the afternoon) and said that when both win it is 'my perfect day'. The Arsenal way, based on a clear understanding of the role of staff and management, began to emerge as the match progressed. Dein stayed on the touchline keeping himself to himself and hardly spoke to the coaches or manager until the game was over. As he greeted the boys, the senior players and the coaching staff on his arrival, they each responded in identical manner, with a respectful 'Good morning, Mr Dein'. It was like a well-drilled army unit on the arrival of the senior officer. The vice-chairman appeared to know all the boys well and spent extra time chatting to two players, one a substitute, the other a recent graduate to the reserves. Dein's son Gavin observed: 'My father is like a butterfly. He likes to have a word of congratulation for all the team but he never lingers.' In contrast to this impressive turn-out by Arsenal, none of their Spurs counterparts was anywhere to be seen.

The game itself was even more revealing. The Arsenal team played to the Arsenal system, like a mirror-image of the first team, tactically aware, hard-working and professional. Perhaps too professional, since goalkeeper Jim Will was sent off early in the second half for bringing down an opponent who was through on goal, which left Arsenal happy to draw the match 2–2. There was no doubting, though, that this team played to a pattern based on that employed by the senior side. Furthermore, it was not just the system of play that had the first-team look about it. The individual players often bore an uncanny likeness, either in looks or in movement and style of play, to their more famous elders. Adams, Davis, Thomas and Merson, all of whom had emerged through the Highbury youth system, each had younger versions on the pitch that day.

Of all the big First Division clubs, Arsenal is the one with the most successful youth policy by far in recent years. Started in the Bertie Mee/Don Howe era during the seventies, the policy began to bear fruit as more and more talented players moved through the ranks to the first team, where they were good enough to win the League Championship in 1989. The importance attached to the youth policy was underlined by the attendance at the training ground and by David Dein's comment that 'there was a chance for Pat Rice to move up but we told him that along with George Graham he has the most important job in the club. Apart from the team spirit and camaraderie it [the youth policy] engenders, it will save you a million if you can get a first-team player out of it.'

The policy at Arsenal, then, is to build from the youth team. Scouts throughout the country as well as in London look for players who are not simply skilful or quick, but who can be classified as 'Arsenal types', a category exemplified by the whole-hearted commitment to the cause, in their different ways, of Tony Adams and Paul Davis. Indeed, it was the importance Arsenal attached to its youth teams that was the determining factor in Davis joining the club. A number of clubs wanted to sign him as a youngster, but, as he later recalled, 'None of them had a number of players who had come through the youth side. I looked at Arsenal and they had about six players. I thought, if they can do that then it could happen for me.' At the youth stage players are allotted their role within the system, and decisions on whether to keep any young player are based as much on his ability to play the Arsenal way as they are on any objective view of his talent as a footballer. All boys who come to Arsenal are considered good raw material for the system, but even so only a few make it all the way to the first team. In Arsenal's case, the percentage is numerically higher than at most clubs, and qualita-tively better than anywhere. 'It's the hardest thing we have to do,' remarked David Dein on having to tell a boy he was no longer wanted. 'It's difficult enough with a player of twenty-eight but at least he's a man of experience. With a kid of seventeen it's heartbreaking.'

Once a positive decision is taken, however, the club seems to stick by its choice through thick and thin. Jim Will, the goalkeeper who was sent off against Spurs, for instance, although rebuked for his impetuosity, was allowed to play that same afternoon in the testimonial match, presumably to give him a taste of the big time and restore any dent in confidence the morning's incident may have brought about.

That Saturday morning, Spurs had a number of extremely gifted individuals in their side, including an exciting but erratic attacker, Ollie Morah. Spurs had won the double of League and Cup the previous season and skill for skill were the more talented side. But they could not display the organization and team spirit of Arsenal, who managed to get themselves together after losing their keeper. Whereas Arsenal look for players who can adapt to the club system, Spurs want skill and ball control – they are constantly searching for another Glenn Hoddle – and boys who fail to live up to these requirements rarely become established first-team players. As a result, whereas David Dein can realistically expect 'three or four' of the current youth squad to become regulars at the higher levels, Spurs would be content if one came through.

This does not mean the Spurs youth system produces players who do not make the grade in English football. On the contrary, a number of youngsters who perhaps had other qualities, or who were late developers, have done very well indeed at other clubs. One of them, Steve Sedgley, had to be bought back at a cost of £750,000. Another could not be bought at almost any price. Des Walker was a Spurs fanatic who was discarded at seventeen because his ball skills did not measure up to the demands of the coaching staff. The fact that this youngster was full of dedication and more than willing to work to improve his game went unnoticed until he came under Brian Clough's wing at Nottingham Forest. It is inconceivable that Arsenal would have let such promising material slip through their fingers. The list of other recent products of the Spurs youth system who have found favour and confidence elsewhere is prodigious, and includes Bowen, Crook, Culverhouse and Polsten, all of whom flourished at Norwich. Indeed, as soon as a promising youngster appears, Spurs fans anticipate he will be bound for Carrow Road, just as in a previous generation Keith Weller and Derek Possee had to go to Millwall before their careers took off. As a Spurs scout explained, '[even] if they don't make it to the first team they have been taught good habits and know how to play.' Others who remained at White Hart Lane have mainly filled the role of fringe players, like Paul Moran and Vinny Samways. The difference is stark. While Spurs are looking for the brilliant individual, Arsenal are looking for a team, and while there is only a loose conception of what a Spurs player should be (exciting, skilful), there is an extremely tight conception of what constitutes an Arsenal man (a team player).

The sense of team spirit instilled into the Arsenal players breeds success on the field. At the same time everyone is constantly reminded, often in subtle ways like the ever-present bust of Herbert Chapman in the marble entrance hall at Highbury, of the traditions that they have inherited. It is the embodiment of the 'all for one, one for all' philosophy, which, while promoting positive features such as team spirit, also has a downside that must be kept in check in a volatile contact sport like football. The main manifestation of this downside is a tribal mentality, which is infused into the boys' thinking by the time they reach seventeen years of age. The indoctrination of 'You are Arsenal, you are different' cannot fail to have an effect on an impressionable teenager. The logical conclusion to this is the emergence of a 'them and us' syndrome, so when things go badly wrong on the field, even when the team is actually winning the game as was the case at Old Trafford, they all feel victimized and resort to collective action. This kind of wound-up intensity is bound, sooner or later, to spill over into bad behaviour unless the pressure is relieved in some other way. The explosion might not necessarily take place on the pitch, as the Paul Merson and Steve Bould incidents showed, but it will find expression somewhere. Perhaps the situation is inadvertently fuelled by George Graham. He tends to watch the first half from the stand and the second from the dugout. It appears that he winds them up at half-time and then keeps up a constant barrage of encouragement, advice and criticism, all delivered with a high decibel count. It surely is no coincidence that Arsenal are one of the best second-half teams in terms of performance and one of the worst in terms of behaviour.

The more freewheeling approach of Tottenham was in evidence on the day of the Manchester brawl. The Sheffield United manager, Dave Bassett, who appears to be a master of the psychological ploy, decided to use the pre-match media interest in the days before his team faced Spurs at White Hart Lane to pressurize Paul Gascoigne through the press. Taking his cue from Poland's manager, Andrzej Strejlau, who had said before the midweek European Championship game that Gascoigne's antics might get him the red card, Bassett really went to town. 'There are double standards,' he claimed. 'Gazza is getting away with lots of things that would get Vinny Jones and other pros into trouble. All of a sudden Gazza is a national hero and everyone is letting him off. They are always making excuses for him.'

Bassett's team seemed to want to carry on where their manager left off by attempting to impose a physical game on Tottenham. During the first half the tactics paid off, as Tottenham gave as good as they got in an attempt not to be intimidated. Pat Van Den Hauwe and David Barnes tussled and were shown the yellow card. By the end of the game, Steve Sedgley, Vinny Jones and Simon Tracey had followed them into the referee's notebook, while Barnes was sent off for a second bookable offence. However, the impression was never given that the Spurs players were about to lose their collective temper, and in the second half Bassett's plans came badly unstuck as Spurs hit four goals without reply.

Gary Lineker had suffered a cut head while playing for England against the Poles in midweek, so his place against United was taken by Paul Walsh, Lineker sitting the match out in the role of substitute. After the first-half niggles, Terry Venables insisted the team begin to play some football. Walsh took his chance by scoring a superb hat-trick, the second of which was a brilliant solo effort that inspired the chant 'Going down' from the Spurs fans. The insult was quickly returned with interest. 'Going bust' was the amusing riposte of the Sheffield contingent. Nayim added the other goal, while Venables pulled off Gascoigne when Spurs were 3–0 up and replaced him with a home-grown player, John Moncur, another of the fringe performers.

'Walsh has been playing well and not scoring,' commented Venables after the game. '[Today] he took his goals with a vengeance.' Unfortunately for Walsh, no matter how well he played there was not the remotest possibility that he would keep Gary Lineker out of the side when he recovered. 'It's a nice situation to be in,' was how Venables summed up the position.

There was nothing amusing in the after-match comments of Dave Bassett and the Sheffield United chairman Reg Brealey. 'He [Gascoigne] behaved like a buffoon, waving at me during the game and giving it "the boot" in mockery of our style,' Bassett raged. 'He has a big temperament problem . . . Take a look at the game against Aston Villa. He almost decapitated Gordon Cowans but nothing was done. He goes around ruffling hair and making gestures and gets away with it, but if my kids behaved like him they would get a smack and be sent to their room. For his own good I hope he grows up.' On the sending off of Barnes, Bassett remarked, 'Barnes' second offence was to kick the ball away, yet Gazza does it a few minutes later and nothing happens. There is one rule for some players and another for Gascoigne. If Vinny Jones behaved like Gascoigne he would be sent off every week.'

For his part, Vinny Jones called Gazza 'flash', and said that he 'bottled' the midfield confrontation between the two of them. Jones went on to warn: 'He will get hurt one day with all that standing on the ball and taking the piss.' Brealey concentrated his venom on the referee, Martin Bodenham, saying, 'I will be writing to the FA about this man. I want him suspended while videos are studied ... [he was] a dangerous man to have in charge of a game like that.' As it turned out, Bassett and Brealey were hoist on their own petard. Having tried to wind up the game in general and Gascoigne in particular, they had seriously misjudged the atmosphere at White Hart Lane. Their comments were relayed to the FA which dispatched a letter to Bramall Lane asking for an explanation of the outbursts. In addition, there was every possibility that a disrepute charge could follow.

Thus a situation that could easily have got out of hand on the pitch was avoided by the belief that the best answer to intimidation or injustice is to play football. At Old Trafford a game that should have produced the best that English football has to offer, somehow degenerated into a free-for-all. The first instinct of the Arsenal players was to become involved, and it proved all too easy for them to go completely over the top, just like Dave Bassett at White Hart Lane.

After the weekend it became increasingly clear that both Arsenal and Manchester United would have to take action, if only to convince the FA not to deduct League points. On Tuesday 23 October, the Arsenal board met to decide on what punishment to mete out to those considered responsible. In an unprecedented move at any football club, the directors announced that George Graham would be fined two weeks' wages (approx £9,000) as would five players, Winterburn, Davis, Limpar, Rocastle and Thomas (approx £5,000 each). The board's decision was strongly influenced by chairman Peter Hill-Wood, who appeared genuinely embarrassed by the affront to the good name of the club and concerned that the lesson of the Norwich game had not been heeded. 'Twice in two years is too often,' he said. 'The name of Arsenal has been sullied and that is why I have taken this action. The ultimate responsibility for the conduct and behaviour of the team lies with the manager and that is why a fine has been imposed on George Graham as well as five players. It is not the tradition of this club to have a bad reputation and I hope it will not recur.'

George Graham took the fine, and more importantly the public rebuke, on the chin. 'The fine does not really surprise me,' he revealed. 'If I am in charge of the behaviour of the players, I will accept responsibility. It is something I am not proud of. It is paramount that the club's good name does not suffer and also for the game in general. Team spirit has always been one of my priorities here and the players and myself accept that we have responsibility.' Manchester United, meanwhile, left disciplinary action to the manager, Alex Ferguson, who fined three unnamed players (widely believed to be Irwin, McClair and Ince) an undisclosed amount (believed to be £1,000 each). The United secrecy was in direct contrast to the openness and candour displayed by the Arsenal board. Ferguson later criticized the Graham fine, saying, 'What they did to him was degrading . . . I don't think it should have happened.' Other managers, including Terry Venables and Howard Kendall, also condemned the action against Graham. Venables made the interesting point that 'by fining George and putting him on the same level of employment as his players, the Arsenal chairman has assumed responsibility for discipline at the club.' Support for the Arsenal action, however, came from PFA boss Gordon Taylor, who viewed the fine as 'a positive step'. Taylor outlined his association's policy on discipline, adding, 'We have always argued that managers have an influence on, and a responsibility for, teams' behaviour.' Other arguments in the wake of events in Manchester centred on the supposed 'trial by television' aspect of the affair. Video evidence had been accepted by the FA for some time, however, most notably in the case of Paul Davis. It is also a fact that a big club like Arsenal receives many benefits from television, not least of which is a large amount of money, over £750,000 in 1989–90. When accepting these benefits it also has to be realized that television can have other effects, not all of them guaranteed to please clubs.

It had been a turbulent week at Highbury. Before the next home game, against Sunderland, George Graham admitted that he was uncertain about the effect the affair would have on his players. All five disciplined men were in the first team, and Graham was aware of the extra pressure on them. 'I am about to find out what reaction the week has had,' he said. 'A crisis can either split you up or pull you together. I expect a positive reaction.' After closing the book on the Manchester incident, Graham welcomed his errant Swedish star back home. 'Thank heavens for Anders Limpar,' he said. 'He creates excitement every time he's on the ball, and scored another brilliantly cheeky goal at Old Trafford.'

In an uninspiring game against Sunderland, the Gunners shaded it 1–0, the goal coming from a Dixon penalty after Limpar had been brought down. At one point Rocastle once again looked to be threatening physical intervention, after the Sunderland defenders accused Limpar of play-acting when he went sprawling following a tackle by Bennett. Limpar, having spent some time in the Italian First Division, where all the best German actors perform, is sometimes guilty of making challenges look worse than they are. It is a trait that could easily be cured once the player absorbs more of the culture of English football, but it none the less annoys opposing teams. Graham described Rocastle's presence as 'peacemaking', an interpretation that obviously did not occur to the referee, who had strong words with him after the incident. Paul Davis once again emerged as the best player on the pitch, Gabbiadini included, although even he lost concentration once or twice and needlessly gave the ball away. David Rocastle seemed totally out of sorts, appearing agitated and frustrated at the way his game was going, and it was no surprise when he became involved in the Limpar–Bennett incident. Tony Adams, meanwhile, picked up his fourth yellow card of the season. The focus on this side of the game obscured the fact that the win meant Arsenal had enjoyed their best start to a League campaign for over forty years. If anything could restore George Graham's equilibrium, it would be statistics such as these.

Despite the win and the unbeaten run, Arsenal were still four points behind Liverpool, whose stuttering performance against Norwich was put into perspective with a clinical, if at times unconvincing, 2–0 demolition of Chelsea at Anfield. Spurs remained third, two points behind the Gunners, after coming from behind against Nottingham Forest to win 2–1. This was a match of high quality in which both sides produced some flowing football. After the emphasis on the more violent aspects of the game it was refreshing to see two teams committed to playing attractive football. Nottingham Forest are known for their sportsmanlike behaviour, and to see them accept refereeing decisions and bad tackles with equanimity made Arsenal's approach seem that much worse. Interestingly, the two Spurs goals which beat Clough's team on the Forest boss's twenty-fifth anniversary in management were scored by the one player in the Spurs line-up who had progressed from the youth side to a regular place in the first team – David Howells. The winner, in injury time, came just seconds after Howells had denied Forest a goal by clearing off his own line. Howells' performance gave Terry Venables the opportunity to spotlight a player who was beginning to receive praise for his part in Tottenham's improvement.

'When I came to Spurs, Howells was on the fringe of doing it or not,' commented the manager. 'I have said before that he is one of the best attackers in the club but he doesn't always get the chances ... when Forest switched Clough to a deeper role we moved Howells in front of the back four. He showed that tactically he is a very good player.'

Both Arsenal and Spurs made further progress in the Rumbelows Cup during the following week. Arsenal's victory over Manchester City at Maine Road saw the team produce another disciplined away performance, this time with no relapses, while Spurs made heavy weather of beating Bradford City 2–1 at

White Hart Lane, despite a virtuoso Gascoigne display in the first half. When the draw for the fourth round was made, Arsenal found themselves due to play none other than Manchester United at Highbury, while, to complete the kind of coincidence that football occasionally throws up, Spurs were to visit Sheffield United.

The draw once again brought thoughts of disciplinary matters to the fore. Arsenal, building from the youth team and only dipping into the transfer market when absolutely necessary, have created players whose spirit, knowledge of each other and 'all for one' attitude have added an extra dimension that has significantly contributed to the club's success. At the same time, the excesses that these very traits bring have boiled over too often for the players' own good. It is a successful, though potentially lethal, cocktail, which may have gone just too far in the game against Manchester United. By contrast, Spurs and Gazza could look forward to renewing their acquaintance with Dave Bassett with confidence. Before that, however, there was the little matter of a televised game against Liverpool at White Hart Lane to consider. Liverpool had just lost their first game of the season, in the Rumbelows Cup to Manchester United, a defeat almost entirely due to appalling goalkeeping by Grobbelaar, who would surely not be so profligate again. It has become a cliché in football that Liverpool are never more dangerous than when they have just lost a match. White Hart Lane was about to witness the truth of that, but in a manner that raised more questions than answers about the relative merits of both teams.

8

Red-eyed

After two months of the season, the supporters of Arsenal and Spurs could reflect with quiet satisfaction on the way the campaign was going. Both clubs were undefeated; Arsenal's start was the best in four decades, while the Spurs team had given Terry Venables the sort of solid foundation that had been signally missing from his previous two seasons in charge. The euphoria was tempered, however, by the awesome inevitability of Liverpool's position at the top of the table, having won nine and drawn one of their first ten games. There had been signs of vulnerability as October drew to a close, but with Liverpool, this could just be the calm before the storm. A draw against Norwich destroyed the scenario of Liverpool coming to White Hart Lane trying to take the record of eleven successive League wins at the start of a season from the Spurs double side of 1960–61. This blip was followed by the victory over Chelsea and a traumatic 3–1 defeat in the Rumbelows Cup at the hands of Manchester United, the Anfield club's first defeat since the FA Cup semi-final the previous April. Crucially, Liverpool's stutter coincided with a hamstring injury to John Barnes, which revealed how important he had become to the team's effectiveness in attack.

It seemed that the Championship challenge of the two north London clubs would hinge on the results of their matches against the Mersey machine. The first of these was due at White Hart Lane on Sunday 4 November, in a televised game that would show a waiting nation whether Spurs, the last team to beat Liverpool in the League, back in March 1990, and undefeated themselves in thirteen League and Cup games, were the stuff of champions, or whether the team was again flattering to deceive. Graeme Souness, the manager of Glasgow Rangers and former Liverpool star who started his career at Tottenham, sounded a warning of what Spurs could expect: 'That 3–1 defeat by

United was the worst thing that could have happened to Spurs
... Going back even before my days I know Liverpool are never
more dangerous than when they have lost ... Until they lost to
United in the week I was ready to sit on the fence and go for a
draw. But now I am not so sure. Liverpool will be fearsome on
Sunday and thirsting for blood.' In a reference to the intense
rivalry between the two northern giants, Souness concluded,
'They will be furious at having lost to United of all teams.'

The Sunday schedule for televised matches lent further drama to
Saturday's fixtures, because it gave Arsenal the chance to go within
one point of Liverpool if they won at Coventry. If that were to be
followed by a Spurs win, or a draw, the Championship race would
be thrown wide open. The Gunners duly fulfilled their role in the
weekend's excitement by winning 2–0 at Highfield Road through
two late goals from Anders Limpar, who was fast proving that his
game went far beyond being just a tricky and skilful winger. In fact,
he was now Arsenal's top goalscorer, with seven in the League.
George Graham started the game with Smith and Groves filling the
front two places, while Limpar and Merson operated from wide
positions in midfield. Smith injured an ankle after half an hour,
which necessitated some reorganization, although a ready replacement was on hand in the shape of Kevin Campbell. Subsequently,
Graham pulled off Groves and sent on an extra defender, O'Leary,
in a move that was seen at the time as a way of holding out for a
draw. The change actually had the effect of allowing Dixon and
Winterburn, probably the best pair of attacking full backs in the
First Division, to push forward, giving Arsenal's attacking play more
options. Just after Coventry had hit the post, Limpar left the two
inexperienced central defenders, Emerson and Edwards, for dead,
before firing in the perfect left-foot finish. There were only seven
minutes left. With Coventry pushing forward in a last attempt to
salvage a point, Arsenal received a stroke of good fortune as they
broke away, and Limpar's close-range shot, this time with his
right foot, took a deflection to leave Ogrizovic with no chance.
Arsenal were within one point of Liverpool, George Graham was
naturally 'ecstatic', and it now fell to Spurs to complete the job of
closing the gap on the leaders twenty-four hours later. For once,
the aspirations of Arsenal and Spurs supporters converged.

During the weekend's build-up to the televised game, Irving Scholar made an appearance on the *Saint and Greavsie* television programme. In trenchant style Scholar defended his actions in the recent turmoil at White Hart Lane, at the same time ruling out any thoughts of selling Gascoigne and Lineker. Scholar had been forced to resign as a director of the parent company in the week leading up to the match, though the public and shareholders had not received any hard information on the situation and the promised circular had failed to materialize. Referring to the club's financial troubles, Scholar asserted: 'There is an easy way out, and that is by selling our main assets. Newspapers have tried to sell Gary Lineker and Paul Gascoigne for us since the World Cup in Italy. I have maintained all along that they would not be sold and nothing has changed. If Lineker and Gascoigne have to be sold to solve the problems, which were not created by the football club which I am in charge of, then I am wasting my time here. I would not do it. I would prefer to go before that happened. I would not agree to it because it would be letting down the club.'

The game itself was an unmitigated disaster for Tottenham. The shrewd tactical brain of Kenny Dalglish was once again in evidence, as Liverpool lined up with a plethora of defenders and proceeded to stifle the midfield. Yet many would later argue that the 3–1 Liverpool victory owed more to the vagaries of the match officials' decisions than any inherent superiority on the part of the Merseysiders.

When talking to ordinary fans, particularly those of Liverpool's big-city rivals like Arsenal and Tottenham, it immediately becomes clear that there is little liking for Liverpool. The most that is ever expressed is grudging admiration. The justification for such an outlook is generally twofold. First, they complain that the media go completely over the top when Liverpool are being discussed, praising every move in a craven display of sycophancy unmatched by anything said or written about other teams, even the big clubs of Europe. Then there is the view that Liverpool, because of their pre-eminent position over so many years, receive preferential treatment from referees.

While there is no doubt that much of the antipathy towards

Liverpool stems from envy born of the simple fact that Liverpool keep winning trophies, it would be unwise to dismiss these opinions totally. Examination of television coverage does reveal a slavish uniformity in the analyses offered by pundits and commentators alike. In the press the bias is less pointed but still exists, and some journalists are as brazen as their television colleagues in promoting a tone of reverence whenever Liverpool are discussed. Terry Venables became very animated when asked about a piece by David Miller in *The Times*, in which Miller praised the skills of Liverpool, then, using a comment made famous by Ian Hislop, the editor of *Private Eye*, implied that if Paul Stewart was a First Division attacker, then he (Miller) was a banana. Venables' response was cutting. 'I thought that was not a criticism but a cruel personal attack on a hundred per cent player.'

The point about referees also contains a grain of truth. The propensity of officials to grant penalties to Liverpool at Anfield is legendary, whereas Liverpool's own excesses are rarely punished in the same manner. A long list of hard-men, stretching back from Steve McMahon through the likes of Graeme Souness and Tommy Smith, testifies to the physical side of Liverpool's game. But the opinion that Liverpool receive favourable treatment gained credence in the match against Manchester United, when David Burrows committed a blatant professional foul on Danny Wallace when the latter was through on goal. Having been told by the FA and FIFA to clamp down on this type of foul by using the red card, it was astonishing to see Burrows remain on the pitch after his transgression.

The match against Spurs confirmed the feelings of the die-hard anti-Liverpool faction with a vengeance. The general consensus of opinion in the press after the game was that Spurs had been outplayed, out-thought and outrun by a superior Liverpool team, but Terry Venables offered another interpretation. The first half, according to the Spurs manager, was even or perhaps shaded by Spurs up to the point when Liverpool's first goal went in, scored by Ian Rush. That goal, said Venables, should have been disallowed for offside, not against the scorer but against Steve Nicol, who was running back from an offside position when the ball was played by Molby to Rush.

'That affected our game completely,' claimed Venables. 'Worse than the result, I still don't know how we would have fared against Liverpool if that [goal] was not allowed.'

After the first Rush goal, Spurs were forced to chase the game, leaving them vulnerable to a classic Liverpool counter-attack, which came just after half-time and ended in another goal for Rush. Thereafter Spurs managed a period of sustained pressure. Lineker pulled a goal back (his sixth of the season) two minutes after Rush got his second, picking up the pieces following a Howells shot that rebounded off the post, and for a time Liverpool were looking distinctly shaky at the back. Then, with Liverpool's defence creaking, they got another crucial break when substitute Peter Beardsley was not given offside in the build-up to the third goal, which he scored himself and which killed off the Spurs challenge.

There has to be a certain amount of sympathy for Venables' view, particularly concerning the third goal. When teams play the offside game, it is only a matter of time before a linesman makes a mistake and a goal is conceded – but Spurs were not playing the offside game. When Rush scored the first goal, television replays showed Nicol to be in an offside position, but the question was whether he was interfering with play. In a now famous phrase, Bill Nicholson once said, 'If a player is not interfering with play, what's he doing on the field?' However, if it is accepted that referees are allowed the discretion to rule that a player is not interfering with play even when in an offside position, then the decisions are as likely to go one way as the other. On this occasion George Courtney gave Liverpool the benefit of any doubt, but it has to be admitted that permitting referees to exercise discretion in such important circumstances invites inconsistency. It was this that really upset Venables.

'This has been going on for too long,' he said. 'It is something that people can hide behind. You are either offside or you are not. It should not be open to dispute.'

The third goal was more clear-cut. Television showed Beardsley to be clearly offside when the ball was played out wide, and he must have been interfering with play since he finished the move off himself a couple of seconds later. Unfortunately for Spurs, the linesman did not see it, and the referee was in no position to give the decision himself. It was cruel but, as everyone knows, these things happen in football. What made it particularly galling was that it had happened against the League leaders and had severely dented Tottenham's title ambitions. They were now nine points behind.

Against this, Spurs contributed to their own downfall, as even Terry Venables conceded when he said, 'A little naïvety crept into our play . . . there was plenty of time. We should have kept our shape and our patience but instead left ourselves very light at the back at times.' Gascoigne never got to grips with the close marking of Burrows, who was detailed by Dalglish to follow the Spurs star all over the park. Burrows not only muzzled Gascoigne, who became increasingly frustrated and was eventually booked, but also found the time to go forward and play an important part in Liverpool's attacks. It was his run and pass that set up the second goal for Rush. The subdued performance of Gascoigne may have been due to a niggling thigh injury, but for most observers he never looked like imposing his skills on the game. Johnny Giles, one of the great midfield players of his generation, who won trophies with Manchester United and Leeds, offered this perspective on Gascoigne, a player whom Giles had recommended for the England team long before *Italia 90*: 'Against Liverpool we saw the basic problem. He failed, totally, to dominate the player who was assigned to close him down. David Burrows is an excellent pro, but he should not have been able to both subdue Gascoigne and contribute so heavily to Liverpool's attack. Gazza's challenge was to build on one simple task. He had to win the battle with Burrows and then influence the game. But before he could attend to the latter he had to attend to the first. Why did he fail? It was because of the main current weakness of his game. His success has inevitably led to closer marking and there is a classic way to counter this. It is by being busy, by piling one move on top of another, by the granting of no respite to the man at your heels. Gazza is simply not busy enough to achieve this. Against Liverpool he made a clever pass and then stepped back. Burrows was allowed to gather himself, take time off from marking the player who should have been the game's most influential figure.'

Giles also spoke of what he saw as a temperament problem, saying, 'Within the game there is a sharp prejudice. It is for pros who get on with the game, who do the hard work and take the knocks without flinching. There is also the understanding that some players are different, have special talent and allowances are made for differences of temperament. But Gazza is currently stretching all tolerance. He seems incapable of looking beyond his own situation, of seeing his place in the wider game.'

This view of Gascoigne is buttressed by those who point out that Gazza was not distracted by Dave Bassett's comments as much as he was by Liverpool's spoiling tactics, which culminated in Steve McMahon's elbow in his face. McMahon's wink to his team-mates after he had committed the deed, unseen by George Courtney but perfectly picked up by the TV cameras, gave viewers a rare glimpse of the way Liverpool are prepared to employ rough-house tactics when it suits them. Spurs' physio Dave Butler once employed a lip-reading expert to quash an FA disrepute charge, but any television viewer could have understood what Gazza asked George Courtney to do after the clash with McMahon. Perhaps another player, on another day, would have been shown the red card.

Terry Venables saw the incident in a different light. It proved that Gascoigne was capable of taking punishment. 'No one gave him credit for jogging away from that situation,' Venables remarked. 'Nearly everyone else in the game would have hit him back, there would have been another mêlée and another big problem. There was no criticism of McMahon for that elbow in the face. Jimmy Greaves said on television it was six of one and half a dozen of the other. To me that is the most incredible thing.' McMahon added insult to injury by saying later, 'I don't care about him [Gascoigne],' while the FA decided to hide behind the referee's report and did not call for television evidence.

The incident appeared to take the words of Dave Bassett a stage further, namely, that there was one rule for Liverpool and another for Spurs and Arsenal. Indeed, Spurs fans with good memories will recall the dismissals of Steve Hodge and Chris Fairclough against Liverpool and the exoneration of Barry

Venison for elbowing Nayim in the face. Venables felt the media made 'no big deal' over the Burrows tackle in the Manchester United game and added that Liverpool 'bully other teams around while there is never any attack on them like there is against Arsenal'. The bottom line, he believes, is that 'the press are frightened of Liverpool, and that's unhealthy.'

In addition to Gascoigne's lacklustre display, there were other self-inflicted wounds that contributed as much to Spurs' defeat as poor refereeing. When Rush scored the first goal, Erik Thorstvedt was slow to come off his line and attack the ball, and the third came after Paul Walsh gave the ball away with most of the Spurs team out of position. Walsh's precipitous free kick to Howells was intercepted by Ablett, who carried the ball from the edge of one penalty area to the other without having to face a serious challenge. Collectively, the Spurs team, having got back to 2–1, failed to display patience, throwing everybody forward. Moreover, Spurs in theory faced a weakened Liverpool team, as Barnes, whose inclusion after his hamstring problem surprised everyone, had to go off after eighteen minutes. The Liverpool team also took the field without Houghton and Beardsley, who were substitutes, and Whelan and Hansen, who were injured.

Whatever view is taken, whether Spurs were robbed or whether they were outplayed, Liverpool had again surged forward in the championship stakes. Matthew Stone, co-editor of *The Spur*, subscribed to the latter view: 'We thought, just maybe, we were as good as them. But we were wrong, we weren't.' Stone's description summed it up for all Spurs fans when he called the game a 'numbing disappointment'. Spurs were still in third place but were now three wins behind the Merseysiders and facing an uphill climb to close the gap. Arsenal remained second, but instead of being one point behind, the deficit was now four points. George Graham's old friend had been unable to do both of them the favour that was required. With the approaching FA hearing over the brawl at Old Trafford, Graham could have been forgiven for thinking that the gods had turned against him as much as they had against his Tottenham counterpart.

9

The Manager who Would be King

The entrance hall at the Football Association's headquarters in Lancaster Gate is not adorned with marble, but the oak-panelled opulence of the ground-floor waiting room does provide the sort of comfortable surroundings in which the four representatives of Arsenal Football Club could feel a measure of reassurance. As they sank into the plush armchairs, Peter Hill-Wood, Ken Friar, Richard Carr QC and George Graham could keep apprehension at bay with the belief that the quick and decisive action the club had taken over the brawl at Old Trafford had forestalled any possibility of the FA deducting League points. The optimistic mood was not to last for long. In fact it had already been dented somewhat by an amazing article in that morning's *Daily Mirror*, which extensively quoted the Crystal Palace chairman, Ron Noades, who claimed that the outcome of the FA disciplinary hearing into the Old Trafford affair had been fixed in advance. Noades began with a now familiar refrain.

'There are different laws for the rich and the poor,' he said. 'There's a lot riding on this inquiry. Liverpool are walking away with the First Division and only Arsenal can catch them. When you talk about the Championship race there's more on this FA commission than a straightforward incident on the pitch. Wimbledon and Sheffield United would stand less of a chance. As the big clubs are involved they will get a suspended sentence with points deducted if it happens again. Whether points are deducted or not, I want Crystal Palace treated the same. I want consistency in refereeing and disciplinary measures. I want Halifax treated the same as Arsenal ... I want my players treated the same by referees as Gascoigne and Limpar.'

Noades' extraordinary intervention came after he had seen his high-flying team held to a goalless draw by the Gunners at Selhurst Park. Perhaps his outburst was due to emotion after

Palace had failed to breach an Arsenal defence that looked impregnable. George Graham left out Alan Smith, who had not scored in the League since the opening match against Wimbledon, and reverted to the system of three centre backs that had been so successful in the title-winning campaign. This meant a recall for David O'Leary but still left no place for Andy Linighan. With Paul Merson operating in a wide role and Kevin Campbell occupying a lonely position up front, little was seen of the Arsenal attack, but Palace were unable to take advantage of the situation, and their own attacks were stifled throughout the game. The Arsenal defence was so secure that the Palace manager, Steve Coppell, described Arsenal as 'without doubt the best team in the country. They are so well-drilled, organized and disciplined. They are past-masters at taking the sting out of the game and then putting their foot down on the pedal in the closing stages.' In Coppell's view, 'Liverpool have more individuals who can win a game but Arsenal are the best team, and at the end of the season there won't be much daylight between them.'

A more likely explanation for Ron Noades' outburst, however, is that he knew exactly what he was doing and wanted to remind the FA that there was a world out there waiting and watching for its decision. It is also the case that if points were deducted from Arsenal, then Palace, at the head of the chasing pack outside the top three, would be one of the main beneficiaries. Whatever the case, Noades' public views lent weight to those who were arguing for a points deduction. Arsenal could easily absorb any financial penalties, the argument went, and, as Colin Gibson pointed out in the *Daily Telegraph*, 'If Arsenal escape . . . The rest of football will be given carte blanche to conduct themselves in any manner they feel fit. How could the FA deduct points from a first-time offender when they have shown leniency towards Arsenal?'

None the less, the majority would probably have agreed with Ron Noades about the outcome. It was unlikely, given the nature of the altercation, that removing League points would be the result.

After a three-and-a-half-hour hearing, during which the five-man commission watched three different video recordings of the incident and heard from referee Keith Hackett, the Arsenal and Manchester United contingents left quickly, without any comment to the waiting media. It fell to Graham Kelly, chief executive of the FA, to read out the verdicts. Both clubs were fined £50,000 and would indeed have points deducted, United one and Arsenal two. Kelly explained the decision by saying, 'The disciplinary committee felt that mass confrontations had to be stopped once and for all. We wish to emphasize our determination to eliminate them.'

Reaction to the commission's sentence was mixed. While some thought the loss of points correct, it was also viewed by large sections of the press as a poor decision, which was ironic considering how the media had been dining out on the incident for over two weeks and had supported government and UEFA calls for severe punishment. Martin Edwards, the Manchester United chairman, put forward the opinion that by establishing the precedent of deducting points, the FA had opened the way for 'the championship being decided not on the field but in the committee room. Which is worse, a flare-up lasting eighteen seconds or a team with a bad disciplinary record all season which has kicked its way constantly to points?' With the benefit of hindsight and television replays, the FA effectively rendered referee Hackett's report useless and his two yellow cards an inaccurate reflection of what actually happened. Thus the verdict and the punishment undermined the final authority on the pitch – the referee, who is right even when he is wrong. Calls by the Professional Footballers' Association for trial by television to be employed for the defence as well as the prosecution now sounded far more reasonable. Perhaps the worst aspect of the affair was that the innocent were punished along with the guilty, just as in the case of Swindon Town at the end of the previous season. Rather than concentrating on the guilty parties, the FA saw fit, firstly to ignore the fact that many of the players were acting as peacemakers at Old Trafford, and secondly to punish the fans.

'As a Spurs fan,' wrote Hunter Davies, 'I don't even feel any pleasure in seeing Arsenal penalized. Liverpool will just get further ahead. They have been given an unfair advantage for doing nothing.'

Terry Venables concurred, declaring, 'I don't agree with taking points off teams, it makes supporters suffer.' His solution was to 'study the videos . . . that way it would be far easier to sort out the guilty players and ban them for three or four games.' If that was insufficient for the hawks, then a suspended sentence of a points deduction would have ensured an early resumption of normal service. Better the sword of Damocles than the guillotine.

The reaction at Highbury was predictably gloomy. David O'Leary was utterly devastated and moved enough to say, 'It is very sad. The champagne will be out at Liverpool tonight because this makes our task very much harder. Without being disparaging to all the others in the First Division, we were the team that could have provided Liverpool with a genuine challenge. They have as good as handed the title to Anfield at Lancaster Gate today.'

Anders Limpar was a shade more optimistic. 'It seems very harsh,' he said. 'It makes it a little bit harder to catch Liverpool, but it is not impossible.'

The one person who did not feel it appropriate to comment was George Graham. The manager had already displayed his stoicism when he accepted the fine his club had imposed without a hint of criticism. Now he was equally determined not to rush to the nearest journalist with complaints about the injustice of it all. If he had done so he might have pointed out that by taking strong internal action, both Arsenal and Manchester United were placed in a 'double jeopardy' situation by the FA inquiry. In theory, since the FA action was against a club rather than individuals, the sentence handed down could be justified but the effect fell on those same people who had already been disciplined, the manager and players.

Graham's silence was all the more effective for being unusual. It prompted David Dein, after the Arsenal board had taken the decision not to appeal against the FA verdict, to say, 'George Graham took it with dignity, so, we felt, should the club. In no way did we want to be seen as whiners.' It also showed how Graham's public image – the strict disciplinarian who brooked no interference – was a one-dimensional construction at best. In fact an examination of Graham's career tells a completely different story and reveals just how limited the media version of the man had become.

In the years following the Second World War there were few cities in Europe as disadvantaged as Glasgow. The coal-mining village of Bargeddie, a few miles from the centre, was one of many on the fringes of the town in which the mines were rapidly being run down and abandoned, leaving behind a bleak landscape of barely disguised slag-heaps, a legacy of the open-cast mining system which was widespread throughout Scotland. Glasgow itself was entering the period of razor gangs and gratuitous violence which would tarnish an already tough reputation for the next twenty years. Like so many Scottish youngsters in those villages, George Graham's life revolved around football. Unlike the majority, however, he was a good enough player for the game to provide his escape.

Graham's progress into the professional arena began at the local club, Airdrie, where he was a useful centre forward and target man. For young players at most Scottish clubs the dream was to be transferred to one of the giants, Celtic or Rangers, or to be spotted by a scout from England. Graham slipped through the net of the big Scottish clubs but attracted the attention of Aston Villa. After only a handful of games for the Birmingham club he was bought by Tommy Docherty, who introduced him into his Chelsea side of the early 1960s. That team included a number of exciting youngsters, one of whom was Terry Venables, it was the move across London to Highbury, though, after the same row that signalled the end of Venables' time as a Chelsea player, which changed the course of Graham's life. Whereas Venables' potential was never really fulfilled after he left Stamford Bridge, Graham's career blossomed at Arsenal, where he developed into a midfield player of the highest class.

In those early days at Chelsea, Graham admits he was a bit of a 'Jack the lad', who often came into conflict with his coaches and managers. For a youngster taken from the streets of Bargeddie to the bright lights of London, Graham's reaction was not atypical. What was more important was the capacity he showed for not only overcoming adversity and conflict, but also for actually prospering through the changes of direction they brought to his career. When Docherty decided to offload Terry Venables, he went to Spurs, a great club but with a team past its best. When Graham left Chelsea (in a straight swap for Tommy Baldwin), he arrived at a club which was about to be transformed by the management duo of Bertie Mee and Don Howe, and Graham would become an integral part of the double side. Another example of Graham's ability to overcome setbacks or deficiencies can be seen in his metamorphosis, midway through his career at Arsenal, from fading striker to cultured midfielder. His lack of pace would have seen many players fail to shine in the English First Division, and they would perhaps have had to drop to the lower levels. Graham turned lack of pace into a positive virtue, treating the football pitch like some personal domain where events unfolded at a pace that always seemed to suit him, a characteristic (shared by Bobby Moore) that earned him the endearing nickname of 'Stroller'. He was, of course, also fortunate to have George Armstrong alongside him to do his running.

This was probably Graham's happiest period as a player, and those fans who today accuse him of adopting an aloof and humourless approach would be astonished if they could speak to the people who knew him during this period. One of them was Morris Keston, a Spurs supporter and friend of Terry Venables. Keston would often run into Graham, particularly when Arsenal were due to meet Spurs. When Graham saw Keston before a derby game, it always seemed as if Arsenal won, and the two began to believe that their meetings were not coincidences but harbingers of fate. So when games against Spurs approached, Graham began to seek out Keston, his lucky omen, who in turn took evasive action, thinking that Spurs' chances of success depended on him avoiding Graham before the game. On the eve of one such derby match, Keston thought he had managed it, as there had been no sign of Graham for weeks. However, late on Friday evening, the doorbell rang at his flat. It was George Graham, who ignored the protests of Keston's wife and began to systematically search the flat. Eventually he came to a locked door, the toilet. Graham got a chair and knocked on the glass above the door, whereupon Keston looked up and was amazed to see Graham's face.

'I've seen you,' shouted Graham. 'Now we will win tomorrow.' And, of course, Arsenal did.

Again in contrast to his friend at White Hart Lane, Graham's period at Highbury saw his international prospects flourish. He had played for the Scotland youth team in 1962–3 and made two appearances for the Under-23s in 1964–5. He did not win the first of his twelve full caps, however, until the double triumph, in October 1971.

A year after the double, Graham was transferred to Manchester United – whose manager at the time was, ironically, Tommy Docherty. He left behind a playing record that boasted seventy-seven goals in almost 300 appearances, and took with him an abiding appreciation of a club where he spent seven successful years. 'It taught me how to organize my life, that there are certain ways of doing things with dignity, with a certain professionalism that has got to be attained.' The move to Old Trafford, though, began a period of relative failure. Graham never really fitted in, and, as the team was going through a sad decline after the great days of the 1960s, he was identified with the problems that led to the unthinkable – relegation. Another move, to Second Division Portsmouth, also ended in disappointment as the club was relegated in his first season. This experience in the twilight of a great career might have caused others to hang up their boots, but not George Graham. Suddenly the call came from his old mate Terry Venables, who had just been appointed manager of Crystal Palace, and Graham's career took on a new lease of life. After helping Palace gain promotion to the Second Division (twenty-three appearances, two goals) injuries curtailed his playing career. Graham admitted, 'I was always a slow player – I didn't do it on purpose, I couldn't go any faster. After I broke my leg and [had] an ankle operation I almost went into reverse.' It was time to call it quits.

As Venables' Palace team began to take off, George Graham, for the first time, had to think of a future outside football. It was during one of his frequent conversations with Terry Venables that Venables suggested he could make the grade in coaching and eventually management. Graham had never thought about the possibility seriously before, but Venables persisted with the idea, and as he did so, it began to seem an attractive option.

'It's fascinating looking back', recalled Graham, 'that it took me so long to get it into my brain that I could be a potential coach or manager. Terry was the one person who sat down with me and said "you've got a lot to offer".' When a vacancy occurred in the Palace ranks at youth level, Venables offered the coaching job to Graham, telling him to try it for a year, and if he didn't like it, leave. Amazing himself, Graham found that he had a gift for teaching youngsters and had the ability to instil in them a spirit that had previously been lacking. 'I loved it, absolutely loved it,' he said, 'I took to it like a duck to water.'

Graham followed his mentor, Terry Venables, when he went to QPR, once again in the capacity of coach to the juniors. The move into management proper was now only a matter of time, but when the offer came it was from an extremely unpromising source. Millwall was known throughout the country for the violence of its fans, had never been in the First Division in the whole of its history, and was reeling under the appalling state of its finances. Yet the situation was tailor-made for a canny Scot who was used to tough streets, unruly reputations and lack of money. By carefully husbanding the available resources, Graham began to produce a useful side, and promotion to the Second Division was achieved in 1984–5. The team performed well in the Second Division, and by the time Graham left to take over at Arsenal the foundations had been laid for eventual promotion to Division One. With no money to spend and Millwall forever in a precarious financial position, Graham's achievement was immense. He had displayed the ability that all successful managers and coaches must, the knack of getting the best out of the available players whatever their standard. It was also during his time at Millwall that Graham developed his ideas and tactics, particularly the belief that successful teams play from the back and always keep their shape in defensive situations, a way of playing which would reach its apogee at Highbury.

When the chance came to manage Arsenal, it was the perfect time for George Graham. In his own words he was 'astounded, it came like a bolt out of the blue'. Although things had not been going too well at Highbury, there were a number of players emerging from the youth policy who were regarded as special.

Graham, with his background in youth coaching, was in an excellent position to take advantage of the potential that existed. The chance to put what he had learned into practice with such an outstanding crop of players was like manna from heaven and could not have been provided by any other club. The years of financial constraints had also made Graham wary of spending big money on star players. When just about everybody expected a spending spree to revive the fortunes of the Gunners, Graham did the opposite, and made a positive virtue out of not buying. Further, after his first season he sold a number of Arsenal's more experienced players, including Kenny Sansom and Steve Williams. It was, in Graham's opinion, far better to work on welding together the remaining staff into a team. 'Football is eleven units,' he explained. Stars could so easily disrupt the side. 'Why shouldn't all eleven enjoy the success? Why should only three or four star players enjoy it? They should all go away with a feeling of satisfaction.' Graham is adamant that he is not against stars *per se*, merely those 'who don't perform'. This opinion was reflected in the manager's first controversial act when he arrived at Highbury, which reduced the one real star of the Arsenal team – Charlie Nicholas – to a marginal figure. Although Nicholas managed to score both goals in the defeat of Liverpool in the Littlewoods Cup Final in 1987, it was obvious that what Graham saw as inconsistency meant that Nicholas did not loom large in his manager's plans for the future. Nicholas, though, was a firm favourite with the fans, and most were genuinely upset that no place could be found for him. It led many to question Graham's suitability, but the manager, with a firmness of purpose that would become more overt as his reign at Arsenal progressed, took no notice and sold Nicholas regardless. It was this decision that made his reputation as a man who knew his own mind and would do anything he thought necessary in pursuit of his objectives. Nicholas told the press that Graham had set out 'to destroy' him, adding, 'He hardly ever spoke to me.' Graham's single-minded determination over Nicholas was confirmed by his assistant, Theo Foley, who said, 'His handling of Charlie Nicholas was excellent. Nobody other than George would have dropped him, because Charlie was the North Bank's darling.'

Since then, George Graham has been treated with wary respect by the Arsenal faithful. There has never been the outpouring of affection for him and his achievements that someone like Bill Shankly could generate. It was well known that Graham had negotiated an enormous salary for himself, as much as £250,000 a year with bonuses, whereas his refusal to sign big names was said to be due to the fact that the Arsenal players were not receiving as much as those at other First Division clubs and that Graham would not pay the level of wages required to tempt players like John Barnes, Tony Cottee and Frank McAvennie, all of whom attracted Graham's interest but not his cash. While there may be an element of truth in this, it is the case that during his stewardship, players' salaries have increased to the point where the club can now match any without distorting the pay structure. None the less, Graham has retained a reputation for being parsimonious in financial matters and cautious when contemplating a dip into the transfer market. In John Barnes' case, the failure of Arsenal to buy the player hinged on Graham's assessment of whether Barnes was a star who was prepared to 'dirty his hands and feet'. There was a 'big question mark over John's approach to the game, it's very laconic,' stated the Arsenal manager. What he said about another star, Anders Limpar, explains best why Barnes is not an Arsenal player. Of Limpar, Graham said, 'He's got to do what everyone else does.'

While criticized for a lack of imagination in his transfer dealings, Graham has nevertheless won grudging respect for the shrewdness of some of his buys. Lee Dixon, Steve Bould, Nigel Winterburn, Perry Groves and Alan Smith have all performed crucial roles in the development of the manager's plans, and all are team men, bought to fit into the Arsenal pattern. There seems to be no lack of salesmanship when players leave Highbury either, Graham having received large sums of money for players like Charlie Nicholas, Kevin Richardson, John Lukic, Niall Quinn and Martin Hayes, among whom only Lukic was an automatic choice for the Arsenal first team in 1990–91. Graham's own view, that dealing in the transfer market is one of his strong points, is supported by his employers. David Dein said that he prided himself on being a good negotiatior, 'but George has me beaten into a cocked hat.'

Another area in which Graham attracts respect, if not love, lies in the way he is seen to be the boss of the club from top to bottom. His approach can be likened to that of Alf Ramsey, in that he believes the only way to build success in the English game is to have complete control. Paradoxically, this is more important to a manager who does not as a rule spend large amounts of money on players. To put together a First Division side based on a youth team can only be accomplished if each player possesses an undying commitment to the cause. This attitude of mind depends on a strong leader, one who is seen to be in charge, whose decisions cannot be reversed by anyone else at the club. Thus at Highbury a hierarchy has developed which defines areas of responsibility. Administrative matters are the province of Ken Friar, commercial development and expansion are run by David Dein, and all matters related to the playing side are handled by George Graham. Since at Arsenal everything is based on the football team, Graham effectively runs the club. This suits the club because, as Graham says, 'If the control goes to the business people then it becomes more important than the football. Football clubs weren't meant to make a profit. The profit should be ploughed back into the football club and here at Arsenal it is.'

While this may be an enviable position to someone suffering the constraints that Terry Venables was under at Spurs, it is salient to remember what happened to Alf Ramsey. While he was winning, all was well, but once results started to go against him, all the residual bitterness surfaced and the knives were not long in coming out.

Graham is well aware that he is walking this particular tightrope, but insists: 'I'm going to do things my way, and if I'm wrong I'll be the first to hold up my hands and say so.' He feels he has earned the right to approach the job in this way because, he says, 'you're only given that freedom if you can do the job.' Since the Arsenal board set great store by loyalty, they know that, according to one director, 'George is an Arsenal man', and are therefore prepared to give him the space and time to carry out his policies.

Graham baulks at being called a disciplinarian. He prefers to describe himself as 'professional', with all the implied responsibilities the word entails. He has won over at least one of his critics, Johnny Giles, who admits to seeing in Liverpool 'weaknesses which George Graham would not permit – weakness of organization, attention to detail and required work-rates'. As for players, Graham feels they 'are looking for leadership and that comes from managers and coaches. I'm a demanding person. I like people to reach the standard I know they can attain. When they play well I'm absolutely delighted.' None the less, another, more self-critical, side of Graham emerged when he wistfully said, 'Maybe I don't show it enough.'

Johnny Giles summed up Graham's success by saying, 'Perhaps the thing I admire most about Graham is his apparently implicit understanding that being a successful manager is not to be involved in a popularity contest. Graham is said to be unpopular in the Highbury dressing room. I do not hear this as a criticism, only that he is doing his job.'

This single-mindedness, which allows Graham to control his feelings as well as his dominion, is a double-edged sword, however. He knows what he is doing and is under no internal pressure to explain himself; the resulting insularity encourages a somewhat ambivalent attitude towards him on the part of many fans.

An incident at the end of last season gives support to this view. Graham was reported to have said, when asked if the demonstration of support for John Lukic might make him change his mind about selling the goalkeeper, 'It's not up to the fans. I am the manager and therefore the only person who decides what is best for this club.' The gut reaction of *Gooner* (an Arsenal fanzine) editor Mike Francis was perhaps over the top, but the sentiment understandable. 'I think it's disgusting that a man in his position, manager of one of the biggest clubs in the country, if not the biggest, should make a comment such as that about the life and soul of the game,' he wrote. What irked the fans, of course, was the tone, rather than the substance of Graham's remarks, since they all realize that the manager has to be in control of what players are bought and sold.

All the elements that marked George Graham out as a natural manager of Arsenal came together in the Championship-winning season of 1988–9. Although the team had led the table for a period, Arsenal were always second favourites to Liverpool. Few gave them a chance of overhauling the Merseysiders in the last game of the season at Anfield, but the spirit of the team that Graham had created was perfect for the occasion. Being dismissed as no-hopers merely added to the collective belief that they could do it. Of course, tactics and player selection over the season were the crucial ingredients in the success, but the resilience and togetherness that the manager had nurtured were equally important. The players in any team managed by George Graham will always be well organized and tactically aware, but they will also contain a remarkable *esprit de corps*, which will sometimes boil over but will also overcome great obstacles. 'Every successful team must possess a great spirit of togetherness,' he said, 'we have that at Arsenal.' The senior pro, Paul Davis, said, 'There's a lot of respect for each other, not just as players but as people, and that's more important, because from the respect you can do anything together.'

Graham's record is testimony to the fact that he is well on the way to becoming one of the great Arsenal managers, along with Herbert Chapman and Bertie Mee. His ambition is to be the greatest, which would be fulfilled if he could take a team to success in the European Cup. He believes the fans at least recognize his commitment to this cause. 'They know my heart is here,' he said, then added with less certainty, 'I'm sure they do.'

Thus it was only to be expected that when the Arsenal team faced Southampton on the Saturday after the points deduction they would be more than fired up. Graham, eschewing his usual place in the stand for the first half, cajoled and harangued from the bench, and Arsenal went in at half-time leading 3–0. The final 4–0 victory was significant for another reason than the confirmation that the team refused to be affected by the FA verdict. Alan Smith scored his first League goals since the Wimbledon game on the opening day of the season. If this signalled the end of his personal famine then it was good news indeed. With Merson and Limpar adding the other two goals, the match provided a highly satisfactory diversion from the knowledge that the loss of two points now left Arsenal eight points behind

Liverpool. A relieved George Graham said, 'I think the boys are a bit perturbed, obviously about the stick we have been taking. They have responded magnificently.' The manager went on to remove any thoughts of complacency and sounded a warning to his rivals. 'We can get better,' he asserted. 'In the Championship year we scored a lot of goals away from home. Now we're just winning. To change things you have got to go back to basics; be dour, hard to beat. We're not going to be beaten easily now.'

Two days after the FA hearing, England played a European Championship qualifier against the Irish in Dublin. Manager Graham Taylor left out Paul Gascoigne on the grounds that 'it would not be his type of match', though quite why he believed that Gordon Cowans, who was Gascoigne's replacement, would cope any better mystified critics and fans alike. Taylor said that Jack Charlton's tactics of hustle and bustle would pass Gascoigne by. The manager was somewhat vindicated by a 1–1 draw, but it seemed a strange decision that someone who frequently dominated fixtures in the English First Division could be considered unsuitable for the game against Ireland, which was the closest to a First Division match that the England team would encounter. Perhaps Gascoigne's poor performance against Liverpool had persuaded Taylor that Dublin was the wrong place for his talent. Gascoigne was man-marked in that game, however, which was unlikely to be repeated against the Irish. Moreover, his performance the previous Saturday, while not one of his very best, led Terry Venables to compare him to one of the great players of all time.

'I remember going to watch Michel Platini play for Juventus when I was with Barcelona in the European Cup,' he said. 'I saw him three times, and every time he couldn't get into the game. Yet he made the winning goal on every occasion.'

Venables' eulogy came after Gascoigne had provided pin-point accuracy from corners for two of Spurs' goals in the 4–2 win over an improving Wimbledon. The game once again showed that Tottenham were not about to relinquish their Championship ambitions without a fight. It was a game they might not have won in previous seasons, but two late goals from Walsh and

Lineker to add to first-half efforts from Stewart and Mabbutt saw them home. The performance of Gascoigne notwithstanding, the real Spurs hero was Paul Walsh, who came of the bench in the seventy-seventh minute to transform a seemingly inevitable draw into a clear-cut victory. It was hard luck on Wimbledon, for whom Terry Gibson missed a good chance just before Walsh scored, but the Dons' manager, Ray Harford, recognized the influence of Walsh, describing his introduction as 'the turning point' of the match.

Gazza's answer to being left out of the England team, delivered in typical style, was to turn on a brilliant performance in a televised game away to Everton the following Sunday. After falling behind against the run of play early on to a McCall header, Spurs came back strongly, equalized with a superb headed goal from David Howells and should have won the match in the second half. Gascoigne produced some defence-splitting passes but also made several runs from deep positions, arriving on the edge of the penalty area at crucial moments to pick up the momentum of the attack. It was a superlative display, for which he deserved to win the title of Man of the Match. Lawrie McMen-emy, the England manager's No. 2, instead gave the award to McCall, perhaps thinking that a vote for Gazza would imply criticism of his omission from the Ireland game, but even McCall was moved to say that it was a poor decision. 'I got the award,' he commented, 'but if it had been left to me, my vote would have gone to Gascoigne.' His view was echoed by another Everton player, Tony Cottee, who said, 'I don't understand why Gazza doesn't play in every England game. I'd have him in every time because he is the best midfield player in the country.'

Spurs, however, were now eleven points behind Liverpool and the defence was starting to creak. Terry Venables knew what was required – a couple of new players – but could do nothing about the situation. The freedom to control events at the club had not been given to him at White Hart Lane, where Irving Scholar intervened far more than Venables ever thought he would. The contrast with George Graham's position at Highbury could not be more marked. For his part, Graham now faced the task of making up those two lost points, but his team were in a better position to do that than perhaps any other. And there would be an opportunity to make some inroads into the deficit in the near future, since Liverpool were due to play at Highbury in two weeks. If any single match was to exert an undue influence on Arsenal's own title aspirations, it would certainly be that one.

10

All's Well that Ends Well

At 4.28 p.m. on Saturday 24 November, with only twelve minutes to go before the end of that day's League fixtures, the outlook was decidedly favourable for Tottenham Hotspur. The team was leading Norwich 2–1 and heading for another victory, but, equally important, Arsenal were a goal down to Queen's Park Rangers at Loftus Road and, incredibly, Liverpool were losing at Anfield, 1–0 to Manchester City. Then, in the space of a few short minutes, the picture was totally altered as Arsenal hit three goals without reply and Liverpool took a 2–1 lead, eventually drawing 2–2. It was if the gods were toying with Spurs, providing hope one moment only to dash it the next.

Despite what might have been, Terry Venables was happy enough with the three points, coming as they did on the third anniversary of his appointment to the manager's post at White Hart Lane. 'Norwich are a very interesting team and they cause a lot of problems,' he said afterwards. 'But I thought we dealt with them well. I was hoping for a third goal to finish it off, but at least we kept making chances.'

Most of the chances he was referring to fell to Gary Lineker, who scored the two goals but failed to take advantage of at least two more opportunities. Lineker might already have had a hat-trick before a cross from the right by Van Den Hauwe found Stewart at the far post. As Stewart tried to get the ball under control, it fell into Lineker's path. He pushed it forward before shooting past Gunn in the Norwich goal. The visitors claimed Lineker had controlled the ball with his hand, and television evidence seemed to lend weight to their protests, but referee Roger Milford was having none of it. For his part, Lineker claimed that 'the ball spun up viciously and struck my arm but it certainly wasn't deliberate. I don't blame Norwich for being upset, but I've had so many valid goals disallowed in my career that there was no way I was going to volunteer anything about this one. It was a very advantageous strike on the arm and I would have fully understood had the ref not given it, but I didn't push it through on purpose.'

The incident fired Norwich up, and they equalized two minutes later through a superb free kick from one of the many members of the Spurs old guard who had found a home in East Anglia, Ian Crook. Some thought Thorstvedt should have saved the shot, which spun into the net off the post, but this view detracts from a strike of pin-point accuracy that would have beaten most keepers. Once again, Spurs came out for the second half with more determination, and went ahead again after fifty-two minutes. Another cross from the right, this time by Allen, was headed on by Stewart to Lineker, who drew Gunn before rolling the ball beyond him into the far corner. A big plus for Spurs was the performance of Stewart, whose aerial power dominated the Norwich defence for long periods. Although his goalscoring record remained poor, Stewart took comfort from his display, saying, 'I was the target for the crowd, but now I'm enjoying the best and happiest time of my career at Tottenham.' One reporter was even moved to suggest that Lineker and Stewart reminded him of Smith and Greaves. Perhaps the one area of concern for Terry Venables was the ease with which Norwich had exposed the defence. On this occasion, Thorstvedt made good saves and the visitors spurned chances, but the flaws were there for all to see, and, as the Liverpool game proved, a good team will punish poor defenders without mercy.

Luckily for Spurs, Sheffield United were not a good team. Unluckily, the bad feeling engendered in the League match at White Hart Lane was still in the minds of some of the Sheffield players when the teams met in the fourth round of the Rumbelows Cup at Bramall Lane on the Tuesday after the Norwich match. Vinny Jones was lectured after five seconds for a foul on Paul Gascoigne, and the niggling continued throughout the opening exchanges. In the twenty-sixth minute Brian Deane lunged at Steve Sedgley, who immediately collapsed in obvious pain. The referee, Keren Barratt, did not see the incident as a foul, which led to remonstrations from Terry Venables. The irate Spurs manager eventually had to be pulled from the pitch by his assistant, Doug Livermore. Sedgley was carried off and replaced by David Tuttle, a youngster who had come through the junior ranks and had won England caps at youth level. Venables' intervention in the Sedgley injury was given some justification when it transpired that the player needed eight stitches in a nasty leg wound and would be out for some time.

In the game itself, Spurs tended to be over-elaborate, until Paul Walsh came on for Vinny Samways in the seventieth minute. Bringing a more direct approach to the Spurs attack, Walsh crossed for Stewart, who had missed two earlier chances, but now made amends by putting Spurs one up. In the dying seconds a Walsh shot was parried and Gascoigne tapped in the rebound. Spurs had made it to the quarter-finals, but not without cost.

There were other portents that did not augur well for Tottenham's immediate future. The deal with Robert Maxwell looked further away than ever. At a football writers' lunch, Maxwell revealed he had been infuriated by the League's 'mismanagement committee' and its inference that there was something underhand about his involvement with Spurs. He demanded an apology, which, if not forthcoming, might result in him notifying Tottenham that he would refuse to go ahead with the deal to underwrite the rights issue. 'To ram the point home,' he concluded, 'I could say that in the case of Derby County and Oxford, if they are not sold by the end of the season to fit and proper people, I will pull out and invite the management committee to pick up the deficit for running the clubs.'

In addition to the new problems with Maxwell, no new statement had been prepared for shareholders, which led to renewed speculation concerning the possible sale of players. Vinny Samways had expressed a desire to leave the club, but more worrying was the news that Terry Venables had been linked to the vacant manager's job at Real Madrid following the departure of John Toshack. While giving the lie to the rumour, Venables still kept the door open for a possible move away from Spurs.

'I loved my time in Spain,' he enthused, 'but I'm a Londoner and this is where I want to live. My intention is to win the League Championship in my own country and I'm getting close now with this Spurs team. My ambition is to leave an indelible mark on our game here. But my contract does expire after the end of this season and I'm waiting to hear something sensible from the directors.'

The bad omens were confirmed in full when the team went to Stamford Bridge for the next League game against Chelsea. The problems started before the match, when the club coach was towed away by police for being illegally parked outside the Royal Lancaster Hotel, where the players were enjoying their pre-match meal. A fleet of black cabs was hailed to take the stranded players to Stamford Bridge, while a Spurs official had to be dispatched to the pound at Camden Town to retrieve the kit.

'When someone told me what had happened,' commented Terry Venables, 'I refused to believe them, because I thought it was Jeremy Beadle . . . I think it's incredible the police did not come and ask us to move the coach to another position. It could have been an old ladies' outing or something.'

The fiasco led to the kick-off being delayed by ten minutes. What with tow-away fees, taxi fares and a possible fine by the League for turning up late, it had turned out to be one very expensive lunch.

Perhaps the disruption got through to the players, or perhaps Chelsea simply came out full of fire and fight. Whatever the case, Spurs found themselves a goal down before they had hardly had time to draw breath. Somehow, without ever being convincing, the Spurs defence had built one of the best records in the division, particularly away from home. All the good work was now to go spectacularly off the rails as Steve Sedgley's absence proved fatal. His replacement, David Tuttle, had a nightmare forty-five minutes until his manager withdrew him from the fray. By then Chelsea were 2–0 up, but it would be unfair to lay the blame for that solely at Tuttle's door. The whole team seemed lethargic until the later stages, and there were more than one or two below-par performances. Tuttle was unfortunate to have to face a probing ball from Townsend after five minutes that caught him on the turn, allowing the experienced Kerry Dixon to race past and hold him off before placing a low shot past Thorstvedt. Durie's snap shot in the forty-fourth minute would have bemused any number of defenders, but it was Tuttle who was marking him and Tuttle who took the blame when Durie's effort was palmed away by Thorstvedt only as far as Bumstead, who scored easily. Spurs did conjure up one moment in the first half when Lineker put the ball in the net, only to be denied by the referee for handball.

Gazza pulled a goal back with another brilliant free kick early in the second half, but Spurs' joy was shortlived, as just four minutes later Durie struck Chelsea's third. It was only then that Spurs began to play, but it was too late. Lineker was brought down by Beasant but amazingly blazed his penalty way over the bar. Walsh came on for Nayim after sixty-three minutes and immediately provided another good chance for the England captain, which he put wide. Eventually, Lineker did manage to get on to the scoresheet, when he volleyed home Stewart's centre. Despite goal-line clearances and missed chances as Chelsea tired and Spurs came forward towards the end, there were few complaints afterwards in the dressing room. Spurs had truly succumbed to the boys in blue, and the job of catching Liverpool seemed ever more difficult. Seven days before, when Spurs were beating Norwich and both Arsenal and Liverpool were on the verge of defeat, the gap between Spurs and Liverpool might have been cut, with Arsenal and Tottenham level. Now, for the first time in the season, they were out of the top three, losing their place to Crystal Palace, who were 2–1 winners over Coventry. Spurs were three points behind Arsenal and nine behind Liverpool, but had played one game more than both of them, since neither had been in action that day. They were due to meet in a televised game at Highbury the following afternoon.

The three goals that Arsenal scored in the last twelve minutes against a weakened QPR lifted the spirits of everyone at Highbury. With Liverpool held to a draw by Manchester City, the Gunners were now six points behind the Merseysiders with the match against them to come. Arsenal had been on top for most of the game at Loftus Road, George Graham said, 'They [QPR] retreated and they almost played like an away team. It was embarrassing in the first half. Had it been a boxing match it would have been stopped.'

Rangers were a side decimated by injuries and so had tried to contain Arsenal. None the less, the Gunners had fallen behind in injury time at the end of the first half, when Tony Adams was judged to have pushed Roy Wegerle inside the penalty area. It looked a harsh decision, but Wegerle wins those sort of penalties regularly; this was his fifth of the season. Adams had to take some stick from the crowd for the rest of the game, but this appeared to make him more determined than ever to atone for his mistake. As the second half wore on it looked as if it might not be Arsenal's day, but the team never gave up. Campbell came on for Groves in the sixty-eighth minute but it was Adams, foraging forward yet again, who slammed in a shot in the seventy-eighth minute, which was blocked, but which fell kindly for Paul Merson. Merson smashed the ball past goalkeeper Tony Roberts to equalize. Seven minutes later Alan Smith showed he was back on the goal trail with a vengeance, as he coolly finished a three-man move with a low strike from the edge of the area. Two minutes after that, Kevin Campbell provided the perfect finale by keeping his head when put clean through by Lee Dixon, placing the ball low in the corner and giving Roberts no chance. It was Rangers' fifth defeat in a row, and Don Howe had good reason to be worried. So did Tony Adams, since a complaint had been made to police that during the celebrations following Merson's equalizer, the Arsenal captain had given the V-sign to the QPR supporters who had been baiting him. The police were to report the matter to the FA.

George Graham told Frank McLintock that the midweek Rumbelows Cup tie against Manchester United at Highbury was 'more important' than the following Sunday's League encounter with Liverpool. 'You only get one chance in a Cup tie,' he said. 'If we lose to Liverpool we have the rest of the season to put it right, but if we lose to United that's it.'

Manchester United are a strange team. The two games against Arsenal showed them at their worst and at their best. Whether events at Old Trafford made the Arsenal defence freeze, or whether Graham's reversion to a flat back four unbalanced the side, there was no disguising the fact that United carved gaps in the Arsenal defence of a magnitude that had not been seen at

Highbury for a very long time. The 6–2 defeat was the worst at home for seventy years. The most miserly defence in the League conceded as many goals in one match as they had in all their previous League games in 1990–91 put together.

The first half was a complete disaster, as United went into a three-goal lead that could have been larger. For a time in the second half Arsenal looked to have pulled themselves back into the match after Alan Smith put home two rebounds, the first from a Michael Thomas shot, the second from a Tony Adams header. But the only crumb of comfort from the whole catastrophe was that Smith had now scored five in three games. At 3–2, everybody expected the Gunners to play patiently, but for the first time in the season they lost their heads and chased the game. Although chances were created around Sealey's goal, United always looked more dangerous when they came out of defence and could have doubled the three more goals they actually scored.

George Graham readily agreed, saying, 'We had to play with fire in our bellies at the start of the second half and we did. But once we had pulled the two goals back the approach should have been a bit calmer. We allowed United to hit us on the break.'

While acknowledging the superiority of the opposition on the night, particularly the young Lee Sharpe, who scored a brilliant hat-trick, Graham complained about United's second goal, scored by Mark Hughes, which he claimed should have been disallowed as Steve Bruce was offside. It was yet another decision about what constitutes interfering with play, and added fuel to Terry Venables' argument over the need for some kind of formal clarification. No one could accuse the Arsenal team of interfering with play. It was a truly awful performance, which made thoughts turn to how they would respond in the toughest test of all – the visit of Liverpool four days later.

The players' public spokesman was Nigel Winterburn, who said, 'The dressing room was like a disaster area after the match. It was more disbelief than anything else. Real shock. We're ashamed and we're sorry.' Looking ahead, Winterburn expressed a more positive attitude: 'It was a one-off. I'm sure of it. You can't go unbeaten as long as we did and not believe that, not believe you are a good team. What we have to do is get it back for Sunday. If we beat Liverpool – and victory can be the only thing on our minds – it will wipe out this memory.'

Arsenal had gone seventeen League and Cup games unbeaten, and had they won the Manchester United clash would have set a new post-war record. George Graham reminded everyone that it was also a personal catastrophe: 'It's my heaviest defeat as manager and I never lost six as a player. It's not enjoyable.' Graham didn't mention a particularly emphatic loss he was involved in as a player with Arsenal, a 5–0 trouncing at Stoke. That game came early on in the 1970–71 season, and the team replied to the humiliation by trouncing Nottingham Forest 4–0, then embarking on a fourteen-game unbeaten run that propelled them towards the title – and the double. If that was to be the manager's example, there would be some interesting weeks ahead.

When the Arsenal players left the pitch at the end of the Manchester United game they were in a state of shock and utter disbelief. They were apprehensive of the manager's reaction and fully expected to be called in for extra training and not have the following day off as was customary after a match. In the event, Graham was not angry, nor did he intend to deprive the players of their rest day.

Paul Davis didn't go anywhere on Thursday. 'I just sat at home and thought about the game,' he revealed. 'I relaxed a little bit and even watched some of the game, just to see what happened. It was like a shock, the next day I was trying to analyse it, dissect the game a little bit. Come Friday I was starting to forget about it.' Davis was putting into practice the lessons he had learned as a player who had spent his entire career at Highbury. George Graham had set the tone by promoting the philosophy that after a traumatic defeat you work out what went wrong quickly and decisively. Then you put the loss behind you and concentrate on the match to come.

On Friday the players had a training session at London Colney. There were no recriminations, no lectures, no haranguing of individuals. The manager told the players to forget about what happened, to still believe in themselves and their ability. The players took their cue from the positive attitude which the coaching staff exuded. 'Football is a lot about the mind and confidence,' explained Paul Davis. 'So we concentrated on keeping our confidence together and keeping together as a group. I think that helped us for the Sunday game.'

After another light training session on Saturday morning, everyone met up again that evening at a hotel in South Mimms. At 8 p.m. they had tea and sandwiches and watched television until half past nine. Paul Davis described the atmosphere: 'The spirit was good amongst the guys ... everybody wants to be together, it's a nice feeling.' Arsenal never train on the day of a game, so on Sunday they had a late breakfast in the hotel at 11.15, before attending George Graham's twenty-minute team meeting at 12.30.

When Kenny Dalglish announced his team at 2.30 p.m., it surprised everyone. Peter Beardsley had been dropped and was not even named as one of the substitutes, Ray Houghton was out of the starting line-up, though he was on the bench, and there was no Steve McMahon who was injured. In came two full backs, Venison and Burrows, which meant Liverpool were to start the match playing six defenders, the others being Ablett, Molby, Hysen and Gillespie. In a bizarre turn of events, Peter Beardsley put in an appearance in the television studio but was not allowed to say anything of note. Most spectators and pundits were caught on the hop by Dalglish's selection and the Arsenal camp were equally stunned.

Paul Davis told how they responded: '[The composition of the Liverpool team] was completely different to the one we had been talking about. We had another team meeting half an hour before the game. We still weren't sure of their system of play even though we knew the team − whether they were going to play five at the back or four, one up front or two ... so we tried to make provisions. If they played five at the back, we would do this, if they played one up front we would counteract it by doing that. We found out what was happening once we got out there and we kind of worked it from there. As it happened, they did play four at the back, but we knew what we were going to do [in that eventuality] before we went out, so there weren't any problems.'

By playing the two full backs, Burrows and Venison, in midfield, Dalglish was making his intentions clear. Liverpool were six points ahead and they had come to Highbury to defend that lead. Dalglish had brought in Burrows against Tottenham but had used him specifically to mark Gascoigne. Moreover, in that game the Liverpool manager kept the option of Beardsley by naming him as substitute, and Beardsley it was who came on to great effect. Against Arsenal, it seemed that Dalglish was even more committed to a policy of stopping the other team from playing. In a way it was a tribute to the respect Liverpool were paying to the Gunners, whom they regarded as their only serious challengers. None the less, for the first fifteen minutes Arsenal did not play particularly well and were fortunate that Liverpool did not sense their vulnerability. In the end the Gunners also benefited from some favourable refereeing decisions, which on another day might well have gone against them.

Liverpool were unable to take advantage of Arsenal's obvious nerves during the early part of the first half. With Beardsley and Houghton not playing, Rush was isolated up front and drew little support from Barnes, while the return of O'Leary stiffened a defence that had looked so porous against Manchester United. Paul Davis was surprised Liverpool were so defensive: 'If they'd maybe been a bit more positive then it may have been a different result.' Once Arsenal realized that this Liverpool line-up was not going to present them with insurmountable problems, their confidence began to return and they put some sustained pressure on the Liverpool defence. In the twentieth minute Michael Thomas, who seems to save up his best performances for games against Liverpool, won a corner through some clever play that took him deep into the heart of the Liverpool penalty area. Paul Davis's corner was headed away to the edge of the area, where it was met by a superb Thomas volley. A slight deflection by O'Leary wrongfooted Grobbelaar and the keeper could only parry the ball, which was immediately knocked back towards the danger area. Merson's header beat Grobbelaar, and although Venison hooked the ball away, referee Alan Gunn judged that it had already crossed the line, a decision that was hotly disputed by Kenny Dalglish and the Liverpool players after the game. Dalglish also said that Liverpool accepted the referee's opinion.

'That we didn't go chasing after him is to our credit,' he said. 'That's why we have won the Fair Play Trophy for the last three years.'

George Graham was pleased that the team went into the interval in the lead but urged the players to do more. It didn't take long for his message to get through, as Arsenal tore into Liverpool at the start of the second half. Within three minutes Merson released Limpar, who burst into the penalty area between Ablett and Gillespie, then went crashing to the ground. Referee Gunn made his second crucial intervention of the match by awarding Arsenal a penalty, which Dixon put away to make the score 2–0. It was another decision that could have gone either way, but it showed that the 'one rule for Liverpool' argument did not always hold good. The question of an Arsenal fan – would he have given it at Anfield? – seemed unduly cynical in the circumstances. Later in the game Limpar went down again in the penalty area after a challenge by Hysen. This time the referee awarded nothing, and Hysen quite clearly demonstrated to Gunn that Limpar had dived. Barry Venison later admitted that they were 'asking the referee to book him for ungentlemanly conduct'. However, the following Saturday an interesting close-up of the incident was shown on the *Saint and Greavsie* television programme. Jimmy Greaves himself was certain that this second incident was a foul and that a penalty should have been awarded. The camera angle showed that Limpar's reputation as a diver, which was fuelled by a number of Liverpool players in interviews with the press after the match, might well have been exaggerated.

Dalglish reacted to events by sending on Houghton and Rosenthal, but there was no way back. With two minutes to go, Arsenal underlined their by now absolute superiority with a goal of real class. Merson produced the perfect back-heel into the space behind the Liverpool defence, and Smith raced through and beat the unprotected Grobbelaar with a clinical low shot into the corner of the net. It was his sixth goal in four games.

Back in September, David Lacey, the football correspondent of the *Guardian*, had asked if any of the Arsenal players were worthy of a place in the Liverpool side: 'Of the forwards only Rocastle would be seriously considered; Groves would not get into the

Liverpool car park,' he wrote. It was interesting that neither the praised nor the damned played a role in Liverpool's heaviest defeat for over a year. Afterwards, George Graham applauded the players for lifting themselves in the days since the Manchester United humiliation.

'I've worked with these players for four years,' he exclaimed proudly. 'Their attitude has always been superb and they deserve all the credit.' Graham went on to explain both the euphoria the result had engendered and its limitations in the overall scheme of things. 'Psychologically it gives everyone a lift, including the fans, but the victory doesn't mean we're going to win anything – it's still only three points for us.'

Kenny Dalglish, who would have to take a fair amount of flak for his selection, was uncharacteristically critical of his team, saying, 'Even if we had twelve players we wouldn't have won. We didn't do ourselves justice. We're still three points ahead and in the position everyone wants to be, but we've got to do better than that.'

Paul Davis, who with Michael Thomas had dominated the midfield, was ecstatic. 'We felt it was a team performance. No one was really outstanding, but all of us had the togetherness again. We felt that everybody played a part in the victory. The manager was pleased, it was a good feeling afterwards, especially to beat Liverpool.' None the less, Davis was not above admitting that after all the recent problems 'there was a bit of relief afterwards'.

Arsenal were now within three points of Liverpool, and the title race had been thrown wide open again. Those two lost points were beginning to look even more crucial, since a one-point gap would have exerted even more pressure on the champions. Perhaps equally important, Arsenal had come back from the Manchester United defeat with style and class and, now that Liverpool were beaten, remained the only undefeated team in the First Division. Only six goals conceded in fifteen League matches told the true story – the game against United could now safely be put down to a one-off freak performance that was unlikely to be repeated in the foreseeable future. It is interesting to note that while the press unanimously condemned Dalglish for his defensive formation, few linked these criticisms with a comparable situation at Arsenal. When Graham left out the extra centre back against Manchester United, the inclusion of an attacker, Perry Groves, did little to achieve a balanced team. It was only with the reappearance of O'Leary, and thus on paper a more defence-minded system, that Arsenal looked capable of playing to their potential.

Selection problems were not restricted to George Graham and Kenny Dalglish, however. Terry Venables had a few of his own. The loss of Sedgley exposed the limitations of the Spurs squad, but there was no money to buy cover and Terry Fenwick was still completing his recovery from a long period of injury on loan to Second Division Leicester. In addition, the Spurs boss had the form of Paul Walsh to consider. Venables had thought from the beginning of the season that his first-choice strikers were Lineker and Stewart. Now Walsh was continually forcing himself into the picture, and his manager was coming under increasing pressure to give him a place in the starting line-up. How Venables resolved these difficulties would probably determine the fate of Spurs' season.

11

Three into Two Won't Go

Paul Walsh could be forgiven for thinking that football, far from being a 'funny old game', is actually the cruellest of endeavours. When he burst on to the scene as a teenager at Charlton in the early 1980s, his close skills and goalscoring prowess led to a widespread belief that here was an England player in the making, one whose career would surely blossom when he was able to perform on the First Division stage. When the call came, however, it was not from any of the big teams as might have been expected, but from Luton, a club not without merit but whose ambition at the time was more about survival than winning trophies. Nevertheless, Walsh continued in the same vein as he had at Charlton, and most commentators thought that it was only a matter of time before his undoubted talents drew the interest of a club with bigger aspirations. When, in 1984, Liverpool stepped in, Walsh must have thought that at last his time had come. Filling the position previously occupied by Keegan and Dalglish was perhaps the biggest job in English football, but Walsh's natural ability was of a sort that won the hearts of supporters. Everything was set up for the fulfilment of that early potential. Somehow, it didn't quite work out that way.

At first, things went well for Walsh at Anfield. His record of twenty-five League goals in seventy-seven appearances, while not outstanding, stands comparison with most, but by the time Terry Venables paid £500,000 to bring him back to London in 1987, he had become something of a marginal figure at Liverpool and did not command a regular first-team place. The arrival of Peter Beardsley, John Aldridge and John Barnes meant his chances would be equally restricted in the future. As one of Venables' first signings for Spurs, Walsh seemed to have been presented with a new lease of life, the centrepiece of the new Spurs attack. It may have been that the Liverpool experience adversely affected his confidence, but Walsh did not perform to the high standards expected when he came to White Hart Lane, and his career once again looked as though it might stagnate. When Venables bought Gary Lineker from Barcelona, Walsh was again facing the prospect of being reduced to the role of understudy. The downturn was confirmed in Lineker's first season, during which Walsh made only twelve full appearances, was substitute on a further fourteen occasions, and scored just two goals. Meanwhile, he gained a reputation among the Spurs fans for ill-luck. 'Whenever he gets on the field and has a strike at goal,' said one, 'the next thing you're bound to say is "unlucky Walshy".'

At the start of the 1990–91 season, it seemed that Venables knew in his own mind who his first-choice strikers were: Gary Lineker and Paul Stewart. In the early games, although Stewart failed to find the net, results were good enough for Venables to feel his decision justified. Once Stewart began to score a few goals himself and improve his all-round play, Walsh was even more likely to fade into the background. Just when many players would have given up in despair, Walsh found inspiration from somewhere and began to seize with both hands the limited chances that came his way. While those chances were mainly as substitute, Walsh's hat-trick display against Sheffield United, when he deputized for the injured Lineker, brought pressure on his manager to give him a run in the first team. This presented problems for Terry Venables, since it would mean changing the pattern and shape of the Tottenham style. Walsh himself clearly felt he had proved his point, not least to some of the Spurs supporters. An incident after the game against Norwich in November demonstrated the depth of pressure he was under. Walsh and fellow substitute Vinny Samways were jogging round the pitch when Walsh was abused and provoked by two spectators, who had stayed behind after the vast majority had long departed. As this went on, Walsh became so incensed that he jumped over the perimeter wall into the seated area, where a scuffle took place, eventually broken up by the intervention of the police. Reports the following day claimed that two men had made a complaint of assault against Walsh to the local constabulary.

The affair did not seem to affect Walsh's renaissance on the pitch. He came on again as substitute against Sunderland at White Hart Lane on 8 December and delivered an early Christmas present to the Spurs supporters. In this game the enforced absence of Steve Sedgley through injury exposed the lack of defensive cover available to the manager. The young David Tuttle was clearly not yet ready to take on experienced First Division strikers, and the club had sold two centre backs – John Polsten and Guy Butters – since the previous season. With Terry Fenwick getting back to match fitness while on loan to Leicester, the Spurs back line was inevitably makeshift in character, containing three left-sided full backs (Thomas, Van Den Hauwe and Edinburgh) and Gary Mabbutt. The hole in Spurs' finances was beginning to show itself on the pitch, and there was little Venables could do to fill it. Suddenly, the Tottenham midfield, perhaps made insecure by the troubles at the back, was overrun. And this time it was not by a great side like Liverpool, but a modest Sunderland team which, while capable of attractive attacking football, had its hands full fighting to stay out of the relegation positions. To make matters worse, Lineker was not firing on all cylinders and did not present the options that would normally be expected, possibly due to a heel injury he had been carrying.

Just as in the previous game, against Chelsea, Spurs got off to a bad start. Gascoigne, who was later booked, lost possession to Bracewell after eleven minutes, and a quick counter-attack ended with Pascoe putting Sunderland ahead. Worse was to come after twenty-two minutes, when Davenport raced through a porous defence to make it 2–0. At half-time the match was apparently lost. Although outplayed for long periods, it was again a credit to the players that they were able to turn the game around, though much of the praise was reserved for Paul Walsh. First he touched in Gazza's free kick, then got the bit of luck he deserved when his shot was deflected by Armstrong to bring the scores level. When Pascoe grabbed his second to put Sunderland ahead again after seventy-five minutes, many teams would have given up the ghost. But Walsh made one more surging run down the left in injury time, conjured up an inch-perfect cross and Lineker did the rest. Spurs had escaped with a point from a match many observers felt they deserved to lose, but there was no denying the contribution of Walsh, nor the fighting qualities of the comeback.

Terry Venables paid full tribute to the part his substitute had played: 'He turned the game once again and I thought he was outstanding.' The draw did little, however, to enhance Spurs' title ambitions, and the lack of strength in depth was now abundantly clear.

Another substitute that day was Vinny Samways, who was the subject of transfer speculation concerning a possible move to Nottingham Forest. Samways came on to replace Paul Stewart after he limped away from the game with an ankle injury. The inevitable question was now posed – will Walsh retain his place, especially if Stewart's injury clears up? Stewart himself was generous and honest in his assessment of the situation.

'Paul Walsh is breathing down my neck and is unfortunate not to be in the team,' he said. 'In the last two matches he has come on and been absolutely brilliant . . . but I've got five goals in the last eleven games and I believe I should be there on merit. So does Gary Lineker and so does Paul Walsh.'

Stewart's direct appraisal was entirely in keeping with his style of play. His no-nonsense approach to the game has often seen him overstep the line between enthusiasm and recklessness. Sometimes he appears so wound up that he tries too hard, makes rash tackles and looks clumsy as a consequence, perhaps all born of a desire to justify the £1.7 million that Terry Venables paid for him. His effectiveness hinges on achieving a balance between his natural instinct for a scrap and infringement of the laws of the game. Stewart has had a hard time winning the wholehearted allegiance of the Spurs faithful because of these characteristics, and has fallen foul of referees for the same reasons. Indeed, when he first arrived at White Hart Lane he was serving a suspension and was sent off in a Littlewoods Cup game against Southend in 1989–90. But Venables was firmly of the opinion that Stewart brought an extra dimension to the team and that a squad of largely cultured footballers needed an injection of aggression to be fully effective.

Paul Stewart had made his name in one prolific goalscoring season in the Second Division with Manchester City, when he netted twenty-four times in forty League appearances. City had bought him the previous season from Blackpool, where his scoring ratio was somewhat less convincing – fifty-six League goals in 201 games over six years. In his first season at Spurs, his return of twelve goals in twenty-five games was more respectable, but his progression was interrupted in 1989–90 by injury, suspension and omission from the side. The failings of the team in general were aggravated by Stewart's apparent awkwardness, and the striker had to shoulder increasing criticism from the supporters. The fans' opinions began to change at the end of the season, first when Stewart headed a fine winning goal in a televised match against Liverpool, then when he carried on to score five goals in the last nine games, a sequence which included a superb volley against Coventry which was voted the goal of the season by Spurs' supporters. When the crowd had been on his back, Stewart had seemed to get more irascible, but those goals, particularly the one against Liverpool, marked a turning point in his fortunes at Tottenham, a testimony to the player's determination to succeed.

As the 1990–91 campaign got into full swing, Stewart again found goals hard to come by. But a more positive attitude, fuelled by fulsome praise from Terry Venables, saw his general play improve considerably, and after he had broken the ice in the Rumbelows Cup tie against Hartlepool, goals began to come more regularly. One noticeable change was a more responsible approach to his role in the team and a willingness to forge an effective partnership with Gary Lineker. He appeared to have realized that he cannot get away with explosive play and behaviour like Gazza can. Gascoigne accomplishes the feat through his extreme skill and national status, whereas Stewart must control his temperament in the interests of the team. Any success he enjoyed had come slowly and, even though the 1990–91 season had seen a new Paul Stewart, the fans were not yet completely won over. 'When I see him take a shot on goal,' said one after the game against Forest in October, 'I almost want him to miss, because I know he is not good enough.'

As far as the supporters and the media were concerned, the decision for Terry Venables was whether to pick Walsh instead of Stewart, whose ankle injury had healed by the time of the next game, or whether to play three up front from the start, even if it meant changing the pattern of the side. Players of clubs who had faced Walsh spoke glowingly of his contribution. The pass that had set up Paul Allen for the winning goal against Aston Villa was described by Kent Nielsen as one that completely split the defence. The Villa defender went on to say that Walsh 'has the ability to dribble, show close control and is very sharp'. Chelsea's Ken Monkou was equally complimentary: 'When Walsh came on, John [Bumstead] had another dangerous player to keep an eye on and it gave Gazza more freedom.' Terry Venables, on the other hand, made a cogent case for maintaining the status quo. On the day before the away game at Manchester City, he ventured the opinion that 'football is a thirteen-man game. On the Continent they sometimes have their best players on the bench. In some ways it is an ideal situation for a manager, having players pushing each other for a place. Paul hasn't come to see me about the situation but I'm the first to say how well he is doing.' Venables concluded his argument by describing how Walsh's inclusion would necessitate tactical changes. 'The shape of our midfield makes it very difficult for him to play anywhere but up front,' he said. 'There are certain games I can play three up front, but I doubt if Manchester City will be one of them.'

Having put forward such convincing reasons for leaving Walsh on the bench, Venables then did exactly the opposite and included all three strikers for the game at Maine Road. Perhaps the media pressure had finally told on the manager, or perhaps he had been indulging in a disinformation exercise to confuse the opposition. Whatever the case, it certainly seemed a strange turn of events. In a game where a ball winner was surely needed to combat the fighting qualities of Peter Reid and Gary Megson, the manager dropped Paul Allen, one of the few players at his disposal who could compete with the opposition midfield. At first it seemed as if the ploy would pay off. Venables was relying on the recovered Steve Sedgley to stiffen the defence and Paul Gascoigne to produce some magic. Gazza duly obliged with a magnificent solo goal to give Spurs the lead in the twenty-fifth minute. Once again, frustration got the better of him later in the game and he was booked for kicking the ball away. In the last half-hour Tottenham were unable to hold the midfield and Manchester

City pushed them to the limit. With fifteen minutes remaining the Spurs defence finally cracked and Redmond equalized when he deflected a shot from Wayne Clarke past a wrong-footed Erik Thorstvedt. Seven minutes later, the ultimate irony, Paul Walsh conceded a penalty when a cross from Brightwell hit him on the arm. It was an unlucky decision that cost Spurs the game.

Gary Mabbutt summed up the cost to Spurs of their run of poor form: 'We are really disappointed because we believed we could put ourselves right back in the title race. Instead we have now lost eight points in three games and that is not good enough – it is certainly not Championship form.'

No one, of course, dared suggest the unthinkable – that perhaps Gary Lineker's performances left something to be desired. And why should they? After all, Lineker's record speaks for itself and the goal machine was still functioning somewhere near maximum efficiency. Yet there were occasions when the merest hint of frustration seemed to be etched on the face of the player the *Spur* called NMOE (the Nicest Man on Earth). On anyone else, such looks would be interpreted as mild annoyance, but coming from the undemonstrative England striker they spoke volumes. Maybe Lineker was having to come to terms with the fact that Spurs' Championship aspirations were fast disappearing, but it certainly seemed at times as if he wasn't pleased with what was happening around him. It could also be that any displeasure Lineker felt was accentuated by a series of niggling injuries, not bad enough to prevent him from playing, but perhaps proving the difference between taking and missing chances, or making those telling runs time after time for ninety minutes.

When Lineker first came to White Hart Lane, he admitted that his primary reason for returning to England was to ensure a place in the World Cup team. This led many fans to conclude that his heart really wasn't with Spurs, but probably lay with his home-town club, Leicester City. While there may be some foundation for this view, there were other important factors. The prospect of playing with Chris Waddle, for instance, was one. Lineker said that of all the players he had ever played with, Waddle 'knows my game, sees my runs and provides the most accurate passes I have ever had'. His disillusion after Waddle was sold to

Marseille must have been immense. Nevertheless, Lineker stated that he would like to pledge his future to Spurs. Commenting in November on the club's financial problems, he said, 'It would be a shame if the Spurs team was broken up but everything depends on what happens in the boardroom. I would be content to spend the rest of my career at Tottenham. I don't want to leave, but in the end the club will decide.'

Despite these assurances, there is a certain ambivalence running through the moves in Lineker's career. When it became obvious to everyone that he would have to leave Leicester he openly professed his desire to stay, and challenged the directors to build a team round him. But the Leicester directors had neither the ambition nor the will to keep a player of Lineker's calibre. Few could have predicted, on a frozen January afternoon in 1979, that the seventeen-year-old making his début against Oldham would be hailed by no less an authority than Jimmy Greaves as 'the greatest goalscorer England has ever produced'. Lineker was overshadowed in that game by two other youngsters, David Buchanan and Andy Peake, and his chances were restricted for the next two years. But once Lineker got a run in the first team the goals began to flow with an astonishing regularity. They were often the result of searing physical pace, equalled only by speed of thought, both allied to a willingness to chase lost causes. In his first full season he scored seventeen goals in thirty-seven League appearances, following that up with twenty-six League goals, the highest in the division, which were instrumental, along with thirteen from Alan Smith, in Leicester's promotion to Division One. The higher level did not deter Lineker. If anything, his pace was even more effective, and his haul of twenty-two League goals in a struggling side remains a tribute to his ability. The next season, his last for Leicester, he scored a total of twenty-nine goals in forty-eight games, twenty-four of them in the League, to make him the division's top marksman.

A move to a big club can go either way for a player who has made his name for one of the smaller outfits. It took Lineker precisely one month and six games to win over the Everton fans, when he hit four goals in a 6–2 win at Sheffield Wednesday. Lineker went on to score thirty League goals in his one season at

Goodison, once again the division's leading scorer. The Championship medal he craved, however, was snatched away by rivals Liverpool, as was a Cup-winner's medal, despite his opening the scoring at Wembley. When it became clear at the end of the season that Everton were prepared to accept the offer from Terry Venables' Barcelona, the pragmatic approach of England's leading striker began to assert itself.

Lineker was transferred to Barcelona at the same time as Mark Hughes of Manchester United. But where Hughes never adapted to life in Spain, Lineker made great efforts to learn the language and present a positive image of himself. His command of Spanish even became good enough for him to commentate on television. On the pitch, the goals continued to flow, and he ended his first season second in the goalscoring chart with eighteen goals, behind Hugo Sanchez of Real Madrid, whose total was swelled by a large number of penalties. What brought him the undying loyalty of the Catalan fans, however, was a hat-trick against Real Madrid in the Bernabeu, in a match Barcelona won 4–0 and which is still spoken about with reverence. Lineker had gone to a team which had won the Spanish Championship and reached the European Cup Final in the previous two seasons, yet in Lineker's début season the title was clinched by arch-enemies Real Madrid. Moreover, Barcelona went out of the UEFA Cup in the early rounds. When the team once again trailed behind Real the following season, the writing was on the wall for Venables. The consolation of twice finishing second in the League could not save him and he left, to be replaced by Johan Cruyff. Cruyff publicly voiced his doubts about Lineker, reinforced perhaps by the striker's poor showing in the 1988 European Championships and the subsequent diagnosis of hepatitis. However, thirty-six goals in fifty-nine appearances in the Spanish League made it more difficult to leave Lineker out than Cruyff imagined, so the new coach played him out of position on the wing. It is a paradox that Lineker won his first major honours, the Spanish (King's) Cup and the Cup-Winners' Cup, playing out of position for a coach who didn't really want him in the team.

Lineker's response to the challenge posed by Cruyff was a testament to his temperament. He simply knuckled down, never criticized either Cruyff or the board, and always professed his love of Spain in general and Barcelona in particular. And he seemed prepared to fulfil any role asked of him. Lineker won many friends and admirers for the way he handled this tricky period, but it reinforced the growing belief that a footballer cannot expect loyalty and commitment to be repaid by a club as a matter of course. More often than not, changes take place and you can be in favour one minute and out the next. Far better to look after your own interests than expect your club to do it for you.

When Lineker came back to England he was nearly twenty-nine years old, a time to think seriously about the future. Thus he gradually took up more activities outside the game. All of these received a massive boost, first by the twenty-four League goals he scored for Spurs in his first season back, yet again the highest total in the division, then by his success in the World Cup. The time in Spain had been well spent, both on and off the field. 'As a result,' Lineker said of the improvement he discerned in his play, 'I've got greater awareness around the penalty area, I'm better able to make the positional adjustments that are necessary.'

His international scoring record, which had begun with two goals against the USA in 1985, was now among the elite: he was the third-highest England goalscorer of all time, behind only Bobby Charlton and Jimmy Greaves, both of whom played in an era when international goals were easier to come by, particularly against the smaller nations. And his ten goals in eleven matches in the final stages of the 1986 and 1990 World Cups is unparalleled by any Englishman. Many have been the pretenders to the crown of Jimmy Greaves – Trevor Francis, Tony Woodcock and Kevin Keegan among them – but Lineker has outstripped all of them at international level.

Lineker has become positively Keeganesque in his extra curricular excursions. He is a regular analyst on ITV and commentates on BSB's Italian football programme. In addition, he has appeared on television talk shows, radio's *Desert Island Discs* and in a children's comedy-drama show called *Spatz*. There have also been commercials and participation in a debate at the Oxford Union. He even made a personal appearance at the House of

Lords. Interestingly, no one has questioned his ability to do all this and still keep his mind on football as they have with Paul Gascoigne. Perhaps it is thought that he is mature enough to handle it, and his self-effacing charm ensures that this image is maintained. Perhaps Lineker had come to the conclusion that the upheavals behind the scenes, and the lack of money to buy adequate cover in case of injuries or suspensions, meant that Tottenham were no longer serious title contenders. As the realization pressed home, Lineker's frustration became more obvious. At the same time his outside activities provided insurance against future problems at White Hart Lane. When Torino made an offer for him at the start of the season, Lineker was prepared to go. Of course, the prospect of playing in the Italian League was challenging, but there was also the pragmatic consideration of what such a move would mean for his career overall.

It would be madness to suggest that Lineker be dropped for these minor distractions or because he was not consistently performing to his own high standards. At the time of the Manchester City game, and the debate about the merits of Walsh, Lineker had scored ten goals in sixteen games, more evidence of how necessary his contribution had become to Spurs' fortunes. But it would be equally wrong to think that Lineker is above normal human frailties, and while missing chances might always have been part and parcel of his game, it becomes more galling when, along with each miss, the Championship slips further away. Other players miss, of course, but Lineker's record makes his somehow less forgiveable.

Lineker's public standing was enhanced after the World Cup when Graham Taylor made him captain of England. Taylor said he chose Lineker 'because to be England captain you have to have status and standing on the field and off it'. Though obviously proud, Lineker played down the importance of his new job.

'I don't think I'll change,' he said. 'I've always been fairly communicative on the field. If I see something I think is wrong I'll mention it. But I don't shout. On the field players should be talking all the time. I know it's a bit of a cliché but I think a team should have eleven captains.'

Two goals in two and a half matches – he missed the second

half against Poland through injury — were evidence that he could handle the extra responsibility the position undoubtedly brought. The honour went alongside the tribute of Jimmy Greaves, who said, 'I recall watching his semi-final display against West Germany during *Italia 90* while sitting alongside 1966 World Cup hat-trick hero Geoff Hurst and that master goalkeeper, Gordon Banks. All three of us were lost in admiration for his display.'

Greaves had marked Lineker out as special in his days as an analyst for Central Television in the Midlands. 'For the first time in years I was really excited about the potential of an English-born striker. He has more than lived up to everything I expected of him. His equalizing goal against West Germany was a gem that included just about every ingredient that goes into the cocktail of class finishing. He had to be brave under pressure from two defenders, needed nerves of steel to look for a path to goal when it would have been easier to lay the ball off, and he had to show quality control and split-second timing. Once he had got himself clear by cleverly directing the ball with his thigh he then had to show finishing accuracy, and if he had been guided by radar he could not have placed his shot better.'

Further accolades were forthcoming. Don Howe called him 'the best in the world', adding, 'people talk of Dutchman Van Basten, Schillaci of Italy and Brazil's Careca but Gary is ahead of them all, because he has scored regularly over a longer period.' Franz Beckenbauer said Lineker was one of 'the best and most experienced strikers in the world'. Perhaps the greatest honour came in December when Lineker's career, during which he has never been sent off or even booked, was acknowledged by FIFA, who awarded him the coveted Fair Play trophy, worth 50,000 Swiss francs (£25,000). Lineker was cited for his 'exemplary conduct'. FIFA considered him 'a living example of how the spirit of fair play can be crowned with personal success'. Only one individual, the German Frank Ordenewicz, had previously won the award, in his case for persuading a referee that a penalty should have been given against his own team.

So, although Gary Lineker was the automatic first choice in the Spurs front line, it was also the case that both Walsh and Stewart deserved consideration. The decision to play all three had badly backfired on Terry Venables, though, as he said himself, in some games the formation might work. Moreover, the debate about the attack directed attention away from the real problem for Venables, the leaking defence that had now conceded eight goals in three games. If three into two wouldn't go up front, what equation would solve the gaping holes at the back?

Spurs' troubles had left them trailing in the Championship race. Arsenal, on the other hand, had recovered from their own adversity and were still within shouting distance of Liverpool. The 3–0 victory over the Champions had provided just the tonic the title-race needed, and the Gunners were back in the frame. While Spurs were being held by Sunderland, Arsenal faced a trip to Luton. Arsenal's poor record on the plastic pitch did not augur well, but the news that Liverpool's game against Nottingham Forest had fallen victim to the vicious snow-storms that were sweeping the country gave the team a special incentive. If they won, they would go top of the First Division on goal difference.

In the event, the headlines were provided by the hapless Arsenal captain, Tony Adams, who added to his disciplinary woes by getting himself sent off. In another example of 'double jeopardy', Adams brought down Dowie to concede a penalty as well as attracting the red card from referee Philip Don. Don had adjudged Adams guilty of a professional foul, which FIFA had decreed must be dealt with by dismissal. Television supported the view that Adams had been harshly treated, but while the FA had used video evidence to supplement the referee's account of the Old Trafford affair, there was no suggestion in this case that it be used in the player's defence. The punishment was complete when John Dreyer slotted home the penalty to secure a draw for the home side. An angry George Graham claimed, 'There is an issue here. Does this mean in future that every time a penalty kick is given . . . the player should be sent off?'

Graham received support from the Luton manager Jim Ryan, who said, 'If that happened to one of my players, I'd be quite upset. All he did was trip him in the box, and a penalty is a just punishment for that.'

The incident took the gloss off the first-half goal of Alan Smith, who powerfully headed home a Paul Davis corner. Arsenal's defensive tactics saw O'Leary operating at right back in a flat back four, with Dixon pushed forward into midfield, a formation designed more to contain the opposition than win the game, and in the end Arsenal probably did not deserve to take all three points.

Back at Highbury the following week, Arsenal encountered a Wimbledon team reverting to type after gaining something of a reputation for playing football since Ray Harford's appointment as manager. At Highbury, the Dons knew they had to stop Davis and Thomas getting into the game, which they achieved by continually punting the ball over their heads. Consequently, the first thirty minutes saw hardly anything that could be interpreted as creative play. Then Paul Merson raced through to get on the end of a Smith touch, moved sweetly into the penalty area, and clinically shot past Segers. Four minutes later Tony Adams thumped in a header from the inevitable Paul Davis corner to apparently put Arsenal on the way to a comfortable victory. Shortly before half-time, however, Kruszynski exploited a gap left by Adams to reduce the deficit, and Wimbledon were back in the game. The second half became a long procession of high balls into the Arsenal penalty area, where Fashanu rarely got the better of Adams and Bould. The source of much of the aerial bombardment was the goalkeeper, Segers, who continually rolled the ball out of his area before unleashing stratospheric assaults in the general direction of Fashanu. It was a tactic David Seaman would also employ before the game was out as Arsenal were dragged down to Wimbledon's level. Three minutes into injury time, Wimbledon won a free kick in their own half. Curle blasted one last ball into the Arsenal box. Seaman came off his line but never looked like getting there. Bould and Fashanu went up together while Seaman flapped in the vague proximity of their heads. Television pictures showed that Fashanu probably got a touch which Seaman then palmed into his own net.

Amazingly, Arsenal had been pulled back to 2–2, and the fact that the unbeaten League run was creating new records was little consolation, particularly since Liverpool had come back from the defeat at Highbury with a 2–0 win over bottom club Sheffield

United at Anfield. The Merseysiders now led the table by four points and had a game in hand. With the Christmas programme approaching, Arsenal would be without Adams, who would get an automatic ban for being sent off against Luton. No one realized, however, that the loss of the captain would come even earlier, in the most dramatic of circumstances.

12

Season of Goodwill?

The courts of Essex are renowned for the hard line they take on drinking and driving. For a number of years this attitude was seen at its sternest around Christmas, when the penalty was often elevated to the ultimate – a spell behind bars. The reputation had not extended as far as the Arsenal dressing room, however. The banter at the training ground on the morning of Wednesday 19 December centred on the possible fate of Tony Adams, who was facing just such charges in Southend that same day. 'We laughed and joked that Tony would be doing porridge,' Paul Merson revealed. 'Now the laughter has turned to sorrow inside Highbury.' 'Merson was commenting on the news that Adams' sentence had indeed been severe, nine months in prison for reckless driving, five of them suspended, and a further three-month concurrent term for driving with three times the permitted level of alcohol in his blood. He was also disqualified from driving for two years and ordered to pay £500 costs.

The incident that led to this latest ignominy had taken place on a hot afternoon the previous May, which the Arsenal captain had spent at a barbecue party in Rayleigh. According to the host, Mick Hynes, it was something of a wild affair where the drink flowed freely. Hynes claimed that Adams left in his 'souped up' Ford Sierra, after having already downed 'about ten cans of Fosters and Budweiser'. Whether or not this is a true account, what is certain is that Adams roared off along the quiet residential street, lost control of the car at about 70 mph, then mounted a pavement, collided with a telephone pole and went straight through a wall before coming to rest in a garden. Judge Frank Lockhart told him in court: 'You were out of control for 130 yards, the length of a football pitch. It is incredible that you came out of that car alive, let alone unscathed, and a merciful relief there was nobody there to be killed or injured. You have not been in prison before, therefore I must consider if there is any alternative to prison today. But because of the serious nature of the offence I see no other practical alternative.'

Not surprisingly, the sentence became front-page news and was accompanied by an explosion of media comment. Emlyn Hughes, though generally sympathetic, thought that Adams 'may have blown his career', while ex-Arsenal manager Terry Neill was less forgiving: 'I have no sympathy for him. The authorities have made it clear they are clamping down. I have two daughters who drive and I worry every time they go out at night.' PFA chief Gordon Taylor, however, was completely stunned by the sentence.

'I think this is a case of a famous figure being made an example of at this time of year,' he said. 'I am shocked at the severity of the sentence. No one could argue that players should be above the law of the land, but their fame puts them under a heavier spotlight and sometimes they may have to pay a higher penalty because of that.'

Support for Taylor's view came when it was revealed that on the day of Adams' court appearance, a pensioner whose car had killed three people and injured a further ten incurred only eight penalty points and a fine of £300. Much of the analysis concerned Adams' international future, particularly as Graham Taylor had instituted a campaign against drink-driving since becoming England manager. Having forced his way back into the national team in the game against Ireland, many now believed that the jail sentence would force the FA to veto Adams' future selection.

There were no such qualms at Highbury. When Adams appeared in court, he was accompanied by a bevy of Arsenal officials and players, all ready to sing his praises and lend their support as character witnesses. George Graham told the judge that when he first arrived at Highbury, 'Tony had the qualities of professionalism and leadership that I wanted in the Arsenal captaincy. I think he handled the responsibility admirably. He has been a first-class captain.'

The following day the club was even more adamant in defence of Adams. Ken Friar said, 'As far as the club is concerned, he will continue to be an Arsenal player and will receive our full support.

There is no question of him being sacked.' The PFA followed suit, Gordon Taylor declaring that the Association would 'do anything to help Tony if we can'. The support Arsenal were prepared to give turned out to go far beyond mere words of comfort. Unlike Liverpool, who stopped Jan Molby's wages when the Dane was jailed for similar offences in 1988 and underwent a heated internal debate as to whether they should retain the player at all, Arsenal announced that they would continue paying the £2,000 plus a week that Adams was receiving, and he would resume the club captaincy on his release.

The response by the club brought criticism from those who believed that Adams was, at the very least, no longer fit to hold the position of captain. A letter to *The Times* asserted that the player was 'an English international professional footballer in the public eye. He has thousands of people looking up to him and he has a duty to behave in a decent manner.' Being the captain of a team that had grudgingly earned respect for its pragmatism rather than its flair, Adams was never likely to receive the sort of popular sympathy and understanding that accompanied the excesses of George Best or Ian Botham, and it is impossible to imagine Gazza being condemned in the same way. Against those who saw the incident as serious enough to warrant further sanction was the view that the courts had already imposed a severe sentence. Once Adams had paid his debt to society, he should not have to suffer further punishment. Yet it is the case that the vast majority of those imprisoned for a criminal offence do not receive full pay while inside. Nor are they generally welcomed back with open arms by their previous employers. What, one wonders, would Arsenal's reaction have been had a member of the clerical staff committed the same offence? The club's admirable show of loyalty may become a rod for its own back, since it is surely now obliged to extend the same sympathy and support to others in its employ who may transgress the law in future.

For its part, the club was reeling from the disciplinary problems and resulting controversies of the previous two years, which, as the Adams case revealed, showed no signs of abating. Tony Adams himself was still embroiled in the V-sign incident against QPR, although the police had announced that they were leaving any action to the FA. Perhaps the long-running saga, which began with Paul Davis's assault on Glenn Cockerill in 1988, had led to the development of a 'bunker' mentality at Highbury, where the 'all for one' ethos saw a closing of ranks whenever problems occurred.

It is, however, a natural reaction to support one of your own. As David Dein put it: 'We were certainly not going to kick the lad when he was down, it would break his spirit.' Moreover, this latest problem was the culmination of a series of misfortunes to befall the player Bobby Robson had hailed as a future captain when first selecting him for England. Robson repeated the claim shortly before casting him into the international wilderness in 1989 after a World Cup qualifier against Albania, which England won 5–0. Whether or not Robson was influenced by the criticism Adams had to suffer from the press and opposing fans, he never selected him again. The vitriol reached its height when the *Daily Mirror*, picking up on the 'donkey' jibes, superimposed a pair of ears on his picture after he had given away an own goal against Manchester United in 1989 (conveniently forgetting that he also scored at the right end). This was almost too much for Adams to bear, particularly as his family was deeply upset by it, and he contemplated seeking legal redress against the newspaper. In the event he kept his own counsel and stoically decided not to proceed with the court action but to do his talking on the field. That he succeeded was demonstrated not only by him being one of the few Arsenal players to keep his form in a generally disappointing 1989–90 season – he scored five League goals – but also by getting back into the reckoning for a place in the England squad for *Italia 90*, only to be pipped at the post by Mark Wright.

For his commitment to the cause, Adams is adored by the Arsenal fans. As one North Bank regular said, 'Tony is Arsenal through and through. He is 110 per cent in every game – that counts for a lot.' Without a conventional hard midfield man like Peter Storey, it is not merely incumbent on Adams to win the ball but to ensure it is available for Davis and Thomas to orchestrate the play.

Adams also commands the respect of those in the game. On the eve of the Wimbledon match, the Dons manager, Ray

Harford, called him 'my kind of pro', and went on to put his performances in perspective. 'He has had to put up with terrible stick for a long time and yet has remained one of the most consistent and influential players for Arsenal in that time.' Harford might also have added that, until the Luton game, Adams had never been sent off or suspended. His resilience was proved when he was recalled to international duty by Graham Taylor to play alongside Des Walker and Mark Wright in a reinforced central defence that performed creditably in the 1–1 draw against Ireland in November. With the court case hanging over his head, it was no mean achievement for Adams to have maintained, even improved, his level of performance. According to one of his predecessors as Arsenal captain, Frank McLintock, he was playing 'better this year than he has ever played'.

For the fans, natural sympathy for Adams' predicament was superseded by the question of how the team, particularly the defence, would perform under the weight of this latest blow. Whatever view is taken of Adams' football abilities, or his off-the-pitch troubles, his inspirational qualities and influence on those around him cannot be denied. Yet again, as George Graham prepared the team for the next game, a televised confrontation with Aston Villa in Birmingham, he found it necessary to lift the players and point out the need to respond positively to adversity.

In the match against Villa, Graham used a flat back four, with a central pairing of Bould and Linighan. There was no place for David O'Leary in the starting line up, and the formation meant that the full backs could not take up attacking positions with any regularity. Perhaps Graham thought they would have their hands full containing Villa's threat down the flanks, especially from Tony Daley, so the system was essentially one of caution and the game turned into a sterile 0–0 draw. About the only moment of note came when Anders Limpar was substituted late in the second half and David Rocastle made his first appearance for two months. 'We were losing our shape,' was Graham's explanation. It was a shape plainly built on defence, and it worked, at least to the extent that Villa's attacks looked ever more ineffectual. To withdraw the one player who seemed capable of breaking the deadlock because, according to Graham, he was 'drifting inside and that wasn't what we wanted', then replacing him with an obviously ring-rusty Rocastle, made it clear that 'shape' and a draw were the order of the day. It was hardly the stuff of champions, though in some ways understandable in the circumstances.

Andy Linighan did nothing wrong, sticking to the simple things, and this in itself was a bonus for his manager. Up front, chances were created, but Alan Smith for once had an off day, Nigel Spink was inspired in the Villa goal, and a confident appeal for a penalty when Groves was felled in the area was turned down. It was Arsenal's eighteenth League game without defeat since the start of the season, a new club record. The main thing to cheer for the Arsenal fans, however, was the fact that the team had yet again displayed its competitiveness, and although the weekend's results left them six points behind Liverpool, having played one game more, it did not seem beyond their capabilities to make up the ground.

The Christmas programme gave them an opportunity to begin the process. It often happens that teams' aspirations are significantly enhanced or severely jolted by the three or four games that occur during the holiday period. With a month's worth of fixtures telescoped into a few days and the disruption caused to the League programme in January due to Cup commitments, any ground lost or won at Christmas can take a long time to reverse. In theory, Arsenal's away games at Villa and Manchester City provided the sternest tests, while the home matches, against two lowly clubs, Derby and Sheffield United, should have ensured the six points needed to exert some pressure on Liverpool.

For the Boxing Day encounter with Derby at Highbury, George Graham retained Bould and Linighan at the centre of the defence. Those in the crowd of 25,000 (the lowest home gate of the season, owing to the lack of public transport and dreadful weather), must have thought that the Derby players were taking collective seasonal employment as Santa Claus as they presented the game to Arsenal gift-wrapped. First, Dean Saunders missed a handful of the kind of chances he had regularly put away all season, as Bould and Linighan looked ponderous and devoid of confidence at the back. Then, Derby's goalkeeper, Martin Taylor, who was deputizing for the injured Peter Shilton, made three mistakes that Arsenal punished unmercifully. In the fourth minute Taylor was rooted to his line as a cross came in from Anders Limpar. Mark Wright was equally indecisive and Alan Smith headed his eighth goal in as many games. Another cross from Limpar led to the second goal after twenty-seven minutes. This time Taylor could only flap the ball away to Paul Merson, who hit a precise shot from a narrow angle to put the Gunners two up. In the seventy-seventh minute a wind-assisted clearance by Seaman eluded everybody, Taylor included, although the keeper did manage to tip the ball on to the bar, from which it rebounded perfectly for Smith to get his second of the match with a diving header.

For George Graham, the performance of Paul Merson was the most praiseworthy contribution to the victory, although overall he admitted that Arsenal had not performed particularly well. 'We have played better in two of the three recent games we have drawn,' he said. On the debit side, the reappearance of David Rocastle, who played in place of the injured Perry Groves, ended in the fifty-ninth minute when he limped off. Rocastle's injury was diagnosed as a broken toe resulting from a tackle in the first minute, a cruel blow for a player who had been desperate to get back into contention after loss of form and other injury problems. For the team, two clean sheets in two games was pleasing, though luck certainly played a part in the Derby match, but the biggest cheer of the day came with the announcement of the result from across London at QPR, where Don Howe's team had done his old club a considerable favour by holding Liverpool to a 1-1 draw.

Three days later Arsenal faced Sheffield United at Highbury. United, who had failed to win a game in four months of trying since they returned to the First Division, had suddenly awoken and emerged victorious in their previous two outings. They started as if they were determined to continue their winning form. For the first half of the match it appeared that Arsenal would be lucky to escape with a point. The Gunners looked completely at sea and went behind in the twenty-sixth minute when Bryson exploited gaps at the back to head home from a Vinny Jones cross. Well though he performed against Villa, in this game Andy Linighan was again looking uncomfortable. His confidence, particularly in front of the Highbury crowd, seemed at a low ebb, and the player was unrecognizable from the gifted defender who had turned in so many excellent performances for Norwich. He was therefore unable to assume the commanding role that is usually provided by Tony Adams. While much of the credit for keeping the opposition out in these games can be claimed by Steve Bould and David Seaman, the feeling persisted that really, Arsenal got away with it.

The truth of this was nowhere better illustrated than five minutes into the second half of the Sheffield United game. Up until that moment the Gunners had never looked like scoring and might well have fallen further behind. Then Perry Groves took the ball into the penalty area, where he was impeded. The referee later said that Jones had pulled his shirt. The outcome was that Arsenal were awarded a penalty from which Lee Dixon equalized. The reason for Arsenal's remarkable qualities of resilience and the explanation of why they had established a better opening sequence of League results than any of their illustrious predecessors was revealed in the minutes following the penalty decision. They stepped up at least two gears and ruthlessly destroyed United, who finished a beaten and demoralized side. Dave Bassett was fully aware of the penalty's importance to the result.

'It just proves my point,' he said, 'that big clubs get penalties and little ones don't. I've got nothing against Arsenal but I wish we could get penalties like that. We haven't had one all season. If we do get one, I'll have to check whether the referee's name is Bassett.'

After the equalizer it was a different match. Arsenal generally stormed forward, Winterburn in particular foraged along the left, and three more goals followed. A low cross from the full back looked to have been turned into his own net by Beesley, but television showed that the goal belonged to Alan Smith. Then Paul Merson reached the byline and cut the ball back for Thomas, who swung a foot and made a connection that wrongfooted the whole defence, the ball creeping into the corner of the goal.

Arsenal were now irresistible, Davis found Smith on his own, and Smith gratefully added the fourth.

George Graham was pleased. 'Some of our play in the second half was as good as we have played all season. Even I enjoyed it,' he enthused. 'The attitude here has always been first class, and we now have players who can adapt to different positions. These players know what is expected of them and they like the way we play.'

The adaptability to which the manager referred was exemplified by Paul Merson, who floated between the roles of partner for Smith up front, midfield creator, and wideman on the right. The United defence never got to grips with this interchange once it began to work in the second half. Arsenal had seized the moment that the penalty decision had offered. By the end, that elusive quality – confidence – was flowing through the side. The following day their resurgence gained further momentum when Crystal Palace continued Liverpool's dismal Christmas by beating the Merseysiders 1–0 in a televised game. The gap had now closed to one point.

A traumatic month by anyone's standards had at least ended for Arsenal with promise, and the knowledge that Liverpool were at last in their sights. If it had not been clear before, the most blinkered observer must have realized by now that it was a mistake to write Arsenal off, as many had done after the sequence of draws earlier in the month. The new year game away at Manchester City, where the Gunners had already won in the Rumbelows Cup, now looked a little less daunting than it had before the holiday period.

George Graham seemed to have got the message about the overall performance of his defence since the loss of Tony Adams. At Maine Road he reverted to three centre backs, O'Leary making up the numbers once more. After half an hour of stout defensive resistance, O'Leary clashed accidentally with his team-mate Linighan, suffered concussion, and had to leave the field. He was replaced, not by Colin Pates, whom many would have thought next in line, but by another youngster not long out of the youth team, David Hillier. Hillier made a solid contribution to the Arsenal tactics of stopping Peter Reid while looking to embarrass the home team on the break. He even found the time to play a part in Arsenal's winning goal. A break in the fifty-eighth minute led to a corner, from which Hillier fed the ball to Smith, who smashed it into the roof of the net. Despite looking the more polished side throughout, it was a classic theft of three points, prompting Derek Hodgson to write in the *Independent*: 'Unpalatable though it may be north of Golders Green, the fact is Arsenal are now the best team in England.'

It was also a necessary victory, since Liverpool had ended their own Christmas programme with a 3–0 win against Leeds at Anfield, so the gap remained one point. The Manchester City player-manager, Peter Reid, became the latest in the line of growing Arsenal admirers, saying, 'There is no question that they are a very tough side to beat.' Interestingly, in all four games over the holiday the Gunners used the ploy whereby Seaman would bring the ball out of his area to unleash a long punt upfield towards Alan Smith, completely bypassing the midfield. It was pure Wimbledon, but none the less effective for that. While such unsophisticated play makes a worthwhile variation, it hardly seemed in keeping with Arsenal's more familiar pattern of playing from the back and through the midfield.

Controversy was again in attendance at Maine Road. George Graham was enraged by an article in the City programme that catalogued Arsenal's recent problems. 'The programme notes were a disgrace,' the manager fumed. 'This game was very easy for us because when I arrived and saw the programme I didn't need to motivate the players.'

Graham's outburst had some effect, as City chairman Peter Swales apologized for the offending piece. None the less, it seemed a needless argument to air in public. Perhaps the outside pressures were taking their toll, if not on the pitch, then in the sense of isolation that a bunker mentality can produce. Incredibly though, the team had come back with a vengeance and the defence had not only survived, it had conceded just one goal in the four games since Adams' unhappy departure.

The Spurs defence was also under pressure, although for different reasons. The team approached the Christmas games knowing that any more slips would make it hard to keep in touch at the top. Losing third place was a bitter blow, particularly as it was another London club, Crystal Palace, who were now making the running in the chase behind Liverpool and Arsenal. A good Christmas was essential, and that depended on the first-choice back line – Thomas, Van Den Hauwe, Sedgley and Mabbutt – rediscovering their early-season form.

The day before Arsenal's televised match against Aston Villa, Spurs faced Luton at White Hart Lane. The most influential figures in the proceedings were Paul Gascoigne, Paul Stewart and the referee, David Elleray, a Harrow schoolmaster. Gascoigne provided some exquisite touches, Stewart grabbed two goals, while Elleray sent off three players and brandished his yellow card with something approaching abandon. The match got off on the wrong foot when Steve Williams clattered into David Howells. Williams continued to exert a malign influence on the game through a constant barrage of verbals. The breakdown of control spread from there, although it was indiscipline of an individual nature, rather than the collective transgressions that characterized Arsenal's problems. It was no more excusable for that, however, and led some to question the professionalism of those who refused to heed the warning of Elleray's early flourish of the yellow card.

The first to go was Nayim, who had already been cautioned for a foul when he was slow retreating ten yards for a free kick in the thirtieth minute. He said something to the referee and was dismissed for 'foul and abusive language'. Seven minutes later Pat Van Den Hauwe joined Nayim in the dressing room after he committed a disgraceful foul, scything down Dowie in a manner calculated, according to one report, 'to separate his legs from his body'. Many Spurs fans in the West Stand, who got a perfect view of the action, were incensed at Van Den Hauwe's indiscretion. The general consensus was that the full back was 'not a Spurs player', while one fan was extremely forthright. 'The manager should never play him again,' he said. He then paused, before concluding, 'But of course he will.'

Fifteen minutes into the second half Hughes brought down Lineker, the crowd screamed for his dismissal, and Elleray obliged. A member of the Luton team, John Dreyer, later complained that Lineker had made the most of the tackle and helped get Hughes sent off, an allegation the England captain vehemently denied. Dreyer later withdrew the accusation and apologized, saying that his remarks were tongue in cheek, not meant to be taken seriously, and were uttered 'in the heat of the moment'.

Although attention was afterwards naturally focused on the sendings-off and the bookings, there was some good football on view from both teams. Luton took the lead in the thirteenth minute when a superb cross from Black found Dowie, who swept the ball home first time. After the sendings-off of Nayim and Van Den Hauwe, the extra players seemed to disconcert Luton and they were unable to convert their numerical superiority into more goals. In fact, the loss of the two players became the cue for Gascoigne to turn in another breathtaking performance as he held the ball up intelligently, allowing Spurs to make the most of their depleted forces. It was Gascoigne who fashioned the equalizer with a run to the byline that took out two defenders, from where he crossed perfectly for Paul Stewart to head the all-important first goal. When the nine forced a corner in the fifty-seventh minute, Gascoigne took it and Stewart scored his second. Terry Venables had again started with Paul Walsh, but the striker was substituted in the second half as Venables looked to protect the lead. It was Stewart who caught the eye, producing perhaps his best ever display for Tottenham, particularly in the more withdrawn role that events during the game had forced him to adopt.

The victory was certainly welcome, perhaps even 'sensational', which was how Venables described it. But looming up was the loss of Van Den Hauwe from the defence through the automatic three-match suspension that results from a red card for serious foul play. Nayim would also be banned, although hopefully for a lesser period. Venables decided to call Terry Fenwick back from his spell on loan to Leicester, and there were many who felt that despite this win, the old stalwart would be more than needed.

The day after the Luton game, another story about events behind the scenes at White Hart Lane hit the headlines. Whenever Spurs were mentioned now, there was somewhere a reference to the millions of pounds of debt. In the absence of discernible progress in the talks with Robert Maxwell or any other benefactor, and because there was still little prospect of the Stock Exchange lifting the share suspension, speculation was rife. In the week before the Luton match it was reported that Terry Venables was to attend fresh talks with Irving Scholar, having earlier rejected an offer from the chairman that entailed a cut in basic salary of £25,000, in return for a bonus scheme. This really upset Venables, who retorted, 'What do you think of a man who says "I now believe you are the best coach in the world and I'm offering you £25,000 a year less"? It doesn't really make sense, even if you want to believe it.' Other press reports claimed that Venables was about to purchase Queen's Park Rangers, while QPR owner Richard Thompson bought out Spurs in some kind of reciprocal arrangement.

But the real drama came on the Sunday, two days before Christmas, when Jeff Randall of the *Sunday Times* reported the existence of a consortium, led by boxing impresario Frank Warren and including Terry Venables, that wanted to buy Spurs. Warren was best known to the general public through the trial and acquittal for attempted murder of one of the boxers he used to manage, former World Champion Terry Marsh, following a shooting that almost cost Warren his life. The new consortium, according to Randall, would reserve the post of managing director for Venables, while Osvaldo Ardiles would be brought back from Swindon to take the job of coach.

Any possible rescue package or takeover would, of course, have to meet with the approval of Irving Scholar, who was the main shareholder. Scholar showed little inclination to consider seriously any plan that would lead him to offload his stake in the club, and although Venables confirmed that he was involved in discussions, there was little that could be accomplished over the holiday period, particularly since an Annual General Meeting was due before the end of the year. The hiatus complete, attention turned once again to Spurs' chances of hauling themselves back into the title race.

These were dealt a huge blow in the Boxing Day game against Coventry at Highfield Road. The Spurs defence was cut to shreds, and the fact that they managed to hold out until half-time without conceding a goal owed everything to Erik Thorstvedt.

Just after the restart, a seven-man move carved a swathe through the defence once more and Gallacher put Coventry in the lead. A long through ball was next to undo the Spurs back line, and Gynn settled the match after Thorstvedt had blocked Gallacher's shot.

'We didn't do too badly in the first half,' said Venables afterwards, 'but the early goal after the interval tore us apart. We played poorly after that, but just how much damage it has done, we shall have to wait and see.' They were brave words but they could not disguise the fact that Tottenham's title aspirations had just about vanished into the blustery wind that had swirled around Highfield Road all afternoon. The first-choice defence had again proved vulnerable and the malaise was now affecting the confidence of the whole team.

Another tough away game at Southampton followed four days after the Coventry débâcle. This time matters went from bad to worse as Spurs were again well beaten, this time by three goals without reply. Gazza failed to appear, having contracted a stomach bug that left him asleep in the dressing room, and Spurs' hopes were lost with him as the defence was once again cruelly exposed. It was Spurs' heaviest defeat of the season thus far and Southampton's biggest victory. Southampton had a former Tottenham player, Neil Ruddock, at the centre of their normally fragile defence, which on the day looked the more secure. Later, Ruddock compared the current Spurs line-up unfavourably to the team of his era, David Pleat's side of 1987.

One of the main reasons Spurs had kept six clean sheets in the first ten games was Gary Mabbutt. 'There is a certain type of central defender,' said Erik Thorstvedt, 'that every goalie loves to have in front of them, and Gary Mabbutt is one of those types. He is . . . a link between you and the rest of the team. You can always trust him.'

Mabbutt modestly discounted his exceptional form and placed great emphasis on the virtues of a settled side: 'We had a very solid pattern. We knew the way we wanted to play and really believed the way we were playing was the right way.' Spurs' longest-serving player, he was determined to add to his thirteen England caps. His performances within a surprisingly cohesive defence in those early weeks prompted a recall to the international set-up. In November he captained the Football League against the League of Ireland and the following month played for England's 'B' team in Algeria.

Mabbutt's pragmatic approach to life has enabled him to come to terms with his diabetes and take in his stride an onerous daily routine of injections, blood counts and 'exchange' eating (mainly carbohydrate to compensate for the insulin injections). Although Bobby Robson was reluctant to sign him for Ipswich, he had no such qualms about picking him for England and called him 'The Bionic Player'. This inspired the *Spur* to reveal that his real name was Mabot, that he must be some type of robot, invented and controlled by the machiavellian Dr Scholar, because of his 're-markable lack of aggression to anyone or anything other than the ball'.

With two successive defeats following several poor defensive performances, perhaps because Mabbutt was carrying an injury for much of that time, it looked as if Spurs were in danger of dropping out of the title race altogether. The unease was obvious.

'We started to panic a bit,' revealed Mabbutt, 'and rather than keeping the same shape and continuing to believe in the way we were playing, we tried to complicate things on the pitch and players weren't keeping to the role they were selected to do, and in the end we began to lose our pattern completely.' The matches over the holiday period compounded the problem, there being little opportunity to retreat to the training ground in an attempt to find the necessary answers.

Before the team had the chance to put matters right in a televised match against Manchester United on New Year's Day, behind-the-scenes events again came to the fore. The Annual General Meeting had been called for 31 December, the last day possible to comply with legal requirements. It was a short meeting, however, lasting only an hour. No new financial information was forthcoming, nor were company accounts fully prepared. A motion to adjourn the meeting was voted down on a show of hands, but was carried after a formal vote through the exercise of proxies held by the acting chairman Douglas Alexiou. Although a number of shareholders tried to ask questions, Alexiou refused to disclose anything further and the meeting broke up, despite angry protests. It was a reverse also for the fledgling Tottenham Independent Supporters' Association, which had been set up when the Maxwell bid was announced. TISA had attempted to find a way of bringing pressure to bear on the board but had been largely ignored by the directors, although they later agreed to discussions with the Association. Another piece of bad news for fans followed, when it was announced that Spurs were to increase admission prices in the new year (midway through the season), which was an atypical move, both for Tottenham and for football in general. Already charging the highest prices in the league, Spurs were now set to raise the minimum price of a main-stand seat to £17.

The team, which seemed as full of holes as the club's finances, had now to face an in-form Manchester United. The game encapsulated all that had gone wrong, both on and off the field. Spurs were outplayed for long periods but managed to snatch the lead through a fortuitous penalty after Phelan fell on the ball during a mêlée in the United penalty area and was adjudged to have handled. Lineker, who had missed two chances by then, made no mistake with the spot-kick. Unlike Arsenal against Sheffield United, when the Gunners grabbed the chance that the referee presented to them with both hands, Spurs allowed United to get back into the game by conceding space in midfield. The Manchester side took full advantage and increasingly put the Spurs defence under pressure. Eventually, Pat Van Den Hauwe completed a miserable Christmas by clumsily tangling with Hughes and conceding the game's second penalty, from which Bruce deservedly equalized.

Tottenham started the second half well and might have taken the lead when suddenly everything collapsed around them. Lineker went down after a challenge by McClair, but referee Vic Callow this time waved away penalty claims. Then Gascoigne appeared to say something to Callow, who had no hesitation in producing the red card. Gazza, who had just been named BBC Sports Personality of the Year, had been sent off for the first time in his Spurs career, in full view of the watching nation (10 million people viewed the game, one of the biggest audiences since live

League football began to be screened). Although Spurs almost held on for a draw, one last Manchester United attack in the ninetieth minute led to a momentary lapse in concentration at the back. Bruce crossed, Hughes, who had been a thorn in Tottenham's side all afternoon, chested the ball down, it bounced nicely for an unmarked McClair and the United striker could hardly miss.

Gazza said he was gutted. 'I let myself down and the rest of the players,' he said. It was particularly unfortunate because, as Gary Mabbutt remarked, 'Had Paul Gascoigne not got sent off . . . we were beginning to take control of the game and create chances, the whole side was playing well . . . and I believe we would definitely go on and win the game.'

If there were any lingering hopes of a Championship revival, they disappeared in that moment. The game left Spurs a massive fifteen points behind Liverpool, in sixth place. While Arsenal took ten points out of twelve over Christmas, Spurs managed only three, and had lost the last three games. Mabbutt looked half fit, and the team now faced the prospect of losing three players through suspensions.

Not unnaturally, Gazza's sending-off made most of the headlines. It was pointed out that he had been the victim of at least two bad fouls, one when he was surging into the United penalty area, but had taken them in good heart. Explaining that the offence was 'foul and abusive language', Terry Venables said, 'If everyone got sent off for swearing you wouldn't have many players left.'

Gascoigne was still under the most intense media scrutiny. He was often criticized by other sportsmen as well as journalists and pundits. After the Manchester City game the *Mirror* ran a front-page non-story of how he was alleged to have sworn at some schoolchildren. Those who had predicted trouble, including Alf Ramsey and former World Cup referee Clive Thomas, could say 'I told you so', and the newspapers were guaranteed some more good copy. The real effect, though, would be felt by Gascoigne's team-mates, already in a depressed state, when the important games of January arrived. Since losing to Liverpool on 4 November, after being unbeaten in their first ten games and yielding only four goals, Spurs had dropped nineteen points out of thirty and had conceded twenty goals. Success would now be confined to the cup competitions, and Gascoigne, like Nayim and Van Den Hauwe, would miss vital matches, including the Rumbelows Cup quarter-final against Chelsea.

Before that though, there would be a precious chance to put aside League form, if only for an afternoon. The next weekend saw the third round of the FA Cup, the day of dreams for supporters across the country. But Tottenham could not even prepare for that game without further press revelations concerning the club's finances. Southampton had threatened to sue Spurs for £20,000, which they claimed was owed as a result of a deal under which Spurs supplied the Southampton club shop. That matter was resolved out of court, but two other similar cases quickly followed; one for a mere £600, which was claimed by a Hampshire company over a contract to sell programmes at the Southampton shop, and another from Chelsea, for a more substantial £45,000 ticket bill. There was bad press relating to a delay in the settlement of monies from Danny Blanchflower's testimonial game at the end of the previous season. It was as well for Spurs that the venue for the FA Cup tie was Blackpool, where the talk would be bound to focus on the club whose past is so intimately bound up with the competition. As a seaside resort designed to transport visitors from the mundane world of everyday reality to the ephemeral fantasy of the Golden Mile, it was better placed than most football towns to help Spurs forget the troubles that beset them.

13

Seaman Keeps the Ship Afloat

For over a hundred years the FA Cup has exercised a special magic over generations of football supporters, but its enduring appeal is not confined to fans alone. The unique atmosphere affects players, managers and owners alike, and often whole cities are caught up in what is aptly termed 'Cup Fever'. Tottenham Hotspur's record in the competition is second to none, and the seven wins the club has achieved over the years have contributed significantly to the traditions of the greatest domestic football tournament in the world: the victory in 1901, for instance, when Spurs were still in the Southern League, or sixty years later when the club became the first this century to do the double. Since the arrival of Terry Venables, however, Spurs have suffered humiliating defeats against lower-division opponents, Bradford and Port Vale. When the draw for the third round was made and Spurs came out of the hat with an away tie against Blackpool, there were many who viewed the trip north with a degree of wariness.

Blackpool, of course, possess their own rich FA Cup history, largely based on one sensational victory over Bolton Wanderers in 1953, the Stanley Matthews final, in which the maestro was instrumental in turning a 3–1 deficit into a 4–3 triumph. Since those heady days, Blackpool, in common with a number of Lancashire clubs, have slipped down the divisions, and important matches against class opposition are now few and far between. The build up in the seaside town in the week before the game was typical of the increased profile the FA Cup brings. The knock-out format of the tournament, its relatively few matches, which often pitch David against Goliath with the prospect of the same result, raise the status of every game to that of an event. In recent years, television has played a big part in boosting this further.

When the big five League clubs split the united front presented to the television companies in the negotiations of 1988 by agreeing a deal with ITV, Ted Croker, then General Secretary of the FA, made his own arrangements for the FA Cup and England international matches with the BBC and the satellite service BSB. With far less football to screen after the loss of League action, the BBC, of necessity, decided to make more of the FA Cup. For the first time there were highlights of rounds one and two, and from the third round on the BBC put out highlights and a live game, turning Saturdays and Sundays into 'FA Cup weekends'. These programmes were extremely successful, so the BBC increased its coverage even further until, by 1991, Cup matches and replays were screened throughout the week. Originally, the BBC did not think such expanded coverage would be popular, but the ratings success forced a rethink. Almost by accident, then, the effect of separating the FA and the League in television negotiations led to increased exposure for the Cup and a concomitant upturn in awareness, interest and excitement for what was already a national institution.

Thus it was no surprise when the media descended on Blackpool, most looking for reasons to predict another Spurs upset. By the time the match started, amid 90 mph winds blowing off the Irish Sea, Bloomfield Road was once again a place of passion and drama. For a brief moment, decayed and delapidated conditions forgotten, the clock was turned back, and with Gazza filling the role of Len Shackleton, 'the Clown Prince of Soccer', the nostalgia evoked by the occasion was complete.

Despite all the fascinating elements, Spurs could not shake off the spectre of financial troubles. On the day of the match, Blackpool went into the transfer market and bought Dave Bamber from Hull. The purchase focused attention once again on the fact that Spurs, the First Division club, one of the big five, could hardly afford a new pair of boots, let alone a much-needed addition to the playing staff. Indeed, that same week, Terry Venables was forced to sell reserve goalkeeper Bobby Mimms to Blackburn, leaving him with no experienced cover. One consolation was the return of Terry Fenwick, who had completed a successful comeback from injury while on loan to Leicester. Fenwick could have stiffened the heart of the Spurs defence, but

Venables played him at full back, which is not his natural position. This was possibly due to the suspension of Van Den Hauwe and an injury to Thomas, but Fenwick is an experienced central defender, something Spurs obviously needed, and with Sedgley dropped and Mabbutt's leg heavily strapped, Venables, unlike George Graham, was hardly spoilt for choice through the middle of the defence. The manager's lack of defensive cover was compounded by the loss of Chris Hughton, the last link with the Cup-winning sides of 1981 and 1982, who went on a free transfer to West Ham, probably in order to reduce the wage bill.

With Nayim suspended and Howells partnering Mabbutt at the back, Tottenham's midfield consisted of Gascoigne, Allen, Samways and Stewart. Paul Moran came in to partner Lineker up front in the absence of the injured Walsh, but the makeshift formation had difficulty establishing any sort of dominance over its Fourth Division opponents. While the conditions played a part, it was also the case that Blackpool adapted to them better and might have won the game, or at least secured a lucrative replay at White Hart Lane. In the event, Spurs weathered Blackpool's pressure and the storm, and scored with a rare foray into the opposition penalty area. Paul Gascoigne was one of the few players capable of keeping the ball on the ground but most of his play had been contained by the Blackpool midfield, which used the tactic of funnelling two or three players back as cover whenever Gazza got the ball. In the sixty-eighth minute he took a swerving free kick, Lineker knocked the ball back, and Stewart completed a happy homecoming – he scored over fifty goals as a Blackpool player before being transferred to Manchester City – when his half-hit shot rolled into the net for the winning goal. Blackpool manager Billy Ayre said, 'We were beaten by the quality of that free kick.' Terry Venables agreed: 'The ball moved all over the place and must have totally confused the Blackpool defence.'

While the performance was not wholly convincing, the win was more than welcome. In previous seasons, Spurs had succumbed to sucker punches from less talented opposition. This time they overcame appalling conditions, which Terry Venables described as a 'lottery, the worst I have ever seen', and were good enough to snatch the game. 'I could not have asked more of them,' said Venables. 'They kept their discipline and what I got was a display of the highest moral fibre.'

The victory also put an end to a losing streak of three straight defeats, which had dented their League ambitions so badly over Christmas. Perhaps the result would galvanize the team enough for it to recapture its early-season form. As Gary Lineker remarked afterwards, 'We're going through a bit of a trough at the moment and hopefully this will get everybody going.'

Venables' reshuffled team had responded well to the setbacks of suspensions, injuries and defeats. Before anyone got carried away, however, Blackpool were still a Fourth Division team, and a much more searching test would have to be faced in a week's time, when George Graham brought his undefeated Arsenal to White Hart Lane.

If Spurs' tie at Blackpool was an archetypal FA Cup encounter, pitting unfashionables against aristocrats, Arsenal's was a classic confrontation of a different, though potentially no less exciting, order. The match against Sunderland at Highbury provided the variety only available in a competition like the FA Cup – a clash at the first opportunity between two teams from the First Division. In these games form can mean little. After a hard slog through to Christmas, even the most fallible side can forget the weight of League results for the duration of a Cup run, and often the fancied team gets beaten.

Sunderland is another club with a fine Cup tradition, although its record since the sensational victory at Wembley over Leeds in 1973 has been poor. Having attained First Division status by the back door when Swindon were demoted, the team had struggled, and to make matters worse they arrived at Highbury without the two forwards who might have given them a chance, Gabbiadini and Davenport. Losing these two showed the paucity of Sunderland's squad – a sad demise for a club which in the 1950s was known as 'The Bank of England'.

Robbed of their potential match winners, Sunderland were hard pushed to rise to the occasion, although they did threaten a shaky Arsenal defence in the opening moments when a youngster bearing the name of another illustrious goalscorer – Rush –almost gave them the lead. Once Arsenal settled, however, the match began to take a more predictable course. The high winds, while not reaching the force of the gales in the North-West, were nevertheless bad enough to all but destroy the game as a spectacle. Groves looked the liveliest player on view, and it was his run and cross after a quarter of an hour that enabled Smith to stretch and poke home his fifteenth goal of the season, his thirteenth in eleven games. The game was decided on the stroke of half-time, when Rush, with Sunderland pressing forward, shot straight at Seaman, who immediately set up an attack. The ball reached Limpar and he coolly lobbed the ball over Norman, the Sunderland goal-keeper, to send Arsenal in at the interval leading 2–0.

The second half should have been a formality, and so it proved for thirty minutes. O'Leary came on with twenty minutes to go in place of Limpar to shore up the centre of the defence but did just the opposite when he knocked an attempted clearance over David Seaman to put Sunderland back in the game. It was the Irishman's first own goal in 690 appearances and brought the wry comment from George Graham that he expects his substitutions to lead to goals. The mistake did not alter Graham's new-found determination to keep O'Leary at Highbury when his contract ran out at the end of the season. After a disagreement following O'Leary's decision to go on holiday after the World Cup, it looked as though he would be leaving, a view seemingly confirmed when Graham bought Andy Linighan. But with Linighan struggling and Adams in jail, the Arsenal manager was forced to rethink his plans.

'The way it was looking I was on my way,' commented O'Leary. 'Centre halves were signed and I was the odd man out. In fact, 9 October was the first time I got on the subs' bench this season. But from being totally out of it, all of a sudden I'm involved and now the manager says he wants me to stay.'

Graham's legendary attachment to his plethora of central defenders was substantiated that same weekend when Charlton manager Lennie Lawrence revealed that he had tried to buy Colin Pates, but the Arsenal manager had 'refused to entertain the idea'. Like Spurs', Arsenal's performance had not been particu-larly distinguished, but the 2–1 victory saw them in the draw for the fourth round, and that was the most important thing.

The excitement of the Cup over for a couple of weeks, attention turned to the return derby match at White Hart Lane on 12 January. Whereas the first encounter that season was between two unbeaten teams vying for the right to challenge Liverpool at the top, Spurs' title chances had receded over Christmas and it now seemed that the prize for them was pride and a possible place in Europe through a high League position or a win in one of the Cup competitions. Arsenal goalkeeper David Seaman did not agree with this analysis. He thought Spurs were still serious title challengers. The day before the game he said, 'I know they've been written off after a bad run, but I don't think they're out of it at all. A few wins and they could pose a threat to us and Liverpool. We can't afford to let Tottenham start a Championship charge by beating us.'

In many ways, the game was a mirror image of the match at Highbury in September. In a total reversal of recent form, Spurs went on the offensive and put Arsenal's defence under the kind of pressure it had not experienced since the Rumbelows Cup débâcle against Manchester United. For all their attacking, though, Spurs could not break the deadlock. The 0–0 scoreline said nothing about the quality of the play produced by both sides in a match which Trevor Brooking described as one of the best he'd seen all season. The result might have been different had Lineker not stayed upright after David O'Leary pulled his shirt in the seventeenth minute when the England captain was through on goal. A penalty and perhaps even a sending off could have resulted had Lineker fallen, but although the chance had all but disappeared, he kept his feet to get in a shot, which Seaman pushed away for a corner. 'If I were a diver,' said Lineker, 'I could have gone down.'

With O'Leary playing for the injured Perry Groves, George Graham had reverted to playing five at the back. All three central defenders – O'Leary, Bould and Linighan – looked ponderous and were often exposed through the middle by the pace of Lineker and the returning Walsh. David Seaman produced outstanding saves, particularly from Allen and in the last minute, from Lineker, pushing away a shot which was on its way to the back of the net. 'When you pay top prices,' said Graham of

Seaman, 'you get top players.' Terry Venables concurred, saying, 'He was quite exceptional.' Seaman was more than pleased with his performance. 'I enjoy making saves like that,' he said. 'It's a great feeling, just like scoring a goal really.'

Terry Venables had again left out Steve Sedgley and persisted with David Howells in a back four that still contained Terry Fenwick at right back. Sedgley had incurred his manager's wrath after a performance against Southampton that was probably his worst since rejoining the club. Meanwhile, Mitchell Thomas was pushed into midfield alongside Stewart, leaving Walsh and Lineker up front. The lack of height at the back forced Erik Thorstvedt to take a more commanding role in his penalty area, particularly when Arsenal managed to get in a decent cross. Thorstvedt was also seen to great effect racing out of his area to deny Limpar. A pulsating game had finished with no goals, but Venables was not exaggerating when he said, 'I don't think I have seen so many chances against Arsenal. We could have had four or five. It was a shame we just couldn't finish it off.'

Frank McLintock agreed: 'That was probably the best perform-ance from them [Spurs] I've seen all season. As a team there was not a weak link in it and they really should have beaten Arsenal.' George Graham put the result in perspective: 'We have this horrible thing called resilience, we don't lie down.' Graham's analysis could hardly be denied. It was Arsenal's fourteenth clean sheet and the twenty-second League match of the season without defeat.

Paul Davis added some detail: 'As far as character and resil-ience are concerned this is the best Arsenal side I have played in. The team spirit couldn't be better. We all get on and play our hearts out for each other. We've formed something special. I can't believe there is a better team spirit anywhere in the game . . . We don't sit in the dressing room shaking our fists at one another and shouting "let's not get beaten". But there is something there. Call it an an inner feeling. We just know we're going to do it.'

With Liverpool also drawing 0–0 away to Aston Villa, the day's results left Arsenal still one point behind, although Liverpool had a game in hand. Spurs, by contrast, were in sixth place, a massive fifteen points behind the champions. Before the game, Terry Venables had agreed with Seaman that Spurs were not yet out of the race for the title, provided they took three points off their rivals. 'We can get back into it,' he said, 'but we must beat Arsenal to get us on our way.' After the failure to convert territorial superiority into goals, even the optimistic Venables must have begun to harbour doubts.

While the draw was in part due to missed chances and a subdued performance from Paul Gascoigne, the lion's share of the praise for the goalless outcome deservedly went to David Seaman. Seaman's transfer to Arsenal had not met with universal approval from the Highbury fans, who not only believed that John Lukic was a good goalkeeper but also took him to their hearts. In addition, George Graham's protracted and public stalking of Seaman drew sympathy for Lukic, who made it clear that he did not want to leave, but did feel he deserved better terms than he was being offered. Graham insists that Lukic turned down a new contract, but it is surely inconceivable that Leeds were in a position to offer a more lucrative deal than Arsenal and equally unlikely that Seaman's personal terms were less than anything Lukic demanded. The impression remains of one player being forced out to make way for another.

Of course, none of this was Seaman's fault. The new keeper did, however, have to make a special effort to win over the fans and match the high level of consistency produced by Lukic over seven years. After dramatically failing to join Arsenal just ninety minutes before the transfer deadline the previous season – the deal broke down because Lukic refused to go to Loftus Road on loan – Seaman had to return to Shepherd's Bush to face the music from fans who were sure to give him some stick for wanting to leave. His performances were not affected, however, and he did well enough to be included in England's World Cup squad. He also won a measure of grudging respect from Rangers' fans for not going public with his grievances against the club, a stance which ironically bore the hallmark of an 'Arsenal man'. When the transfer finally went through in the summer of 1990, Seaman was obviously pleased finally to be at Highbury. On the pre-season tour to Sweden, he was left in no doubt that he was replacing a great favourite, but the fans had marked his card for him. He was told he was expected to do 'the twist', which his predecessor did on request during the pre-match warm up. That he did so willingly, together with his confident start, enabled him to ease himself in. As one fan put it, 'If you have got a player on the pitch who is answering your calls, you respect them because they acknowledge you are there.'

At Birmingham and Queen's Park Rangers, Seaman had been prone to the odd mistake, and hints of this were in evidence in his early games for Arsenal, particularly when dealing with crosses to the near post. However, the solid Arsenal defence in the early games allowed a short acclimatization period and thereafter the clean sheets began to multiply. A modest man, Seaman character-istically underplayed his performance against Spurs, the great saves notwithstanding, saying, 'I just keep concentrating and leave it down to that. You can go through a game when the most important thing you do is organize. Then you get games like this.' Seaman was now being touted as a better candidate to take on the mantle of Peter Shilton in the England goal than the other contenders, including the incumbent, Chris Woods. Of course, not many London-based pundits had seen much of Woods, who plays in a league few English pressmen ever take account of, let alone watch. It could not be denied, however, that Seaman had made significant advances as a goalkeeper in his first season at Highbury. It is to his credit that while Arsenal fans still reserve an affection for John Lukic, Seaman has won them over with a vengeance. The Arsenal fanzines, which had always supported Lukic, were now ready to heap praise on the newcomer. The *Gooner* reported that George Graham was entitled to say 'I told you so', and continued, 'He took a lot of stick for ditching John Lukic in favour of Seaman and deserves the credit for making such a bold and unpopular decision.' *One-nil Down, Two-one Up*, in its players review of 1990, put the feeling most succinctly. 'Lukic was a good goalkeeper,' it said, 'but Seaman is a poten-tially great one.'

Johnny Giles ran his eye over the prospective England goalkeep-ers in his *Daily Express* column. After the Spurs game, Giles claimed that Seaman could win the Championship for Arsenal.

'A 4–0 scoreline would not have flattered Spurs,' he wrote. 'Instead, Seaman made a series of outstanding saves to give his side a draw they hardly deserved on general play. [His performance] preserved the Gunners' unbeaten run, preserved the confidence and high morale such a record engenders and preserved the momentum of their season. As I watched the Spurs–Arsenal game . . . I was reminded of the contribution Bob Wilson made to the double-winning side of 1971. They pipped my Leeds team and, looking back, the difference was in goal . . . I haven't seen anyone play better in goal for a long time than Seaman did against Spurs.'

Wilson himself compared Seaman in style and temperament to Pat Jennings, saying, 'There can't be another goalkeeper in the First Division who's made so few mistakes.'

The importance of a class keeper as the last line of defence is a view not confined to Johnny Giles. When Brian Clough took his Nottingham Forest team to the League Championship, he proclaimed the signing of Peter Shilton as the last and most important piece in his jigsaw, and certainly Shilton's performances, spurred on by Clough's confidence-building assertions to all and sundry that he had bought 'the best goalkeeper in the world' (at the time Shilton's, career was in something of a trough and Ray Clemence was England's first-choice keeper), did much to spread a feeling of invincibility throughout the team. While many were now taking Seaman's credentials as seriously as Clough once took Shilton's, few heaped similar praise on his opposite number at Spurs. Could it be that here was the crucial difference between the results of the two clubs thus far? Both defences had looked wobbly at times, but Seaman's displays not only kept Arsenal in games they should have lost, they also infected the rest of the players with the confidence that only clean sheets can bring. 'If the forwards have confidence in us keeping a clean sheet, they know that one goal can clinch a game,' claimed Seaman. Could the same be said of Erik Thorstvedt?

When Thorstvedt arrived at Tottenham from IFK Gothenburg, he was something of an unknown quantity to English fans. He had trained previously with Spurs, Arsenal and QPR in an attempt to play in the English League but had not been offered the contract he sought. Eventually he went to Borussia Moenchengladbach, in Germany, where he spent two largely uneventful seasons, before returning to Scandinavia. When, in 1988, he heard of Spurs' renewed interest, he was cautious and refused to become elated at the prospect. 'I had had so many knocks,' he recalled, 'I said to myself, "I don't believe in this."' It came as a pleasant surprise when Terry Venables, true to his word, paid Gothenburg £450,000 to bring him to White Hart Lane permanently.

Thorstvedt did himself no favours when he let a shot from Nigel Clough through his hands in the first live televised game of his Spurs career (he repeated the gaffe, again against Nottingham Forest, in a Littlewoods Cup tie a year later). The early games proved something of a struggle as he fought to adapt to the demands of the English game. He remembers one incident that he thinks was decisive, against Southampton. 'I raced out of my box,' he said, 'there was this guy, he got a foot to the ball and I cut him down, I was very scared of what the ref might do but he dragged up a yellow card. If I'd got a red card then it could have been the end of it really.' The support and confidence he drew from Terry Venables during this period was fundamental to his eventual success. 'He [Venables] was very good at that time and I pulled through,' he commented.

The Norwegian international later admitted that his play in those early days lacked a vital attribute: 'You must be aggressive in the Football League, particularly when you are a goalkeeper; the game is very physical. When I go back to Norway [on international duty], no one says a word in the dressing room. It's a big difference. You really notice it but it doesn't come that natural to me. I never had fights at school, it wasn't in my nature. Even today I'm the same laid-back guy off the pitch, but I have had no option but to change my ways during games.'

Paradoxically, it was probably his placid nature that enabled him to come to terms with his initial mistakes. 'What can you do?' he asked rhetorically. 'You've got no option, you've got to keep battling.' Thorstvedt has conceded roughly a goal a match since coming to White Hart Lane, but he is a keen student of his own game, and it is significant that in 1990–91 that ratio was

1. George Graham trying hard
not to enjoy himself . . .

2. . . . while the players celebrate as the Championship is finally won against
Manchester United.

3. It is lucky for Spurs when the year ends in 1.
Skipper Mabbutt is a worthy winner.

4. History in the making.
Gazza's tremendous free kick sets up victory in the first ever FA Cup semi-final at Wembley.

5. From the sublime . . .
Gascoigne's wild tackle in the Cup Final was felt as far away as Rome.

6. Ciao Italia 90, hello White Hart Lane.
Hopes run high at Tottenham at the start of the season.

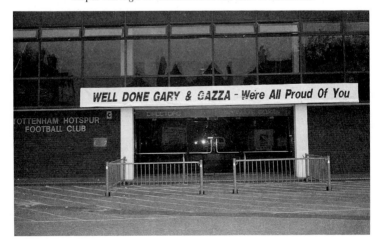

7. Jubilant Arsenal fans greet the team at the civic reception at Islington Town Hall.

8. For some it is just too much.

9. Happier times for Scholar and Venables, as Lineker joins Spurs in July 1989.

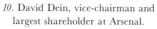

10. David Dein, vice-chairman and largest shareholder at Arsenal.

11. End of the beginning?
Alan Sugar, Terry Venables and Tony Berry at the press conference to
announce the Venables–Sugar takeover.

12. Nat Solomon, the super-sub plc
chairman who kept the club going
into extra time.

13. Bartlett of Notts County is caught between 'the Rock' and Erik the Viking in the sixth-round FA Cup tie.

14. Paul Walsh, looking good as usual, turns Andy Linighan at White Hart Lane.

15. Paul Allen demonstrates those famous scrapping qualities against Gareth Hall of Chelsea.

16. Bould forces Lineker to shoot in haste at the White Hart Lane derby.

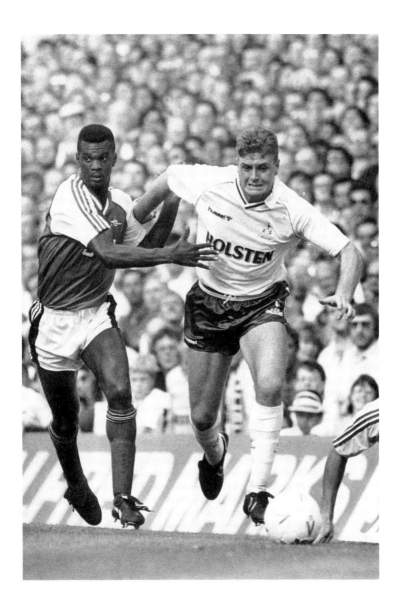

17. Davis's day in midfield, in the early season goalless draw at Highbury.

18. The start of Adams's black period.
Harshly sent off at Luton for a professional foul on Dowie.

19. Back in style – with the winner against Cambridge United in the
sixth-round FA Cup tie.

20. Two finds of the season.
Kevin Campbell . . .

21. . . . and David Hillier.

22. Limpar shooting his way into Graham's good books against Wimbledon.

23. 'The Merse' back on the road again, with a fine goal against Wimbledon.

24. David Seaman – England's No. 1 – with Wimbledon's Hans Segers.

25. Chelsea's Beasant foils Smith – who finished as the First Division's top
marksman – in Arsenal's only League defeat.

appreciably improved until the Christmas disasters. 'I am playing better – I'm catching the ball more. The gap has closed between the defenders and myself, we are a much tighter unit,' he said. His coach at Spurs, Ray Clemence, concurred: 'Erik works very hard at his game, and as a result there has been a noticeable improvement this season.' In training, whenever he misses a ball he thinks he should get, he yells 'bastard'. When it was pointed out that this was hardly in keeping with his soft-spoken character, he laughed and retorted that 'swearing doesn't seem so bad in someone else's language.'

Of course, it cannot automatically be assumed that a poor defensive record is evidence of a fallible goalkeeper. Even Peter Shilton was unable to prevent Leicester from being relegated in 1969, and Pat Jennings played in over half of Tottenham's games when they were relegated to Division Two in 1977. Thorstvedt's openness brought admiration from the supporters. He has become something of a cult figure, throwing his gloves into the crowd after a victory, but until recently 'too ashamed' to acknowledge them after a defeat.

If Seaman's displays spread confidence through a sometimes sluggish defence, at Spurs the process worked in reverse. Enforced changes at the back led to a reshuffled midfield. Strikers began to miss chances and the drop in confidence these things engendered spread back through the team until the defence began to crack with alarming regularity. It is ironic that as Thorstvedt improved, the rest of the team looked more and more insecure, and on many occasions it was the goalkeeper, coming out to play the role of sweeper, who saved the day.

'The turning point,' according to Thorstvedt, 'was the Liverpool game. Before, we were rock solid. I think we lost a lot of confidence there. We didn't really pick it up again afterwards.' As Seaman remarked, the Arsenal team know that if they don't score, they can rely on a sound defence to get them out of trouble. If Spurs failed to find the net, the likelihood now was that the side would concede at least one goal and lose the match.

There was one aspect to the derby game that escaped most commentators. White Hart Lane was full to capacity, with over

34,000 watching the match. In fact, there would have been little difficulty in attracting double the number, such was the level of interest. When the stadium goes all-seat the capacity will suffer a substantial reduction. The truth is, neither Arsenal nor Spurs will soon be able to house the number of spectators who will want to attend the big events. As the game was not chosen to be that week's live TV encounter, those excluded saw only thirty seconds of it on television.

The Taylor Report recommended that clubs in the First Division should be playing in all-seat grounds by 1994 and should move towards that figure by reducing standing room by 20 per cent per year from 1990–91. Although the Football Licensing Authority, which was created to enforce these and other provisions in the Taylor Report, was not fully operational by the beginning of the 1990–91 season, both Arsenal and Spurs, in common with all the First and Second Division clubs, had already accepted the need to comply. While a rearguard action was still being mounted by some fan groups, once the major clubs had embraced the idea, the argument was effectively over. Moreover, instructions emanating from FIFA and UEFA meant that from 1994, the final stages of all tournaments played under their direct jurisdiction would have to take place in all-seat stadia. FIFA had also decreed that these strict guidelines would be applied to countries wishing to host the World Cup Finals, which ensured a direct interest in the issue on the part of the FA.

If the opinions expressed in club fanzines – the first real forum most supporters have had to air their views (and still largely shunned by those in charge at Arsenal and Spurs) – are a reliable guide, the Arsenal fans see the writing on the wall as far as Highbury is concerned. As late as January 1991 the club had carried out no real dialogue with supporters regarding its policy for the transformation of the stadium in line with the 1994 deadline. There was merely some comment in the match programme, which promised, at some point in the future, to outline 'the steps we are taking to redevelop the stadium and how they will affect our supporters'. The club sought to justify its position by claiming, 'We have no choice if we wish to continue as a major football club.' It was a *fait accompli*, with no role for fans in the decision-making process. There was a belated effort to adopt a consultation policy, again through the programme, which announced that David Dein would hold a series of meetings with supporters, but this appeared to be little more than a public-relations exercise. The decisions had already been made.

Despite the proposed discussions at Highbury, the battle to retain standing areas is almost certainly lost. Most fans would probably accept this if they could be sure that capacity and prices would be kept at the same level, but this will not happen. Capacities will go down, prices will go up, probably sharply, and many of the most loyal fans will be forced out unless they can afford to buy a season ticket, which will become the only way to guarantee a place. A more realistic objective, and one on which fans ought to concentrate their efforts, is to secure their place in the scheme of things by demanding stadia with sufficient capacity to meet demand. While the prime concern of supporters is to attend the live event, clubs cast their gaze towards the Europe-wide television audience, which they believe is on the horizon, as the most important revenue provider in the future. It was to this end, in February 1991, that Arsenal opened a state-of-the-art media centre as part of the refurbishment of the East Stand offices and reception area. The centre provides the manager with facilities for conducting press conferences more in keeping with the club's status than was previously the case. It is a far cry from the draughty cloakrooms, corridors and car parks he is forced to endure on many away trips.

It is the professed aim of Arsenal and Spurs to compete with the best in Europe. However, each club is spending precious resources to create two grounds which in European terms can never be more than adequate at best. In Spurs' case the decision has contributed to the disastrous debt of over £20 million and its consequent interest payments, which will be running at more than £40,000 a week every week for the foreseeable future. While Arsenal's finances may be considerably healthier, their plans envisage a ground, the capacity of which, by the most optimistic forecasts, will be hard-pushed to reach 40,000. Spurs' all-seat capacity will be even less than the 34,000 who watched the derby match. At present, Highbury has 18,000 seats, while White Hart

Lane has 16,000. Both these figures fell short of 50 per cent capacity in 1990–91, so both clubs are going to have to work out ambitious redevelopment policies to keep capacity at existing levels.

Two upgraded but low-capacity football grounds in north London will not bear comparison with the likes of Italy, where monies from the central government and local authorities have created superb stadia. But one of the reasons they do not mind funding new facilities in Italy is that Italian clubs do not insist on owning and maintaining their own grounds and are perfectly prepared to share in order to provide the best possible surroundings. The lesson of this is that Arsenal and Spurs must, at some point in the future, seriously examine the prospect of sharing or be prepared to sacrifice home advantage and play big games at Wembley. Most League and Cup games could be played at White Hart Lane and Highbury, even though capacities would be reduced. European matches, and possibly big domestic contests such as the local derby, could be moved to Wembley. The unique qualities of European football might just make Wembley an acceptable compromise venue – the first step on the road to true ground-sharing in England.

Any decision to share should not be taken without real consultation with the fans of both clubs. Indeed, it may be that, on reflection, fans themselves might press for this solution if there were certain guarantees. Many, for instance, might be more disposed to the idea if they believed that resulting cost savings would be released to improve the team. George Graham certainly believes this would happen. 'Instead of spending so many millions annually on the two stadiums,' he said, 'Terry Venables and I would have five to ten million to spend on players. Don't the fans want the best players playing for Arsenal and Spurs?' In fact, Arsenal fans came up with a variety of negative responses when their views were sought in an informal investigation, but the common thread was that the idea offended against their sense of history.

There is an overwhelming emotional attachment on the part of most fans to their traditional home, which is rightly felt to be part of their heritage and which, if taken away, would change the character of their club irrevocably. Many claim they would stop going to games if Arsenal moved out of Highbury, and their rejection would be compounded if the club shared with its north London rival. 'It's the same as putting seats in, it's against the traditions of football,' was how one supporter voiced his opposition. 'Football is a game, it shouldn't be a business,' said another, adding in conclusion, 'Support for a club contains a mixture of many things. At Arsenal, it's Highbury, it's the team, it's everything about the club, but it's not sharing with Spurs. And anyway, Highbury is a good stadium. I am proud that there are no fences, that there is no racism in the crowd, that children and families are welcome and the atmosphere is fantastic. If they [the directors] turn their backs on that, they turn their backs on me. The game isn't only about building new grounds.'

A contributor to the *Gooner* was even more forthright: 'I don't want to share a ground with anyone, especially that lot. We are too big to have to share. Forget what they do in Milan and Turin, this is London.' For another, the issue was simple. 'It's not about sharing with Spurs,' he explained, 'it's about losing Highbury.'

The trouble with these kinds of views is that although they are sincerely held, they have often allowed directors to shirk their responsibilities by hiding behind the argument that the fans wouldn't wear it. The opposition to ground-sharing was fierce in a survey conducted by the *Gooner*, which found that 91 per cent of respondents would not support sharing with Spurs and 80 per cent were not in favour of moving at all. But the question is always posed in the wrong way. It is not good enough to ask, would you prefer to move out and share a new stadium or stay where you are? This does not express the real choice. With the inevitable reduction in capacities and concomitant price increases, the correct question should be, would you prefer to move to a new stadium and be guaranteed a place, or stay where you are and lose access to the big games?

The issue is anyway academic, as the fans are informed of decisions after they are made and are rarely canvassed for their opinions beforehand. This is a shame, particularly as Spurs fans appear to take a more positive stance. White Hart Lane, it seems, does not exert the same hold over Spurs supporters as does

Highbury for the Arsenal faithful. 'The main thing is that I'm sitting in a stadium watching Spurs play, and provided they don't move Tottenham to Derby I'd be very happy to share with Arsenal,' was a typical view. Another said, 'When I go to watch Arsenal play Tottenham at Highbury, I'm thinking about Tottenham. I don't think I'm in Arsenal's stadium contributing to their profits. It doesn't go that deep. I can eat at Arsenal and not choke on their food.'

Spurs were amazed when their UEFA Cup Final home leg in 1984 against Anderlecht realized record gate receipts of £250,000. Now, they beat that with virtually every home game. When this regular income is added to the extra revenue from increased prices, more games priced in the grade-A range, an expensive programme, money from 0898 numbers and merchandising, it is no wonder that the footballing activities of the club are profitable. There is a story told by a Spurs fan. A Spurs commercial executive asks, 'Have you seen our new merchandising catalogue, it's tremendous?'

'Have you seen the Arsenal shop?' the fan replies.

'Yes, it's OK . . . but we're taking more money than them.'

'You can imagine in five years' time,' added the supporter, 'losing 6–0 to Arsenal at home and Irving Scholar turning round and saying, "Yes, but our shop takes more money than theirs."' The emphasis on commercialism, however, has not noticeably helped Spurs to fashion a Championship-challenging team, let alone a stadium of European class. In contrast to the club's directors, Spurs fans seem to have focused their attention where it matters – on the field, not off it.

The Football Trust is providing £137.5 million to football clubs as part of a five-year plan to help fund the move to all-seat accommodation. Much of this will come from a reduction in the pools betting levy from 42.5 per cent to 40 per cent, the first time the Government has taken active steps to help the game financially. People in football, when arguing for a further reduction, often say that the betting levy is money taken from the game, but this is a spurious argument. The money does not come from football at all, but from the members of the public who gamble on the games. Football is paid for the use of its fixtures. If the amount received is considered insufficient, then football should seek to negotiate a better deal with the pools companies. It should be remembered that when the League tried to run its own pools competition, the venture was a dismal failure. Football's case for government money would carry far more force if the clubs, particularly the big clubs, were seen to be taking bold decisions for the future.

Both Arsenal and Spurs will take up the maximum grant on offer to First Division clubs from the Football Trust, £2 million. For Arsenal, this figure will cover some of the cost of the proposed North Bank development. By sharing a purpose-built, large-capacity stadium, the two clubs could not only double the money on offer from the Football Trust, their action could also release other purse strings, from government, financial institutions and the FA, which is seeking to implement a National Plan For Stadia, in order, among other things, to enable England to mount a credible bid for the World Cup in 1998.

In a report prepared in 1990 by the financial information company Jordans, Arsenal emerged as 'the best run club in the League', having made over £3 million profit in the three years to 1989, a performance unmatched elsewhere. The club managed this despite having a smaller turnover than either Liverpool or Manchester United. But even the best run club in the League cannot see itself providing the size of stadium necessary for it to join the exalted company of the wealthy European clubs. A survey of Europe's top clubs in the *Sunday Telegraph* showed just how far both north London clubs need to travel if there is to be a realistic possibility of living with Europe's best. All the top clubs in the *Telegraph* survey boast stadia of at least 50,000 capacity, many all-seated. In the paper's Top 40 of European clubs, Arsenal crept in at number 38, while Spurs failed to make any impression. The picture is confirmed in the Jordans report, which shows that Arsenal's income of £6.3 million in 1989 was not enough to appear in the European Top 20, and was way behind the £29.6 million of AC Milan.

In 1989, 15 per cent of Arsenal's income came from television. In future, this percentage, and that from other commercial activities, is set to rise. If the fans wish to secure a place in this future they need to press for stadia with a capacity commensurate with the numbers who want to attend. In this, they would gain crucial support from the FA and the Government. They may well have to bite the bullet of ground-sharing to accomplish the task, but since fans expect clubs to mend their ways post-Hillsborough, so should supporters themselves not be blind to what may, in the end, prove to be in their own best interests. Many problems need to be overcome, not least the lack of suitable sites on the northern fringes of London for a new stadium. What is needed is a greater understanding by all concerned, and an attempt to view the future in more rational, less emotional terms.

This issue has yet to receive its full prominence, although Spurs' financial plight might bring it to the agenda faster than many realize. For the moment, thoughts could turn back to the teams. While a number of Arsenal players would be representing the Football League in a match against the Italian League in Naples during the coming week, a game designed primarily for Italian television, Spurs would have no such distraction. For them the quarter-final of the Rumbelows Cup against Chelsea at Stamford Bridge beckoned. And Spurs would be without Gazza, who was due to begin his suspension for being sent off against Manchester United. Progress was more important than ever, both for financial reasons and to keep Spurs' season alive. Having all their eggs in one FA Cup basket was courting the kind of trouble they really needed to avoid at all costs.

14

Saved by Singular Men

Tottenham's performance in the Rumbelows Cup quarter-final at Stamford Bridge was variously described as inept and appalling. Without Gazza, the team struggled badly. That the game ended in a 0–0 draw owed more to some wayward Chelsea finishing than any solidity on the part of the Spurs defence. The blue tide, which had all but overwhelmed Spurs in the League meeting in December, again created chance after chance, all of which were spurned, saved, or cleared off the line. It was a lamentable display by Spurs and they were lucky to get another chance. Those supporters who did not make it to the Bridge were spared the sight of their side's vulnerability when war broke out in the Gulf just as *Midweek Sports Special* was about to show highlights of the game on television.

Yet again, events on the pitch were eclipsed by happenings off it. A new chairman of the public company had been announced, Nat Solomon. Solomon was well known in the City as a trouble-shooter, and his appointment had been made to placate those in the Stock Exchange and the Midland Bank who were calling for an administrator to run the club's affairs. In fact Solomon's commitment could only be part-time, since the sixty-five-year-old former chairman of the Pleasurama casino and leisure group already held a number of other directorships. It turned out that Solomon was a Spurs supporter who had first gone to White Hart Lane in the 1930s. 'The first great Spurs team I saw was Arthur Rowe's push-and-run side,' he said. The appointment of Solomon, however, had been accompanied by a statement to the Stock Exchange that talked of 'selling assets'. When asked if this could mean players, Solomon replied, 'It could do, yes. I don't rule it out and I don't rule it in.'

This statement caused further speculation about the sale of Gascoigne and Lineker, which was fuelled at a news conference in Naples before the game between the Italian and English Leagues. Napoli boss Alberto Bignon admitted that Gazza could fill the breach when his club lost the services of Diego Maradona. 'He has the qualities of skill and fantasy we look for and need from footballers in this country,' enthused Bignon. 'Gascoigne could give us exactly what we require.' Others in Italy weren't so sure. Francesco Morini, the sporting director of Juventus, one of the clubs that had been linked to Gazza after the World Cup, said, 'In Italy, temperament is so important. Gascoigne can have such a positive influence on a team but other times he loses his head.' Roma goalkeeper Giovanni Cervoni was equally ambivalent: 'He is an authentic phenomenon. In the World Cup he was a revelation. He comes across as a born leader, a man capable of winning any game at any time. When he has the ball at his feet he is a genius. But football in Italy is not just about what you do with the ball. It is a way of life . . . If he came to Italy, he would have to change. I have watched him a number of times and if he acted in Italy as he does in England he would be sent off.'

Nat Solomon was caught in something of a dilemma. As a supporter, he claimed to recognize 'the value of not only Gascoigne and Lineker but other players of great ability in the squad', while as a hard-nosed businessman he also knew that Tottenham's debts were increasing and required urgent action. The company accounts, in addition to revealing an overall debt position of £24 million, showed interest payments of £2.3 million in 1990 and £1.3 million loss incurred in ending the agreement with Hummel earlier in the year. It was left to Douglas Alexiou to spell out exactly what these figures meant. 'No asset is bigger than the club and we have a duty to our shareholders. Players are assets and if the circumstances were right and we couldn't raise money except by selling star players, we would have to consider letting them go at the right price.'

It was a far cry from Alexiou's words back in 1982, when Irving Scholar took over the club. 'We want to emulate Liverpool,' he had said then. Now Spurs were more in danger of emulating Accrington Stanley.

The comings and goings behind the scenes, and the statements emanating from the public company, were only the tip of the iceberg. Since the start of the season, Terry Venables had sought to insulate his players from the financial problems, but now here were the chairman and former chairman both making it clear that Gascoigne and Lineker might well be sold. Venables himself had become embroiled in the manoeuvres by being associated with the Frank Warren consortium, and relations between himself and Irving Scholar had markedly deteriorated. Solomon's appointment was another slap in the face for Scholar, the major shareholder, who could not be removed but who could not satisfy Stock Exchange conditions either. Venables had not been consulted over the statements and was more than a little upset when he found out. 'If it is the case that anyone has to be sold,' he said, 'I wish they would let me know. We have two vital Cup ties next week and I don't want to be distracted from the importance of that.'

No one had bothered to ask the players concerned what they felt about it all, particularly as they were now viewed primarily as 'assets'. It was the press who asked Lineker for his response to the developments. 'I don't want to go,' was his adamant reply. 'I'd like to spend the rest of my career with Spurs.'

Match days arrived as merciful relief from the unending series of revelations that had so blighted Tottenham's season. Now even they were no longer sacrosanct. On the day before Spurs were due to face Derby in a televised game at the Baseball Ground, it was reported that Venables had been offered the job of coach to the United States World Cup squad, in preparations for the 1994 finals. The story, which appeared in the *Sun*, was soon contradicted by its rival, the *Mirror*, which claimed the Americans had denied any interest in Venables, quoting US Federation official John Polis, who called the story 'an invention', and went on to say: 'There is no substance to it. No one from the Federation has contacted any British club or their manager.' Whatever the truth of this particular story, supporters faced the prospect of losing Gascoigne, Lineker and Venables, in addition to any other players who could be offloaded to help balance the books.

Luckily for Spurs, Derby were, if anything, in an even worse mess. A position among the relegation candidates had been the team's lot since early in the season, and disillusionment with the regime of Robert Maxwell had set in on a grand scale. Indeed, Derby fans made a special effort to protest against Maxwell in front of the television cameras by unfurling a number of banners bearing slogans on the theme of 'Maxwell Out'. One said, 'Give Tottenham a Bob', another, 'Give Spurs our Czech'. Such an atmosphere was not likely to induce feelings of confidence in the Derby team, and so it proved. Maxwell, who unsurprisingly did not attend the game, had raised the temperature by launching a two-page attack on the club's supporters in the match pro-gramme. That Maxwell had part-financed the move of Gary Lineker from Barcelona to Spurs, and had offered to underwrite a £13 million share issue while Derby were poverty-stricken, added to the fans' annoyance.

Gazza was again missing, as was Gary Mabbutt, but the enforced absences had less of an effect on Spurs' performance than in the game against Chelsea. Samways, Allen and Nayim established a firm grip in midfield after a frenetic opening, and thereafter Spurs controlled the game. Derby still managed to create the odd chance, and Saunders always looked dangerous, but the points were wrapped up by a simple goal from Lineker in the twenty-seventh minute, his twelfth of the season. Brian Clough, appearing as a pundit for ITV, summed up the situation perfectly when he offered some advice to Terry Venables. 'Terry ought to be on the first plane to America – I would be if I were him.'

The Tottenham manager, sensing the amusement in Clough's tone, could not resist adding his own comment: 'He must be telepathic. Perhaps I should be on the next plane . . . I think he is right.'

The win at Derby proved a temporary respite from Totten-ham's struggles against the balance sheet. Two days afterwards Emlyn Hughes hit out at Terry Venables in the *Mirror*.

'Stop moaning about not having any money, mate,' was Hughes' message. 'Spurs are skint and you've spent all they can afford to give you.' Hughes went on to detail the expenditure of £9 million on players during the Venables era, following this up with another broadside: 'Venables may claim he's recouped £7.25

million, but it's not who you sell but who you buy that surely makes a successful manager. For the millions spent, Tel Boy should have produced a better team than he has.'

It was clear by now that Terry Venables had just about had enough. Having done his best to shield his team during four months of intense speculation punctuated by morale-sapping revelations, the Spurs manager himself now decided it was time to go on the offensive. The negotiations over a new contract had recently been revived, but had not really progressed very far. Moreover, attacks like those of Emlyn Hughes questioned his ability as a manager. Venables had earlier felt it necessary to defend his position when Irving Scholar had attempted to cut his salary. Now Venables decided finally to go public. 'For heaven's sake,' he told the directors through the back pages of the tabloids, 'sort this mess out.' Venables went on to discuss his fears for the future if nothing were done. 'No one has a clue what will be happening next season. Will the star players still be here, or will the manager? Spurs could be playing in Europe but we wouldn't know who leads the team out or which players would be left to play.'

Venables' public outburst perhaps unwittingly removed the last vestiges of the shield he had thrown around his players. On the day the stories appeared, Spurs faced Chelsea in the replay of the Rumbelows Cup tie. Having got away with a poor performance at Stamford Bridge they now had the return of Gascoigne and Mabbutt to bolster the team, although Sedgley was once again left out. In their most disappointing display of the season, Spurs were taken apart and humiliated on their own ground by Bobby Campbell's blend of experience and youth. It was an intense match, with plenty of bone-crunching tackles, all carried out at breakneck speed. For the first fifteen minutes Spurs looked the better side as they launched a series of assaults on the Chelsea defence. During this period Gascoigne surged into the penalty area and was brought down by Cundy. Referee Hill waved play on and Chelsea began to look as if they might weather the early storm. They took charge of the game after fifteen minutes when Durie helped on Beasant's long clearance to Dixon, who passed short to Townsend. Townsend's run had taken him between

Mabbutt and Howells, and he beat Thorstvedt from an acute angle. Apart from one more run by Gascoigne, which was stopped by sheer weight of numbers, Spurs were never really in the match after the Townsend goal and it looked at times as if their heads had dropped.

Although Chelsea didn't score again until the seventieth minute, the Spurs response never looked likely to trouble a defence led ably by Monkou, a £100,000 buy from Feyenoord. Floundering up front on the rocks of Monkou and Cundy, Spurs were also outgunned in midfield, particularly by Townsend, who won his running battle with Gazza despite a surreptitious hand-off which left the Chelsea player on the floor. It was Townsend's shot which rebounded off the post for Dixon to make it 2–0, then Edinburgh brought down Durie with eight minutes left and Wise completed Spurs' misery by scoring from the spot.

Tottenham's season was now in danger of completely going off the rails. Atonement for the defeat in the Rumbelows Cup could only be made by a long run in the FA Cup, and the second cup tie of the week was due in three days, when Spurs lined up against another Maxwell team, Oxford United, in their fourth-round match at White Hart Lane. Although Oxford were languishing in the bottom half of the Second Division they had a reputation for playing good football going forward and had already knocked Chelsea out of the Cup in a thrilling 3–1 victory at Stamford Bridge. In the event, Gazza turned in a virtuoso display, scoring two and having a hand in two more, as Spurs ran out 4–2 winners. There were times, though, when Oxford's enterprising football threatened to embarrass their opponents, and two goals from Foyle were just reward for their contribution. Part of that contribution was that Oxford did not detail anyone to man-mark Gazza, and he took full advantage. In fact, he was totally irresistible and virtually won the match by himself. It was his shot that rebounded for Mabbutt to open the scoring, and then after nineteen minutes he brought into the game the one part of his anatomy that many say is severely under-used – his head – when he nodded the ball perfectly into Lineker's path. Lineker took the pass in his stride and lashed the ball into the top corner. It was twelve minutes into the second half, however, when Gascoigne really clinched the match. Taking the ball off Fenwick's toe, he played a one-two with Walsh on the edge of the area to open the way, went past Foster, seemed to have been forced wide by the goalkeeper, Veysey, but calmly sidestepped him to slide the ball home from the narrowest of angles. When Foyle scored his and Oxford's second eleven minutes from time, Tottenham might well have wavered, but almost immediately a square ball from Allen found Gazza, who feinted, then lashed a left-footer beyond Veysey.

After the game, Terry Venables was at his most fulsome. 'Over the years,' he purred, 'you can always compare a current player with somebody from the past, a player always reminds you of somebody. But in the case of Paul Gascoigne I don't know anyone who has played like him. He has the attitude of Dave Mackay towards the game, the hunger for the game. But he is more than a hard wing half, even though he has that same barrel-chest of Dave Mackay and is a good tackler. Also, his football's as good as anybody's and he has that great ability to run with the ball. Little Tommy Harmer didn't run with the ball so much, he played one- and two-touch football, but Gazza can do that as well, he can also play that early pass . . . he has that upper-body strength, just like Maradona, enabling him to hold opponents off.'

Oxford manager Brian Horton was equally forthright in his assessment of Gazza's influence: 'He was so sharp it was unbeliev-able. You can't stop him. We needed twelve men out there but even if we had put someone on him, he would still have done the things he did. He is a special player and you wouldn't want that talent to be lost from England.'

There could be no doubt that Gascoigne had saved Spurs' season. While the media praised his general performance, it was his goalscoring prowess that caught the eye. At a time when international teams are crying out for a midfield player who can come through and score vital goals, Gascoigne would surely walk into any team – except England's, which has always been ill-at-ease in accommodating wayward genius. Surely, for Totten-ham to sell such an 'asset' would be crazy. Stuart Jones, writing in *The Times*, put the case succinctly: 'As the bankers consider the financial balance, more than a few of the club's supporters might view the equation in a different light. Tottenham minus Lineker, and particularly Gascoigne, equals nothing.'

The same day that Tottenham faced Chelsea in the first Rumbelows Cup game at Stamford Bridge, the English League played the Italian League in an all-star game in Naples. Owing to cup commitments, most of the English team was provided by Liverpool and Arsenal. George Graham complained bitterly over losing players at such a crucial time for what he saw as a meaningless game. 'We have a big match against Everton on Saturday and I face having half of my team returning from a hard game in Italy with one full day to prepare,' he said. 'For competitive international matches, countries want their players rested for a week before. Yet I have a vital League match and the preparations are being disrupted because of a friendly. You'd think they wanted less football, not more.'

Graham had a point, though a League spokesman pointed out that the game had been arranged to help foster good relations and with 'the European future of our clubs in mind'. The row brought the old 'club v. country' conflict to the fore once again. Try as they might, the clubs and the authorities, be they FA or League, could never shake off the friction that always seemed to exist between them. The match itself was a disaster for Lawrie McMenemy's League side, which crashed to a 3–0 defeat.

The League game at home to Everton was a tricky prospect, as George Graham was trying to make clear when he let loose his diatribe against the Naples adventure. The return of Howard Kendall had rejuvenated the Merseysiders, and they came to Highbury on the back of five successive wins. The game was, in the main, a struggle for midfield supremacy. Everton almost created a number of openings but could not produce the required sharpness to unduly trouble Seaman and a more solid-looking defence in which O'Leary replaced Linighan. Paul Merson grabbed the only goal of the game three minutes after half-time, following a superb run and cross by Perry Groves. It was a triumph for spirit and the sheer will to continue on the unbeaten League trail.

The win, and the manner of it, were less important than the effect on the League table. Liverpool had become the latest team to succumb to the Wimbledon method, and the 1–1 draw at Plough Lane meant that Arsenal had achieved what many thought was impossible just a few weeks before – they were top of the First Division by one point, though Liverpool still had that game in hand. George Graham was naturally a proud man. 'We seem to have responded to setbacks,' he said. 'The spirit within the club has grown even stronger. That we will reach February without losing a League game is a tremendous achievement, especially after what has happened.'

Graham was less pleased when he heard the news that ITV had switched the League game at Anfield from 2 to 20 March. Under the terms of the League contract with ITV, the television company was allowed to alter the dates of up to four matches a season. What incensed Graham, and those at Liverpool, was the fact that they had not been consulted, and only received the news from the press. Given that Graham's own vice-chairman had been instrumental in pushing the contract through a largely reluctant Football League in 1988, it was difficult to feel too much sympathy. However, it showed once more how the League's decision-making process was simply not up to the task. The result of the change meant that Arsenal now faced five games in seventeen days, more if there were cup replays or bad weather. When it was pointed out that the next round of European Championship qualifiers came in the middle of the run, the Arsenal manager exploded. 'It is incredible that Kenny Dalglish, Terry Venables and Howard Kendall, who have been at the top of the profession for twenty years, are not asked their opinions,' he fumed. 'We are just middle-men between directors and players. I don't want to read about this in the papers. You would have thought that we have had to get over enough already this season without that as well, wouldn't you?'

In the Cup, the tie of the round and the one chosen by the BBC to screen live was between Arsenal and Leeds at Highbury. Since some tentative performances in the early games of the season, Howard Wilkinson's team had emerged as a true force once again, and the midfield of Batty, Strachan and McAllister was a match for any in the First Division. On the day, the teams all but cancelled each other out. Neither wanted to lose, but equally, neither was prepared to take the chances necessary to win. Leeds just about shaded it, although Davis had what looked like a perfectly good goal ruled out for offside. David Seaman was once again the Arsenal saviour, making a number of important saves, one in particular from a thundering McAllister drive in the dying seconds. Eleven successive victories at Elland Road made Leeds favourites for the replay, particularly since another centre back was out, this time David O'Leary, who limped off with hamstring trouble in the second half at Highbury. Howard Wilkinson was less sure. 'It would be foolish for anyone to suppose that just because we've drawn here, it will be anything other than another hard, tight game. I can see this one running to a few replays.'

The replay promised to be a titanic struggle. In a more open game than the Highbury encounter, Leeds stormed forward on a crescendo of noise. The pressure on the Arsenal defence, which had Linighan and Bould at its centre, became ever more intense and something had to give. In the frenzy that followed half-time, Leeds stepped up the pace even more. Whyte had a goal disallowed for offside against Chapman and Winterburn cleared off the line from Speed. Then Chapman, who had spent such an unhappy time at Highbury under Terry Neill, headed the Yorkshire team into the lead. Two minutes later, with Leeds still celebrating their goal, the ball broke to Limpar in his own half. Limpar had been the main threat to Leeds throughout the game, and this time he set off on a run of such electrifying pace that it took him to the edge of the Leeds area before anyone could challenge him. He cleverly cut inside the only Leeds player in the vicinity, Whyte, and beat Lukic at the near post. It was a goal of real skill and flair – and it kept Arsenal in the Cup.

George Graham was in trenchant mood afterwards. 'We are no southern softies,' he declared. 'We didn't come up north to lie down. That just doesn't happen when we travel. For the first twenty minutes, when they came at us, we had to do very well to hold out.'

Howard Wilkinson again presented a pessimistic face: 'I was

never confident we would win, even when we took the lead. I always thought it would take two goals to win this match.'

There can be no doubt that Leeds stretched Arsenal to the limit over the two games and perhaps won the midfield battle in both. Arsenal were pleased to win the toss for choice of venues for the second replay and the fans looked forward to the saga starting again at Highbury in two weeks' time. But if Leeds provided the most cohesive play, Arsenal, in the shape of Anders Limpar and David Seaman, contributed the inspiration.

It was ironic that the man who saved George Graham's FA Cup run was a player whose style was not normally associated with the Scotsman's professed liking for order, shape and resilience. When Anders Limpar was transferred from Young Boys of Berne in Switzerland to Cremonese in the Italian league, he was known as a skilful but moody and erratic central midfield player. The reputation had clung since his beginnings in Sweden, where he continually frustrated his English coach, Bob Houghton, over his fitness and attitude. With just cause, George Graham fancied himself as a bargain hunter in the transfer market, and when Cremonese were relegated and Sweden had an abysmal World Cup, he stepped in. Graham thought Limpar could perform in a wider role and bought him to supply the crosses to Alan Smith, which Brian Marwood had done to such great effect in the Championship-winning season. In the event, the Swede was versatile enough to play in either role. As the season got under way, it soon became clear that he could also score goals, a feature which had been lacking during his Italian sojourn. He won over the crowd early on with some scintillating performances, none better than when he destroyed Chelsea in the 4–1 win at Highbury. He had grabbed the two goals that preserved the unbeaten League record at Leeds as well as providing the match winners at Coventry and Manchester United.

However, as the bunker mentality set in, George Graham's priorities began to change. Draws and hanging on became the order of the day. The imperative was not to lose. As this change gradually took place, Graham became less tolerant of his 'star'. Previously, when Limpar drifted inside, Graham was happy enough; now, as the goals came with less regularity, he felt the

Swede was destroying the pattern of play he had carefully set out. Notwithstanding Limpar's eight goals in the first fourteen games, the manager still had reservations.

'Anders has a terrific shot in both feet,' commented Graham, 'so there's no excuse for not scoring more . . . In the role we have given him, he has more chances to shoot at goal and I have been on at him to do it more often.' If Limpar refused to stay out wide in his 'given role', he would be substituted. As the sense of attrition mounted at Highbury, this increasingly occurred. It happened in the Rumbelows disaster against Manchester United, as if Limpar were alone responsible for the defeat. The Aston Villa game provided a classic example of cutting off your nose to spite your face. With a conservative defensive alignment (it was the first match without Tony Adams), the possession of one point was more important than the possibility of three, and Limpar was pulled off with almost twenty minutes to go. In the absence of any discernible injury it could only be assumed that Graham saw Limpar as something of a luxury who could not be afforded when the chips were down. Yet, as results proved, Limpar added the kind of flair Arsenal desperately needed and could win or save games on his own with a rare degree of skill. In fact he was probably the difference between the lacklustre team of 1989–90 (when Marwood was sidelined through injury for much of the time) and the Championship contenders of 1990–91.

George Graham, however, was still not satisfied. After Limpar scored the equalizer against Leeds his manager lambasted him for not contributing more: 'I expect a lot more from him. He is playing in spasms and I want him attacking the full back. At Leeds we kept waiting for him to take on the full back.'

Perhaps Graham was doing what his good friend and golfing partner Frank McLintock said was needed. 'Limpar is slightly lazy and wanders about the pitch drifting out of a game,' McLintock claimed. 'He is the type who needs a kick up the arse every now and again.'

Anders Limpar, a great admirer of both Arsenal and English football, was more than pleased to come to London. 'The Italians tend to be more skilful overall than here,' he said, 'but their top teams are no better than Liverpool or Arsenal.' While he professed to have enjoyed his time in Italy, he had never looked the player there that he did once he came under George Graham's wing, and most would agree that he was a revelation to English fans, the more so when he curtailed his appetite for throwing himself around in the penalty area. Graham's instinct, especially when things got rough, was to fall back on the pattern of play that had served him so well. No one knows better than the Arsenal manager that Limpar as a player possesses the potential for greatness and can produce the unexpected that can turn a game. Yet this goes against the grain. Players at Arsenal are asked to perform a role and are expected to stick to it. Once shape is lost, as Limpar encroaches into the midfield, Graham's sense of order and discipline is violated. How he resolved the paradox could well determine Arsenal's season. As he pondered on the problem, it is to be hoped that he recalled the words of Leeds' mercurial Gordon Strachan, who said after the Elland Road replay, 'Limpar is a fabulous player. He has absolutely great feet, the quickest and deadliest in British football at the moment. He is what every team wants, a match winner of unquestioned class.'

As February arrived, though, George Graham was entitled to feel he had got his selection policy right and that any criticism was mere carping. Arsenal were top of the League and unbeaten. Another lucrative FA Cup game against Leeds was due in two weeks and, now they had survived the Elland Road confrontation, the Gunners were once again favourites. Before that, Arsenal were set to follow Spurs to a revitalized Stamford Bridge. Having disposed of Tottenham, Chelsea were sure to approach the Arsenal game in a much better frame of mind than they showed in the first match at Highbury. The Blues' confidence in fact must have been sky-high after White Hart Lane, a game which had put them on the brink of a Wembley final. It promised to be another fascinating encounter.

15

He who Laughs Last

The feeling among the Arsenal players was that they could have been two or three goals up by half-time. Just before the break, though, Steve Bould was caught by a late tackle that damaged his ankle, and he failed to appear for the second period. With David O'Leary injured, Arsenal had lined up against Chelsea with four at the back, and although David Hillier did well as Bould's replacement, the defence rarely looked comfortable after the latter's departure.

That no lesser a judge than George Graham should view the loss of Bould as 'the turning point' testified to the player's quiet success since coming to Highbury from Stoke. While rarely attract-ing headlines (except, on occasion, for the wrong reasons, such as an early return from Singapore and a fine for excessive celebra-tions at the Supporters' Club dinner), in the absence of Tony Adams, Bould had become central to the team's strategy. It was not that he was asked to play in a different way. Rather, with Andy Linighan finding it difficult to slot into the central defensive role, it became imperative that Bould won every challenge, every 50–50 ball, every battle with opposing forwards. He put in some outstanding performances, with headers going prodigious dis-tances, tackles that brooked no argument and a new positional awareness that gave him the space to improve his distribution.

It was an uncharacteristic error by Nigel Winterburn that opened the way for Chelsea to become the first team to beat Arsenal in the League. A free kick was headed on by Kerry Dixon, and as Winterburn tried to head clear, he instead directed the ball across the face of his own goal. David Seaman, possibly wrong-footed by the defender's mistake, was unable to get to the far post quickly enough and Graham Stuart headed Chelsea into the lead. After that the game opened up, but although Arsenal might have grabbed an equalizer in a goalmouth scramble, it was

Chelsea who looked the more likely to add to the score. In the eighty-eighth minute Wise found Stuart on the left, and the youngster produced a telling pass to Damian Matthew, who left Linighan for dead before squaring the ball to Dixon. Dixon had time to pick his spot and wrapped up the victory with a clinical low strike. Although Alan Smith pulled a goal back in injury time, it was too late, and the unbeaten run had come to an end at the twenty-fourth time of asking – the third longest this century, after the twenty-nine-match sequences of Leeds in 1973–4 and Liverpool in 1987–8.

George Graham was not overly disturbed by either the defeat or the end of the unbeaten run. 'I was expecting it to end but I was hoping it would be in May,' he joked. He was also able to put the loss in perspective, when he added, 'If someone had told me at the start of the season that we'd lose our first game in February I'd have said "thank you very much."' Many thought the hard midweek FA Cup match against Leeds, with its energy-sapping extra time, had left its mark on some of the Arsenal players. Graham did not agree and neither did most of the team. Lee Dixon echoed Graham's point that the loss of Steve Bould was the real reason for the defeat.

'That was the difference,' he said. 'It put a lot of pressure on Andy Linighan and Dave Hillier . . . and we didn't stay together as a back four. A few holes appeared and we lost it through that more than anything the Leeds game contributed. I didn't feel any more tired than I normally do.'

The following day, Liverpool could only draw at Old Trafford, so the two front-runners were locked on 51 points each, although Liverpool still had a game in hand.

While Arsenal were struggling at Stamford Bridge, Spurs met Leeds at White Hart Lane in a poor game that ended scoreless. Gazza did not play, having been sent home from training with a fever the previous day, although Terry Venables made the telling comment that 'he would have played if it had been a cup tie'. This could only mean that the Tottenham manager had given up the League and believed that the Cup was now the club's only chance of glory. However, with League position vital in the quest for European places, the decision was somewhat surprising. Against that, it was clear to Venables that Gascoigne, who had been carrying a groin injury that was not healing as had been hoped, needed to be rested as much as possible. Many fans were annoyed that the decision to leave out Gascoigne was not announced until just before the kick-off. With justifiable cynicism they felt the club had deliberately withheld the information since it might have an adverse effect on the gate. The impression was compounded when a seemingly hale and hearty Gazza was spotted in a restaurant on the day of the game.

The match itself contained just one dramatic incident, when Lee Chapman was accidently kicked in the face by the returning Steve Sedgley after just two minutes. The impetus of the blow sent Chapman crashing on to the cinder track surrounding the pitch. The Leeds striker was obviously seriously injured and required immediate medical attention. In fact he was unconscious for almost five minutes.

'I've never been so frightened before,' said Sedgley. 'His eyes were rolling and the whole situation made me feel sick. As soon as I caught him I knew he was out. He was unconscious when he hit the floor.' Leeds' manager, Howard Wilkinson, revealed afterwards that Chapman had suffered 'concussion and shock'. He had also lost a lot of blood. 'There was bleeding internally and externally from the nose,' Wilkinson continued. 'The blood was in his windpipe and throat.' The whole of the Spurs crowd was stunned by the incident. There were no whistles or cat-calls, as was the case when David Howells was left prostrate, apparently concussed, at Elland Road. Then, there were cries of 'let him die'.

The Leeds contingent at White Hart Lane did nothing to temper their reputation for the worst type of partisanship. They greeted the entrance of the Spurs team with a vile antisemitic chant, which was ironic considering their own chairman is Jewish. Unless Leeds can eliminate the sickening behaviour of this section of their support, the club may well receive some swingeing penalties when the new law against racial abuse and chanting at football matches, which is contained in the 1991 Criminal Justice Bill, reaches the statute book.

With Leeds missing Batty, Chapman and, after half-time, his replacement, Pearson, and with Gazza out for Spurs, the match was not one of the season's better offerings. Venables preferred Mitchell Thomas to Vinny Samways in midfield, but Thomas was ineffectual for much of the time. When Samways finally came on with just over twenty minutes to go, the midfield congestion had become endemic and he was unable to change the pattern of the game. Sixth place, thirteen points behind Arsenal and Liverpool, was the result, and most Spurs fans now agreed with the manager's tacit admission that the Cup was their only realistic hope.

The second week in February saw snowfalls disrupt much of the country. Football was as affected as everything else, and the week's fixtures were almost entirely lost to the weather. The day before the snow arrived en masse, England played a historic game against Cameroon at Wembley, the first time a team from Africa had appeared at the famous old stadium. At first, the FA received universal approval for inviting Cameroon to England after their exploits in *Italia 90*. The atmosphere was soured, however, when the African team's officials became embroiled in an unseemly financial dispute, resulting in the non-appearance of Roger Milla, who refused to play after his demands for appearance money were rejected by the FA. The game itself, played in sub-zero conditions, drew a crowd of over 60,000 but failed to live up to the classic encounter in Naples. There was still plenty of interest for Arsenal and Spurs fans, though. David Seaman was chosen ahead of Chris Woods, a testament to his recent form, while Lee Dixon was picked for the fourth time. Dixon recalled with pride his selection in Graham Taylor's first England team against Hungary back in September: 'I was more thrilled to get that cap than the first one. It was the first time I'd been picked on merit. The last time, I was picked by Bobby Robson because someone was injured.'

Gazza was in the side once more, which undoubtedly helped swell the attendance, but his groin was troubling him and he went off after an hour. 'It was my decision to come off,' he explained. 'The groin is not good but now I must wait and see how it goes.'

Graham Taylor warned of the possible dangers ahead. 'During the half-time interval,' he said, 'the injury stiffened up and it was uncomfortable for him out there. It's now a bit of a problem for him and it's something he and Spurs will have to look at.' Taylor was obliquely referring to the stark choice for the player and his club. The type of groin problem Gazza was suffering from could only be properly cured by an operation. Sometimes it can be alleviated by rest but not when the rest is interrupted by the intense activity of an English First Division match. The dilemma was whether to get Gascoigne into hospital as soon as possible in the hope that he could do what Chris Waddle did after suffering a similar injury. Waddle was back playing first-team football within five weeks. But so reliant were Spurs on Gascoigne's presence that the overriding concern was of what might happen without him, particularly in the Cup.

There was better fortune for Gary Lineker, who scored the two goals that beat the Africans, the first from a penalty. Lineker's incredible record of goals at international level showed no signs of drying up. He was now, with thirty-nine goals to his credit, only five behind Jimmy Greaves and ten behind Bobby Charlton. For Spurs' fans, his England performance was tantalizing. For Tottenham, his form had dipped, and his scoring rate, while respectable, was not up to the high standards he had established for himself in the past.

One of the few other matches to survive the weather was Liverpool's game in hand, a derby encounter with Everton at Anfield, where a 3–1 victory for Liverpool ended Arsenal's brief spell at the top. For the moment there was little the Gunners could do, since League action would not be resumed for at least another ten days. And before any further League encounters there was the little matter of the second replay against Leeds, which was to go ahead as planned thanks to the undersoil heating at Highbury. The postponements at least gave George Graham breathing space to get his first-choice central defenders fit and back into the side.

In fact, Steve Bould and David O'Leary had recovered in time for the Leeds showdown, so Andy Linighan dropped out. Incredibly, Lee Chapman, his face a mass of scars and stitches, also played, his second appearance since the awful injury he sustained at White Hart Lane. Once again the teams cancelled each other out, and extra time could not produce a goal. Howard Wilkinson's prediction that the tie would run and run was coming true, and instead of the winners visiting Shrewsbury the following Saturday, another game at Elland Road was necessary. The tie was approaching the proportions of the titanic struggle with Sheffield Wednesday in 1979, when Arsenal finally won in the fourth replay and went on to lift the Cup. Unfortunately for Arsenal, Anders Limpar was carried off towards the end of extra time with badly damaged ankle ligaments. The game was again dominated by the goalkeepers, both of whom made important saves, but the result turned on an incident halfway through the second half. A cross from Nigel Winterburn hit Mel Sterland on the arm, and the referee awarded a penalty. The normally reliable Lee Dixon, who had scored four penalties from four attempts during the season, blasted his spot-kick over the bar and into the North Bank.

'There was a lot of pressure on the penalty,' Dixon said. 'But I've had pressure before – it was no different to when we were 1–0 up against Liverpool and I scored to make it 2–0. I just tried to get a good strike on the ball. I got a good strike but too much elevation.' Dixon's team-mates thought that the presence of John Lukic in the opposition goal might have put him off, but he refuted the suggestion. 'I didn't really notice it was John in goal until after the game,' he maintained. Whatever the cause, Dixon was sure it was his worst moment since arriving at Highbury.

Dixon was bitterly disappointed with his miss. 'Twenty past eleven I left the ground,' he said. 'It seemed like it took me about three days to get home. There were a few Leeds fans on the motorway going back with their scarves out. I watched the game when I got home and I had a couple of drinks to get myself to sleep, but I didn't sleep at all that night.'

The sleepless night helped get the incident out of the full back's system. 'I watched the game and read the papers,' he said. 'It wasn't going to change the fact that I'd missed a penalty . . . You can't hide from it . . . it's still going to be reported on, it's still going to be shown on TV. If you try to bury it, it seems to keep cropping up. My attitude is to take the bull by the horns and say, "Look, I made a mistake." '

Any lingering doubts in the player's mind were expunged the next day, which he spent at home relaxing after taking his son to playschool. 'Kids take your mind off things,' he ventured. 'When you switch on the telly and see people getting killed in the Gulf it brings it home to you. I'm sat there worrying about a penalty and people are sat there worried about their relatives. It brings it down to earth.'

The squad had a light training session on Friday. In typical George Graham style, the manager did not criticize Dixon, nor was there any question of anyone else taking the penalties in future. Graham had decided that the best way to break the stalemate, particularly in view of the loss of Limpar, was to play the alternative system of five at the back. Lee Dixon explained the thinking behind the change: 'It was dragging on a little bit, it had become a stalemate, everyone knew what everyone else was doing ... [Leeds] caused us a lot of problems with Gordon Strachan in the middle, floating around. We had not been causing them enough problems. The manager changed it for the fourth game.'

The training session included a period of 'shadow play', where the players go to their positions and pass the ball around, to get a feel of the system. It instils the shape of the team, and the duty of each player, into the minds of the side. This versatility, which meant that opponents could never be sure of Graham's tactical plan, had been an important factor in Arsenal's success all season. The ease with which the players switched roles was such that, as Paul Davis explained when talking about the defeat of Liverpool at Highbury, the team did not decide on their exact alignment until the game had started. The tactic was about to pay its biggest dividend so far, and as Lee Dixon said, 'It proved a masterstroke'. The training session concluded with the viewing of a video of the first half of the last Leeds match. Graham felt they had not performed well, and pointed to a number of mistakes he felt could be eliminated.

The Elland Road atmosphere was electric. 'It was incredible to listen to the noise,' said one Arsenal fan. 'They must have been handing out song sheets.' This was a reference to the chant – in cha cha cha style – of 'Let's all laugh at Dixon, ha!'

The revised Arsenal formation confused Leeds from the start. Howard Wilkinson's team had played exceptionally well over the previous three games and might have already won the tie had it not been for the individual brilliance of David Seaman and Anders Limpar. George Graham paid Leeds the compliment of comparing them to his Arsenal side of two years before and predicted that they would become a permanent force in the First Division. Nevertheless, they were incapable of altering their basic tactics to nullify Graham's game plan, and were caught brilliantly on the break. After seventeen minutes, Strachan lost the ball to Michael Thomas and it broke to Kevin Campbell, who had come in for the injured Perry Groves. Campbell gave the ball to Merson, operating on the left in the absence of Limpar. Merson set off on a forty-yard run, culminating in a right-foot shot that beat Lukic low to his right. Leeds' best chance fell to Lee Chapman after half an hour, but the usually lethal striker shot wide with the unprotected goal gaping in front of him.

Apart from that, Arsenal controlled the first half, and it was fitting that the second, and winning, goal was brilliantly scored by Lee Dixon just before the break. Dixon received the ball on the right and attacked the penalty area. When he hit a wall-pass and went for the return, Andy Linighan appeared on the edge of the box to play the perfect ball. Dixon held off Batty's challenge and shot low and hard beyond Lukic. The Leeds fans were stunned, while the Arsenal contingent gave them their version of the Dixon cha cha cha.

The second half was going much the way of the first until Chapman finally produced a moment of class, when he turned past the entire Arsenal defence, held off Linighan's challenge, and beat Seaman with a low cross-shot. With twenty minutes left, Leeds were rejuvenated and put Arsenal under considerable pressure, but the Gunners held out to record a famous victory.

Lee Dixon felt, as did most observers, that the change of system had made the difference. 'We stopped their midfield, which is their biggest strength,' he said. 'Nigel and I pushed forward, while Micky Thomas and Paul Davis played it tight. Once you've nullified their strengths you can work on your own, which is going forward on the break.'

The game was a personal triumph for Dixon. He would now have the pleasure of playing at Shrewsbury in the fifth round, a club managed by John Bond. Bond had got rid of the young Dixon when they were both at Burnley some years previously. He would soon publicly admit his mistake.

Lee Dixon's road to the top is marked by some tough times in the lower divisions, which may go a long way to account for his balanced approach to the success he has enjoyed at Highbury.

'I loved the club [Burnley],' he said. 'I knew everybody there and I wanted to stay, but John Bond decided he didn't want me there.' Bond gave the teenage Dixon a free transfer, and he eventually went to Chester, then bottom of the Fourth Division. The experience, Dixon believes, actually helped him in the long term.

'What Bond did was a kick in the guts,' he remembered, 'but it definitely toughened me up. It was like my world had come to an end, but at the end of day I ought to shake his hand and thank him because he set me on the road to coming here.'

After eighteen months at Chester, Dixon asked for a transfer and moved to Third Division Bury for £3,500. Twelve months later, Mick Mills, then manager of Stoke, offered £40,000 for him and he was on his travels again. In the Potteries, Mills tutored Dixon in the art of full-back play to the point where George Graham was prepared to pay £350,000 to bring the player to Arsenal. Once again, Graham had made a shrewd purchase. The determination of Dixon's performance in the final Leeds game exemplified all that Graham expected from his players.

The four games against Leeds had not quite matched the record marathon against Sheffield Wednesday, but they threw up some interesting statistics. Seven hours of football had been watched by 110,000 spectators live and by millions more on television. The first game was screened live and highlights were broadcast of the others. Over £1 million pounds was taken in gate receipts. Amazingly for such an important series of matches, not one player was booked.

*

As Lee Dixon was relaxing at home the day after the third match against Leeds, Tony Adams was tasting freedom for the first time in eight weeks. The coaching staff at Highbury were impressed with the way Adams had kept himself fit during his detention. The weather had put paid to a scheduled reserve game away to Reading, but in order to give Adams a game as soon as possible, Arsenal offered to switch the match to Highbury, where the undersoil heating would enable it to take place. Reading, having not played for some time because of the snow, readily agreed and decided to send their first team for some much-needed match practice. So while his team-mates were fighting the final battle at Elland Road, the Arsenal captain made his comeback. Adams, who had been fined £1,000 by the FA for the V-sign incident at QPR while still in prison, could never have suspected the greeting he was about to experience from the Arsenal faithful. A crowd of 7,000 turned out, ten times the normal gate for such a match, and they gave Adams a hero's welcome.

Adams had been whisked to the stadium in a limousine and he was just as quickly whisked away again at the end. In between, he gratefully acknowledged the fans' support with an emotional gesture to the crowd, and helped Arsenal recover from a 2–0 deficit to draw 2–2. The result was unimportant, however; what mattered was that the captain was back and looked as though he meant business. He was genuinely surprised by the reception he received.

'It brought a lump to my throat,' he said. 'I felt totally overwhelmed by it all. The fans were absolutely tremendous and it's great to be back at Arsenal.'

The crowds that came to applaud Adams' return were not condoning the behaviour that resulted in his prison sentence. They had come to express their feelings to a man they recognized as one of their own, someone wholly committed to the Arsenal cause who had made a mistake but taken his incarceration with the dignity befitting an Arsenal captain. The loyalty shown to Adams and his family during this period by the club and his fellow players was reciprocated when they turned down large sums of tabloid money to tell their story. There was never any argument over whether Adams would return as captain; it was just a matter of when. Paul Davis, who had been given the job in Adams' absence, summed up the feelings of all at the club when he said, 'I won't mind handing over to Tony. He was a great captain before – he'll be even better now.'

Tottenham's game that weekend was a fifth-round FA Cup tie away to Portsmouth. Terry Fenwick, who had been slowly coming back to full fitness, was involved in a freak accident as the players were warming up, which resulted in another broken bone, this time in his ankle. Having so recently fought his way back from a long-term injury, it was a cruel blow and compounded the makeshift nature of the Spurs team, which had already lost Howells and Walsh to injuries and Stewart to suspension. Neither of the two ex-Spurs players who had been transferred to Portsmouth played in the match. Guy Butters was left out and Gary Stevens, who had often been injury-prone in his Tottenham career, unluckily missed the game after a run of fifty consecutive appearances for his new club

As it was a Cup tie, Gazza played and once again stole the show, shrugging off his painful groin injury. Portsmouth, like Oxford before them, gave him the room to create chances for others and himself. Gascoigne's ability to find the net proved essential, since Lineker seemed once again to have mislaid his sharpness in the box. Lineker spurned three good opportunities before former England winger, Mark Chamberlain, put Portsmouth ahead just before the interval. It was left to Gazza to turn the match, aided by Paul Allen, who was the only other Tottenham player to trouble Gosney in the Pompey goal. On the hour, Gascoigne initiated a four-man move and completed it himself with a powerful header from a pin-point Allen centre. Gazza ensured victory with his second goal after eighty-two minutes. Fastening on to a hopeful punt from Van Den Hauwe, he wrongfooted the Portsmouth defence before drawing Gosney and calmly planting the ball in the back of the net.

Terry Venables summed up the importance of the result: 'We've had a difficult season but we're in the last eight and that's uplifting for everyone.' The win was more important than the manner of it and Spurs could look forward to a sixth-round home tie against Second Division Notts County. If Arsenal got past

Shrewsbury, Third Division Cambridge at Highbury was the prize. It looked as if both clubs could make it through to the semi-finals, and the draw presented the intriguing possibility of a north London Cup final for the first time. Before that, however, Arsenal had some ground to make up on Liverpool and Spurs needed to find their true form before the luck, and Gazza's stunning displays, ran out.

16

Pressure, What Pressure?

Reporters invited to the press conference at Anfield on Friday 22 February were convinced that a new signing was about to be unveiled. Their preconceptions exploded with the sensational announcement by Noel White, Liverpool's chairman, that Kenny Dalglish had resigned with immediate effect. What made the revelation all the more astonishing was that Liverpool were at the top of the First Division with two-thirds of the season gone, and were still in the FA Cup, following a 4–4 draw with Everton two days previously, which was described by many as the finest derby game ever seen on Merseyside.

Dalglish's record as player, player-manager and manager was unparalleled, even by his distinguished predecessors. He arrived at Anfield from Celtic in the summer of 1977 for a British record transfer fee of £440,000 to wear the number seven shirt vacated by Kevin Keegan, who had departed for Hamburg after having helped win the European Cup for Liverpool the previous May with a scintillating display in Rome's Olympic Stadium. Most thought Keegan irreplaceable, but Dalglish scored on his début and went on to write himself into the history books by snatching the only goal of Liverpool's second successive European Cup triumph against Bruges at Wembley. Five League Championships followed, along with two more European Cups and four League Cups. When he became player-manager after the Heysel tragedy, he took the club to its first League and FA Cup double and failed by the narrowest of margins to repeat the feat in 1988 and 1989. It was the way in which Dalglish broke up the double-winning side, though, and his signing of Barnes, Beardsley and Houghton, which marked him out as a great manager, producing in the process the class of 87–8, which played a quality of football not seen in the Football League since the great Manchester United side of the 1960s. Unbeaten in the League until mid-March that season, one performance in particular, when they routed Nottingham Forest 5–0 at Anfield, prompted no less a judge than Tom Finney to remark that it was 'the best team performance I have ever seen'. A complex and much analysed personality, Dalglish's dignified bearing after the Hillsborough disaster, and his identification with the relatives of the victims as if they were his own family, drew universal acclaim. Perhaps also the tragedies of Heysel and Hillsborough left a deeper scar than many realized. When confronted with death at such close quarters, priorities can undergo a seismic shift.

As the 1990–91 season progressed, for all Liverpool's strengths, something had started to go badly wrong for the first time in Dalglish's career as a manager. Initially, no one, probably not even Dalglish himself, realized what was happening. When Liverpool won at White Hart Lane in November, Dalglish had picked a team packed with defenders to shut out Gascoigne. The success at Spurs may have led to a false sense of security, because Dalglish used the same tactics at Highbury in December, a ploy that went disastrously wrong as Liverpool were beaten 3–0. In the past, Liverpool rarely allowed the opposition to dominate selection policy; now it was becoming the rule. Never forthcoming with the media, Dalglish revealed more about himself in the short statement that accompanied his resignation than he had in five years of after-match comments. He spoke of 'the pressure I put myself under to be successful'. Such was the intensity of that self-imposed pressure – and Dalglish had never developed the art of delegation – that he had burnt himself out at the age of thirty-nine.

There were those who could not accept the finality of the manager's decision, and speculation was rife that he might return after a break from the game. This view was encouraged by the fact that for the first time in thirty years there was no clear line of succession. The club had not only lost its manager, it had lost its most precious asset, the sense of continuity that had been present since the Liverpool dynasty was established by Bill Shankly.

Many managers and pundits pondered over the nature of the pressure Dalglish might have been under. Several wild theories were advanced, including rumours of a rift between Dalglish and his team after the Everton game. George Graham was asked how he coped with the pressures of being a top football manager and claimed that he found relaxation in gardening. 'I plant things,' he said. 'Daffodils, tulips, crocuses, snowdrops – it's quite creative, I cut off mentally.'

Long-term injuries to key players, such as Whelan, Gillespie and McMahon, obviously had a bearing on the make-up of Dalglish's teams. Nevertheless, it seemed to most outsiders that his selection policy became more bizarre as the season progressed. Peter Beardsley, for instance, was left out when he was the First Division's top scorer. When goals were hard to come by, Ronnie Rosenthal, whose strikes at the back end of the previous season had helped win the Championship, languished in the reserves, even when Rush was injured. In the Cup tie against Everton, the Liverpool defence made a series of uncharacteristic errors to let their rivals back into a game they should have sewn up. Dalglish's transfer activity also seemed at odds with the Liverpool tradition. The purchase of David Speedie was especially mystifying, the player being thirty-one years of age and Scottish, when what Liverpool surely needed were more young Englishmen in order to be able to field the required number of qualified players in European competitions, as demanded by new UEFA regulations. Suddenly it was as if the wheel of fortune had begun to turn. Arsenal, although plagued by adversity, had somehow clung on. Now there was a chance that the disruption caused by Dalglish's resignation would give them the break they had been waiting for. Moreover, Liverpool's first game minus their manager was to be played on plastic at Luton, where the team had often struggled in the past. Although some semblance of order was restored when Ronnie Moran, who had been at Liverpool for thirty years, was put in temporary charge of the team, it was not enough to stop the Champions crashing to a 3–1 defeat. Dalglish's timing had left everyone bewildered. After the Luton game, the team had to face two hard matches – the Cup replay against Everton and the visit of Arsenal to Anfield the following Sunday.

While Liverpool were losing at Luton, Arsenal celebrated with a 4–0 home win over Crystal Palace at Highbury, which took them back to the top of the table on goal difference. There never seemed a four-goal difference between the two sides, but on a windy afternoon Palace made the mistakes and Arsenal capitalized on them with a vengeance.

Palace, who, like Arsenal, employed a sweeper system for the game, shared the first-half possession but still found themselves two goals down by the interval. O'Leary forced home the first after just three minutes, when the ball bounced awkwardly from Linighan's knock-down. Then Eric Young, perhaps fooled by the wind, made a mess of what should have been an easy clearance, Merson took the ball off him and ran on to beat Nigel Martyn in the Palace goal. The strike of the game came from Alan Smith, a superb chip from the edge of the penalty area which put the Gunners three up. The victory was sealed a minute later when Martyn failed to hold a Winterburn shot, a mistake punished by Campbell.

'A good, combative performance,' was how George Graham described it, adding, 'we could have scored more than four but I'll settle for that.' Although Palace might have considered themselves unlucky to lose by such a wide margin, it was difficult to argue with Steve Coppell's candid judgement that they were simply 'not in the same class'.

An injury to Andy Linighan in the second half saw Colin Pates at last get an outing, and David Rocastle came on for Paul Merson for the final eight minutes. The quality of Graham's squad was once again emphasized by the substitutions, neither of which disrupted the seamless web that characterized Arsenal's style. One minus point was a below-par performance by Paul Davis, who looked strangely out of sorts. One incident in particular, when he allowed himself to be caught in possession by Geoff Thomas, just about summed up his afternoon. Every player has a bad game from time to time, but with Limpar and Groves coming back to fitness, Arsenal's strength in depth meant that anyone who did not perform to the standards set by the manager could soon find himself out in the cold. And from there it could be a long road back, as David Rocastle would be the first to admit.

One Arsenal player who was definitely not out in the cold was

Tony Adams. After playing three reserve matches in the thirteen days since his release from prison he had proved his fitness and would almost certainly resume his place in the rearranged fifth-round FA Cup tie away at Shrewsbury, which was due to take place the following Wednesday.

Gay Meadow might have proved one of those difficult grounds for a First Division side, but the Arsenal steamroller refused to be turned back by the occasion or the muddy conditions. As expected, Adams was recalled, but interestingly, Graham preferred David Hillier to Paul Davis in midfield, citing the youngster's strength as the deciding factor. Although Shrewsbury attacked fiercely for the first quarter of the match, they could not quite manage the breakthrough, and gradually Arsenal began to take control. After fifty-eight minutes the Gunners scored the goal that won the tie, and it was a classic worthy of any match. Nigel Winterburn broke from defence and spotted Michael Thomas on one of his famous runs from midfield. A precise through-ball allowed Thomas to outpace two defenders before producing the perfect chip shot over goalkeeper Hughes. After that, Arsenal could have had more as Smith hit the post and Dixon had a shot cleared off the line.

'Shrewsbury were full of enthusiasm for the first twenty minutes,' said Graham. 'But once we saw that through, we were comfortable and could have had three goals.'

The Shrewsbury manager, John Bond, the same John Bond who had discarded Lee Dixon at Burnley, joined the growing list of Arsenal admirers, saying, 'To me Arsenal are the best team in the country. They seem to have everything, including a bigger will to win than anybody else.' With only Cambridge, another Third Division side, standing between Arsenal and a place in the semi-finals, the talk in the media inevitably began to turn to the possibility of another double. The idea, which would have seemed preposterous when the two points were deducted by the FA, gained impetus when Liverpool lost their replay against Everton by a single goal from Watson, an Everton defender rejected by Liverpool as a youngster.

Attention now switched back to the League, in particular the clash between Liverpool and Arsenal at Anfield. After the furore over the way ITV had altered the date of the game, the television company had a change of heart and the match reverted to its scheduled weekend. While it would not in itself decide anything, there was no question that the winners would receive an important psychological boost.

Liverpool might have lost their manager and their last two games, but the decline was relative – they had not lost three matches in a row for over five seasons. Moreover, there could be no denying the quality of their players, and with Beardsley back in the team and Molby's silky skills in full working order, they pounded Arsenal from the start, creating a handful of good chances in the first half. That they didn't score was due to missed chances by Rush and the goalkeeping heroics of David Seaman, who made five world-class saves. One, in particular, from a John Barnes free kick, was an example of goalkeeping perfection. Barnes, who has scored many goals from set pieces in his career, hit his curling shot precisely, but Seaman had read the player's intentions. Still he had to make ground, but he clutched the ball out of the air and held on to it with a panache reminiscent of the young Gordon Banks.

Despite Liverpool's attacking verve, the defence continued to look less than effective. Gillespie in particular, returning after an absence of six weeks and playing out of position at full back, looked vulnerable whenever Merson ran at him. Although Liverpool were creating chances at one end, they were allowing Arsenal to counter-attack in a manner previous Liverpool sides would never have countenanced. It was difficult to remember a Liverpool team defending with the ineptness they had displayed against Luton, Everton and now Arsenal. In fact Arsenal had two good chances in the first half, both falling to Paul Merson. The first ended up as a wild shot, while the second, a free header at the far post, followed a similar course over the bar.

If there is a flaw in Merson's game, it is his occasional impetuousity. He is at his best when running at defenders with the ball, and when those opportunities present themselves he is more often than not devastating in his finishing. This aspect of Merson's talents was seen dramatically in the sixty-sixth minute, when he scored the only goal of the contest. Beardsley, who had hardly put a foot wrong, tried to find Gillespie. Merson saw the pass coming, intercepted the ball and set off on a direct route towards Grobbelaar, exploiting the space vacated by Gillespie. A one-two with Alan Smith saw him clear of Liverpool's crumbling back line, and with consummate coolness he slipped the ball past the advancing Liverpool goalkeeper.

As the Arsenal celebrations began, the Liverpool fans had no answer. They had looked downhearted before the match started, and the visiting supporters rubbed it in by mockingly chanting 'Dalglish'. The Anfield faithful were forced to suffer in silence a rendition of 'We've got that double feeling'. Liverpool's third defeat in succession was their first at Anfield since they conceded their League title to Arsenal forty-three matches ago. It was only the second time Arsenal had won at Anfield in fifteen years.

Paul Merson, echoing Kenny Dalglish, spoke afterwards about the pressures a young footballer can come under. In his case, he had sought escape from the goldfish bowl through drink and gambling.

'I'd bet on anything,' he remarked. 'Gee-gees, snooker, darts, dogs, even indoor bowls. Then I started drinking heavily because I became so worried about my gambling debts.' Merson was no stranger to trouble. He had fallen prey to the footballer's habitual offence – drinking and driving – which had led to a club fine to add to the one imposed by the court. He was also suspended from the club for a period, an unprecedented act at Highbury. Before that episode he had been involved in a poolroom brawl and sent home in disgrace from a tour of the Far East.

Before the season started, with some powerful figures at the club wanting the player to be thrown out, his manager gave him 'one last chance'.

'He told me it was a make or break season and that he'd stuck his neck out for me,' Merson revealed. 'I was ready to pack up the game. I just didn't fancy it anymore. I got the feeling I was thought of as nothing but a troublemaker . . . George kept me when he probably shouldn't have.'

The combination of marriage, the arrival of a son and Graham's support, gave Merson the motivation to respond. Extra training to shed excess weight and a deliberate withdrawal from drink and gambling were the basis of the regime the player set himself. The results of his perseverance could now be seen in the fifteen goals he had scored and the improvement in his all-round play. His versatility had enabled the attack to cope with Limpar's absence. As George Graham put it, 'He is comfortable on the ball, and if you are comfortable on the ball it doesn't matter where you are on the pitch.' The goal against Liverpool completed his rehabilitation, and he drew new accolades from his manager, who said of his display at Anfield, 'He was superb. He can do it for me as a central striker, or in midfield, and on the right flank.' Gone was the despair of the last year, and Merson was now in serious contention for a full England place. Now, the player claims (paraphrasing what was said of Stan Bowles, the legendary gambler and sometime QPR and England midfield genius), he can 'pass betting shops as well as passing the ball'.

Paul Merson is not unique in his experiences. As he said himself, 'When you're a young footballer with nothing to do in the afternoons, temptation can get to you.' Other players had suffered a similar fate, although Merson's single-minded attitude once he decided to mend his ways was uncommon and deserves admiration. As with Tony Adams, Arsenal, or at least George Graham, stuck by Merson, but the point is surely that by the time the symptoms were treated, the disease could already have proved fatal.

Most young footballers who make it to professional status have been dedicated to the sport since an early age. Paul Merson himself wrote to *Jim'll Fix It* more than twenty times as a boy in order to get to meet his idol, Ray Wilkins. This obsessive attitude means that, with some individuals, the difficulties of coping with other facets of life are immense. While the gifted young player is intensely coached in football, he is not really helped to withstand the inevitable and unique pressures that accompany progress to the first team. At a club like Arsenal, where success is more or less expected and all involved come under the closest media scrutiny, young players are subjected to the kind of pressure most of us would find intolerable. To be judged, as a person as much as a player, every week by 30,000 partisan spectators, or millions of armchair fans if the game is televised, would be daunting enough for anybody. A successful young pro at a top club also has to cope with the large amounts of money he suddenly starts to earn. It is the equivalent of a senior managerial salary, but the recipient has not undergone any of the experiences or taken on any of the responsibilities that would normally have been accumulated over the years before that level of income is attained. The standard response of football clubs has been to encourage players to get married young and start a family as soon as possible. In Merson's case it seems to have been good advice, but perhaps, as often happens at the leading Continental clubs, the criterion for care and consideration should be age and temperament rather than the assumption that if a player is in the first team, he can handle all that life can throw at him.

George Graham must have been overjoyed when that goal went in at Anfield. In a team performance that had so much to admire, there were plaudits for virtually every player: Alan Smith had produced an exhilarating display of centre-forward play; David Hillier gave a solid performance in place, once again, of Paul Davis; Tony Adams marshalled the defence; Steve Bould was, as usual, like a rock; and David Seaman made the saves when necessary. In a first-class exhibition of the art of counter-attacking, eight out of the thirteen players deployed by George Graham were products of the Arsenal youth system, a quite staggering achievement. The Gunners were truly on top of the world, three points ahead of Liverpool with twelve matches to go.

The day after Kenny Dalglish resigned, Spurs, with their fifth-round Cup tie at Portsmouth out of the way, had to visit an improving Wimbledon. Unfortunately, events off the pitch and some poor performances on it had rendered Spurs incapable of taking advantage of Liverpool's plight. Indeed, if Liverpool were in trouble, what words could be used to describe the horrendous situation at White Hart Lane? At Plough Lane, fielding a make-shift side without Gazza, Tottenham just about hit rock-bottom, the high expectations of the early part of the season finally ground into the mud by the division's most basic team. Spurs crashed to a shambolic 5–1 defeat, their worst of the season. To complete the wretched story, Wimbledon, by virtue of this result, moved above Spurs in the table, and Venables' side dropped to eighth place. It is not an exaggeration to say that Spurs' entire future could now be determined by the fluctuations of fortune that decide the FA Cup.

On the morning of the Wimbledon game it was reported that an unnamed Italian club had bid £7 million for Paul Gascoigne. When asked about the bid, Terry Venables claimed ignorance. 'It may be true,' he said, 'although I don't know anything about it. But I wouldn't think they will consult me about it.' It is a strange state of affairs indeed when the manager knows nothing about the possible departure of his most influential player, the bedrock of his team. 'What has to be done is out of my hands,' Venables continued resignedly. 'I don't want Gazza to go . . . there is no point in me getting involved in it, getting frustrated. It will happen one way or the other . . . yes, of course it is a lot of money to turn down. It will be difficult for the club.'

Gascoigne, whose groin injury was keeping him out of the team unless absolutely necessary, was not the only absentee at Wimbledon. Paul Stewart, Pat Van Den Hauwe, David Howells, Terry Fenwick and Paul Walsh were all sidelined, and Venables revealed that he would have liked to have rested Gary Lineker too. 'Gary has had a few knocks,' he explained, 'he could do with a break but I couldn't afford to leave him out as well.' In fact, he might as well have left Lineker out for all the service he received during the match.

The porous Spurs defence, consisting of Edinburgh, Sedgley, Mabbutt and Bergsson, cracked as early as the ninth minute, when John Fashanu reached the byline and pulled the ball back for McGhee to score a simple goal. A less than coherent Spurs somehow stemmed the tide until the second half when Curle bent a free kick around the wall to give Wimbledon some daylight. After that, Spurs showed a bit of fight and even pulled a goal back when Bergsson turned up in the box to take advantage of some neat work by the substitute, Gray. The goal, instead of galvanizing Spurs (as it surely would have done Wimbledon if the situation were reversed), signalled a complete collapse, as the home side hit three more, two from left-wing crosses finished off by Gibson and Fashanu. Cork ended the humiliation with the fifth, three minutes from time. Despite the loss of so many first-choice performers, it was a shameful defeat, with the team showing none of the determination that had been so evident until the Liverpool defeat. The defence that had conceded so few goals early on (eight in the first thirteen matches) was now only a vague memory.

The Wimbledon coach and former Tottenham player Joe Kinnear offered an interesting perspective on his old club's problems in his comments after the match. 'It looks as if the club is in disarray,' he said. 'We are talking about one of the biggest clubs in the land, but now all you ever hear is talk about them selling and not buying, which was never the case in my day. During my time at White Hart Lane I was the only player in the team who was not bought.'

Terry Venables did his best to put a brave face on things, and to his credit he refused to criticize the team. Perhaps his own attention was being diverted by other matters. He was, after all, part of a consortium seeking to take over the club, and the outcome of that would determine his future. While the incumbent administration was in no position to provide money to strengthen the squad, Venables had taken his players just about as far as they could go. What made the situation more pressing was that the adjourned AGM was due in a few days, and the club's problems would soon have to be resolved one way or the other.

The meeting was convened in the Chanticleer restaurant, the one part of the White Hart Lane complex large enough to cater for the anticipated turnout of shareholders. The Tottenham Independent Supporters' Association (TISA) had distributed leaflets severely critical of the board in general and Irving Scholar in particular. Scholar himself expected to face some flak and still had to decide whether he was prepared to sell his stake in the club. The main thrust of his defence would be that he always acted in what he believed to be the best interests of the club. However, the Ashurst Morris Crisp report was critical of his actions, which resulted in Scholar resigning from the board of the plc because he had allegedly infringed the Companies Act in his dealings with Robert Maxwell, and meant he was only attending as a director of a subsidiary company – the football club.

The atmosphere surrounding the meeting was intense. A demonstration had been planned to take place outside and TISA had prepared a list of probing questions to which the board did not have proper answers. That things did not get entirely out of hand was due to the skilful and experienced handling of the meeting by Nat 'Stonewall' Solomon.

The new chairman accomplished the difficult feat of appearing to be forthright without actually saying anything of substance. He managed to defuse a potentially volatile situation by allowing the TISA questions to be put, even though direct answers were few and far between. He answered those who questioned his commitment to Tottenham's future by trenchantly declaring, 'After fifty-five years as a supporter, I have not accepted the chairmanship to preside over the demise of the club.' No detailed, up-to-date accounts were available, however, an incredible state of affairs considering the importance of the year's figures in any assessment of performance. Chief executive Ian Gray revealed some basic financial information, although it was by now well out of date – football activities were in profit by £2 million; non-football losses were £700,000; and interest payments reached £3.9 million, leaving an overall loss of £2.6 million. Total debts stood at £13.6 million and liabilities at £22.9 million. The directors were unable to say how these figures were made up, although Solomon said that the Midland Bank debt of £10 million could be called in at any moment should the bank so decree. This was because the club had exceeded its borrowing limit. The Midland had agreed to provide short-term support, while Solomon was installed to raise new capital and/or dispose of assets.

Solomon made it clear to the 700 shareholders that the choice for Spurs was stark. Either a new source of finance had to be found, or the big names would have to be sold, there was no other option. 'Regarding star players, namely Gascoigne and Lineker, I would like to say very clearly that I speak for the whole board when I say we fervently hope we can find a solution to our problems that will not require them to be sold. Nevertheless, if an offer is received by the board, we will have an inescapable responsibility to look at it carefully in the light of the prevailing circumstances.' The chairman added that 'no guarantee' could be given that any player would not be sold.

As far as new funds were concerned, Solomon stated that 'discussions' were in progress with three possible buyers, and that if a firm offer was forthcoming, the board of directors was prepared to go. Presumably, such a move would bring intolerable pressure to bear on Irving Scholar to sell his 26 per cent stake. One consortium, according to Solomon, included Terry Venables (but was now minus Frank Warren), a second was on behalf of the financial services company Baltic, while the identity of the third could not be revealed. This third option was apparently unconnected with Robert Maxwell, as Solomon reported that as far as he was concerned, 'All that is finished'. Maxwell, of course, was in a difficult position, since he had been unable to dispose of Derby and Oxford. Discussions were also taking place to sell one of the subsidiary companies, Martex, the textile operation, which Solomon said were 'at an advanced stage'.

Although Solomon's robust manner managed to avoid open warfare, there was still an air of hostility among the small shareholders, who knew they could be outvoted by the board and Irving Scholar at any stage. This was illustrated when votes were taken to re-elect the officers of the company. Nat Solomon, untainted by failure, was easily elected on a show of hands, but both Tony Berry and Ian Gray failed to gain enough support to retain their positions on the board. One shareholder considered it astounding that they were being asked to cast their votes for those responsible for the disastrous state of the club.

'I see no proposal in the report and accounts for the resignation of directors,' he said. 'Who is going to carry the can for this total disaster that you present to the meeting today?' After muttering some generalities about the directors being 'aware of their responsibilities', Solomon called for a full vote, produced over two million commitments from shareholders, and both Berry and Gray were re-elected. This move produced some booing and hissing, and allegations of 'financial hooliganism' were directed at the board, along with calls for their resignation.

Just about the only new information to come out of the meeting emerged when Irving Scholar was closely questioned about the interest on the loan made to Spurs by Robert Maxwell, which was channelled through Scholar's company, Holborn Property. Scholar, backed by Solomon, made it clear that he had not taken the extra 1 per cent interest that Holborn charged Spurs, over and above that charged by Maxwell to Holborn, nor had he cashed any dividend cheques from the years of profit.

Scholar's position eased when Paul Bobroff lost his temper and incurred the wrath of the meeting by saying that delays and increased costs in the construction of the East Stand were the result of having to take account of supporters' protests over the removal of the Shelf. As chairman of the plc at the time, Bobroff was the obvious person to blame, but until this meeting most of the opprobrium had fallen on Scholar. Scholar may well have infringed the Companies Act, but no one could say that he made any personal gain from the club, even in the profitable years, unlike several other First Division chairmen. On the contrary, he had dug deep into his own pockets on a number of occasions. However, being obliged to resign as a director of the plc should have alerted fans and shareholders to the possibility that this was nothing to do with technical breaches of financial law, which were anyway hardly on a par with insider trading, but more to do with Scholar's policy of acting in the best interests of the football club, rather than the banks. Solomon was their man precisely because they knew he could be relied upon to do what was necessary. Scholar may have been incompetent in his dealings, but there was no denying he would do everything in his power to keep Gascoigne and Lineker at the club. None the less, with the Maxwell deal seemingly dead and buried, his days as king were surely numbered. Either a consortium would take over, in which case he would be forced to sell, or Gascoigne would be sold, which he had publicly stated was a resignation issue. Although the long term may see him vindicated, for the moment Irving Scholar was truly caught between a rock and a hard place.

The League game against Chelsea the following Saturday came as a welcome intrusion into the saga of Tottenham's finances. Gazza played but looked less than fit, was booked and eventually substituted. All in all, it was a nothing game. Gary Lineker earned a penalty, which he himself put away, when Beasant brought him down, a goal that equalized an earlier header from Durie that had given Chelsea the lead. After that, the game simply petered out. Chelsea's season had ended when they were beaten in the semi-final of the Rumbelows Cup by Sheffield Wednesday and they contributed little. Spurs fared no better, apart from the occasional foray by Gascoigne.

With only the Cup left to aim for, Spurs looked forward to the sixth-round tie at home to Notts County, which was to be the BBC's live televised game of the round. Somehow, in a season when the wheels had come off the rails with increasing frequency, the team had clung to the dream of an FA Cup final. Such dreams, though, can be as precarious as Tottenham's finances. While Arsenal were on course for the double, Spurs had to win to keep the season, and perhaps the club, alive.

17

Easier Said than Done

By the first week of March, the worst of the winter weather had begun to recede. When half-time arrived in the FA Cup sixth-round clash between Spurs and Notts County at White Hart Lane, Spurs' fans must have wished the disruption had continued a little longer. It was not that Spurs were losing to what Terry Venables described as a 'miracle goal' that hurt so much, but the fact that Tottenham had been completely outplayed for forty-five minutes by the Second Division side and could have been even further behind. During the interval, Venables reminded the players of their plight. Paul Allen described the scene: 'He's not a shouter but there were some harsh words. He said, "They're first to the ball and first to the tackle. We've got to show the same attitude."'

According to Erik Thorstvedt, it was a chilling moment. 'He told us, "You haven't got much choice, you really have to go for it. It's forty-five minutes and if you don't do it you're out and that's the end of it." Everyone then really understood the serious nature of things.'

Underlying Venables' words, which could have been uttered by any losing manager during an FA Cup tie, was a deeper meaning. This Spurs team, unlike any in history, was playing for the club's very existence. When the manager said 'that's the end of it', he was not referring to some metaphorical fate, nor was he indulging in the rhetoric so beloved of football managers. It was nothing less than harsh reality. None of the possible sources of finance mentioned by Nat Solomon at the AGM had yet materialized and even Venables' own consortium seemed to have stalled for the time being. Lazio of Rome had stepped into the vacuum and it was no secret that they were seriously in pursuit of Paul Gascoigne. In the absence of any firm bids for the club, Solomon once again refused to rule out the sale of any player. For Spurs, exit from the FA Cup would not simply mean the end of a dream for another twelve months, it would cut the club off from perhaps the only avenue of salvation that did not entail the transfers of Gascoigne and Lineker, the sale of the club, or its demise. These were the stakes for which Spurs were playing and which weighed so heavily on the minds of Erik Thorstvedt and the rest of the team. At half-time, Spurs were literally forty-five minutes from oblivion.

Anyone who had seen Notts County in the Second Division would have known that, on their day, they were capable of producing attractive and effective football. Manager Neil Warnock could also field some of the most gifted young players in the lower divisions, particularly defender Dean Yates, midfielder Mark Draper and forward Kevin Bartlett.

'We knew it was going to be a difficult game,' said Paul Allen. 'For them to have got as far as they did they were going to be no pushover, and for the first forty-five minutes they gave us a fright.' During the build-up to the tie, Spurs had practised playing against the system they thought the opposition would employ. Erik Thorstvedt talked about what Spurs believed they would face by comparing the County approach to that employed by teams back home in Sweden. 'The Swedish game,' he said, 'is very tight, and no one gets any time on the ball. The one place where there is any room is between the goalkeeper and the defence and they keep knocking balls in there all the time. That's what we were expecting Notts County to do, so we trained quite a bit on that.'

In the event, County played the ball to feet, and Draper used his close control to run at the Spurs defence as much as possible.

Spurs created chances in the first half, but in the main they seemed to be nervous and looked a yard slower than County. Gazza played, but it was now obvious to everybody that he was not even half-fit. Overall, he did not enjoy the best of matches. On television, Jimmy Hill called him 'a liability', and that judgment could hardly be denied given that it was Gascoigne who lost possession in a crucial area to set up County for the opening goal, four minutes before half-time. As the ball came out of the Spurs penalty box, Gazza tried to flick it round the onrushing Harding, who made a timely interception. The ball reached O'Riordan on the left, who unleashed a mighty shot from thirty yards. It flew between the outstretched legs of Paul Allen – what it would have done to him had its course been marginally elevated hardly bares thinking about – and comprehensively beat Thorstvedt, as it would have any keeper.

It was no more than County deserved. Before the goal Spurs had enjoyed a number of escapes around their six-yard box. Draper revelled in the freedom given him by the Tottenham midfield and, supported by Thomas, began to hit some telling balls that caught the Spurs defence square time and again. Harding stuck close to Gascoigne and since Gazza was unfit, he was moved up front to ease the strain on his groin. The change of role, however, disrupted both the Spurs midfield and the attack. When Tottenham left the pitch at half-time they looked a thoroughly demoralized team.

It is to Venables' credit that, as against Portsmouth, he was able to lift his side's spirits sufficiently to produce a much improved performance in the second half. In a tactical switch, the manager pushed Paul Stewart further forward, while Gazza resumed his usual position in midfield. At last, Spurs began to exert some serious pressure on the opposition defence. It did not take long to crack, but there was more than an element of good fortune about the equalizer. Gascoigne took a short corner to Nayim, who turned and shot low and hard to goalkeeper Cherry's right. The ball was deflected and beat Cherry, going in off the keeper's left-hand post. Soon afterwards, Venables made another tactical move by sending on Vinny Samways and Paul Walsh for Nayim and Mitchell Thomas.

Harding marked Gascoigne the whole afternoon. It is a tactic Gazza does not like, and he eventually responded to being held back with an elbow in Harding's face. Although he claimed afterwards that he did not mean to fell his marker, Gazza was lucky to stay on the field. The break ensured that he was able to perform the moment of magic in the eighty-second minute that won the game for Tottenham. Both Sedgley and Mabbutt had pushed forward, and the former tried to play a one-two with the latter on the edge of the County penalty box. The ball somehow reached Walsh, who helped it into the area. Instead of Sedgley collecting the return, Gazza appeared from nowhere and hit a perfect first-time shot that flashed into the net. Gazza had once again risen above the limitations placed on him by his injury, this time with the winning goal. It had, as Venables admitted, been a gamble to play him, the more so after the double substitution, but it had paid off, just. County could justifiably claim to have been unlucky, especially when conceding the equalizing goal. But Gascoigne had once again delivered the goods and Neil Warnock made it clear afterwards that, in his opinion, even a half-fit Gazza 'was the difference between the teams'. The feeling in the Spurs camp was generally, as Erik Thorstvedt put it, one of 'joy and relief. I even hugged Steve Sedgley!'

The Tottenham management confirmed after the game that Gascoigne's injury had made his appearance touch-and-go. David Butler, the Spurs physio, revealed that Gazza had almost not made it past the pre-match warm up.

'He ran over to the bench and said he could feel the injury,' Butler said. 'We immediately had substitute Vinny Samways warming up, but in the end Gazza was fine.'

Terry Venables talked about Gazza's move into the attack, saying, 'We allowed him periods to play up front because we did not feel he could motor up and down in midfield for ninety minutes.' The player's immediate future was going to present a dilemma to his manager. 'If we had drawn today,' said Venables, 'he would not have been able to make the replay. He needs longer and longer to recover. I would not rule out surgery this week, but I just don't know yet. It was a risk to play him, but I was going to leave him on the field unless he complained.' Clearly, the situation could not continue. Yet so important was Gazza to the Spurs team that to lose him for possibly two months was too awful to contemplate. It was not only the contribution Gascoigne made to Spurs' play on the pitch: he also wielded enormous influence behind the scenes on the morale of the whole squad.

Spurs' improved display in the second period was exemplified by the performance of Paul Allen. Even Allen's famed scrapping qualities were not enough to keep County at bay in the first half, but after the interval he was instrumental in helping Spurs to push forward, and two runs in particular, made into the heart of the Notts defence, gave both team and supporters fresh heart.

'It was a difficult game,' he said afterwards. 'It wasn't a passing game, it was just a very committed game where you're closing people down. It was very tight but I enjoyed it, especially the result.'

Paul Allen came to Spurs in 1985 with a big reputation. Not only was he on the fringe of full England honours, he also belonged to one of Britain's most illustrious footballing families, two of whom, besides Paul, played for Spurs with distinction. Les Allen will always be remembered by Spurs fans as a member of the double-winning team, while his son, Clive, had already played for England when Paul arrived and went on to score forty-nine goals for Tottenham in the 1986–7 season. The family has also given two other members to London football, Martin at West Ham and Bradley at Queen's Park Rangers. Paul was renowned for being the youngest player to appear in an FA Cup final, a record he achieved in 1980, aged seventeen years and 236 days.

Allen joined West Ham, the club he had always supported, as a youngster. Having been part of the Cup final team that beat Arsenal, he went on to play in the following season's European campaign, when the Hammers reached the quarter-final before going out to Dynamo Tbilisi after one of the most memorable performances by a foreign side on English soil (the Soviets beat West Ham 4–1 at Upton Park). Under-21 and Under-23 honours followed, and he was picked for the England 'B' team but had to withdraw through injury.

A down-to-earth individual, Allen is unassuming to the point of modesty. He has no discernible interests outside football and his family, and is unconcerned by the attention lavished on his more famous colleagues. Nevertheless, he was sufficiently aware of his momentous Cup final appearance to savour every moment. Not for him the oft-heard lament that the day 'passed me by'. Years later, as he spoke about the experience, it became obvious that even as a youngster he was willing to listen and learn.

'So many people said to me, "It goes by and you don't remember the day,"' he recalled. 'So I made a big thing about it to make sure I took it all in and didn't forget it. It was a great experience, the whole day and the whole weekend. Travelling through the streets on the coach with the Cup . . . I'll never forget it.' This trait is also apparent in his attitude to football, as he explained when he talked with something approaching reverence of his team-mates during his period at White Hart Lane. 'I've enjoyed it since I've been here and especially to play alongside some of the great players at this club. I've been fortunate to play with the likes of Glenn Hoddle, Ossie Ardiles, Chris Waddle, Gary Lineker and Paul Gascoigne. You can learn things from them, you watch what they do in training and learn.'

Allen's style of play has not always endeared him to the fans, although they realize he is a totally committed player who always looks to be giving everything. He enjoys the role of closing opposing players down. 'Everyone loves to see skill,' he said, 'but I think the crowd also appreciate the other side of the game, when you get behind the ball and win it back.' The importance of his role is reflected in the prevailing view that when he plays well, Spurs play well. Perhaps the one area in which he has not fulfilled his potential is goalscoring, though he believes it is more in his style to 'make things happen' for others.

The early success at West Ham was not repeated, as the club failed to build on the achievements of promotion, Cup success and Europe. His last season at Upton Park was a good one for the club, but since his contract was coming to an end, he decided to move on.

'There was paper talk of Arsenal under Don Howe being interested, but when it came to talking it was between Liverpool and Spurs,' he said. Joe Fagan, and later Kenny Dalglish, came to London to offer terms, and Allen was tempted. In the end, domestic considerations played the biggest part in his decision. His wife was pregnant, they were both Londoners, and a move north was too much of an upheaval in the circumstances. 'Perhaps if we'd had the children,' he mused, 'or if we were married with no children, it would have been different.'

The honours Allen wants desperately to win have not been forthcoming since his move across London. Having been picked once more for England's 'B' squad, when he again had to withdraw because of injury, he has since been consigned to the international wilderness. But, at twenty-eight, Allen was certainly not dismissing the possibility of an England future, and has a good few years at the top ahead of him.

The day before the Spurs–Notts County game, Arsenal met Third Division Cambridge United at Highbury. It was the second year running that Cambridge had reached the sixth round of the Cup, the previous season as a Fourth Division team. While Arsenal were obviously hot favourites, nothing could be taken for granted, particularly when 10,000 Cambridge supporters turned up at Highbury to create a marvellous atmosphere and lift their side. They were determined to enjoy themselves at perhaps the biggest match in which the club had ever taken part. A good example of their idiosyncratic approach was evident when David Seaman was taking goal-kicks. Instead of the usual 'you're shit . . . aaargh', the Cambridge contingent adapted the chant to incorporate their emblem, the moose. Accompanied by a series of intricate hand movements that culminated in a passable imitation of the animal's antlers, the crowd chanted 'Ooh . . . ooh . . . ooh . . . ooh . . . MOOOOSE'. The strange ritual had started when goalkeeper John Vaughan arrived from Fulham. His unkempt hair and subsequent use of liberal amounts of gel led to the fans likening him to a moose (or mousse?). So popular did the image become that it ended up on Cambridge products sold in the club shop.

When the game started it became clear that the Cambridge manager, John Beck, was going to ensure that if his team went down they would go down fighting. He had the audacity to play a 4-2-4 system, with two out-and-out wingers in Philpott and Cheetham. Arsenal lined up with five at the back, Bould, Adams and O'Leary filling the heart of the defence. Merson was asked to play in the position the injured Limpar would usually occupy – wide on the left. More surprising was the omission of Paul Davis in favour of David Hillier. Once again, George Graham was showing his belief in the strength of his squad, while at the same time reminding Davis that no one was indispensable. Graham may also have been seeking to influence the long-running contractual negotiations he was having with the player.

For the opening twenty minutes Cambridge gave as good as they got. Indeed Lee Dixon and Nigel Winterburn were made to endure such a torrid time from the two wingers that they hardly ventured forward. Gradually, Arsenal began to gain a measure of control, although they displayed little in the way of flair. When the full backs did advance, both produced telling crosses. First Dixon found Kevin Campbell at the near post, but the striker put his shot wide. Two minutes later, Campbell made amends by scoring with a perfect glancing header, this time from Winterburn's cross. Soon afterwards, Dixon delivered another pin-point centre. Campbell missed it but Alan Smith was right behind him and his shot brought an excellent save from keeper Vaughan. Merson almost added to the score just before half-time, but his header went across the face of the Cambridge goal before being scrambled away. A 1–0 lead at the interval may not have seemed comfortable, but there had been little evidence after the first twenty minutes that Cambridge could come back. Then, after five minutes of the second half, the visitors equalized with a splendid goal. Cheetham left Winterburn for dead and crossed to the near post, where Dion Dublin met the ball on the volley. It seemed to take a slight deflection off Tony Adams before looping over Seaman into the opposite corner of the net.

The outcome of the match turned on two crucial incidents involving the Arsenal captain. Ten minutes after the Cambridge equalizer, Arsenal won a corner on the right. The ball came to Adams, who bulldozed his way forward before finding Bould. Bould chipped sweetly for Smith at the far post, Vaughan managed to palm Smith's header on to the bar, but it dropped perfectly for Adams, who had continued his run, to apply the finishing touch. A minute later Taylor was clean through for Cambridge but Seaman blocked his shot with a brave dive at the striker's feet. The ball spun to Dublin, but in the time it took for him to produce a shot, Tony Adams had thrown himself into the ball's intended path and it was deflected away. Cambridge were not finished, and could have snatched another equalizer on at least two occasions as the Arsenal defence creaked. At one point a heated argument ensued between Dixon and Adams and the pair had to be separated by Dublin. Somehow, the Gunners held out, but it had been too close for comfort.

The confrontation between Adams and Dixon showed the nervousness Arsenal still occasionally displayed at the back. For Dixon, it seemed totally out of character. He had been caught upfield when Cambridge won the ball and swept it out to Philpott, who was lurking in the space Dixon had been occupying. Philpott took the ball on and very nearly scored. Adams had a go at Dixon for being out of position, and Dixon, in the pressure of the moment, exploded, believing that Adams should have covered for him. Although it was Dixon who appeared to lose his temper first, he was mindful of how Adams had been particularly psyched up before the game. 'He was buzzing around in training like I've never seen him buzzing before,' Dixon revealed later. Adams was certainly important to Arsenal, as his winning goal had proved, but since his release from prison he had appeared to some observers to have exceeded even his own high threshold of commitment. George Graham had recognized as much, saying, 'He'll admit he's not back to top form. I brought him back [after his release from prison] because I knew he had the character. He's still a little rusty, but his performances have been satisfactory.'

After the game Graham was predictably asked whether the double was now a possibility. 'If we win every game,' he quipped, 'we've got a chance.' The Cambridge manager, John Beck, had no such reservations and was fulsome in his praise.

'They've got something special,' he said. 'They've got strength, desire, character, quality passers, quality finishers. The list goes on. I don't think they've got any weaknesses.'

Graham gave an insight into the reasons why his team had not looked particularly fluent. He had studied a video of Cambridge's fifth-round victory, when they thrashed Sheffield Wednesday 4–0. 'Wednesday approached the tie believing they would out-football them with passing, and just got completely overrun. They play the percentage game, and there's always been a problem with teams that play that system. You've just got to beat them.'

Graham was dismissive of the altercation between his two defenders. 'There was nothing wrong with it,' he asserted. 'In fact, it was great. I like to see passion in my players. That is how determined we have become. If someone is not doing their job, the others react to sort it out.' Graham must have been putting a brave face on things. The referee, Ron Groves, praised Dion Dublin for intervening, and while he agreed that the argument never got out of hand, he also said that it could have resulted in at least one sending off had it not been for Dublin. Dublin was sure 'they would have exchanged blows' had he not pulled them apart. In a typical gesture, Adams, once the tension of playing had disappeared with the final whistle, went to the referee and apologized. Although the flare-up was over in just a few seconds, it once again illustrated the way Arsenal walked the thin line between commitment – the desire, in Graham's words, to throw off the image of 'southern softies' – and a breakdown in discipline. They had overstepped the mark at Old Trafford and paid a penalty that might still cost them the Championship. This time they had, thanks to an opposing player, stopped just short of disaster.

While Arsenal were otherwise engaged in the Cup, Liverpool were announcing that their Championship challenge was by no means over. A 3–0 defeat of Manchester City at Maine Road, courtesy of two debatable first-half penalties converted by Molby, put the Merseysiders on fifty-seven points, the same as Arsenal, although Liverpool had now played twenty-seven games to Arsenal's twenty-six.

Before thoughts could return to the League, the FA Cup had one last twist to deliver. Hopes of the first all north London final were dashed when Arsenal and Spurs were drawn together in the semi-final. It was the first time it had happened at this stage of the Cup, although they had met in the two-legged semi-final of the Littlewoods Cup in 1987. The FA immediately decided to break with tradition and hold the semi-final at Wembley. It may well have been the case that two sets of London-based fans heading up the M1 for Villa Park at the same time would have proved chaotic. Wembley, therefore, was the obvious choice, and there was little dissent except from supporters of the other semi-finalists, West Ham and Nottingham Forest, and those who felt that playing a semi-final at Wembley detracted from the mystique of the place.

The scene was set for one of the biggest confrontations in the history of games between the two clubs, the most important since

1971, when Arsenal clinched the League title in front of over 50,000 people at White Hart Lane. The draw also meant that at least one of the two teams would end an incident-packed season with a Wembley Cup final. The 80,000 at Wembley would be the biggest crowd in the history of north London derbies, an unusual record in these days of reduced capacities.

For Spurs, the match was a matter of survival: they had to win to keep themselves in business. And as Terry Venables was involved in a consortium to buy the club, and Irving Scholar was hanging on in the hope that victory in the Cup might yet save him, the further Spurs progressed, the more difficult it would be for Venables to assume control.

Wembley would be no place for a half-fit Paul Gascoigne. And Arsenal would surely not give him the space that the lower-division opponents had allowed him in the earlier rounds of the Cup. Before the week was out, the decision had been taken and Gazza entered hospital for surgery on his injured groin, which had been diagnosed as a double hernia. It was now touch-and-go whether he would make it at all for the semi-final, but in the circumstances it was the only decision the player and the manager could realistically take.

Spurs' next match was away to Aston Villa, who welcomed back David Platt after a lay-off with a similar complaint to Gascoigne's. Spurs must have wished his reappearance had been delayed a while, as Platt hit a hat-trick in a 3–2 defeat. The Villa goals were all described by Venables as 'lousy', but in truth the Spurs defence put in a poor performance, failing to close down the opposition and naïvely relying on an offside game. This was meat and drink to Gordon Cowans, who spent the match chipping the ball over Spurs' square back line. In the twelfth minute, and again twenty minutes later, Platt made runs from deep positions to latch on to passes over the top from Cowans. This straightfor-ward tactic put Villa two up. Just after half-time, the Spurs defence got in a real mess when defending a corner and, left with the task of turning and beating Thorstvedt, Platt again made no mistake. A late rally saw goals from Samways and Allen reduce the deficit, but they were as much due to Villa's nervousness as any new-found purpose on the part of the Spurs side. Lineker was substituted on the hour by Philip Gray after complaining of a bad back. The England striker, like the whole team, looked out of sorts. The absence of Gazza, and the problems of Lineker, had reduced the side to the ranks of the ordinary. Tottenham had now dropped to ninth place.

Liverpool, meanwhile, were beating Sunderland in a match at Anfield that the Wearsiders dominated for long periods and at least deserved to draw. For twenty-four hours Liverpool would be back heading the League, and the pressure was on Arsenal to beat Leeds in a televised game at Highbury the following day to replace them once more at the top.

The Leeds match was the sixth of the season between the two clubs, and the cliché that familiarity breeds contempt could be seen in the size of the crowd, at 26,000, the second lowest of the season. A dull game was won in the end by two second-half goals from Kevin Campbell, who was at last proving that his prolific goalscoring record in the youth and reserve teams could be reproduced at the higher level. The first came after an astute Smith pass at last unlocked the Leeds defence and left Campbell with only Lukic to beat. The second resulted from a David Seaman punt, which was touched on by Smith. Chris Fairclough should have cleared the danger, but a terrible back pass went straight to Campbell, who hooked the ball into the net.

The way George Graham had handled Campbell's raw talent was proving to be just right. When criticized for not buying a striker at the beginning of the season, he had pointed to the potential of Campbell as one of the reasons why. The youngster, another product of the Arsenal youth policy, had been brought on carefully, with limited exposure to first-team action. Two loan spells with Leyton Orient and Leicester had been hugely success-ful. Nine goals in sixteen games helped Orient win promotion to the Third Division in 1989. At Leicester he had been an immedi-ate hit with the fans; his five goals in eleven games helped the club stave off relegation to the Third Division and, according to manager David Pleat, 'gave the whole place a lift'. Campbell possesses, according to Pleat, 'the ability to galvanize a team, to turn a close situation into a winning situation, [and] a raw, powerful, surging run, where people bounce off him or just can't cope with him'. When Pleat had arranged the loan, George Graham made it clear that Campbell was not for sale and Pleat agreed not to attempt to sign the player permanently. Such was his impact, however, that the Leicester directors told Pleat to make Arsenal an offer. When Pleat refused, the directors contacted Arsenal themselves to see if they could arrange a transfer. But as Pleat said: 'They are not fools at Arsenal. George Graham knew how good Campbell was, and there was no way they were going to sell him.'

The lack of chances at Arsenal was explained by Graham. 'It's a matter of timing when to bring players into the team to maximum effect,' he said, 'and I couldn't have plotted it any better. He [Campbell] has hardly been in the team all season, and when I brought him in it was like the beginning of the season for him and he was just raring to go. It was almost like a new signing prior to the [transfer] deadline.'

The injury to Anders Limpar gave Campbell his first opportunity of a sustained run in the first team, and he responded to it with those priceless commodities − goals. He scored four in five games, even though he was playing out of position for much of the time, being pushed out wide when he is more of an old-fashioned striker in the mould of a Bobby Smith or, more recently, Ronnie Rosenthal. The experience that comes with regular First Division football could well see Campbell emerge as the most effective partner for Alan Smith in the Arsenal attack. It could be a lethal combination. Smith's clever positioning (often with his back to goal) and adroit control could provide Campbell with the opportunity to run at defences and open up avenues to goal.

Arsenal's chief scout, Steve Burtenshaw, says Campbell is improving all the time: 'He's not just running straight, which he used to do, he's making runs which make it difficult for people to stay with him.'

Howard Wilkinson blamed the defeat on a poor display by his team. 'We just weren't at the races,' he said. 'Arsenal didn't have to do much to beat us . . . It was a scrappy, untidy game and it probably looked awful on television.'

Arsenal's overall performance might have been less than convincing, but again they had ground out a result when it mattered, just like the Liverpool of old. Their reward was to regain their place at the top on goal difference, with their game in hand due the following Wednesday, at home to Nottingham Forest.

The day after the Leeds game, Graham Taylor announced his England squad to face the Republic of Ireland in a vital European Championship tie at Wembley the following week. The surprise was not the selection of Seaman or Dixon, or that Merson, Smith and Thomas were placed on standby, but the recall of Tony Adams. Taylor justified his choice by saying that after Adams had got back into the Arsenal team, 'it was just a question of what my eyes were telling me. They told me to put him back in.' Taylor was either looking at Adams through rose-tinted glasses, or a bout of tunnel vision precluded him from noticing that it was Steve Bould, playing the best football of his life, who was anchoring the Arsenal defence. Surely Bould was more likely to slot in smoothly alongside Mark Wright and Des Walker in a strengthened defensive formation than Adams, who had still, as his manager had noted, not regained peak form and fitness.

George Graham changed the system again for the visit of Forest. The midlanders' season had been in and out, some good performances and some awful ones, but Graham knew they were capable of playing flowing football, and their confidence must have received a boost when they made it to the semi-final of the FA Cup. David O'Leary came in at right back, presumably to prevent the forward runs of Stuart Pearce. Dixon was pushed into a midfield role to stifle Roy Keane, and Graham decided to play with four at the back. The line-up was designed to stop Forest's explosive counter-attacks and the threat of Nigel Clough, a player with the ability to unhinge a defence with one pass.

On the night, Forest were largely bereft of attacking ideas. This could hardly be blamed on the high wind blowing around Highbury, since Forest's game entails playing the ball to feet. Arsenal took control from the start and Kevin Campbell got his fifth goal in six games after half an hour to put the Gunners ahead. Paul Davis, back because Hillier was suffering from tonsillitis, headed on a Seaman goal-kick to Michael Thomas who instantly set Campbell free. Campbell's strike past Forest keeper Crossley bore all the hallmarks of a player full of confidence. Merson looked increasingly effective on the left, often making incisive runs into the Forest box, but somehow the goals that would have sewn the game up refused to flow.

Seven minutes after half-time, Forest made their one committed excursion into the Arsenal penalty box, and it brought them the equalizer. Adams was harshly penalized for handball in a dangerous position near the edge of the box, Clough hammered the ball into the wall and it ricocheted to Jemson, who turned and volleyed into Seaman's left-hand corner. Anders Limpar, recovered from injury, came on with Perry Groves with fifteen minutes left, but although Limpar drove a free kick against a post, the winner simply would not come. Instead, Arsenal had Groves to thank for a last-ditch tackle which denied Parker as Forest began to put together some menacing breaks.

The result meant that Forest had ended Arsenal's run of six successive victories and had prevented them going three points ahead of Liverpool. Still, with both contenders having played twenty-eight games, Arsenal were a precious point ahead. In 1989, Graham's team had come from behind to snatch the title from Liverpool at the last gasp. Now the question was whether they could keep their nerve from the pole position.

George Graham remained philosophical. 'It was just one of those games,' he said. 'You are going to get quite a few of those over the course of a season, so you just forget about them and say, "Who do we play next?"'

As the Championship race entered the final straight with ten games to go, Graham could reflect with some satisfaction on the achievements of his team so far. The title was theirs for the taking, its destination entirely in the hands of his players. There was also the encounter with Spurs at Wembley to look forward to. Those connected with Tottenham would have liked to have been able to feel the same. Unfortunately, this was not possible, as yet again speculation concerning the sale of both the club and Paul Gascoigne overshadowed their exploits on the field. By the time of the Wembley clash, it was conceivable that Gascoigne would be gone or that the club would be under new management.

18

Buongiorno, Roma!

On the evening of Wednesday 13 March, an executive jet from Rome touched down at Southend airport. The Essex seaside town was an unusual destination for someone heading ultimately for London, but the passengers on this particular flight were eager to avoid any possibility of being spotted by the media, so much so that the plane had flown via Geneva and Zurich to throw reporters off the scent. The next day, Gian Marco Calleri, Carlo Regalia and Maurizio Manzini waited patiently at Claridge's hotel for the arrival of Nat Solomon, Irving Scholar and a leading agent, Dennis Roach. They had come to finalize the transfer of Paul Gascoigne to Lazio.

After the World Cup, there had been much speculation concerning the possible sale of Gascoigne to an Italian club. Juventus had reportedly made the running and offered £10 million, which Spurs had turned down. Another bid came via an Italian company called Studio Legale, which, as the name implies, had carried out legal work for a number of Italian clubs, including Lazio. Ostensibly acting on behalf of one of the Milan clubs, Studio Legale contacted a Leeds-based agent, Majid Muhammed, and asked him to approach Tottenham for Paul Gascoigne and Gary Lineker. He was authorized to bid £8 million for both players. Irving Scholar turned the offer down flat.

Then in mid-February, Majid received another call from Studio Legale. This time he was told that Lazio wanted to make a bid for Gascoigne and were prepared to offer £5 million. He later told BBC Radio's *File on Four* what happened next.

'I thought I wouldn't go to Irving Scholar because last time he refused completely. I thought the person who would make the decision would be Nat Solomon . . . so I approached Nat Solomon. I spoke to him in his office in Berkeley Square. He said that none of their players was for sale but "if you make an offer in writing I'll take it from there."'

Majid obliged and sent Solomon a fax on 18 February confirming that 'a client from Italy' was interested in purchasing Paul Gascoigne for £5 million. Nat Solomon's reply was tersely negative. Majid relayed the news to Studio Legale, who told him to raise the bid to £7 million. Again Solomon said Spurs were not interested. The rejections must have had an effect in Italy, because Studio Legale began to pressurize Majid into producing some movement.

Majid decided that there was only one way of bringing pressure to bear on Solomon. He leaked the story of Lazio's £7 million bid to the press, just as the Spurs AGM was due to take place. Majid did it, he said 'to let the creditors know'. The offer was then increased to £8 million. The reply from Solomon this time was more welcoming, but only just. Provided that the identity of the prospective buyer was revealed and Majid could produce evidence that he was authorized to negotiate on the buyer's behalf, Solomon would meet him at 4.30 p.m. on 5 March.

Nat Solomon carried the day at the AGM, but he realized the situation was fast becoming untenable. The shares were still suspended, none of the consortia who might make a bid for the club had come up with an acceptable offer, and the Midland Bank had transferred the club's debt to its 'intensive care' division and could at any time appoint an administrator to run the club while assets were sold off. Solomon told Irving Scholar in no uncertain terms that they must take positive steps to ward off creditors. Scholar, who had publicly stated that the sale of Gascoigne would be a resignation issue, was in an invidious position, but it suited his purposes to go along with Solomon's proposal to send a representative to Italy to actively seek out clubs who might be interested in buying either Gascoigne or Lineker. Italy, as the richest football market in the world, was always rife with stories of transfer deals. Often, approaches are made that turn out to have no substance, so it was imperative for Tottenham to know if there was any real interest behind the Majid approach.

The man they turned to was no stranger to either Spurs or the wealthy clubs on the Continent. He was Dennis Roach, a players' agent. Roach had handled the sales of Glenn Hoddle to Monaco and Clive Allen to Bordeaux but had fallen out with Scholar because of what Roach saw as Scholar's interminable interference in the transfer negotiations that took Chris Waddle to Marseille. Scholar was now forced to put any lingering resentment aside and to hope that Roach could deliver the goods. For Scholar, the decision to bring in Roach could be presented as a serious attempt to resolve the club's financial difficulties, as demanded by its creditors. If Roach's mission proved successful and a firm offer materialized, at whatever price, he could claim it was not enough and frustrate the sale. Solomon took the plan more seriously. The transfer of Gascoigne was an easier option than selling the club, which could involve months of negotiations yet still end in deadlock. So at the end of February, Roach left for Italy. The terms of Roach's involvement were clearly laid out for him in writing. He could not agree any deal; the thrust of his task was to conduct a 'market evaluation' of key company 'assets', particularly Paul Gascoigne.

His quest took him to AC Milan, Juventus and Napoli. While Gascoigne was viewed in Italy as one of the best players in Europe, there was a widespread belief that his temperament was 'too English' and it would be an expensive gamble to bring him to the Italian League. Milan, however, seemed prepared to take the risk. Moreover, there was one club president who had been a fan of Gazza's for two years and who had no qualms about the Englishman he believed could help revive his team. He had already used an intermediary to test the waters but had been rebuffed. Soon, a much better opportunity would present itself.

Gian Marco Calleri presided over a club that had seen better days. Lazio of Rome are best remembered for the team of the mid-seventies, which won the club's only Italian championship in 1974 but earned a reputation for cynical manipulation of the rules and officials, and brutality towards the opposition. Two European ties in particular, against Arsenal and Ipswich, are recalled with horror by those who experienced them. After the

Ipswich confrontation, Lazio were banned from European competitions for a year and thus missed their only opportunity to enter the European Cup. Their star in those days was Giorgio Chinaglia, who was brought up in Swansea and later went on to become president of Lazio after a period as one of the few successes of the ill-fated North American Soccer League with New York Cosmos. Chinaglia's Lazio side provided one of the few occasions when a team from the capital overcame the supremacy of Milan and Turin, the traditional power-centres of Italian football. Roma have won two championships, one during the war, the other in 1983, and have had some success in the Italian Cup, with six wins to Lazio's one, but neither Lazio nor Roma have permanently disturbed the dominance of the northern clubs, Juventus, Torino, Milan and Internazionale, although Roma finished in the top three six times in the eighties, reached the European Cup Final in 1984 (when they lost on penalties to Liverpool), and made it to the final of the UEFA Cup in 1991. In Rome, Lazio are the second club, having spent six seasons in *serie B* (the second division) during the last ten years. The club was relegated in 1980 along with Milan for fixing a match in order to aid Milan's championship challenge. However, if Lazio could do well and recapture the days of Chinaglia, the Olympic Stadium, which they share with Roma, would be packed every week.

Between Lazio's triumph in 1974 and Roma's in 1983, the title stayed in either Milan or Turin. The stranglehold was only truly broken when other presidents began to believe they could emulate the rulers at the elite clubs, but these did not come from Rome. First Verona came from nowhere to snatch the championship in 1985, then two unfashionable clubs made the breakthrough to the big time with bold policies. Sampdoria, from Genoa, and Napoli, in their different ways, at last began to seriously upset the old order. Napoli bought Maradona and won the double in 1987 and a further championship in 1990. Sampdoria bought Trevor Francis and Graeme Souness, reached the Cup-Winners' Cup final in 1989, won it the following year and were well on their way towards the *Scudetto* (the league championship) as the 1991 season was reaching its climax. These successes forced the old guard to respond, and the Italian league went from strength to strength. In 1990 – through Milan, Juventus and Sampdoria – Italy provided the winners of all three European competitions.

Football holds a special place in Italian life. Active support for the game comes from all classes. The rich and powerful like to be seen at games, and the presidents of clubs are the focus of attention from both fans and media. The press often portrays matches as personalized confrontations between owners, such as Pellegrini (Inter) v. Agnelli (Juventus), or Mantovani (Sampdoria) v. Berlusconi (Milan). Companies and organizations, as well as individuals and families, are intimately involved in the fortunes of their local clubs. One particular sector that plays an important part in these relationships is the banking industry.

Italy's banks are not national institutions, like the big four in Britain. Rather, they are regionally based. This means that they have to maintain closer ties with the communities they serve than is the case in the UK. One of the ways they do this is through the national sport, football. Banks the length and breadth of the country are associated with football clubs, often as sponsors. In addition, they often sell season tickets as a service to customers. Thus the relationship with the football club goes much deeper than that between sponsor and club in England. The money the banks provide, either by way of sponsorship or cheap loans, is generally spent on improving the team, since Italian clubs do not own their own stadia.

Lazio's sponsor is a savings bank, the Casa di Risparmio di Roma. Many Italian banks ally themselves to overseas counterparts in order to overcome the handicap of being regionally based in their own country. The Casa di Risparmio is linked to a British bank, the Midland.

After stabilizing Lazio's first division status (they finished tenth and ninth the previous seasons), president Calleri, with support from the Casa di Risparmio, went into the transfer market. A promising young winger, Paolo di Canio, was sold to Juventus for £3.5 million, but £4.8 million was spent on Karl-Heinz Riedle from Werder Bremen in Germany. When the spending did not produce the improvement Calleri expected, he turned his attention once again to possible imports. The Casa di Risparmio would have known just how desperate the situation at Tottenham was. It is often the case that feelers are put out in the international transfer market through middle-men. If this fails to bring about the intended objective, other routes are found. When Calleri was alerted to the continuing turmoil at Tottenham, and the pressure the club was now coming under from the Midland Bank, it was not long before Dennis Roach was on his way to Rome.

Majid Muhammed was now out of the picture. His ploy of leaking the story to the press had brought some success, but not to him. Those at Spurs were obviously annoyed at the leak and would not have lost any sleep if Majid were cut out. Similarly, Lazio, once contact was firmly established with Tottenham through Dennis Roach, had no further need of either Studio Legale or Majid Muhammed. In fact, neither party had been officially sanctioned by Lazio to carry out transfer negotiations. Lazio did, however, face competition from Milan, and Roach returned to London with two offers, both valuing Gascoigne at £5 million. Of the two, Lazio appeared the more enthusiastic and committed, so much so that initially Roach thought they were fronting for Juventus. Unlike their English counterpart, the Italian League operates strict financial controls, and participation in transfer activity depends on the status of the club in question. In this system, clubs are divided into categories. In Category One there is no limit to the amount a club is allowed to bid for a player. Roach confirmed that Lazio was a Category One club, therefore the money to finance the Gascoigne deal must have been available.

No matter what Roach achieved in Italy, little could actually be accomplished without the consent of Gascoigne himself. When Gascoigne's advisers, Len Lazarus and Mel Stein, heard about Roach's trip, Stein dispatched a solicitor's letter to complain that Roach had no right to conduct negotiations on behalf of his client, so Roach had to arrange for Tottenham to write to Stein explaining his position. Players' agents are often berated by clubs for the way they have increased their influence in recent years. Here was a role-reversal, with Spurs recognizing that Roach was one of the few people who could walk into any of the big European clubs. Only by using a man with his credentials could the authenticity of any offer be established. Despite Lazarus's and Stein's protestations, they were sufficiently interested in the results of Roach's talks with Lazio to make urgent plans to visit Italy themselves.

Lazarus and Stein arrived in Rome on Thursday 7 March. They had flown from Milan, where they had watched the European Cup quarter-final first leg between AC Milan and Marseille, a game that provided gate receipts of over £2 million from a crowd of 81,000. After two hours of negotiations with Calleri and the rest of the Lazio management, which were continued the following morning in a restaurant near Rome airport, Lazarus and Stein returned to London. They were impressed with what they had been told.

News of Lazio's bid hit the English press just before the sixth-round FA Cup tie against Notts County. Nat Solomon described the reports as 'pure speculation', while Terry Venables claimed no knowledge of the deal and seemed visibly upset that such a thing could emerge on the eve of the most important game of the season. 'If he is going to Lazio,' he fumed, 'I don't know anything about it.'

In Rome, the lack of a positive statement from Tottenham was taken as a negotiating tactic – a typically English ploy which neither confirmed nor denied the reports – one which was described as 'eloquent silence'. On the day of the game against Notts County, more details emerged of the Lazio bid: Gascoigne would be offered a three-year contract with an option for a fourth year; there would be a house in the up-market Parioli area of Rome; the Gascoigne endorsement and promotion machine could transpose itself to Italy with no interference from the club; and there would be a plethora of bodyguards, provided by a security company called Mondialpol, which is owned by Calleri. What did not appear in the press was the enormous signing-on fee that would take Gascoigne's salary package to well over seven figures. Dennis Roach, who had been involved in negotiations like this for many years, had never seen anything to rival it.

When Terry Venables found out about the moves to sell Gascoigne he was undoubtedly agitated. With the active support of a Spurs director, Tony Berry, he had been working for some time to put together a consortium to buy the club, but the retention of Gazza was central to his plans. The Spurs manager had joined forces with a Scottish property developer, Larry Gillick, who had been involved in a failed enterprise comprising a dog track and football stadium in Ayr in 1980, and had since moved to London, where he had been rather more successful. Finance was available to the consortium, although its source remained obscure. With events overtaking them, the Venables–Gillick consortium was forced to declare its hand sooner than its members would have liked, and in the days before the Notts County game they went public with the story that they were about to make a firm offer to the Tottenham board. Meanwhile, another takeover plan, put forward by Michael Goddard, chairman of the finance group Baltic, which envisaged a discounted £6 million rights issue, a share price of 40p and the raising of £5 million in convertible loan stock, was rejected. It was also rumoured that a similar package to Goddard's was being put together by Paul Bobroff, but no firm offer was forthcoming from him.

Nat Solomon had a somewhat different agenda. He believed he could use his City sources to negotiate a rights issue package of his own and had talked with corporate finance companies, one of which was Hambro Magan. Such a plan would not be able to raise the full amount needed by Spurs but could succeed if the club received the cash injection that would come from the sale of Gascoigne. With Tony Berry supporting the Venables consortium and Irving Scholar looking to buy more time in the hope of being able to ride out the storm, the Spurs board were pulling in four directions at once.

The problem for an prospective buyer was not simply raising enough money to purchase the shares. The real stumbling block was the club's debt. Finance not only had to be found for the company's stock, but also for the Midland Bank and the other creditors. Moreover, working capital was required to improve the team, and any deal had to be approved by the Stock Exchange and an extraordinary general meeting of shareholders. These considerations presented massive obstacles, not just to the Venables consortium, but to any possible saviour.

In the week after the Notts County game, matters began to gather pace. Gian Marco Calleri was attempting to set up a meeting with Irving Scholar and Nat Solomon, but the Spurs board were embroiled in takeover talks, and anyway, Irving Scholar for one was in no rush to meet the Lazio delegation. The Venables offer was due to be considered by the board the following Wednesday and was said to include a bid of between 91p and £1 a share, which would have valued Spurs at between £9 million and £10 million. By then, though, the Lazio president had been persistent enough to have arranged his meeting with Solomon and Scholar for Thursday 14 March. Milan, by this time, had dropped out, because, in the view of an insider, president Silvio Berlusconi didn't think that Gascoigne had the right character for his club.

Irving Scholar let it be known that he was prepared to sell his shares provided he received three assurances. The most important of these was that Gascoigne would not be sold. In addition, Scholar wanted evidence that money was available to purchase players and a share price which included a premium over the suspended price of 91p. This meant that any realistic bid had to come up with over £9 million to buy the club and an undisclosed amount for new blood. There was also the £11 million required to cover the debt to the Midland. The stipulation that the Midland loan be refinanced surprised many observers. The Midland, however, were the bankers of Markheath Securities, Paul Bobroff's property company, and it was Bobroff who had brought the bank in to finance the East Stand when anticipated support through Tony Berry failed to materialize. Under the circumstances, Bobroff felt he could hardly sell out and leave the Midland at the mercy of an unproven consortium. For their part, the Venables–Gillick consortium made it a condition of their bid that the Midland guarantee not to cut off lines of credit or call in the debt. The following day, Spurs' financial advisers, Brown Shipley, issued a non-committal statement which said: 'The board of Tottenham Hotspur plc announces that an approach has been received which may or may not lead to an offer being made for the whole of the issued share capital of the company. A further announcement will be made as soon as possible.' In fact, after long negotiations, Scholar believed he had reached an agreement with the consortium and had shaken hands on the deal. It was subject, however, to authorization by Brown Shipley and the Midland Bank. In a public statement, Terry Venables was more circumspect.

'We have been asked about our plans for the club and that is all,' he said. 'We are involved in discussions and that's all I really want to say at this stage. I know the fans are anxious and that's why we are trying to sort something out quickly, but these things take time.'

While Brown Shipley investigated the Venables bid, Lazio re-emerged centre-stage. Both clubs wished talks to proceed in secret, although this was impossible given the intensity of media interest in both countries. Spurs knew that public knowledge of any further negotiations would alienate supporters, while Lazio wanted to conclude a deal before other Italian clubs stepped in and upped the ante. Hence the roundabout journey to Southend on Wednesday evening by Calleri and his negotiating team. Scholar, Solomon and Roach met the Italians in Calleri's room at Claridge's. The benchmark for Tottenham was the Baggio deal (Roberto Baggio had been transferred from Fiorentina to Juventus in June 1990 for £7.7 million). Calleri opened with a bid of £7 million, but by the end of the meeting the amount had gone up to £8 million. Even at that figure, Scholar and Solomon refused to commit themselves, although they agreed to consider it. Scholar left the meeting early, and talks with Solomon continued. Solomon in particular was anxious to keep negotiations with Lazio going in order to satisfy the club's creditors that every avenue was being explored. At the same time he wanted to stall Calleri until he had a better feel for the way the takeover negotiations were going. He explained that as the value put on Gascoigne exceeded 30 per cent of the total worth of the parent company, his transfer might have to be voted on by a specially convened shareholders' meeting to comply with Stock Exchange regulations. There was no point in Calleri getting his chequebook out at this stage, but an agreement of sorts was reached, under which Solomon promised that talks would continue at a later date and that Lazio had first option on Gascoigne's services. Calleri took this to mean that it was only a matter of time before the transfer went through.

That evening, the Lazio contingent went incognito to a restaurant run by Antonio Trapani, an ex-employee of another Italian club, Peronace. All the talk was of Gascoigne going to Italy, but Trapani, unaware of the identity of his customers, was unimpressed.

'For me,' commented the restaurateur to his guests, 'it's madness. That loony will never settle in the Italian League.' As Trapani was about to give full vent to his opinions, he suddenly stopped in his tracks, half recognizing the man to whom he was talking.

'You're not . . . ?' he said.

'No,' replied Calleri. 'I look like him but I'm not him.'

Some enterprising Italian reporters tried to get Gascoigne to comment on the situation from his bed in the Princess Grace Hospital in Marylebone, where he had undergone surgery on his injured groin. Passing themselves off as Lazio supporters failed to gain them an audience, but they did manage to get Gazza on the other end of the phone.

'Sorry boys,' said Gazza, 'you can't come up. Thanks for the good wishes, though. And best wishes to the Lazio fans – good luck in the league.'

Calleri returned to Rome the next day, Friday (clutching a Gazza T-shirt), confident he had got his man.

'He is the best in the world in his position,' enthused the president. 'He's a Benetti with the class of Baggio. Class and power – a Gullit type.'

When asked about Gascoigne's temperament, Calleri was almost dismissive. 'I'll talk to the team about this,' he said, and added that he would organize an 'orientation' for Gazza to settle himself into the club. With many overseas stars failing to live up to expectations in Italy, Calleri was shrewd enough to realize that Gascoigne would need careful handling; it was even reported that Lazio were prepared to buy Gazza's friend

Glenn Roeder from Watford to keep him company. Meanwhile, Gazza was released from hospital, the surgery having been pronounced a success. For most Spurs fans the big question was whether he would be ready to face Arsenal at Wembley in a month's time.

There was the little matter of a League game away to Aston Villa to interrupt the boardroom manoeuvrings. The hiatus did not last long, however. After the 3–2 defeat, Terry Venables was optimistic in the face of the inevitable questions about the prospects, not of his team, but of his consortium. He also made it clear that the deal depended on Gazza remaining at White Hart Lane. 'The offer would obviously be for the club as it is at the moment,' he said.

At Lazio's next home game against Cagliari the following Sunday, a huge banner was unfurled at the north end of the Olympic Stadium depicting a foaming pint of beer, along with another declaring, 'It's ready for you Gazza'. The Lazio president was questioned about Gazza's sweet tooth. 'Just like him,' joked Calleri, 'I like chocolate too. When he's with us, we'll divide it between us. This will give us a reciprocal advantage for both our figures.' Evidently, in Rome, there was no doubt that Gascoigne was Lazio's. Back in London, however, the situation was somewhat less clear-cut. Reaction from Spurs was at odds with the euphoria at Lazio. According to reports emanating from White Hart Lane, their undertaking merely committed Spurs to continue negotiations, and the deal could only be accepted if ownership of the club did not change hands. This led to an abundance of rumours. One was that Milan had undergone a change of heart over Gazza and were about to re-enter the fray with a substantial bid that would allow the player to stay at Spurs for one more season. Another, which had refused to go away, was that the Lazio deal was being financed by Juventus and that Gazza would eventually end up with the Turin club. Such a possibility is not as preposterous as it sounds, since this type of arrangement is not uncommon in Italy, and Juventus had farmed out Michael Laudrup before exercising their option on the player.

Nevertheless, Calleri was annoyed enough about the rumour to vehemently deny it. 'Here am I buying the number one player in Europe,' he said, 'and people are saying we are only a parking lot for Juventus.' The fact was that Lazio, with support from the Casa di Risparmio and a £4 million share of profits from *Italia 90*, were not in need of finance from a third party.

Meanwhile, Brown Shipley had set the Venables–Gillick consortium a deadline of Monday 18 March, by which time all the money had to be in place. According to Scholar, Brown Shipley found some of the details of the proposed agreement 'misty'. Another meeting was arranged with Venables and Gillick to clarify the situation. Scholar maintained that at this meeting, 'the terms were altered downwards', but they again shook hands on the sale, although the Brown Shipley deadline was extended by twenty-four hours to allow the consortium more time to comply with the requirement to make the finance available. The new deadline passed, however, with no discernible movement on either side.

On Wednesday 20 March, as Gazza was in Marseille to watch the second leg of the Milan–Marseille European Cup clash at the invitation of his friend Chris Waddle, Mel Stein appeared on the BBC's *Sportsnight* programme and made an astonishing statement, considering all that had been going on. When asked whether he thought Gazza would be sold, he replied: 'Nobody from Tottenham has spoken to us, nobody from the consortium has spoken to us, which surprises us a little bit. We would have thought if Paul Gagcoigne plays such an important part in everybody's plans then somebody should have come to us, sat down with us and said, "Look, this is what we are planning to do, we are thinking of selling him to Lazio, what do you think about it?"'

Stein was then asked for his opinion of the likely outcome. 'I think . . . that Tottenham would have to sell him in the not too distant future, and if they do sell him at the moment, Lazio are the only bidders. We would look at it very carefully.' Everyone, it seemed, was now jockeying for position. The Tottenham board rejected the bid from Venables' consortium on Friday 22 March, the day before a home League match against QPR. Brown Shipley issued a statement which said that assurances sought by the Spurs board over the amount and origin of the finance had not been received. Irving Scholar claimed that the board 'kept saying, show us your money – but they couldn't'. He was determined to avoid a repetition of the Michael Knighton affair at Manchester United, when the United chairman, Martin Edwards, signed away his control only to discover that the financial guarantees could not be translated into hard cash, to the enduring embarrassment of the club. Moreover, selling Tottenham would have meant the end of the road for Scholar and Bobroff, and probably Nat Solomon too. Neither was about to give up his position at the club unless there was no alternative. The rest of the Brown Shipley statement intimated that the directors did indeed believe there was such an alternative. The Tottenham board, it said, 'was at an advanced stage of preparation of proposals for securing the financial position of the company to the benefit of shareholders, and confidently expects to make a further announcement shortly'. This was probably a reference to Nat Solomon's efforts to reactivate a rights issue with Hambro Magan.

The 0–0 draw against QPR was described as a game of 'mindbending mediocrity' and was completely overshadowed by the news of the failure of the Venables consortium. After the game, Spurs' fifth in the League without a win, Venables insisted that the consortium was not dead. Hinting that there was disagreement over the share price and that the true extent of Tottenham's debts had not been fully revealed, the manager said, 'We are still trying to sort out the final figure. We plan to issue a statement on Monday or within the next few days.'

Venables went on to add that, in his opinion, the Spurs board were not being totally fair. 'I can't see why there has to be a deadline in something you are negotiating, unless there is some other deadline. The board are suggesting we have run out of time, but why should there be a deadline? As far as we are concerned, our takeover is not terminated. The money is there.'

The problems at White Hart Lane had undoubtedly affected morale on the pitch. Gary Lineker certainly thought so, and he blamed the poor form of recent weeks on what was happening in the boardroom.

'All the players are sad at the mess this club has got itself into,' he said. 'The whole thing seems to be a hell of a mess and there is bound to be doubt in the players' minds. I hope someone can resolve the mess, make the club a viable proposition and get things going again. If the club have to sell Paul to survive, then they'll have to do it. We wouldn't want that as players. We are all hoping he doesn't go, because he is irreplaceable. But the club is the most important thing, and if they have to sell him then that would be it.'

By Monday 5 March, Michael Goddard and Baltic were back in the ring, offering a new rights issue. Harry Hyman, Baltic's managing director, said, 'We are not talking about a takeover. That implies 100 per cent control or majority control, which we are not looking for. Our investors want to inject a substantial sum into the company through a deeply discounted rights issue of shares.'

Having originally offered 40p a share and been rejected, the seriousness of Baltic's move would be judged by the meaning of 'deeply discounted'. The nearer the company could get to the suspended share price of 91p, the better its chance of success.

Meanwhile, Gian Marco Calleri was getting impatient and was determined to move the Gascoigne deal forward. On Tuesday 26 March, the Lazio delegation once again flew to England. Using false names, they booked into the Royal Lancaster Hotel in the belief that, as it was known to be the hotel used by Spurs, it was the one place where the media would least expect to find them. It was the same cast and the same script. The meeting began inauspiciously as the Spurs delegation came to the table proposing additional clauses, including a provision for friendly games between the two clubs. This new turn of events came as a complete surprise to Dennis Roach as well as the Lazio officials. Unfazed, Calleri said he was ready to put cash on the table. To show his good faith, he announced he had deposited 17 billion lire (£8 million) in the London branch of the Banco di Santo Spirito. The Tottenham representatives, wanting to discuss the cash bid among themselves, gave their approval for Calleri to leave immediately for further talks with Lazarus and Stein.

When he returned, the Lazio president found Tottenham still stalling. The inertia was just too much, and he gave them an ultimatum. This was the last time he could come to London. If Tottenham wanted to continue with the deal he would be waiting for them in Rome.

In the press, there were more rumours over what was about to happen at Spurs. No statement emerged from the Venables consortium, though by the end of the week both the Baltic and Hambro Magan bids had receded into the background. Spurs had another home game on Saturday – the first of the Easter programme – against Coventry, but League matches now hardly seemed to matter. Since there was no chance of qualifying for Europe through a high League position, Venables decided to give Gary Lineker a break. After suffering from hepatitis in 1988, Lineker had played two seasons back-to-back, with a gruelling World Cup in between. His manager therefore sent him right away from football and he went to stay with his brother, who manages his bar in Tenerife.

The first half-hour of the Coventry match saw the Spurs team hit rock-bottom as the visitors established a 2–0 lead. The Spurs fans were justifiably angry. One section sang 'Where's the money gone?' at the directors' box. They were happier when Nayim managed to pull a goal back just before half-time, but yet again Venables had a repair job to do. Whatever he said worked, as Tottenham's approach in the second half was completely transformed. After a number of chances at both ends, Nayim grabbed the equalizer with fifteen minutes to go.

'I was delighted by the way we got back,' said the manager afterwards. 'We had one eye on the semi-final and it spread like a disease in the first half.'

If the first forty minutes, during which Spurs were embarrassingly outplayed, showed the worst aspect of the team, the second period saw the character that could yet frustrate Arsenal.

After the match, as Spurs prepared to face Luton in the second of the Easter games, Terry Venables went on the offensive. 'If it [his consortium's bid] does not come off,' he said, 'the future of the club doesn't look too good.'

Venables revealed something of the pressure he had been

under during the preceding few weeks: 'I have never worked so hard at anything in my life. I come in to take the players training in the morning, then go straight into meetings, afternoon and evening. What time do I get to go to bed? Some nights I don't even get home. I'm working round the clock to save the club and it has been murder. I'm past the Kenny Dalglish stage, I've gone potty. I've been there and I'm coming back.'

While Scholar was conspicuous by his non-attendance at the Coventry game, Venables was orchestrating the fans' support by working all possible hours to save the club. It was a good tactic, which had the desired effect as the supporters swung behind him. Thereafter, chants of 'Scholar out, Venables in' could be heard with increasing frequency.

At Kenilworth Road on Easter Monday, Spurs and Luton played out a 0–0 draw. Luton were once again engaged in their perennial battle against relegation, and the home fans voiced their displeasure for most of the afternoon. Having seen good players like Wegerle, Breaker and Dowie sold, they were, in their own way, as disgruntled as their Spurs counterparts. Their demeanour was not improved by the match, during which Luton missed a penalty and had Johnson sent off. That Luton dominated the game only made their plight seem worse. Tottenham turned in another poor performance, but there was some good news for the manager. David Howells had recovered from injuries (one sustained in a bar-room fracas) and had played in a friendly against a team from Switzerland with no resulting problems, and Nat Solomon told listeners to Capital Radio that he expected the Venables consortium to assume control at the club 'sooner rather than later'.

Tony Berry added his weight to the view that the takeover was imminent. 'It's just a question of getting contractual arrangements,' he said. 'It will be taking a little bit longer, but we're nearly there.'

The manager was equally adamant that he was on the verge of success. 'That is the way I understand the position,' he said in response to Solomon's pronouncement, adding, 'It is very close. When it is over it will be a big relief to the club and the supporters.'

Venables, more than anyone, should perhaps have realized that public statements throughout the crisis bore little relationship to the true situation. Solomon's claim sounded ominously like one of those notorious votes of confidence with which chairmen presage a manager's downfall

Contrary to Venables' optimistic tone, news from Tottenham seemed to dry up as the Saturday game at home to Southampton approached. Irving Scholar was out of the country, and nothing could happen without his approval. Scholar was now beginning to display some of the acumen that had characterized his original takeover of Spurs in 1982. Under pressure from the rest of the board and the Midland Bank, Scholar had said he was willing to go, but only if his three conditions were met. In truth he must have been aware that fulfilling the conditions was virtually impossible. He had kept a low profile throughout the crisis, unlike some of the others involved at White Hart Lane. The leaks and public statements created a web of misinformation that made it difficult for close observers, let alone the club's supporters, to discern what was actually happening. Only one thing was certain; thus far, Irving Scholar had survived, despite the numerous predictions that he was only days away from being forced to step down.

How he managed it, in the face of opposition from all quarters, is the untold story of the Tottenham débâcle. In essence, Scholar profited from the deep divisions within the Tottenham board and the strict Stock Exchange rules on the way public companies conduct their business. The rift with Paul Bobroff, dating from the Waddle transfer, might, in the normal course of events, have healed with the passage of time. It was exacerbated, however, when the deal with Robert Maxwell was made public. Bobroff had opposed the Scholar–Maxwell proposals, but Scholar could now argue that the arrangement with Maxwell was by far the best that anyone had negotiated. The Baltic offer had priced the shares at 40p, Hambro Magan at 60–70p and the Venables consortium at 91–100p. Under the terms of Scholar's agreement with Maxwell, the shares were valued at £1.30.

The reasons for the failure of the Maxwell offer are complex, but there are two important elements. The Football League had changed its rules in 1989 to prevent multiple ownership of clubs after Maxwell had tried to buy Watford when he still had interests in Derby, Oxford and Reading. Legislation, when drafted quickly in response to a particular event, is generally bad legislation, because all the possible consequences are not thought through. The League rule preventing Maxwell from underwriting the Spurs rights issue actually pushed the club closer to bankruptcy. In addition to the League's rule-change, the adverse media reaction to the deal led to Maxwell's disillusionment. Press comment centred on the public squabbling among the Spurs directors, and a consequence of that was the suspension of the shares, another negative development in the wake of Maxwell's interest becoming public knowledge.

Since Scholar was the main shareholder, the only way he could be forced out was if the Midland Bank called in the overdraft. It was the ultimate poker game and Scholar was about to call the bank's bluff. The gamble was not as foolhardy as it might seem at first sight. Scholar had, after all, heard the Midland cry wolf before. If the bank did foreclose, the bad publicity was likely to be intense – this was no club from the lower divisions but an international name – and there are probably thousands of Midland customers who are Spurs supporters. They might be inclined to shift their business if the bank closed their beloved club down. At the same time, Scholar, like Mr Micawber, was convinced something would turn up to save him. While Spurs were still in the Cup, there was the prospect of a lucrative campaign in Europe the following season. The bank would be mad to foreclose while that was still on the cards. Scholar was also beginning to hear of some startling new proposals emanating from the FA, which could increase the income to all the top clubs immeasurably. FA chief executive Graham Kelly was working on his *Blueprint for the Future of English Football*, which included plans for a premier league of eighteen clubs. If implemented, Kelly's scheme would significantly increase income to the new league's members.

So what Irving Scholar needed to do was buy time. Nat Solomon had come in at the instigation of the Midland and as long as the new man thought there was a possibility of saving the situation, the bank would be unlikely to move against the club. This is why Scholar agreed to the mission of Dennis Roach to Italy, why he countenanced the talks with Lazio, and why he appeared to have put obstacles in the way of the deal at every stage. If Gazza were sold, he might be able to shift the blame for it on to Solomon and the Midland Bank, and somehow survive.

The offers from Baltic, Hambro Magan and the Venables consortium, and the manoeuvring of Nat Solomon, Paul Bobroff and Tony Berry, were manna from heaven to Irving Scholar. He could be seen to be interested in each, yet find others on the board willing to oppose all. For instance, Solomon and Berry would veto the Baltic bid out of hand because the price was too low, while Bobroff and Solomon would come up with reservations about the Venables consortium after advice from Brown Shipley. Paul Bobroff had introduced the Midland to Tottenham and could not afford his reputation in the City to be tarnished. This is why he was against allowing the consortium to take control without safeguards for the Midland. Meanwhile, Scholar could claim that the level of interest was such that the underlying situation was not as bad as everyone believed.

Finally, while just about everybody else could hardly resist talking to the media (with the notable exception of Paul Gascoigne, who refused to comment during the whole business), Scholar left the country, only returning for the important meetings. He even stayed away from a number of Spurs' matches, a most unusual occurrence. In this way, the game could be played out by others, but it was Scholar's ball and he could step in and take it back when it suited him. The bottom line was that Gazza would have to be sold and Venables would leave. Still, as Gary Lineker implied, the club is bigger than any individual, no matter how talented. As the drama continued, there was no reason to think Irving Scholar had misjudged either the situation or his colleagues. The fact that he was still there was in itself a triumph of the first order.

Despite his strategy, Scholar still needed a slice of good fortune. This came his way when a Scottish newspaper, the *Daily Record* (sister paper of the *Daily Mirror*), claimed Larry Gillick had been bankrupt and only discharged three years previously. In addition, he had been savagely criticized by the chartered accountant appointed as his trustee. If anything was designed to destroy confidence in Venables' consortium, it was this story. Indeed, despite talk of libel proceedings, it halted the consortium in its tracks and brought the transfer of Gazza one step closer.

Meanwhile on the pitch, Gary Lineker returned for the game against Southampton, and both he and the Spurs team appeared rejuvenated. Lineker looked a different player from the one who had struggled in recent matches and scored the two goals that beat the Saints. He could have had a hat-trick but missed a penalty, which he had won himself when brought down by Ruddock. Further goals would have been scored but for Flowers, the Southampton goalkeeper, and at least Spurs looked in good shape on the field for the forthcoming encounter at Wembley.

The sorry goings on at Spurs had diverted attention away from a faltering League campaign, but at Highbury, the opposite was the case. Arsenal and Liverpool were now the only realistic contenders for the title, and the remaining games would all be played under enormous pressure. On 23 March, the Gunners secured a point in a 0–0 draw at Norwich. The teams, both employing the sweeper system, just about cancelled each other out. Anders Limpar returned, as did David Rocastle, but Rocastle's day was marred by yet another injury. One incident, when Kevin Campbell was brought down by goalkeeper Gunn, could have resulted in a penalty, but none was awarded. Meanwhile, Liverpool produced an incredible performance at Derby, winning 7–1 to go back to the top of the League. Coincidentally, Arsenal were due to visit the Baseball Ground the following Saturday.

Before that, England faced a difficult European Championship match at Wembley against the Republic of Ireland. Strangely, the First Division programme was allowed to continue unhindered, despite the fact that this was probably England's most difficult home game of the qualifying tournament. A poor

England performance was enlivened by Lee Dixon's first goal at international level after nine minutes, when his shot deflected off Steve Staunton to put England in the lead. Ireland, though, had much the better of things and deserved more than the 1–1 draw they achieved. Three other Arsenal players took part in the game. The only one who could have been satisfied with his performance was David O'Leary, who shut out Gary Lineker so completely that Lineker was substituted by Ian Wright for the last fifteen minutes. Tony Adams, one of three central defenders, was taken off at half-time after enduring a torrid time. Similarly, David Seaman seemed uneasy, particularly when England found themselves pinned back in their own penalty area for long periods. and did not look convincing on the inevitable high balls launched towards the head of Niall Quinn. Graham Taylor, while not directly criticizing the keeper, nevertheless complained that his predecessor would have been more assertive in pushing the defence out: 'If Shilton had been in goal, the defence wouldn't have gone as deep as they did. He wouldn't have allowed that to happen, he'd have been hoarse getting them out of the way.'

George Graham was incensed by the manager's comments. 'I can't see any logic in the argument,' he said. 'You're either a talker or you're not. David doesn't talk a lot, but it never affects Arsenal's performances. One of the greatest goalkeepers was Pat Jennings and he was even quieter than David.'

It certainly did seem to be a strange hypothesis on the part of the England boss. After all, Shilton had been part of the team that drew 1–1 with the Irish in Cagliari, and his presence did not noticeably prevent Jack Charlton's team from imposing their normal long-ball tactics on England. Neither did Shilton stop Ireland beating England in the European Championship Finals in Stuttgart in 1988. Certainly Seaman was not as assured as he had been all season for Arsenal but surely the responsibility for compressing the play belonged as much to the defenders, all of whom knew exactly what to expect. Perhaps the Arsenal players in the England team needed more adjustment, not just to international football, but to the demands of a system different from those imposed by George Graham at Highbury. Successful Arsenal players are those who can perform in the way Graham wants, and the system is more important than individualism. Anders Limpar's talents, for instance, had been sacrificed on numerous occasions to the needs of 'shape'.

Perhaps Seaman, Dixon and Adams, like David O'Leary, would have felt more at home at international level playing under Jack Charlton, whose determination to get players to perform specific roles has much in common with Graham's ideas on how the game should be played.

Three days after the Irish match, Arsenal arrived in Derby to find their opponents already demoralized by impending relegation and rows over the role of Robert Maxwell as chairman. Arsenal won the game comfortably through two identical headers from Alan Smith, which came after Bould had flicked the ball on from corner kicks. Merson, who had been out injured for the Norwich game, was back and played out wide. With Limpar operating on the other flank, George Graham was now using a 4-2-4 or 4-4-2 formation. David O'Leary was the one left out.

'We have such a strong squad now,' said Graham afterwards, 'that we can take players out and put others in and it does not make a great deal of difference.' Amazingly, Liverpool were beaten 3–1 at Anfield by QPR and the Gunners were back at the top of the League, leading Liverpool by two points.

The Easter programme often settles crucial issues, such as promotion or relegation, even if it doesn't actually produce conclusive evidence of who will be League champions. Arsenal's second game over the holiday, against Aston Villa at Highbury, was not played until Wednesday night. By then, Liverpool had lost again, in a televised game at Southampton, this time by a single goal from Matthew Le Tissier, so Arsenal knew that three points would at least see some significant daylight between them and the Merseysiders.

In front of the television cameras and a crowd of almost 42,000, which included the Prime Minister, John Major, Arsenal produced one of their best displays of the season, crushing Villa 5–0. Villa might have scored first when Ormandroyd missed two chances, and could have equalized when the score was 1–0, but once Arsenal settled down, they pulverized Villa with a superb

273

attacking display. The Gunners had created and missed some chances of their own before Limpar threaded a perfect pass through the defence to put Campbell clear in the thirty-seventh minute. Campbell, full of the confidence that goals and a regular place in the team bring, made no mistake, and Arsenal were one up at half-time. Three goals in six second-half minutes killed the game off as a contest. Paul Davis unleashed a tremendous hook shot from the edge of the area to score his first goal for six months; Alan Smith made it 3–0 with a looping header at the far post; then Smith got his second, turning in a low Limpar cross. Villa goalkeeper Nigel Spink had to leave the field after a clash with Kevin Campbell with fifteen minutes to go and David Platt took over. The Villa defence protected him well, until a low shot from Campbell beat him after eighty-two minutes. Arsenal were now five points clear of their rivals, and since Liverpool had no game that weekend because of the Grand National, if Arsenal beat Sheffield United at Bramall Lane they would be a massive eight points ahead. Even John Major, a Chelsea supporter, had to admit that Arsenal were 'a super team'.

Sheffield United, after a dreadful start to the season, were improving all the time, although they had lost their previous game to Nottingham Forest. In bad conditions caused by a combination of high winds and a heavy ground, the match was by no means an easy one. Graham's accent on professionalism, though, was rarely illustrated so well as in this game. Arsenal won with two goals on the break from Campbell and Smith. Steve Bould was once again impressive, although the defence as a whole was exposed several times in the air. Against a side of Sheffield's physical presence and aerial game, David O'Leary was missed at the back, a point which was perhaps obscured by the team's disciplined approach and their excellent goals.

Brian Marwood, a member of Arsenal's Championship-winning side two years earlier, and now with Sheffield United, revealed how players must feel when coming up against a side that has lost only one League game all season: 'Although we put them under pressure today, you could see that they believed they weren't going to concede goals.' Marwood went on to give his opinion on the destination of the Championship trophy: 'I'd be very, very surprised if they lose that lead (eight points over Liverpool) now. They are stronger now, mentally and physically, than when we won it and they have a stronger squad. We won it with thirteen or fourteen players but now they have got sixteen or seventeen, the nucleus of a side to dominate the game for the next five years.'

With one more League game to go before the semi-final, Arsenal were in the best possible position. It was surely inconceivable that any side of Graham's, let alone this one, would blow the advantage they now possessed. As Liverpool faltered, Arsenal had ruthlessly exploited the opportunity, the only club in the First Division with the ability to do so. Spurs' season now rested on the Cup, but they had to raise their game significantly if they wanted to reach the final at the expense of their neighbours. For Arsenal, there seemed no limit to what they might achieve.

19

The Joker Goes Wild

In the week leading up to the confrontation at Wembley both Arsenal and Spurs faced vital League games, although the reasons for their importance could not have been more different. On Tuesday 9 April, the Gunners travelled to Southampton needing a good performance to consolidate their position at the top of the table. From now on, the pressure would be relentless, every game crucial. George Graham decided to give Paul Merson a rest and named him as substitute, along with Michael Thomas. Paul Davis and David Hillier were preferred in midfield. Hillier, however, sustained a badly gashed knee in the first half at the hands of Jimmy Case, which made him doubtful for the semi-final.

Southampton are a useful side at home. Victories over Spurs and Liverpool showed they were capable of living with the best. It was poor away form and home defeats against the likes of Derby and Luton that suggested a brittle streak and led to them being uncomfortably close to the relegation zone. As is usually the case, Southampton pounded their visitors from the start, but they failed to make much serious headway. The game gradually began to lose its fire and the rest of the first half turned into a dour battle. Then, just before the interval, Kevin Campbell went close on two occasions, which seemed to bring the match back to life. A free kick from Le Tissier in first-half injury time reminded everyone how important the contest actually was for both clubs. Le Tissier bent his kick over the Arsenal wall but Seaman, who must have seen it late, launched himself and caught the ball, making it all look ridiculously easy.

With Thomas on for Hillier in the second half, Arsenal began to look more dangerous going forward. If Seaman had saved the Gunners in the first half, Southampton keeper Flowers thwarted them in the second, saving brilliantly from Perry Groves on two occasions and once from Kevin Campbell. Anders Limpar, who had looked strangely ineffective, was substituted by Merson midway through the half, and three minutes later Merson attacked the Southampton defence. His cross should have caused no danger, but Alan Smith stabbed it forward and Saints defender Micky Adams got a touch. The ball deflected past the helpless Flowers to give Arsenal the lead. Adams atoned for his mistake five minutes later when his run up the left and low cross caught the Arsenal defence square. Le Tissier stole in, amid loud Arsenal claims for offside, and scored the equalizer unchallenged. The goal was allowed to stand and Bould went into the referee's book for complaining to the linesman about the decision. A couple of minutes later, Jimmy Case lunged at Paul Davis, then appeared to stamp on him. An ugly mêlée ensued, which could have got out of hand. Thankfully, it blew over quickly, though not before Michael Thomas was booked for dissent. George Graham defended his players afterwards, saying, 'I thought we showed tremendous restraint. The players' attitude was first class because there were some very heavy challenges.'

One point turned out to be more than adequate, since Liverpool again faltered at Anfield, this time in a 1–1 draw with Coventry. So the status quo was preserved, with Arsenal eight points ahead having played one game more than their rivals. With four of their last five League games at home, the Gunners were now clear favourites to win the title. They were also tipped to beat Spurs in the Cup semi-final, and the odds on them winning the double were shortening all the time.

Spurs' game against Norwich the following night was not important in itself, the team's chances of a decent League position having long since evaporated, but it gave Terry Venables the chance to assess the fitness of Paul Gascoigne. Gascoigne had made a remarkable recovery from his operation thirty-one days previously and was desperate to face Arsenal in the semi-final. So vital was he to Spurs' hopes that the match against Norwich was used to give him the opportunity of proving himself. Venables even decided to make him captain for the night. The game provided exactly the same platform for David Howells, also back from injury and surgery. With Venables giving first-team débuts to three youngsters, John Hendry up front, Ian Walker in goal, and Peter Garland (who came on as substitute for Gazza after an hour) in midfield, and with four ex-Tottenham players in the Norwich line-up, the match could have been labelled Spurs Reserves v. Spurs Old Boys.

Venables, who had asked Norwich in vain for the game to be moved back twenty-four hours, made seven changes from the side that beat Southampton. Nevertheless, the team produced some good football and were unlucky not to take the lead when Hendry shot over the bar after a fifty-yard run by Gazza had set him up. Norwich, going through a poor patch themselves, scored first after thirteen minutes through Power. Some nifty footwork by Gazza just before half-time set Nayim free, and his cross was flicked on by Walsh to give Hendry the opportunity to equalize. A minute later, Walsh's flashing shot was ruled out for offside. Both goalkeepers made excellent saves in the second half. Gunn somehow kept out a Gascoigne pile-driver, then Walker, who lost nothing in comparison to Thorstvedt when the two were training together, produced a stunning save to deny Fox. Walker could do nothing, though, about Crook's winner after eighty-one minutes. The former Spurs player picked up the ball thirty yards out and smashed his shot in off the underside of the bar.

It was not a classic game of football, but the return of Gascoigne and Howells was of immense significance for Spurs. Gazza's display had been immaculate, coaxing colleagues and showing the kind of footwork that had bemused opposing teams all season. When he was substituted after an hour, the applause came from both sets of fans and Norwich's David Phillips went out of his way to offer Gazza a handshake.

Venables was more than pleased. 'He was fantastic,' he said. 'I was going to give him one half but I asked him at half-time how he felt and we got the bonus of another fifteen minutes. He picked up the First Division rhythm straight away.'

Norwich manager Dave Stringer agreed: 'A lot has been said about Gazza's clowning. I just wish England and Norwich had eleven clowns like him. The man is brilliant.'

For all the euphoria over the return of Gazza, and of Howells, Tottenham had still lost the match and, as if to rub it in, on the same day the Football League fined them £20,000 – £15,000 suspended – for the late arrival at Chelsea. One interested spectator at Carrow Road was George Graham, who professed himself 'surprised' by Gascoigne's level of fitness and went on to admit he would now have to reassess his plans for the semi-final. 'He will play on Sunday all right, which is something I didn't expect . . . We will have to think again about our approach . . . and we will give him a lot of respect.'

The excitement in London over the forthcoming semi-final now reached fever pitch, spurred on by the news of Gazza's comeback. Although Arsenal were the form team and went into the match as favourites, the outcome was by no means clear-cut. After all, this was the semi-final of the FA Cup, it was a local derby, and the sides had played out two 0–0 draws in the League already. In this situation, anything could happen. While most pundits plumped for Arsenal, one of the few dissenting voices came from the man who had managed both clubs, Terry Neill.

'Beware George,' warned Neill. 'A little voice in the back of my head keeps telling me Spurs could pull off a shock win.'

Inevitably, thoughts of another Arsenal double surfaced again as the game approached. Comparisons began to be made between the sides of 1991 and 1971, in itself a testament to Arsenal's progress under George Graham. Graham was sure the side he managed was better than the side in which he played. 'Whether this team wins the double or not,' he ventured, 'it is a better one, especially in defence. You only have to look at the goals-against column to see that.'

The manager of the double-winning team, Bertie Mee, was more circumspect, pointing to the lower standards of opposition in the modern game. Asked which of the current Arsenal team he would have liked to have had in his day, Mee replied: 'Anders Limpar is one of those players who can turn a game, he has tremendous flair but is a team player as well. We didn't have a player like that. I think David Seaman is outstanding, and a great stabilizing influence as a personality too, but Bob Wilson didn't make a mistake all season in the double year. Frank McLintock was a great captain, a great leader. Adams might become that, but at the moment he hasn't the maturity. Smith and Merson are very good players, but you would have to go a long way to find a better front pair than Radford and Kennedy. So I would take Limpar, although not at the expense of George Armstrong, who used to be the first name I wrote on my team-sheet. I'd probably take David O'Leary, although he is at the end now, so perhaps not at this stage. The goalkeepers are 50–50.'

The double, though, remained the most difficult of targets. Liverpool in 1986 and Arsenal in 1971 had come from behind, in the League and in the respective Cup finals, and seemed to gain the confidence to win both trophies from a late surge. In 1971, on semi-final day, Arsenal were seven points behind Leeds in the League and 2–0 down to Stoke in the Cup. The 1991 team had to lead from the front. If they were to lift both trophies, they would have more in common with the Tottenham side of 1961, which dominated the season from start to finish, than the two most recent winners of the coveted double.

Whatever the outcome on the day, both Venables and Graham would remain firm friends. At their lunch at Langan's earlier in the season, the two managers discussed the possibility of leading their teams out at Wembley, but the FA had decreed that the semi-final should not be treated like the final, so that option was ruled out.

'I've got to cut out the friendship – we both have – for the ninety minutes on the day and be very ruthless,' said Graham. 'Both of us are winners. On the morning of the match I'll want to beat him and he'll want to beat me. On the day we'll be totally against each other, but at the end we'll be friends.'

For his part, Terry Venables was more concerned with the wider questions at White Hart Lane. Although matters had gone quiet, both on the sale of Gascoigne to Lazio and the proposed takeover by Venables' consortium, it was still the case that probably the only thing staving off each, not to mention the Midland Bank, was the Cup run.

Venables tried separating the two issues. 'This is a big game,' he said, 'but the most important thing is still the future of this club and it is increasingly vital to sort it out. To win the FA Cup would be wonderful, and this week the match has been our top priority. But what's the good of winning a trophy, any trophy, if the club goes under?'

George Graham was more than a little worried about the qualities of the Spurs team Arsenal would be facing. 'We're a better side than Tottenham over nine months, a much more consistent side,' was Graham's opinion. But he continued: 'We won't necessarily be better than them at Wembley. If you catch Spurs on their day . . . well I hope we don't.'

Arsenal had switched effortlessly between four- and five-man defences all season. George Graham now had to decide which system to employ for the Wembley encounter. Graham believed Spurs would use a five-man midfield, leaving Lineker alone up front. Spurs had tried this formation in the game at White Hart Lane. That day, Graham played five at the back, but it had not really worked. Spurs dominated the game, produced a number of chances and were only denied by the outstanding form of David Seaman. Moreover, in recent games, Graham had used a 4-2-4 or 4-4-2 system, which had produced the final push towards the League title, including the 5-0 victory over Aston Villa. And in the game against Spurs at Highbury, Paul Davis had dominated a match in which Arsenal played with a flat back four. Against this was the fact that O'Leary had fared well against Lineker when the two met in the game between England and Ireland. In addition, it was the five-man defence that had finally upset Leeds. What weighed heavily on Graham's mind was the loss of David Hillier, who would have marked Gascoigne. Without Hillier, there was no Arsenal midfield player who could perform this kind of ball-winning role.

This was an extraordinary situation. The depth of Graham's squad had drawn praise all season; even his preponderance of central defenders in the end proved to be a strength. The midfield had been shuffled around without any apparent weakness, but the fact was that until Hillier broke into the team, all the Arsenal midfield options involved players who were basically attacking in nature. Thomas, Davis, Rocastle, Jonsson, Merson and Limpar were all of this ilk. When Bertie Mee had compared this Arsenal side to his own he had not commented on the midfield, but this was one time when Graham must have wished for a Peter Storey or even a Kevin Richardson to take care of winning the midfield battle. On many occasions, Arsenal's play bypassed the midfield entirely, hitting long balls (often from David Seaman) to Alan Smith, whose control with his back to goal enabled support to pour forward. The tactic worked best when Arsenal allowed teams to come at them, holding their defensive line on the edge of the penalty area. When the ball was won there, usually by a defender, a break was possible, whether through a strong run by Limpar or Merson, or a long punt upfield towards Smith, with Campbell rampaging through in support. Thus it seemed better to go with the system that had served them so well in recent League games and pick a team designed for this pattern of play, rather than revert to the extra defender which had proved so ineffective at White Hart Lane.

Arsenal's last training session at London Colney before the game consisted of a light work-out. The team met up at their usual hotel in St Albans on Saturday evening for a briefing and a meal together. Most of the tactics had been worked on over the previous few days and, according to Alan Smith, much of the training had revolved around 'working on the Gascoigne thing'. Once Graham had established that Gascoigne was likely to play, it seemed the Arsenal approach was tailored to counter the threat from his direction. In anticipation of Gascoigne being allotted a floating role, Graham sought to reduce his space by shifting Paul Merson to a more withdrawn midfield position and making sure that one of the midfield players would close mark him wherever possible. On another level, David O'Leary stressed how the semi-final preparation was little different to normal: 'It was no big deal, we treat every game very professionally.'

Tottenham, and particularly Terry Venables, had for once spent the week on football matters, putting takeovers aside for a brief period. The day after the game against Norwich, the team went to a health farm, which assistant manager Doug Livermore described as 'a relaxing day, a day off'. Friday and Saturday mornings were taken up with short games against the reserves, mainly to work on set pieces, and with Terry Venables impressing on the players, individually and collectively, what their pattern of play would be. On Saturday evening, the players reported to the training ground from where the coach took them to the Royal Lancaster Hotel. They left for Wembley at ten the next morning.

'We wanted to get there before Arsenal, which we did,' said Doug Livermore. 'We were well relaxed and had plenty of time. We didn't want to get there and be rushing about. Our preparation was excellent.'

Playing the semi-final at Wembley provided a wonderful day out for both sets of fans. It was the only stadium capable of staging such an event, and as the crowds arrived, they created an atmosphere of cordiality which was noticeably free of intimidation and tension (there were only twenty-four arrests the whole afternoon). The noon kick-off may have helped as it reduced drinking time. The fans displayed their colours and seemed far more concerned with the battle to come on the pitch rather than any antagonism towards each other.

With Hillier definitely ruled out, George Graham relied on the formation that had served him so well in recent games – a flat back four with no place for David O'Leary. According to O'Leary, the Spurs camp was more than pleased about his exclusion.

'I know that Tottenham were delighted,' he said. 'I walked up the tunnel and Terry Venables was so pleased when he got the team sheet before the game and I know the other players were delighted when they saw our team. I think that helped Tottenham.'

Venables had indeed decided to give Gazza a place in the starting line-up. It was yet another gamble on the player's fitness. However, it took only a few minutes for George Graham's fears to be realized, as a hyperactive Gascoigne (he needed an injection the night before the game to sleep) took the game by storm. Gazza, according to Venables, was so psyched up, he gave the pre-match talk.

'I didn't do anything to motivate the team,' quipped the manager, 'he did everything in the dressing room, he was magnificent.'

Doug Livermore thought Gazza 'exceptional in the dressing

room' and added that he 'oozes this will to win'. Another risk Venables took was to play David Howells, whose fitness was also in doubt, wide on the left, to counter Dixon's attacking instincts as much as to go forward himself. Howells had missed ten games, and his ability to last ninety minutes at Wembley was debatable. Given these problems, the day did not augur well for Spurs.

After five minutes, Anders Limpar gave away a free kick in a not very dangerous position thirty-five yards from goal. As Gazza shaped up to have a shot, Arsenal failed to construct a proper wall. Just before Gascoigne took the kick, Lineker ran up to him and told him that if he was going to have a dig, not to do anything clever like trying to bend it but just to hit it hard. There are very few players in the English game who would have had the audacity to try a shot from such a position – perhaps Clayton Blackmore of Manchester United might have given it a go – but so determined was Gazza to stamp his name on the occasion that there appeared to be no thought of anything else. Barry Davies, commentating for BBC television, described what happened next in a voice that went from mild suggestion to incredulous disbelief in five seconds. 'Is Gazza going to have a crack?' he began. 'He is you know . . . Oh . . . that's brilliant.'

Gazza had indeed had a crack, which Seaman saw, even managed to get a hand to, but could do absolutely nothing to stop. Some criticized the goalkeeper, arguing that if he got his hand there he should have saved it. The shot went to Seaman's left, but he attempted to bring his right arm over the top and save it with that hand, a style which Peter Shilton perfected over many years. Perhaps Seaman would have done better to attempt the save with his left hand, but even then it is unlikely he would have prevented the goal. Gascoigne hit it with such force and the ball dipped and swerved along the length of its trajectory to such an extent, that Seaman, like many good goalkeepers before him, was faced with an almost impossible task.

Terry Venables was effusive in his description of the goal. 'All things put together it added up to one of the best free kicks ever seen [at Wembley] in all its history. It's easy to bend a ball and lack pace or to just curl it. But to bend it with power and accuracy is very special, especially from that distance. Schuster [who played for Venables at Barcelona] was fantastic. He could slog them as well with the bend. The two of them are the best I've seen.'

There was worse to come for Arsenal. In the absence of David Hillier, Michael Thomas was assigned the role of marking Gazza. After eleven minutes, Gazza, wide on the right, flicked the ball first time off the outside of his boot towards Paul Allen. As it left his foot, Gazza feinted to run along the wing to receive the return pass from Allen, the usual wall-pass manoeuvre. Thomas, of course, went with his man, but Gazza had no intention of running up the wing. A sudden change of direction brought him inside while Thomas was still shadowing his now non-existent adversary along the touchline. The move, which took less time to execute than it took for the ball to reach Allen, created the space that Gazza wanted. Allen, instead of playing the pass up the wing, returned the ball to Gazza and went out wide himself. Meanwhile, Thomas, realizing his mistake, tried to get back to where he should have been, but it was too late. Another Gascoigne flick with the outside of his foot set Allen clear with a direct route to the byline. It was a magical piece of football, a sort of inverted wall-pass that in the twinkling of an eye, or in this case Gazza's boot, had completely opened up Arsenal's left flank. Allen's low cross caused all sorts of panic, though the defence probably should have dealt with it, but as Seaman went down, Alan Smith appeared on his own goal-line as if from nowhere, the ball hit him and rolled free for a split second. That was all the time Gary Lineker needed. If ever proof were required that Lineker had once again found his appetite for goals, this moment provided it. His leg shot out, he reached the ball first, and stabbed it over the line from a yard out, while Seaman, Smith and the rest of the Arsenal defence floundered.

Later, Smith tried to explain what had happened. 'I always have quite a bit of defensive responsibility. It [the goal] came from a set piece . . . there was a bit of play and it came back in. Gary Mabbutt had stayed up the field and as the ball came across I just moved forward. It went past Lee Dixon, it came at me at a very awkward height and struck me on the hip bone. Then it just dribbled out to Gary Lineker.'

Two–nil up, Spurs' fans were delirious, Arsenal's unbelieving and stunned. As the half began to draw to a close, Arsenal, pride now at stake, tried to get back into a match that seemed beyond them. Yet Spurs looked sharper, were first to the ball, and played the more penetrating football. In short, they looked to be hungrier for victory. Then, just before the break, Arsenal were thrown a lifeline by Alan Smith. Smith had ballooned one opportunity over the bar before Dixon managed to get forward to good effect after Edinburgh's header gave the ball away, and his high cross found Smith about ten yards out. Smith's jump and header were superb, beating three defenders and directing the ball to Thorstvedt's left. The Spurs goalkeeper was slightly off his line, but Smith's contact was perfection itself and the ball bounced once before nestling in the corner of the net, beyond Thorstvedt's despairing dive.

At half-time, Liam Brady, who had already professed surprise at the omission of O'Leary, told the television audience, 'Spurs are playing almost Continental football today. They are knocking the ball to feet and it's the old story. If you've got two big central defenders like Adams and Bould and you keep the ball on the ground, they're in trouble.'

It was not only in attack where Spurs had the edge. The defence was a revelation, playing with skill and determination, particularly when defending the second ball. So much of Arsenal's success had come from the team's ability to put pressure on opposing defenders and pick up the resulting loose ends, but Spurs were intent on making sure this did not happen. Terry Venables had hammered home the message in the preparation for the game. 'They've got a lot of tall players,' he said. 'When the ball bounces down it's got to be won.'

The five-man midfield fared better than anyone dared hope. Doug Livermore explained why. 'Terry picked a system that suited us but also stopped Arsenal's full backs from coming on. It's not a system we play week in, week out. It's difficult to play because British players are used to playing 4-4-2, or a sweeper system with two up front. They like to hit the front men and have two options, whereas this system doesn't warrant hitting front players. But we have the players who can adapt and play in that system.'

In the Spurs dressing room, according to Terry Venables, Gazza gave the half-time talk, the manager 'couldn't get a word in edgeways'. Joking apart, Venables had a serious point to make. He knew that, having scored the goal just before the interval, Arsenal would now throw everything at Spurs in an effort to get the equalizer. It was important that his players did not dwell on the concession of a goal so close to the break. He told them: 'If someone had said to you a couple of days ago that you would be winning at half-time, at Wembley, against Arsenal, in the semi-final of the Cup, 2–1, you would have settled for that, so don't let your heads drop.'

Arsenal did pile on the pressure as the second half got under way. Although Spurs had contained the full backs for the most part, and were outnumbering Arsenal in midfield, whenever Dixon or Winterburn came forward the Gunners looked at their most dangerous. At last, Kevin Campbell and Paul Merson began to seriously menace Spurs, and Davis and Thomas found more bite in the middle of the field. On more than one occasion the Tottenham defence creaked. Gazza, having run himself into the ground, was replaced by Nayim, and went off to tumultuous applause. His contribution had been of the highest class, and the price Lazio were prepared to pay looked cheap at £8 million. He had imposed himself on the match in a way no contemporary, and few in the history of the game, could have done.

'I felt he would last the ninety minutes. He did as well,' commented Venables, 'but . . . he put so much energy in the dressing room before the game and at half-time, he knocked himself out there I think.'

Gascoigne's skills had tormented Arsenal and helped Spurs to raise their game, and the whole team showed a desire and will to win that would more readily have been associated with their opponents. Tottenham's League form, and Venables' preoccupation with finance and business, had disguised the fact that Spurs were not only a talented side, they also had deep resources of resilience and commitment. When Nayim came on, Spurs lost nothing; in fact, he offered a new dimension, allowing Samways and Allen more freedom and making some threatening runs himself.

As Arsenal continued to press forward, there was always the possibility of Spurs catching them on the break, and so it proved in the seventy-sixth minute, when Gary Mabbutt intercepted the ball and gave it to Lineker on the halfway line. Lineker stormed off towards goal, while Samways made a diagonal run to pull defenders out of position and create space for Lineker to exploit. Two crucial errors followed, both committed by Arsenal players to disastrous effect. Even when Lineker was well into his stride, there seemed little real danger. But as Samways made his decoy run, Tony Adams decided to attempt a tackle. Lineker saw the lunge coming, evaded it neatly, and left Adams for dead before breaking into the penalty area. Even then his shot should have been stopped by Seaman. Once again the goalkeeper made contact, this time with both hands, but it seemed almost a tired attempt. The ball deflected off Seaman's fingers but instead of going outside the post it hit the inside and dropped into the net. It was a superb solo goal, coolly created and finished by the England captain, with help from Samways' intelligent diversionary run. It was the end of Arsenal's quest for the double; there was no coming back from 3–1.

For the Tottenham fans, the final whistle was the signal for an outpouring of joy. On the Tottenham bench, Doug Livermore recalled, 'Gazza, Terry and myself [were] hugging each other before Gazza ran away to jump all over the boys. It was smashing for the staff. It was nice to be hugging people who had worked so hard to try and achieve the right goal.'

The intensity of the celebrations could not have been less if it had been victory in the Cup Final itself. Eleanor Levy wrote in the *Spur*: 'If people complained about the celebrations at the end it was because they didn't understand the importance of those ninety minutes to Tottenham Hotspur FC . . . it was about pride. Not just in getting to the final but in the way we got there. And after all the snide comments the players and supporters have had to put up with this season, that's worth a quick jig around Wembley stadium in anyone's book.'

While Gascoigne and Lineker provided the inspiration, all the Spurs players emerged as heroes. As Lineker put it: 'The desire to win was exceptional, right through the side.' Jimmy Hill supported this view, saying, when asked which player gave the best display, 'The outstanding performance was by Spurs, the whole team, [with their] classic passing moves. It was an absolute pleasure to watch.'

In addition, Liam Brady pointed to the tactical battle, saying, 'Arsenal didn't cope with the tactics . . . the Tottenham midfield were outstanding. Even Nayim, when he came on for Gascoigne, played superbly.'

By contrast, few of the Arsenal team found their true form. This was particularly so in the case of Anders Limpar, who, having been troubled by a nagging toe injury for two weeks, hardly figured at all. Venables' five-man midfield, and the stifling of Arsenal's full backs, had stopped the Gunners creatively, while the pace of Lineker and the movement of the supporting players caused problems for the Arsenal defence from start to finish. There was also the will-to-win factor. On many occasions, opposing managers had praised this quality in Arsenal, and the team itself, as Paul Davis said, collectively believed it would not get beaten. So why had the tables been so completely reversed? Perhaps the answer lies in David O'Leary's words about treating each game equally – that is, in a professional manner. Such an attitude is admirable most of the time, but, whatever those at Arsenal believed, this game was different. It was the semi-final of the FA Cup; it was at Wembley and on national television; it was a local derby; and the opposition desperately needed to win to stay in business. For such an occasion, passion and total commitment are prerequisites. Spurs, hyped up by Gazza and the manager, found the necessary tenacity. Alan Smith admitted as much afterwards when he said: 'I think at the back of our minds we knew this was Tottenham's only chance for honours. They were going to be putting everything into it – getting Gascoigne fit for this game – we knew it was going to be hard.' Finally, Arsenal's only League defeat, at Chelsea, came after a difficult midweek Cup tie against Leeds, which went into extra time. Once again, defeat had come after an important away game in midweek. However much the Arsenal staff denied it, stamina, and the number of games English teams are expected to play in a season of success, had surely played its part on the demanding Wembley turf.

None of this meant that Arsenal were anything other than bitterly disappointed. David Seaman, in particular, was so unhappy with his display that he was inconsolable afterwards, virtually in tears. Having denied Lineker so brilliantly at White Hart Lane, he had now allowed a shot literally to slip through his fingers. David O'Leary was also depressed.

'There's no bigger disappointment or bigger joy,' he said. 'To lose a semi-final is a sickening thing, to win it is a great thing . . . People say, "I'd rather lose there than in a Cup Final", but I've won and lost Cup Finals and at least you've been part of the occasion in an FA Cup Final, which is a fantastic thing for a player.'

Alan Smith was more philosophical: 'I'm not a person to shed tears over football, whether in defeat or victory. I am an emotional person but that's in my private life, my family life. When it comes to football, it doesn't really work me up enough to shed tears.'

'When we beat Spurs in the Littlewoods Cup semi-final,' wrote David O'Leary in his autobiography, 'Irving Scholar sent a crate of champagne into our dressing room. I thought that was a touch of class.' David Dein concurred. 'Irving,' he had said in admiration, 'you are genuinely a fantastic loser.'

'I've had a lot of practice,' was the retort. Now it was Dein's lot to reciprocate the gift and to show dignity in defeat. George Graham was equally generous. He was convinced that Spurs' incredible start was the cause of the defeat.

'For twenty minutes we were completely outplayed and that's where we lost the game. I warned the boys about it but we didn't handle it. You go 2–0 down and it's really a mountain to climb, isn't it? After the first twenty minutes I thought we played quite well.'

When asked who he thought had inflicted the most damage, Graham, while admitting Gazza's brilliance, singled out Paul Stewart for praise, but added, 'I thought it was a tremendous team performance.' Although obviously disappointed, Graham appeared to have already come to terms with the defeat. 'Part of football,' he said, 'are the highs and lows.' He expected his players to be of the same mind. 'They've had bigger knockbacks than that this season. They came back from those and there's no reason why they won't come back from this one.'

Terry Venables was also keen to stress the group ethic. 'We want to talk about his [Gascoigne's] free kick because that was a special free kick . . . but all the players played magnificently – not just the determination but the football they played.' He went on to emphasize that it was a 'very special moment' and how pleased he was for the fans. 'No one begrudges their [Arsenal's] success, least of all me with George. I'm delighted, but it is very pleasing for our supporters.'

Doug Livermore talked of the period when Arsenal were at their strongest. 'They were bound to put us under pressure, Arsenal are a very strong unit. There's going to come a stage in the game when we are going to come under pressure, and we did. But when you are one goal up you can keep fighting and scrapping, which the defence and the midfield did very well, and Erik did well in goal.'

As the Spurs team coach pulled away from Wembley, everyone on board began to sing along to the tape the driver was playing. As Doug Livermore observed, it was a 'very happy bus'. The word spread around that the bar at White Hart Lane was open for the players and staff, so most went there for a couple of hours to watch, amid the celebrations, the other semi-final between Nottingham Forest and West Ham. Later, the backroom staff and their wives joined Terry Venables at his Kensington club for dinner. Ray Clemence and Doug Livermore produced a passable rendition of old Beatles' songs, while Venables did his Frank Sinatra routine, which Spanish television viewers once had the dubious pleasure of seeing live.

Once again, Spurs had saved themselves at the last. Losing to Arsenal would have had so many damaging repercussions that defeat became unthinkable. For a glorious ninety minutes all the problems were forgotten, replaced by the sheer exhilaration of overcoming an old adversary and reaching the final of football's oldest, and perhaps greatest, competition. Soon, attention would have to turn once again to the massive debt, to the transfer of Gazza and others, to the possible sale of the club and to the immediate futures of Terry Venables and Irving Scholar. For the moment though, with internal strife put to one side, the whole club and its supporters could embrace the same euphoric emotion and bask in the glory those on the pitch had given back to them.

What now of the Gunners? How they responded to this setback would determine their season. George Graham appeared as resolute as ever: 'We're professional people and we've just got to get it out of our system and get back to work tomorrow.'

There was certainly resilience at Highbury; the players had shown that after the Manchester United and Chelsea games. This defeat was the most traumatic, however. They had simply not done themselves justice. David O'Leary thought the tactics were wrong. He was in no doubt they should have played the sweeper system and believed the whole team agreed with him.

'Our full backs, who are called the two Afghans, wanted to play it,' he revealed. 'They said, "let us off the leash", they wanted to. To me it was set up that way and I think I should have played. Our full backs attacking and pushed in would have suited us a great deal. The two lads, Tony and Stevie, could go in hard and know they'd got that safety behind them.'

Alan Smith was less sure: 'The manager was a bit concerned about Gascoigne floating in the midfield and . . . instead of playing as we were playing, we pulled Paul into the middle . . . and I think it disrupted our game. I don't think not playing a sweeper caused us any problems, I think it was the midfield, where we were just outnumbered . . . we'd been playing excellently in the run-up to the Spurs game, scoring goals, keeping clean sheets. I don't think we felt any need to change it really.'

Whatever the case, Arsenal had to get their minds back on the League, fast. The day before the semi-final, Liverpool played their game in hand away to Leeds. By half-time they had raced into a 4–0 lead and looked as if their brooding presence was back to haunt the Gunners. The second half at Elland Road, however, was as mercurial as the first. Lee Chapman hit a hat-trick and had another disallowed. Liverpool eventually hung on to win 5–4. If ever the two sides of this particular Liverpool team were on display in one match, this was it. None the less, both clubs had five games to play, and Arsenal's lead had been cut to five points. If the rest of the season was anything to go by, there was no one better equipped for the job of getting Arsenal back on track than George Graham. What was required now was single-mindedness. To win the Championship, they had to show they possessed grim determination and nerves of steel. Considering their performance two years previously at Anfield, it would be a foolish person who bet against them.

20

It's Not Over Till It's Over

Liverpool's results under Ronnie Moran had been erratic. Even when winning, the side had looked less than convincing, as the astonishing second half at Leeds so graphically demonstrated. But there were moves afoot at Anfield to find a permanent replacement for Kenny Dalglish, and on Wednesday 17 April Graeme Souness arrived in Liverpool as the club's new manager. Souness, manager, director and 10 per cent shareholder at Glasgow Rangers, resigned his positions at Ibrox with the words, 'On the football side, I now feel I have gone as far as I'll be allowed to go in trying to achieve success.' Souness's enigmatic remark probably referred to his long-running disciplinary battle with the football authorities in Scotland: at the time he was in the middle of a two-year ban from the touchline dug-out. He may also have felt that the quest to win the European Cup with Rangers was unrealizable as long as the club were forced to play in a parochial League, dominated, according to Souness, by 'hammer throwers'. Souness had wanted to stay at Rangers until the end of the season, but his chairman, David Murray, thought it best he leave immediately, since Liverpool's interest was an open secret. The Liverpool players enthusiastically welcomed the appointment, and as a result Arsenal were likely to face a renewed challenge over the last few games of the season.

On the day Souness arrived at Anfield, Arsenal took on Manchester City at Highbury in the team's third hard game in nine days, following the draw at Southampton and the semi-final defeat by Spurs. George Graham decided to make one change from Wembley, Perry Groves coming in for Anders Limpar, although the attacking 4-2-4 formation was retained. Referring to any possible hangover from Sunday, Graham said, 'I'm looking for the players to bounce right back, just as they have done before. There's no problem at all to us if we can win our last five games, and that's what we will be going flat out to do.'

As the team came out on to the pitch, the North Bank gave them a tremendous ovation and reserved a particularly warm reception for David Seaman. Manchester City, after three successive wins, began quite well and created a couple of decent chances in the opening minutes. Seaman looked jittery, as though the events at Wembley were not entirely out of his system, and an uncharacteristic error presented Ward with an open goal, which the former West Ham player spurned. Suddenly, however, Arsenal erupted, and powered into a two-goal lead. A long kick from Seaman after five minutes was headed on by Alan Smith. His flick caught the City defence square, Kevin Campbell's pace took him clear and he ran on to notch his eighth goal in ten games. After that, the Gunners' confidence came flooding back and they began to pile on the pressure. Within another ten minutes they crafted a classic goal as Campbell dummied Groves' right-wing cross, Smith laid it off, Paul Merson picked his spot and hit the ball perfectly beyond Coton in the City goal. After that it was one-way traffic, as Arsenal continually pushed City back. A third seemed sure to come. Then, with five minutes to go to half-time, a refereeing decision altered the course of the game.

As Niall Quinn went for a floated free kick, he tangled with Steve Bould and went down. Referee Ian Borrett considered that Bould had been guilty of leaning on his opponent and awarded a penalty. Later, George Graham was adamant that the decision was an error: 'I have watched the incident twice on video and if anything it should have been a free kick to us. Bould was in front of Quinn, who caught his trailing leg.'

Ward converted the spot-kick and within two minutes Arsenal conceded an equalizer. As the Arsenal defence pushed up, Ward's quick pass set David White free from just inside his own half. White outpaced his pursuers and found a clinical low finish to beat Seaman. As the sides went off at the interval, the 2–2 scoreline was barely credible. Although the Gunners could not be faulted for effort in the second half, they could not break down a City defence which drew strength from the way the side had come back into a game they really should have lost. Michael Thomas hit the bar, but that was about the only chance Arsenal created in the second period. The three games in nine days had yielded two draws and a defeat, the team's worst run of the season. If Souness could inspire Liverpool, the season might yet run to a tense finish. Arsenal were now six points clear, but had played one game more.

Liverpool played their game in hand the following Saturday, as Arsenal's home match against Manchester United was postponed because of United's appearance in the Rumbelows Cup Final. Throughout the season, Arsenal had only looked vulnerable after arduous midweek games, so the break was more than welcome. The portents following Souness's first match as manager, a 3–0 win over Norwich that cut the gap to three points with four games to go, were ominous. That weekend, George Graham took his first-team squad to the south coast, to prepare for the run-in. David O'Leary stayed behind to play for the reserves, since it was felt that, having played no full matches for over two months, he needed all the match practice he could get.

While the first team was away, the Arsenal youth team went one step closer to winning the South-East Counties League with a 4–1 victory over Ipswich. It was, however, a bitter-sweet occasion, since five of the players – Kevin Fowler, Richard Faulkner, Danny Walden, Ty Gooden and Stuart Young – had been told the previous week that they would not be offered professional terms. Particularly unlucky was full back Kevin Fowler, who had been injured for much of the season. However, a keen Arsenal fan called Darren Epstein, who had been to over 100 matches featuring Arsenal teams that season, wrote to several clubs on Fowler's behalf. As a result, the youngster received approaches from Aston Villa and Manchester City. The day after the rejections, youth-team coach Pat Rice asked midfielder Stuart Young if he wanted to be substitute against Millwall the following day. An enthusiastic and willing lad, Young readily agreed. As fate would have it, he came on after five minutes after an injury and proceeded to score four goals. It wasn't enough to save him.

'It's unfortunate,' said David Dein, 'but it's like a production line. We have to make room for the next batch and there is always an over-abundance of midfield players.'

As if to prove Dein's point, George Graham was putting his faith in a comparatively untried 21-year-old to anchor the midfield, rather than Michael Thomas, the man whose goal so dramatically won the Championship in 1989. David Hillier, another product of the Arsenal youth policy, had been captain of the side that won the 1988 FA Youth Cup, but his progression into the reserves had been retarded by a series of injuries.

'Last summer was a time for me to think,' he said. 'I'd been in and out of the reserves. I hardly ever put a run of games together.' After demonstrating his versatility by making his début in midfield against Chester in the Rumbelows Cup, then replacing the injured David O'Leary in central defence in the away match against Manchester City on New Year's Day, he came into the first-team squad on a regular basis. When it was most needed, Graham seemed to have found a new Kevin Richardson, whose ball-winning ability was sorely missed, although Thomas and Davis managed to paper over the cracks when they were both playing well. Jan Molby might have wondered why Arsenal were replacing Paul Davis with the ball-boy, but for most of the League match at Anfield, Molby was well and truly shackled by Hillier's marking. 'It was the first time the boy has been to Anfield,' remarked George Graham, 'and he goes out and plays an absolute stormer.'

The manager had no doubt as to the reason: 'He's unflappable, his biggest asset is his temperament.' When Paul Davis got back into the team, it was Thomas who had to make way for him, so indispensable had Hillier's positional and combative skills become to the Arsenal midfield. With Kevin Campbell, David Hillier had rejuvenated a team that appeared in danger of losing its way. His performances were rewarded with a long-term contract and a call up to the England Under-21 squad.

Despite the arrival of Souness, and the dwindling gap between the teams at the top of the table, Arsenal's destiny remained in their own hands. With a massively superior goal difference, should Arsenal win three of their last four games, the Championship would be theirs, whatever Liverpool did. A midweek game the following Tuesday, against QPR at Highbury, now assumed monumental proportions. Arsenal had to win it, to stop any Souness bandwagon from gathering momentum and to get themselves back into the winning habit.

HEROES AND VILLAINS

It would not be an easy task. QPR, after enduring a particularly bad run of injuries and a disastrous sequence of losses earlier in the season, were now on a roll, having lost only one of their previous thirteen games, one victory during this spell coming at Anfield. David Hillier had recovered from the injury that kept him out of the semi-final, and came in for Michael Thomas. Anders Limpar was also back for Groves, but there was no change in the 4-2-4 system. Graham attempted to diffuse some of the tension when he said: 'Nobody here is talking about pressure or even winning titles. You should only talk about winning things after you have.'

Highbury's biggest League gate of the season, 42,393, saw Arsenal dominate the first half but fail to score against some resolute defending. QPR outdoing Arsenal at their own game, played four central defenders, one of them, Peacock, admittedly as an emergency centre forward, but Don Howe's plan was obviously to get as many men behind the ball as possible at every conceivable opportunity. Rangers created only one clear-cut chance in the whole ninety minutes, when Wegerle beat Winterburn and shot, but Seaman produced a smart save. For the rest of the match it was all Arsenal. Hillier had a tremendous game in midfield, harrying opponents, winning the ball, and distributing it simply but always accurately. Moreover, he added Ray Wilkins to the growing list of illustrious opponents he has subdued. Anders Limpar looked to be approaching something like his early-season form, but even so, Arsenal had difficulty finding the final, decisive pass. That same night, Liverpool were playing a much weakened Crystal Palace at Anfield, and as the second half at Highbury progressed with the score remaining at 0–0, news came through that Liverpool were in the lead, followed by reports of a second goal.

The moment of truth arrived in the fifty-eighth minute, and it fell to Lee Dixon to confirm Arsenal's Championship aspirations. The chance came when Paul Davis was brought down by Tillson and the referee gave a penalty. As cool as you like, Dixon put Arsenal one up. After that it was only a question of when another goal would come. It arrived in the seventy-second minute, when Campbell's shot was brilliantly saved by Stejskal, only for the

298

ball to fall to Merson, who gleefully sealed the victory. Liverpool, 3–0 winners over Palace, were now running out of games – three to go with Arsenal still three points ahead. For Arsenal, winning the Championship now depended on how much nerve, guts and desire they could summon up in the few matches that remained.

As the euphoria at White Hart Lane was replaced by the need to gear the club for the Cup Final against Nottingham Forest on 18 May, the financial crisis was temporarily put to one side. It was, however, only a momentary calm, as another episode in the Spurs soap opera was about to break.

Before that there were other things to occupy the club, one of which was even a football match. On Wednesday, Spurs went to Selhurst Park to play Crystal Palace in the League game that was postponed in the worst of the winter weather. David Howells, Justin Edinburgh and Gary Lineker were rested and replaced by Nayim, Mitchell Thomas and Paul Walsh. The game was decided by an early mistake on the part of the Spurs goalkeeper: after six minutes, Erik Thorstvedt dropped the ball and Eric Young put Palace ahead with the simplest of strikes. The Spurs fans could only hope that the big Norwegian was getting any errors out of his system before the return to Wembley. Terry Venables thought Young had kicked the ball out of Thorstvedt's hands: 'I was very disappointed the referee allowed the goal. I thought it was an extremely bad decision.'

After the goal, Spurs took the game to Palace without ever really looking as though they could penetrate a solid Palace defence. Gazza played well, but clearly had some way to go to recover full match fitness, and Venables withdrew him after fifty-four minutes.

'Paul stole the show at Wembley in the first half,' said Palace manager, Steve Coppell, afterwards. 'It was hard for him to reproduce that on a cold and windy night at Selhurst Park three days later.'

The defeat meant that Spurs had won just three times in their last nineteen League games, a statistic that said everything about the side's faltering Championship campaign. They had managed to raise their game for FA Cup ties, but could this continue all the way to the final? And would events off the field fatally compromise the team's preparations?

Although all those connected with Tottenham were ecstatic about the defeat of Arsenal, it did not prevent them continuing to pull in different directions. The Venables consortium had been rejected by the board, but the rejection was promulgated by Brown Shipley and the Midland Bank, who were uneasy with the consortium's ability to find all the necessary finance. Venables was now feverishly trying to come up with an alternative proposal. Irving Scholar was still doing all he could to stall the Gascoigne transfer, while at the same time he was considering a new rights issue to strengthen his hand. Nat Solomon, who was there to carry out the hard decisions, began to talk about the imposition of a 'controlled' board, with some form of administrator appointed by the Midland Bank to run the company. As the pressure for action began to intensify, Solomon, mindful of 17 billion lire sitting in the Banco di Santo Spirito, decided enough was enough. Now he was going to act.

In Italy, Gazza's display in the semi-final was one of the weekend's top sports stories. In typical Roman style, his class was described as 'rugged', and he was called 'the poet and peasant of the kick'. At Lazio, there were pressing reasons why the administration needed to consolidate the understanding struck in March and secure Gascoigne's services as soon as possible. The team had suffered some poor results, the chance of a UEFA Cup place was rapidly disappearing, and a boost in morale was deemed necessary. Beyond that, the Lazio VIP membership scheme was due to be renewed. Five hundred three-year debentures were on offer, costing £5,000 each. With Gascoigne in the team for the following season, the scheme was assured of success. So Gian Marco Calleri was delighted when Nat Solomon told him he was coming to Rome, this time with Len Lazarus and Mel Stein, to finalize the arrangements.

While all this was going on, Tottenham played another football match, away to the rejuvenated Sheffield United. This time Spurs let a two-goal lead slip as United came back strongly to draw 2–2. Mabbutt, Gascoigne, Van Den Hauwe and Lineker were missing. All the scoring came in the second half. Justin

Edinburgh grabbed his first goal for the club to give Spurs the lead, then Paul Walsh netted the second after a Samways shot had been pushed on to the bar by the keeper. Sheffield got one back from a set piece when Beesley headed home a corner, and Deane sealed the comeback in the last minute. Venables, despite his team throwing away a two-goal lead, was not unduly down-hearted: 'I would have been a lot angrier if a more experienced side had been playing. I don't mind too much if the players learn from this. I thought it was all over at 2–0 but the players lacked concentration and look what happened.'

Gazza was rested, according to the manager, because he was 'very, very tired'. As a footnote, Vinny Jones, who had accused Gazza of being 'flash' after the 4–0 defeat at White Hart Lane, publicly revised his opinion.

'Now Gazza is smiling more and laughing things off,' he ventured. 'He has grown up and I am impressed by the way his manager and team-mates have stood by him.'

As Spurs were faltering at Bramall Lane, their opponents in the Cup Final, Nottingham Forest, were putting seven past Chelsea.

Another draw against Everton the following Wednesday, this time finishing 3–3, at least provided good entertainment and goals from Allen, Mabbutt and Nayim, albeit for White Hart Lane's lowest League crowd of the season, just over 21,000. All the headlines, though, concentrated on the fact that Gazza had withdrawn from the England party due to play Turkey in a European Championship game the following week. He had suffered a reaction to the surgery while taking part in a training session, which was why he missed the Everton game.

Terry Venables explained the situation: 'He trained on Tuesday and felt sore, so we sent him to a specialist in the afternoon as a precaution. There is a slight problem with a stitch that goes into the bone. It's nothing, but he needs two or three days' rest.'

The next day Nat Solomon and Dennis Roach caught the 7.25 a.m. Al Italia flight from Heathrow to Rome. There, they were joined by Len Lazarus and Mel Stein. Meanwhile, two representatives of Lazio were conducting some intricate manoeuvres to avoid detection by the media. Maurizio Manzini was with the

Lazio players, who were enjoying lunch at a restaurant. Manzini, the only member of the Lazio staff who speaks English, always remains with the team whenever they are together. For him to be called away was unknown. Suddenly, Manzini was gone. At the same time, general manager Carlo Regalia, who would be in charge of the Lazio negotiating team as Calleri was away in Brazil, disappeared from the training ground. Regalia's house was bombarded by pressmen, but his wife, displaying what Italians called 'Lombardian calm', refused to divulge his whereabouts.

The meeting in Rome was held at the home of Lazio's lawyer and lasted well into the night. As agreement with Tottenham was a prerequisite, without which the player's terms and conditions could not be finalized, the Lazio delegation shuttled between rooms, holding separate negotiations with the two parties, and pausing only to take telephone calls from Calleri in Rio and Gascoigne in London. Progress was slow, but eventually at 3.30 a.m. on Friday morning, Nat Solomon finally signed away Gascoigne as a Spurs player. Naturally, Lazio wanted to parade him immediately, but as the Cup Final was just a week away, and since Gascoigne had yet to sign his personal contract, it was agreed that he would go to Italy in the week after the Cup Final and sign in time to be presented to the fans at Lazio's final home game of the season, against Sampdoria on 26 May. After Stein had confirmed the details of his contract to the player on the telephone, Gascoigne told Manzini he had always wanted to be a millionaire. It was only necessary now to put pen to the paper which Stein would be bringing back with him for Gascoigne's ambition to be realized.

Irving Scholar believed he could prevent the sale right up to the last minute. He had tried to stop Nat Solomon from going to Rome, but his refinancing plans had so far come to nought and Solomon could not wait. When he realized he had failed he confessed to being 'angry and disappointed'. At the Mill Hill training ground Gascoigne remained silent but Venables began a rearguard action, saying that the Lazio offer was 'not all that great', and arguing that Gazza could expect a better deal: 'He is only twenty-three and there are bigger clubs for him. I don't think it will be good for him to go to Lazio and I don't thing there is enough money in it. I don't want to hear any more about Lazio. We want to win the Cup and if Gascoigne doesn't want to go to Italy, no one can make him.'

The Spurs manager pointed to the purported offer from Juventus of £10 million as evidence to support his view. He also insisted that his contract of employment with Spurs gave him the last word on transfers, in and out, and hinted that he might take legal action if this clause were not honoured.

As crowds of joyful fans gathered in ever increasing numbers outside Lazio's Rome headquarters, stopping the traffic in their celebrations, the switchboard at White Hart Lane was jammed with calls from concerned and disillusioned Spurs supporters expressing their anger at the board. White Hart Lane was a gloomy place that day.

One Spurs fan of many years' standing summed up the feelings of all: 'We've been stabbed in the back. It's a disaster, Waddle all over again. Selling our best players hinders any Championship hopes.'

It now appeared that, after the Cup Final, Spurs would lose Gascoigne, Venables and probably a number of other players who would leave in the wake of these two. Irving Scholar had said that selling Gascoigne would be a resignation matter, but to whom would he then be able to sell his shares?

Mel Stein claimed Gazza's sale was not yet totally confirmed, since the player had not signed, even if the clubs had agreed terms.

'If it comes to the stage where the only way Spurs can be saved is for him to be sold,' he said, 'then, rather than let the club go down the tubes, he will go. It is extremely premature, however, to assume that Paul has either gone to Lazio or is on his way. He hasn't even been out to Rome yet and there's no way he'll sign for anyone until he has paid them a visit.'

Despite Stein's assertions, it seemed likely that Gascoigne would go to Rome now that the deal had been as good as completed. The Italian media certainly thought Gazza was on his way. On Sunday 28 April, an Italian newspaper, *Gazetta della Sport*, began a four-part 'Story of Gazza'. There were two other Gascoignes famous in Britain, it told its readers: the quizmaster, Bamber, and the actress, Jill. Discussion of Gascony, from whence the name comes, followed, particularly its historic associations with the UK.

Meanwhile, Gary Lineker expressed his distaste for what was going on. 'It's a terrible time for all this to come to a head, with the Cup Final so close. It's far from the ideal preparation and we are all finding it very unsettling.'

Terry Venables had still not given up hope of mounting a successful bid for the club. His resilience in the matter, after suffering so may reverses, was remarkable. Venables was always careful to court the support of fans, and was seen in many ways as the people's choice. So far, though, nothing had succeeded. Now he was preparing another attempt. Unfortunately for Venables, the public exposure of Larry Gillick's misfortunes had weakened the resolve of the consortium's backers, who from the outset had insisted on anonymity because of the effect that public association with the bid might have had on their own businesses. Now there was the added risk of trial by tabloid. One by one they had withdrawn, leaving Venables to regroup. Despite such setbacks, he seemed determined to fight on.

The new plan unveiled by Venables was a radical departure from what had been envisaged previously. Gone was any talk of £20 million; and gone also was the concept of a consortium that would purchase the entire club. The new offer was made by a private company called Edennote. After the revelations about Larry Gillick's bankruptcy, it was commonly supposed that he had bowed out of the proceedings, and Venables himself hinted at 'new backers' for his bid. Irving Scholar, however, still believed Gillick was involved with the offer. Scholar's view was correct: Edennote was listed at Companies House as having two directors, Terry Venables and Larry Gillick. The terms of the bid were complicated, but essentially they entailed the issue of five million new shares, to be bought by Edennote for £3.5 million. Edennote would then own 35 per cent of Tottenham Hotspur plc, approximately the same percentage that Irving Scholar and Paul Bobroff possessed between them. In addition to the cash, Edennote had prepared a schedule to reduce the debt to the Midland Bank and wanted to install a new board. More significantly, there was the possibility of a sale and leaseback deal for the White Hart Lane stadium. The offer contained two conditions: firstly, 'P. Gascoigne, esq.' could not be transferred; and secondly, the Midland had to agree in writing to the debt reduction proposals.

There were a number of problems with the new bid. Irving Scholar might have supported it, since it kept him as a shareholder – albeit a minor one – provided he and Venables could patch up their differences, but there remained other obstacles. The Midland, which had rejected guarantees from the Venables–Gillick consortium, was unlikely now to accept mere promises to reduce the overdraft over a period. Moreover, under Stock Exchange regulations, if a party gains 30 per cent of a company's shares or more, that party then has to bid for the whole company. The requirement can be waived, but that could not happen without the agreement of shareholders. Selling the ground when property values had slumped seemed injudicious, to say the least. And Tottenham had a binding contract with Lazio. But the part of the bid that would have been most difficult for the board to accept was the price of the new shares, which was set at 60p, 70p less than the Robert Maxwell offer and 30p less than the suspended price.

Venables presented his proposals to the Tottenham board the following day, Monday 29 April. After over five hours of deliberations the meeting broke up with no comment being made. Once again Venables remained undaunted, still insisting that the new offer stood a better than even chance of being accepted.

Some advice for Venables came from Rome, where Lazio's president responded angrily to Venables' claims that Lazio were not big enough for Gazza. 'Please Mr Venables,' he said. 'Join the lifeguards if you are so good at rescues.'

Three weeks before the Cup Final, Spurs' problems were once again at the surface. Yet, despite all the manoeuvring, there was no sign of a solution beyond the sale of Gascoigne. A huge question mark hung over the future of Terry Venables at White Hart Lane, while Irving Scholar, whose demise had supposedly been imminent for six months, was still somehow hanging on. Instead of looking forward to the big game, the morale of the club and its supporters had hit rock-bottom. As one long-time Spurs fan put it: 'The season has definitely been soured for me. I just don't know what's going on. The club has become secondary from what I can see. I'm just angry at everything that's happening.'

A season-ticket holder had similar comments: 'Normally, after a semi-final everybody is bouncing, but you go in now and the staff are very low. "It's alright for Gazza and Lineker," one of them said to me, "but we don't know where the next pound is coming from." A drive down Tottenham High Road confirmed the dismal picture to him: 'Normally, shops are displaying banners and showing their colours. You would not have known there was a Cup Final coming. The whole district is subdued because of the situation.'

A couple of miles along the Seven Sisters Road it was a different story. There, the atmosphere was vibrant, with the expectation that the forthcoming bank-holiday weekend would finish with Arsenal crowned Champions.

21

Champions

The fame of Arsenal Football Club will be forever linked to the
winning of League Championships. Of course, there have been
cup triumphs and success in Europe, but the true legacy be-
queathed on succeeding generations is the worldwide renown
brought about by the remarkable five League titles in the 1930s,
three of which came in consecutive years. Emulating the success
of those days was always an improbable idea, although the
double-winning side went some way towards it. However, Bertie
Mee's team could not maintain its challenge, and, as the only
rewards the club enjoyed after 1971 came in cup competitions,
the feeling persisted that until Arsenal could once again become
League Champions, the club's destiny was left unfulfilled.

George Graham recognized this better than any of his immediate predecessors. Even when the Championship finally returned
to Highbury in 1989, Graham was not satisfied. Not until he
could match the achievements of the Herbert Chapman/George
Allison era would he be entirely happy with his work. At last,
such a goal was now clearly within his sights, and if his team
could just hold its nerve in the three games that remained, a bust
of Graham might one day be placed in the portals of Highbury
alongside that of the old master, Chapman. For Graham, like Bill
Shankly and Matt Busby (Scotsmen all), the quest for success
had become almost mystically bound up with the fate of one
club.

The outcome of the 1990–91 Championship would be determined over the May bank holiday, and television was determined
to be there to broadcast events as they unfolded. The League,
however, refused permission for ITV to show Arsenal's next
match away to Sunderland live, on the grounds that ITV
wanted to move the kick-off time to 5.20 p.m. on Saturday, by
which time all the other results, including Liverpool's, would be

known. Moreover, the League had always set itself against live televised football on Saturdays. When Sunderland found out about the rejection, they were furious. Faced with the prospect of relegation, and the huge loss of income a drop into the Second Division would mean, they desperately needed the cash a live match would bring. Since ITV almost exclusively concentrated on the big clubs, this was the only chance during the whole season for Sunderland to earn the special rights fee ITV paid to the home club in a televised match. Under pressure from the Wearsiders, ITV, and, it must be said, the wider viewing public, the League backed down and allowed the game to be put back to 5.20 p.m. and televised live.

The about-face had implications for the long-term relationship between football, its chief paymaster, and supporters. When ITV won the television-contract war of 1988, it owed its success to the skilful way it exploited the vested interests of factions within the League (a divide-and-rule policy), a strategy played out with the complicity of the big clubs. Now it suited ITV to let a cash-hungry club make the running in the dispute with the League. It was a salutory reminder that money talks. Perhaps the most unfortunate aspect of the affair was the complete lack of consideration for the Arsenal fans, who travel in their thousands to away games. Having become inured to high prices and poor conditions, their endurance of the vagaries of the British transport system was going to be severely tested. With the last trains to London from the north-east leaving before the end of the game, large numbers of the Arsenal faithful would be marooned in Sunderland for at least a night, a situation hardly conducive to the maintenance of public order.

'There were a lot stuck up there,' said one disgruntled Arsenal fan. 'It's disgusting that TV can control football like that . . . I think it's bang out of order that the football supporter is nothing in some people's eyes.'

Liverpool's game against Chelsea at Stamford Bridge went ahead as scheduled at three o'clock. It was absolutely vital that Liverpool win to keep the pressure on Arsenal. They were already three points behind, anything more than that with two games left would make their task impossible. Graham, once again, sought to relieve his players of any pressure, whatever Liverpool did.

'I am not going to talk about pressure because it is tremendous to be involved in the title race going into the last week,' he commented. 'I will happily settle for the same situation next season, whether we win or not.'

In fact, Liverpool soon went 2–0 down, and appeared to be lacking the stomach for the fight, not something readily associated with a Souness team. The Liverpool manager must have found some inspirational words at the break, because a tenacious response after half-time saw the score pulled back to 2–2, and at that stage Liverpool looked the likelier winners. However, in their anxiety to take all three points, Liverpool pushed forward, were predictably caught on the break, and Chelsea won the match with two late goals. So Arsenal ran out at Roker Park knowing they still had the three-point cushion but now also had a game in hand.

With Arsenal's last two games at home, the foremost task at Sunderland was not to lose. Five of the team had been in Turkey on international duty with England the previous week – Seaman, Dixon and Smith for the seniors, Campbell and Hillier for the Under-21s – so tired legs could again prove to be a factor. On the other hand, victory would give the Gunners the title, since their goal difference was so superior to that of Liverpool.

The Arsenal fans were packed into a small section of the ground behind one goal, hemmed in on both sides by the massed Sunderland supporters. The ground, known over the years for the Roker Roar, can be an intimidating place to visit for players and fans alike. It is not often that followers of Arsenal are shouted down, but at Roker Park the home fans kept up a barrage of abuse for almost the entire match. For many of the Arsenal fans, it was a frightening experience and they wondered what might happen after the final whistle, particularly if Sunderland lost. However, at the end of the match the home fans, who minutes earlier had been directing the most offensive torrent of invective imaginable at the Arsenal section, suddenly changed their tune. Almost as one, they turned to the Arsenal fans, and chanted 'Champions'. In return, perhaps tinged with no small amount of relief, the Arsenal contingent sang 'Staying up'.

'They shook our hands and started singing,' said one amazed

Arsenal supporter. 'We all applauded each other after the game and everybody was clapping. We were saying "We hate Luton" and they were saying "We hate Liverpool", everyone was singing at each other, it was a great, great atmosphere at the end.'

In fact, Arsenal were not Champions – yet. They had approached the game displaying little ambition beyond containment of the opposition. David Hillier and Perry Groves came in for Michael Thomas and Anders Limpar, and the safety-first policy was continued when David O'Leary replaced Groves in the second half. In the circumstances this was probably the wisest thing to do, as Sunderland were playing for their First Division existence. They had to win to be in with a realistic chance of avoiding the drop at Luton's expense, so they would be giving everything, urged on by their fanatical support. The plan worked, as Arsenal ground out a 0–0 draw. Their one moment of serious alarm came right at the end when Owers produced a spectacular shot that David Seaman pushed round the post with the tips of his fingers, a save Sunderland manager Denis Smith described as 'world class'.

Afterwards, George Graham explained something of his managerial philosophy: 'The title is won over thirty-eight games and there are times when your performance is not to the standard you would want, and so you have to dig in and refuse to lie down. You may have to concede a little flair to achieve that consistency. We've got to make up our minds what's important. We're here to win.'

The day's results meant that Arsenal would be crowned Champions if they beat Manchester United in the Monday bank holiday game at Highbury. ITV, anxious to cover the dramatic climax to the season, had already committed itself to screening Liverpool's match at Nottingham Forest that day, but it now tried to add the Highbury clash to its schedules. As ITV had used up its allocation of live games with the Forest–Liverpool fixture, Lee Walker, of the League's commercial department, and Trevor East, executive producer of *The match*, had been negotiating a one-off deal for the Arsenal–Manchester United game. Agreement was reached in principle, and the kick-off time was put back to 8.05 p.m. (*Coronation Street* being immovable).

A Forest victory, however, would relegate the game to late evening highlights, as Arsenal would then become Champions before the match against United began.

Not for the first time, the League showed its inability to speak with one voice. 'Trevor East and Lee Walker might have agreed a fee,' said League president Bill Fox, 'but they don't run the League.'

The price, believed to be £400,000, was insufficient for Fox. 'It's simple,' he explained, 'ITV have paid £13 million for twenty-one games this season. Divide £13 million by twenty-one and that is the price for this game [£619,000].'

ITV was insistent that it had a deal for the lower figure, and another unseemly squabble over money threatened to overwhelm the match itself.

In the event, there was no live broadcast, because Liverpool were beaten 2–1 in Nottingham. The Arsenal team met up at their usual Saturday pre-match rendezvous, a north London golf club, had a quick bite to eat, then went into a short team meeting with George Graham. In between, they managed to watch the first half-hour of the Liverpool game, which had kicked off at 5 o'clock. The players left for Highbury separately shortly afterwards. Lee Dixon shared his car with Alan Smith, who wanted to listen to the Liverpool match on the radio.

'Lee didn't want it on. I kept turning it on and he kept turning it off. Then I turned it on and Jan Molby scored with a penalty so he turned it off again. Then we came down Avenell Road and all the fans were going 'two-one, two-one', so that gave us a great lift.'

'By the time most of the team had arrived at Highbury, they knew Arsenal were Champions for the tenth time. As the ground began to fill up, the team went out on to the pitch, bedecked with hats and scarves, to savour the atmosphere and share in the joy of the fans. They were rapturously greeted with the chant of 'Champions', and the captain must have been touched by the massed rendition of 'There's only one Tony Adams'. It was not as dramatic as the victory at Anfield two years previously, but considering the loss of two points at a critical stage of the season, when just about everyone had written off their chances, this triumph was perhaps even more creditable.

Unlike the Rumbelows Cup tie, Manchester United did not turn out to be party-poopers this time. With their own sights set firmly on the forthcoming final of the Cup-Winners' Cup, United were forced to play second fiddle, particularly when Bryan Robson limped off early on, following a tackle from the recalled Anders Limpar. Five minutes later, a low cross from Dixon was hammered home by Smith to give Arsenal the lead. Smith got his second a few minutes before half-time when he was set up by a shrewd pass from Campbell. Arsenal's third came from a rather fortunate penalty decision, when a shot from Tony Adams struck Bruce on the arm. Lee Dixon left the job of converting the spot-kick to Smith, who duly lodged his first hat-trick of the season.

In the last minute, David Seaman gave away a penalty when he brought down Robbins, and Bruce made it 3–1. Although the goal made no difference to the outcome of the game or the Championship, it did prevent Seaman from keeping his thirtieth clean sheet of the season and meant Arsenal had narrowly failed to equal Liverpool's 1978–79 record for the least number of goals (sixteen) conceded in a League season. It was the only negative moment on a night when Arsenal looked worthy Champions and had fulfilled George Graham's wish that they celebrate the title in style.

No one could have been more pleased with the way things turned out than Alan Smith. His hat-trick confirmed him as the First Division's leading scorer, just as he had been in the last title-winning campaign. When he arrived at Highbury in the summer of 1987, Smith was George Graham's biggest signing, at £800,000. It was not only his goalscoring prowess that had endeared him to the manager, but his ability to produce cultured centre-forward play by holding the ball up and bringing other players into the game. This quality facilitated the emergence of Kevin Campbell, who recognizes the way in which Smith's style has helped him.

'He does so much unspectacular, but vital, work,' said Campbell. 'You can't appreciate it unless you play alongside him.' Unusually for a big man, his control on the floor is exemplary, and his phlegmatic character makes him one of the least volatile of footballers. In company with his erstwhile partner at Leicester,

Gary Lineker, Smith has never been booked in his entire professional career.

Smith had already been capped for England at semi-pro level when Jock Wallace took him from Alvechurch in the Southern League to Leicester in 1982. Not long after arriving at the Second Division club, Wallace left, and the new manager, Gordon Milne, teamed Smith up with Lineker to form one of the most prolific goalscoring double acts of the eighties. Smith acknowledges the debt to Milne, saying 'he was the best thing that could have happened to me,' and crediting the manager with teaching him 'good habits'. While Smith was seen as the junior partner in the attack, he was instrumental in providing Lineker with a good proportion of his goalscoring chances, and the two developed an almost telepathic understanding. In their first season together they scored forty goals between them as Leicester were promoted. Neither player was overawed by life in the top flight, and the goals they scored kept what was an otherwise mediocre team in the First Division. During this period, Lineker scored the lion's share of the goals (seventy-seven to Smith's forty-five), but when Lineker left for Everton in 1985, Smith took on the mantle of leading the attack. In a struggling team he scored nineteen League goals the following year and seventeen in his final season.

Smith's move to Arsenal was surrounded by controversy. He was actually transferred towards the end of the 1986–7 season but was immediately loaned back to Leicester for the remainder of the campaign to help in an ultimately unsuccessful bid to stave off relegation. This caused complaints, and League rules were amended to prevent such a situation from arising again. In spite of some settling-in difficulties, Smith ended his first season as Arsenal's leading scorer. An unusual goal-burst at the start of the following season set the Gunners up for their push towards the title, and he finished that season as the First Division's top scorer, with twenty-three goals, an achievement which won him his first full England cap, against Saudi Arabia. The match against Liverpool at Anfield will always be remembered for Michael Thomas' last-gasp goal which gave Arsenal the title, but it is typical of Smith's unsung contribution that his all-important first goal – a delightful glancing header – is rarely mentioned. After a poor start in 1989–90, which turned out to be an anti-climactic season for the whole club, Smith was dropped for a time and was omitted from Bobby Robson's World Cup squad.

The 1990–91 season didn't start too well either for him. With one goal in the first fourteen games (excluding the dubious one against Wimbledon), many fans thought he should be dropped, and this duly happened against Crystal Palace in November. His thoughtful attitude to the lot of a goalscorer enabled him to come to terms with the situation.

'I know there are going to be times when I'm not going to score,' he said. 'That's just the cycle of a striker's game. You've got to have confidence in your own ability. You've got to realize you are going to come out of it.'

Smith returned for the next game against Southampton and promptly embarked on a run of thirteen goals in eleven matches. The early-season malaise then returned for a time as he managed only two goals in the next fourteen games, but it was finally cast off with a flourish as he hit eleven in ten to finish as the First Division's top marksman once again. His form during the run-in was good enough to catch Graham Taylor's eye, and he was reunited with Gary Lineker in the European Championship qualifier against Turkey. Unlucky with a shot that hit the bar, he looked to have done enough to warrant an extended run in the England team.

After the game against Manchester United, the celebrations got under way in earnest. They were somewhat marred, however, by the refusal of the Football League to allow the traditional Championship trophy to be presented. Instead, Barclays made a presentation of their own cup. While the the League insisted that their trophy only be given to the winners after the last match of the season, the real reason was pique because of the dispute with ITV over the television screening. The League's commercial director, Trevor Phillips, bemoaned the lack of acumen which allowed such an opportunity to be missed. 'The only way I'd get the League trophy down here tonight,' he said, 'would be to break into the cabinet room at Lytham St Annes.'

David Dein thought the presentation of the trophy the following Saturday at the game with Coventry would be like drinking 'flat champagne'.

None of this seemed to bother the players and the fans. Spectators at the Clock End spilled on to the pitch, which delayed matters for a while, but order was soon restored. Eventually, the players began a delirious lap of honour, Paul Merson throwing his shorts into the crowd before departing the scene. Brian McClair, who had been at the centre of the brawl back in October, made a point of going to all the Arsenal players to offer his congratulations. United manager Alex Ferguson thought Arsenal worthy Champions. 'Christ, they've only lost one game,' he said. 'When was the last time that was done, a hundred years ago?'

George Graham stood on the touchline, letting the players take the plaudits. Afterwards, he considered the future: 'There is no reason why we cannot continue in this vein. We have a good young team and there are a lot more youngsters coming through. That is exciting not just for Arsenal but for the League as a whole.'

'Graeme Souness, while admitting that Arsenal deserved to take the title, was somewhat faint with his praise, saying: 'Without a doubt over the whole season Liverpool have lost the Championship rather than Arsenal have won it.'

Legions of fans crowded into local pubs, staying until the small hours. 'We didn't stop till 3 o'clock in the morning,' one of their number revealed. 'We were singing "if you're all going to Europe, clap your hands". Everybody was singing and laughing.'

With one more party to come, the final home game of the season against Coventry the following Saturday, it was the perfect time to launch plans for the redevelopment of the North Bank. The Taylor Report required Arsenal, in common with all clubs, to move rapidly to an all-seat stadium. Those in charge at Highbury apparently recognized that they needed to take the fans along with them in any plans for redevelopment. A questionnaire that had appeared in the Leeds programme, however, seemed to be more concerned with building up a mailing list than soliciting supporters' views. The questionnaires were given to the public on 17 March, but the planning application for the North Bank was lodged with the local council three days earlier. Thus the meetings that David Dein arranged with a sample of those who had completed questionnaires were more in the way of explanation of what had already been decided rather than an exercise to allow supporters to have any actual influence on the decision-making process.

The North Bank plan will see it completely rebuilt as an all-seat section. The £20 million two-tier stand will house a museum, crèche and catering facilities, and will be ready for the 1993–4 season. The capacity of Highbury will be reduced to 37,000 (29,000 while work is in progress). The most interesting part of the scheme was not the architecture or the amenities, however, but the way the new development was to be financed.

Mindful of Tottenham's problems following rebuilding, David Dein looked for another method of raising the money. Some years previously he had been impressed when he saw the Joe Robbie stadium in Miami, which was entirely financed by debenture bonds. In the UK, similar schemes had been employed at Cardiff Arms Park and Twickenham, but the only football club that had attempted this method was Glasgow Rangers. Dein therefore went to see the Rangers chairman, David Murray, and came away convinced that this was the road he should take. So enthusiastic was he over what he had heard from Murray that he decided to use the same company of financial advisers, Noble Grossart, to launch a similar scheme to the one at Ibrox to finance the cost of the new North Bank.

Such a scheme carried with it certain legal requirements. Arsenal were incorporated as a private limited company in 1910. By 1991, Peter Hill-Wood and David Dein were the largest shareholders. These two had an understanding that if the need arose they would each have a first option on the other's shares. Although they were from completely different backgrounds, there is mutual affection between the two men. Moreover, both believe that as long as at least one of them remains in control, the future of the club is assured. Shortly before registering as a public limited company on 9 May in order to conform to the rules of the bond issue, Hill-Wood sold the majority of his shares to Dein, making the vice-chairman the major shareholder, with a 40 per cent holding.

Arsenal fans should not be unduly concerned that Dein would do a Scholar. A fan in the boardroom at Highbury cannot run riot, because by definition Arsenal is a football club. Dein has pioneered commercial development, while making sure that nothing be undertaken which could prejudice the reason for the club's existence. It should also be noted that Dein has done all this without taking any salary. His satisfaction is the reflected glory of the team's accomplishments, and the nearest he gets to interfering in the dressing room is by personally shaking each player's hand and wishing him good luck before every game.

Dein originally intended to unveil the debenture plan in June, but the success of the team gave him the opportunity to bring the scheme forward. On the day before the Coventry game, the proposals were presented to the public using the theme, 'Sign for the Arsenal'. At the presentation, Dein spoke of the options the board had considered. Any new stadium would have to be built outside London, which would present huge difficulties with transport.

'Do you see any tube stations on the M25?' Dein asked. 'Moving to Wembley and sharing with Tottenham were discussed, but Wembley is not home. Highbury is the ancestral home, and with so much investment here recently, to throw it all down the pan would be silly.'

Under the terms of the offer, supporters were asked to pay either £1,500 or £1,100, for which they would receive a bond that entitled them to purchase a season ticket in a designated seat for the next 150 years. The bonds could be traded at any time. The price of the new season tickets was to be pegged for an unspecified period so that sitting in the new stand would cost no more than standing in the old one. Thus in five years, in comparison with West and East Stand season-ticket prices, the initial outlay would be recouped. Arsenal had also arranged for the Bank of Scotland to offer loans to supporters who wanted to purchase the bonds, with repayments set at £32 per month.

A debenture scheme such as this is one of the few ways to finance rebuilding work without giving up control (which was why a flotation was rejected) or incurring large debts. Finance for the development could thus be separated from the normal day-to-day operations of the club. This releases money that can then be made available to the manager rather than being siphoned away to pay extraneous costs, as happened at White

Hart Lane. Wherever demand exceeds supply, as will be the case in a reduced-capacity Highbury stadium, debentures can reward their owners by providing added value for their outlay beyond the opportunity to buy a season ticket. If other schemes are anything to go by, the bonds will increase in value over the years and could probably be sold at a profit. Sound though the idea undoubtedly is, it remains the case that a good many of the regular supporters on the North Bank will be unable to afford the £32 per month repayments. Indeed, many could be judged a financial risk and be unable to qualify for the loan at all. They are now in danger of losing their most hallowed place.

'It will also kill off the occasional spectator,' said one fan. 'What if my dad or my girlfriend want to come to a game? If they come they want to be with me, but they won't be able to if I've got my own seat, so they won't come.'

Unfortunately, the inevitable outcome of the Taylor Report is that the cost of rebuilding the country's stadia is so prohibitive that the nature of football's support will change, with many of the traditional supporters forced out. 'I will only be able to go to away games now,' complained another North Bank regular. It was an absurd paradox for the most committed of fans. The spectre looms that football will go the way of the gridiron game in America, where attendance at matches is restricted to the affluent middle class, while everyone else has to make do with television.

For all the publicity surrounding the new debenture scheme – the entire ground was plastered with invitations to buy a bond – nothing could detract from the sheer joy and fun the game against Coventry generated. If Manchester United had been a party, this was a carnival, with what seemed like the whole crowd of more than 40,000 belting out the old Queen classic, 'We are the Champions'. It could only be capped by the presentation of the Championship trophy to the players and the Barclays Manager of the Season award to George Graham. The game itself matched the atmosphere, as Arsenal sealed their triumph with an exuberant 6–1 victory.

The scoreline in no way reflected the bizarre nature of the match. Arsenal moved into a 2–0 lead courtesy of an own goal from Peake and a clinical finish by Anders Limpar. Despite conceding the goals, Coventry looked quite dangerous when they attacked, and the high balls towards Regis caused the Arsenal defence problems. David Seaman again looked uneasy on crosses, and it was his mistake, when he failed to catch the ball from a corner, that let Coventry back in the game. The score remained at 2–1 until late in the second half. Andy Linighan came on for Paul Merson after seventy minutes, but, paradoxically, the move to strengthen the Arsenal defence was followed by the complete disintegration of Coventry's back line, and Arsenal scored four goals in twelve minutes. Limpar completed his first hat-trick for the club, Perry Groves scored another and Alan Smith got his twenty-second League goal of the season. The crowd were almost beside themselves and self-mockingly chanted 'Boring, boring Arsenal'.

The comprehensive nature of Arsenal's triumph could be seen in the fact that they had won the title by a clear seven points, nine if the two that were deducted are taken into consideration. The team's fifty goals at Highbury was the highest at home in the division, and their total haul of seventy-four was second only to Liverpool's, showing that it was not just the defence that had produced outstanding performances. And one defeat in thirty-eight games was a testament to the consistency that so preoccupied George Graham. It was a feat not achieved since the last century, when the League programme was much shorter. No wonder the fans felt able to chant, 'You can stick your — two points up your arse.'

George Graham was, of course, as pleased as punch. He even singled out Anders Limpar for particular praise. 'He has a unique talent,' he said. 'I enjoyed the really good football we played, and I am not easily pleased.' Terry Butcher, the Coventry player-manager, added his voice to the growing number of admirers: 'Arsenal will do well because everything is right throughout the club. George Graham has talked about a dynasty and he could be right. I would not mind having David O'Leary as fourteenth or fifteenth man.'

The Arsenal manager himself looked forward to a campaign in the European Cup: 'We'll be up against the most famous teams and players and it will be another learning process. I am looking forward to working out new tactics.' It was certainly a prospect to savour, and entirely fitting that Graham, the man who understood Arsenal's tradition better than anybody, should lead the club into what promises to be a new era, one which may one day be spoken of in the same breath as that of Herbert Chapman and George Allison. On Sunday 12 May, thousands of Arsenal fans packed the mile-long route from Highbury to Islington Town Hall, where a civic reception in honour of the club was held. As the collection of silverware was displayed on the Town Hall balcony, the biggest cheers were reserved for Tony Adams and George Graham, a 'fantastic occasion', in Adams' words, on which to bring down the curtain on a season when life had proved stranger than fiction.

While the euphoria and excitement were in full swing at Highbury, Spurs were winding down their League programme in anticipation of the Cup Final. It had been a disappointing season in the League, for reasons everyone understood only too well. The final matches of Spurs' programme were meaningless affairs in themselves, although the bank-holiday game against Nottingham Forest at White Hart Lane had a certain curiosity value, as it was a rehearsal for the final. It was also the final home game of the season and perhaps the last time a number of people would be together at the club. Venables, Scholar, Gascoigne, Lineker – who could know how many of those names would still be at Spurs when the players returned in July?

Spurs were lucky to escape from the Forest game with a 1–1 draw, having been outplayed and out-thought for much of the match. With Paul Stewart suspended, Nayim came into the team, and it was he who managed to equalize Nigel Clough's opener. Gazza played, but again looked short of match fitness. Terry Venables was quite relaxed, claiming he found the match 'interesting and helpful'. A number of Spurs fans staged a demonstration at the final whistle, the main thrust of which was that they wanted 'Scholar out' and 'Venables in'. Irving Scholar, wisely, was not there to witness it, and the protest petered out peacefully.

Spurs' penultimate game was at Anfield. At one stage in the season it looked as if they might be travelling to Liverpool to help Arsenal win the Championship, but since the Gunners had managed that under their own steam, the game became something of an academic exercise, which Liverpool won 2–0. The defeat left Tottenham in eleventh place, with only an away game against Manchester United to come after the Cup Final. Whatever the outcome, it would be a disappointing end to a League season that had started with such high expectations. Still, the players had redeemed themselves with their performances in the FA Cup, and the final, the greatest day in the English football calendar, beckoned. With seven days to go to the game that could well determine Tottenham's future, it was to be hoped that boardroom intrigue, sales of players and all the other distractions could be left alone for a short time so that all efforts could be concentrated on the final. Throughout Spurs' traumatic season, it was the team that had managed to preserve the club's pride. Surely now the players deserved the same support from the club's hierarchy. Sadly, it was not to be.

22

Tears and Cheers

On the day before the Cup Final, most people would expect the participants to be directing all their energies and thoughts to Wembley and to how they were going to win the trophy. Apart from the players, focusing entirely on football was something those at Tottenham had singularly failed to do for much of what had turned out to be the most bizarre of seasons. Indeed, a number of the key people involved at Spurs were still trying to negotiate the sale of the club less than twenty-four hours before the most important match in its 109-year history.

Terry Venables' bid to take over Tottenham had continued unabated in the week leading up to the big game and culminated in a late night meeting on Friday 17 May. While the players were asleep (or at least in their rooms) at the Royal Lancaster Hotel, Terry Venables and his business team were attempting to conclude a deal with Irving Scholar, whose rights issue proposal had come to nothing. With Paul Gascoigne due to leave for Rome in a few days, Scholar's shares could well become worthless. Scholar, represented by a lawyer with power of attorney, insisted that agreement had to be reached that night or the deal was off. Interestingly, Scholar's price was £250,000 less if Gascoigne remained at Spurs. Once again, however, the Midland Bank presented a formidable obstacle, as Venables and his partners could not take the risk that their guarantee would be rejected, which had happened previously. So once again the negotiations proved inconclusive, and Venables had to be content with taking his team to Wembley as a manager rather than an owner.

The whole week had been somewhat traumatic for the Spurs camp. On Tuesday, an open-day for the media was held at the Mill Hill training ground. Those newspapers that did not contribute to the players' Cup Final pool were denied access by the agent acting for the team, Eric Hall, and some heated arguments ensued which were only settled when Terry Venables intervened and allowed all the reporters in. This episode was followed by a public plea to Gazza from the Spurs manager, urging him to stay at White Hart Lane.

'I fear for him if he goes abroad,' said Venables. 'I know it will not be easy for him to deal with ... I've said this before and I can only repeat, I don't believe he should go yet. He will have problems on and off the pitch.'

Support for Venables came from the unlikely direction of Michael Laudrup, the Danish international who spent five years in Italy at Lazio and Juventus and now plays for Barcelona. 'I can guarantee now he won't enjoy Italy,' warned Laudrup. 'Such a move could destroy Gazza ... every day he will be pestered and put under constant pressure. It's the same at all the important clubs in Italy. When they've paid so much money for you they think they own you. Someone always wants something from you every minute of every day.'

Whatever Laudrup's view, the pressure on Gascoigne could hardly be more intense than it already was, with an Italian contract on the table waiting to be signed and his manager pleading with him to stay.

If this was bad, worse was to follow. On Thursday 16 May, the *Sun* reported that Spurs were hawking Gary Lineker around a number of Italian clubs. In fact, the Spurs management had engaged Dennis Roach back in February to assess interest in Lineker, Gascoigne and indeed practically every player on the Spurs staff. It was certainly incongruous that the story should appear now, just before the Cup Final. Someone, it seemed, had leaked the information three months after the event for his own purposes. The timing was designed to cause maximum damage, not least to Spurs' preparations for the final, which was less than forty-eight hours away. Lineker, naturally, was extremely upset when he heard about it. His agent, Jon Holmes, tried to be as diplomatic as possible, saying: 'We have decided to say nothing until after the Cup Final. We don't want to rock the boat. We shall wait, but it is safe to say we are disquieted and annoyed.'

On Friday, with the takeover meeting due later in the evening, Terry Venables went to see Mel Stein in a last-gasp attempt to convince him that there were just too many pitfalls in Italy for Gazza. If Gazza were prepared to remain at Spurs, Venables could take over the club and together they could mount a serious challenge in Europe and build a team to win the League title. After that, presumably, Gascoigne's value would be even greater and he could move to a really big club on the Continent. Stein listened politely to what Venables had to say, but was non-committal. The manager left without any encouragement for his plans, and it looked almost certain that the Cup Final and the last League game of the season at Old Trafford the following Monday would signal the end of both Venables and Gascoigne as Spurs employees.

The events of the week almost obscured the fact that the 1991 Cup Final promised to be a classic, with two teams committed to playing the kind of attractive football in which aerial assaults are the exception rather than the rule. Everywhere you looked, there were fascinating confrontations. Not least of them was the battle between the managers. For Brian Clough, twenty-five years in management had brought trophy after trophy. The European Cup twice, two League Championships, five League Cups, everything in fact except the FA Cup. Many neutrals were rooting for Clough, in much the same way that Stanley Matthews had been cheered on to his only winner's medal almost forty years before.

It was thought that a degree of antagonism sullied the relationship between Clough and Venables. If any had existed, it was dispelled earlier in the season when Spurs visited the City Ground and Venables, on behalf of Tottenham, presented Clough with a silver salver to mark his quarter of a century as a manager. (Clough had said he would have preferred to be given Gazza.) In addition to the silverware, Venables gave Clough a present of his board game, The Manager. During the match between the two clubs at White Hart Lane a couple of weeks before the Cup Final, Clough had stood up and shouted across to Venables: 'I should have sold my son to Tottenham, that's what I should have done.' When asked later what he meant, he said that when Venables came to Spurs in 1987 he had enquired about buying Nigel. Clough senior thought that if Nigel had joined up with

Venables, the master tactician and coach, it would have enhanced his international prospects. In the event the move did not take place. 'I recommended him to go,' added Clough, 'but the chairman wasn't too keen, and my son, to be fair, wasn't too keen to go to London.'

In the days before the final, the Spurs manager returned the compliment, paying his opposite number a glowing tribute. 'Clough is the greatest manager in my lifetime. I can't think of anybody to compare. He must be doing something right because he's done consistently well for so long, not just over a period of two or three years. He's not had the financial facility of some of the bigger clubs yet he's still taken them on and won.'

Clough himself remained as idiosyncratic as ever, going on holiday two weeks prior to the final. Upon his return, he imposed a fine on Archie Gemmill, a key member of his coaching staff, because the reserves had turned in some poor performances in the manager's absence. On the eve of the big game, Clough's son was asked what frame of mind his father was in. 'We don't know,' Clough junior replied, 'the players haven't seen him all week.'

These were just the latest incidents in a management career notable for its eccentricity. Clough had always courted controversy with his methods, the like of which no other manager would dream of adopting, however successful they might be for Clough. Clough rules Forest to an extent that even George Graham would envy, and his attitude towards directors is legendary. When he first met David Dein after Dein had joined the Arsenal board, the two exchanged pleasantries, then Clough wagged his finger and said to Dein: 'Now don't you go making trouble for your manager, young man.'

The tactical approach of the two teams also promised an intriguing battle. Forest, natural counter-attackers who built their game on a solid defence; Spurs, full of flair, vulnerable at the back, but given more stability since the introduction of the five-man midfield. Most pundits, with one or two notable exceptions, went for Clough and Forest. Their passing style and the perception of Nigel Clough, not to mention a back line based on Des Walker and Stuart Pearce, were seen as key factors. Moreover, Forest had hit a rich vein of form since their semi-final victory over West Ham, winning five of their last six games, and scoring twenty-three goals in the process.

One of the few who tipped Spurs to win was George Graham. Speaking before his departure for Singapore, where Arsenal were due to meet Liverpool in a lucrative friendly, Graham said: 'I'm as aware as the next man that there is a strong wave of feeling for Clough to complete his trophy collection with a long-awaited FA Cup triumph. But professionals will tell you that such emotion counts for little . . . on the field of play. I think Terry will be triumphant. My forecast: Spurs to win 1–0 in normal time or 2–1 after extra time. I'm convinced it will be as close as that.'

One thing on which everyone was agreed was the crucial importance of Paul Gascoigne. If he performed to the standard he had set himself in earlier rounds, Tottenham would win. If Forest could contain him, then their superior team-work should see them lift the Cup for the third time in their history.

Liam Brady pointed to the significance of Gascoigne's personality: 'To analyse him simply as a footballer is impossible. The personality of the man has always had much to do with the performance of the footballer; and Gascoigne's personality is so outrageous, how can you analyse his talent without taking his character into major consideration?'

Marco Tardelli, the great Italian international and a team-mate of Brady's at Internazionale, told the Irishman that he judged greatness in a player by the ability to perform consistently at the highest level over a number of years. 'Gascoigne can achieve this,' concluded Brady, 'be it in Italy or England. The ball is at his feet.'

Brian Clough had studiously avoided joining the clamour to build up Gazza's likely contribution. However, he was put on the spot when interviewed for BBC Radio. In typical Clough style, he initially played down the Gascoigne factor.

'I haven't seen that much of him actually,' Clough began. 'I'm not into this situation where everybody's obsessed with him.' It was Clough's conclusion that spoke volumes, though. 'I think he's got a lot of talent,' he added, 'and I've asked our coach driver, if he sees him in the tunnel at Wembley, to try to knock him down. I don't think we'll stop him apart from that.'

Gazza himself seemed to be in fine form, relaxed and confident. He told Desmond Lynham in an interview for BBC television that he had been 'waiting for this for six years. I know I may never play in the Cup Final again so I'm going to thoroughly enjoy the whole weekend.'

Gazza managed to avoid the Forest coach and survived his journey down the tunnel, but the calmness he seemed to be displaying when the teams took to the pitch was deceptive. Before anyone could make an appraisal of the tactical formations upon which each manager had decided, Gazza's volatile nature came bursting forth in the most dramatic manner. A full swing of the boot in an innocuous position near the touchline in the opening moments ended with Gascoigne's studs in Gary Parker's chest. It was a wild and unnecessary challenge, which would, in most matches, have brought at least a yellow card, but referee Roger Milford was content to admonish Gazza with no more than a word and a smile. It was enthusiasm and desire gone mad, and there seemed no one, not even the referee, who could bring a calming influence to bear, for a few minutes later came the incident which put a wholly different complexion on the game, Spurs' future, and Gazza's lucrative move to Italy. Forest full back Gary Charles had gone forward in support of the attack and received the ball wide on the right. As he cut inside, his path took him across the edge of the penalty area. In lunged Gascoigne, but Charles had already pushed the ball beyond him. Gazza's leg, however, continued on its course, crashed into Charles, and both players collapsed to the floor. It was a horrendous foul, which probably should have got Gazza sent off, but referee Milford only awarded a free kick.

Forest have a number of players who can be lethal at free kicks on the edge of the area. Nigel Clough, for instance, can bend the ball round a wall with accuracy. Stuart Pearce, though, can blast it with the kind of power reminiscent of Peter Lorimer in his prime. Forest were not above a little gamesmanship to help Pearce in this situation. Lee Glover lined himself up in the Tottenham wall, and as Pearce unleashed his drive he pushed Gary Mabbutt out of the way to create a path for the ball, which flew into Erik Thorstvedt's net before the goalkeeper had moved. Amid the wild celebrations among the Forest contingent, Brian

Clough sat impassive, his arms folded, his face betraying not a flicker of emotion. It was the worst possible start for Spurs, but a further tragedy was to follow within seconds. Gascoigne's foul on Charles had not injured the Forest player but did cause serious harm to his own knee. As Spurs kicked off after the goal, Gazza collapsed in a heap and was carried off on a stretcher, to be replaced by Nayim. The man to whom winning the Cup meant so much had lasted only fifteen minutes and was to take no further part in the proceedings.

There was a perceptible change of mood in the stadium when Gazza left the field. That the damage was self-inflicted added to the air of incomprehension and disbelief. Throughout the season, crowds had flocked to see Gascoigne wherever he played, and it was the expectation of everybody that he would have a major influence on the outcome of the match. Now the hero departed in the most undignified fashion, his image tarnished, a huge question mark hanging over his future. Nobody had done more to get Tottenham to the final and nobody could have done less to help them win it.

It did not take long for the knives to come out. On television, Jimmy Hill reminded viewers how he had been criticized for calling Gazza a liability at half-time in the sixth-round game against Notts County.

'In the mood he was in [today],' said Hill, 'Spurs were lucky they didn't have ten men for the rest of the game ... It's inexcusable. It is beyond the line professionals should not tread.'

It would be unfair to single out Hill in the torrent of criticism that Gascoigne faced afterwards. For instance, Patrick Collins in the *Mail on Sunday* wrote: 'There can be not a scrap of pity for Paul Gascoigne, who entered the game with the mindless fury of a demented child and left, damaged and discredited, upon a stretcher.'

Top sports stars react differently to pressure, and as Liam Brady said, Gascoigne's football prowess and his temperament cannot be separated: they are two sides of the same coin. However, there can have been few, if any, occasions in the history of club football to parallel the enormous expectations heaped on Gascoigne. Quite simply, the whole future of the club had come to rest on his shoulders and he had lived with this since Tottenham's true plight had become public the previous September. Rarely in sport can so much have rested on one man. One wonders how those who were so quick to pillory Gascoigne would stand up under such pressure. And how would, say, George Best have reacted, had Manchester United been about to go bankrupt unless he went abroad? What Gascoigne faced were not the normal pressures with which a top-level sportsman has to cope. Gazza's character, as irrepressible as his play, is as vulnerable to external pressures as the next man's, probably more so. In many cultures his type of extrovert personality is tolerated and understood better than it is in the Anglo-Saxon nations, where self-discipline has been elevated into the ultimate virtue. Far from being 'too English', a criticism levelled from Continental Europe, Paul Gascoigne is a Latin American trapped in a Geordie's body.

Before the final, Terry Venables had hinted at the incredible tension Gazza had been subjected to, when he said, 'I do fear for Gazza with all the pressure he's under . . . The world is watching him. It's too much, and he does feel the pressure. He's only human . . . I have never known anything like it. No player has had to suffer so much in such a short space of time. It does frustrate him. I can see that.'

Whatever view is taken of Gascoigne's contribution to the 1991 final, there could be no denying the paramount role he had played in bringing Tottenham to the brink of success. Now, his injury was so serious that he was rushed to hospital, and it was already clear that his immediate prospects, and those of Spurs, had once again been thrown into total confusion.

The loss of Gascoigne, and the goal, mesmerized the Spurs team for a few minutes. 'The players had to make a decision when he went off,' Venables said later. 'Either that is us gone and people will understand if we lose, or, roll up our sleeves and do it for ourselves and for him.'

Perhaps the real turning point of the game came during this period, when Gary Crosby found himself in the clear after a neat interchange of passes. Erik Thorstvedt came out and produced a brilliant save to smother Crosby's shot. Had Forest gone two up then, it is doubtful whether Spurs could have recovered.

Gradually, however, Venables' tactical plan became clear, and Spurs started to drag themselves back into the match.

David Howells was given the job of marking Nigel Clough. Venables had decided that if he could stop Clough's pivotal role in Forest's build up he could go a long way towards limiting their effectiveness. This was the vital task, because, as George Graham had pointed out, 'Forest's favourite ploy is to encourage their midfield players to run beyond defenders in the knowledge that Clough will sit in for them.' In countering the threat, the Spurs manager was aided and abetted by Clough senior, who left Steve Hodge on the bench. Hodge had been out injured for a number of weeks but had convinced England manager Graham Taylor of his return to fitness – Taylor played him for the whole of the second half of the match in Turkey – but Forest had performed well without him, and the young Ian Woan was preferred for the final. What was lost, of course, was Hodge's experience and his ability to get into advanced positions where he could be found by Clough junior. There was no place either, not even as substitute, for Nigel Jemson, the one heavyweight forward in the Forest ranks. Jemson, as his superb opportunist goal at Highbury had shown, could trouble any defence. His goals had also kept Forest in the competition in the early rounds. Those left to construct Forest's attacking play, particularly Roy Keane, were talented enough, but they were youngsters, and this was the Cup Final.

No matter what tactics or formations are employed, they require players with the ability and character to implement them, especially in the really big games. Beyond that, fortune plays its part. Forest had been on the brink of going out of the Cup on a number of occasions, most notably against Newcastle and Southampton, but they had saved themselves at the last. They had also survived a gruelling three-match epic against the previous year's finalists, Crystal Palace, and had benefited from a debatable refereeing decision in the semi-final when West Ham's Tony Gale was sent off for what appeared no more than a clumsy challenge. After this series of escapes, it was hard to dispel the idea that Forest's name was on the Cup, and that providence had been saving twenty-five years of good luck for Brian Clough to call upon in one glorious campaign.

The rest of the first half at Wembley failed to banish such thoughts from the mind. Just before Thorstvedt's save from Crosby, Spurs had mounted an incisive attack down the right. Paul Allen's cross eluded the Forest defence, and Gary Lineker, stealing in with a perfectly timed run, scored what looked to be a good goal. The linesman thought differently, however, and flagged for offside. Television replays confirmed that Lineker was in fact onside. Then Allen, with a free header, put the ball into Crossley's hands. Still Tottenham went forward in search of the equalizer. After thirty-two minutes, Paul Stewart, who had done much to stem the Forest tide early on, showed that his conversion to midfield was an inspirational move by his manager. Stewart, showing the kind of deft touch of which he seemed incapable when playing up front, released the perfect ball to set Lineker free with only Crossley to beat. The England captain expertly went round the Forest keeper, only to be brought down by Crossley's outstretched hand. Lineker took the penalty himself, but Crossley threw himself to his left and pulled off a superb save, pushing the ball away for a corner.

Despite fighting their way back into the game, Spurs reached the interval 1–0 down. They had been given every possible excuse to lose. Many teams would have folded under the adversity they suffered, and it would have been entirely forgivable had that taken place. For one last time, Terry Venables had to weave his magic at half-time and convince his players that they could still win. When the second half began, Spurs, instead of capitulating, gradually assumed complete control. The only time they looked uncomfortable at the back came when Howells misdirected a back-pass to Thorstvedt, but he immediately redeemed himself by hooking away Keane's lob. Seven minutes into the half the breakthrough came. Nayim, who had been performing well as Gazza's replacement, knocked a long ball from the left into the path of Paul Allen. It came to Allen about waist-height, but he controlled it without breaking stride and surged towards the Forest penalty area. Paul Stewart, who had arrived in the area in support of the attack, was unmarked, and Allen found him with a perfectly weighted pass. Stewart took the ball on and produced a perfect low cross-shot that comprehensively beat Crossley.

Emboldened by Stewart's goal, Tottenham drove forward in search of the winner. Lineker's running was prodigious, Samways, Allen and Nayim supported him constantly, and Stewart stamped his authority on the midfield. On numerous occasions Spurs almost broke through the collapsing Forest ranks, only to be foiled by the magnificent defending of Walker and the calm assurance of Chettle and Charles. Meanwhile, Stuart Pearce was forced back and his dangerous forward runs were curtailed. The tiring Woan was replaced at last by Hodge, but by then the pattern of the game had been set. As the match moved towards extra time, the balance swung in Tottenham's favour, and those early thoughts that Forest were predestined to win the trophy now looked premature. In the last minute, Howells got forward, and a looping header, reminiscent of his winning goal at the City ground earlier in the season, almost gave the Cup to Spurs, but this time Crossley made an excellent one-handed save. Then, after the final whistle and with extra time to be played, the most incomprehensible incident took place. Terry Venables was on the pitch, cajoling his players for one last effort. By contrast, Brian Clough, arms folded, remained sitting on the bench, preferring to leave the crucial task of motivation to his coaching staff. When he eventually left his seat, it was to pass the time of day with a policeman. Whatever was going through Clough's mind, it was inexplicable to everyone else. Surely, if any of the teams needed lifting, it was Clough's youngsters. Bob Wilson, speaking on BBC television, was mystified by the Forest manager's inaction: 'Forest needed help from their leader at the end of ninety minutes. I was absolutely staggered that he stayed on his backside.'

During extra time, Spurs continued to dominate the game. Paul Walsh, on for Vinny Samways, headed a Van Den Hauwe cross against the bar. Crossley wrapped himself around a goalpost in his efforts to retrieve the rebound, and in the panic the ball was turned away for a corner. Nayim's kick was flicked on by Stewart and the ball flew across the face of the goal. With Gary Mabbutt steaming forward on the blind side of the defence, Des Walker tried to head it away for another corner. It was a manoeuvre the England defender must have performed on hundreds of occasions during his career, but this time his aim was not precise enough and he deflected the ball into his own net. It was the cruellest of blows considering the enormous contribution that Walker had made, but there could be no denying that Spurs deserved their good luck. As the whole Tottenham bench leapt into the air in joyful celebration, Brian Clough kept exactly the same demeanour that he had worn for the previous ninety-three minutes, one which could best be described as studied disinterest.

Afterwards, Clough dismissed any idea of sympathy for Walker, saying, 'Des Walker is a handsome young man, very talented and very well paid. But when he puts the ball in his own net that is his responsibility.' In many ways, Clough, the manager, is as irascible and temperamental as Gascoigne, the player. Could it be that the impassivity, the refusal to get involved, were really tell-tale signs that the pressure had got to Clough every bit as much as it had got to Gascoigne, and that the two of them had equally failed to cope with it?

The whole Spurs team were heroes. They had refused to lie down when things seemed to be going against them and had produced one of the most remarkable comebacks of recent years. Everywhere you looked, a Spurs player had risen to the occasion. Collectively, they had overcome the loss of Gascoigne, produced some flowing attacking play, and shown that they could survive and prosper without their injured superstar. It was a display of teamwork second to none; they had stopped Forest from playing and nullified their potential match winners. The performance had been reminiscent of Tottenham's play at the start of the season, when, according to Erik Thorstvedt, 'We battled and battled. We knew we could play good football, so if we could stand up to everything in the first half we knew we had the skills to play and win in the second.'

After the match, the Spurs players were naturally overjoyed. Amid the euphoria, captain Gary Mabbutt managed to sum up his feelings. It was the sweetest moment of his career.

'This means everything to me,' he said, 'because I've been at Tottenham nine years and only ever got a UEFA Cup medal. In 1987, losing the FA Cup really was difficult to take, but coming here to win today as captain has made up for that.'

For Gary Lineker, it was similarly his 'best moment in football'.

It was Paul Stewart's best moment too. 'I've never experienced anything in my life as good as that goal,' he said.

Terry Venables was in no doubt as to the scale of what had happened at Wembley: 'It would be an understatement to say I'm thrilled by the way the lads performed to come back from behind . . . I would say this is my finest achievement as a manager, especially given the year we've had.'

The celebrations of the Spurs fans, at Wembley and the following day when thousands turned up for the victory parade to Haringay Town Hall, were as intense as would be expected. But even as Gary Mabbutt lifted the Cup, the triumphant emotions were tempered by uncertainty. The problems had not gone away, and although their team would be in the Cup-Winners' Cup, they could not be sure who would be playing in it, who would be manager, or indeed who would own the club. The injury to Gazza had only increased their worries. Gascoigne had been taken to the Princess Grace Hospital to undergo surgery once more, this time on the anterior cruciate ligaments in his right knee. It was a serious injury, one that had terminated the careers of many players in the past, including Brian Clough, although surgical techniques have improved immeasurably since Clough's playing days.

Terry Venables spoke of Gazza's, and his own, feelings. 'I've spoken to him on the phone and he's pleased for the lads but obviously very upset about not being involved. I feel terribly sad for Paul. He's devastated. This was the biggest game of his life, and he's missed it.'

For Lazio fans, the weekend had been a bigger disaster than they could have conjured up in their worst nightmares. As Spurs were winning the FA Cup, Lazio were defeated 2–0 by Inter at the San Siro stadium in Milan and finally lost the chance of qualification for the UEFA Cup. Then the news from Wembley hit them like a bomb. The catastrophe became known as Lazio's 'Black Saturday', which, according to the *Gazetta della Sport*, was 'an accursed day for Zoff, who lost Europe and a star'.

One Lazio supporter described his reaction in pure Roman style: 'He would have taken over Italy because he has the kind of personality to make it happen. But now it's all over, and like every other Lazio supporter, I feel like committing suicide.'

Lazio's general manager, Carlo Regalia, had been at Wembley, and watched in horror as his club's new saviour all but destroyed himself. When he briefed Gian Marco Calleri on the extent of the injury, the Lazio president could not conceal his disappointment.

'The arrival of Gascoigne would have been the stroke of the century,' he said. 'Now it's become the stroke of the century in reverse.'

Calleri went on to indicate that his club was now re-entering the market-place in search of someone to fill Gascoigne's role. To most observers in England, that was enough to signal that Lazio had pulled out of the transfer, but this was a misreading of Lazio's intentions. With Gazza likely to be out for most of the following season, Calleri had to find a temporary replacement, but he was not prepared to give up his quest for Gazza completely. In discussions with the other Lazio officials, a plan was devised whereby they would offer to buy an option on Gascoigne, to be exercised if and when the player made a full recovery. In the meantime, they could monitor his progress. Calleri, for one, was not about to cast him adrift. 'We consider him still in our family,' the president said, 'and we won't abandon him.'

Calleri became even more emotional as he blasted the English media for the way it had reported the story. 'We've suffered a mortal blow. Gascoigne is a player of whom we have become very fond, about whom the English press has talked and written a lot of lies. And many in Italy believed them. He's a nice, affectionate lad, a person we really like very much, and I, at this point, say we won't leave Gazza on his own.' It was a somewhat different attitude than was generally on display in England, where Gazza had gone from hero to villain in twenty-four hours, and was being lambasted from all quarters.

The ex-Lazio star, Giorgio Chinaglia, explained why Gascoigne's Wembley performance was viewed totally differently in Italy: 'I know people have been screaming about the tackles he made in the Cup Final, but so what? That sort of tackle happens out in Italy all the time. The only difference is that Italian players are fit when they launch themselves into challenges like that. Gascoigne, obviously, was not. He wasn't just a fraction of a second late, he even had time to send a telegram.'

Maurizio Manzini, Lazio's English-speaking official, concurred with Chinaglia's analysis. After flying to London with Carlo Regalia and medical expert Claudio Bartolini, Manzini emerged from watching a video of Gazza's operation, to say: 'If you think the tackle at Wembley was harsh, you should see some of the challenges over in Italy.' Manzini went on to reiterate that Lazio still wanted to go through with the transfer if at all possible. 'Now that Maradona has gone, Gascoigne is without doubt the best footballer in the world. No club in their right mind would turn down a player of Gascoigne's calibre. He will recover perfectly. We are completely satisfied with the way the operation was performed.' The Lazio delegation went to see Gazza while they were at the hospital. They presented him with a £5,000 gold watch and a Lazio shirt. Mel Stein described the scene.

'Paul was very, very emotional to think that a club he is not contracted to has taken time to come over and wish him well,' he said. Stein then indicated that he was still hopeful the transfer would go ahead. 'We have not discussed any deal with the Lazio officials,' he added. 'That will come tomorrow.'

Irving Scholar was in two minds about what had happened. On the one hand, the loss of income from the now postponed Gascoigne sale might precipitate action by the Midland. On the other, Spurs had won the FA Cup and were in Europe next season. To Scholar, this prospect was 'tremendous. Spurs have got a European tradition. The benefits in Europe are enormous. Glory, glory nights are really what Tottenham Hotspur is all about. There is something about European football at Tottenham that no other competition can bring to the stadium.' Another consideration might well have been that a season in Europe could give Scholar the time to hold on to his fallen star and his shares.

Scholar went on to extol Terry Venables' managerial qualities. 'I have never wanted Terry Venables to leave this club. He will be offered a new contract. That is what I want. You only need to look at what he's done for Tottenham. He's won us the FA Cup.' Scholar then hinted that a one-year contract was about to be offered to the manager, worth £300,000 for the season's work.

Venables was scathing in his response. 'I would have thought,' he said, 'it was plain to everyone by now that unless I can get the equity, the absolute decision-making authority and the position I want within the club, I won't be staying at Tottenham. Not after all that has happened . . . There is no way I can continue to manage the club under the frustrations I have endured for the past three years. Not only have I not heard anything about a new contract since I told the chairman some weeks ago that I could not carry on as manager in the present circumstances, but the propaganda about Tottenham's offer is nothing more than a gimmick to deflect attention from the reality of the situation.' Venables concluded his diatribe by restating his desire to take over the club, and how he still expected his efforts to succeed: 'I am no longer representing a consortium. I am risking funding the takeover finance personally because I believe this great club is worth saving.'

Tottenham's last game of the season, away to Manchester United, went ahead on the Monday after the Cup Final. All the interest centred on the fact that the game was between two cup-winning sides, United having beaten Barcelona 2–1 to take the Cup-Winners' Cup in England's first season back in Europe. Venables delayed his trip north until the last moment, in order to continue his takeover talks. At Old Trafford, a crowd of 47,000 (incredibly, the second highest in the League that season), which had been assembling since 5 p.m., turned out to witness a rare sight, as Bryan Robson and Gary Mabbutt emerged from the tunnel together, holding their respective cups aloft. Before the game started, both sets of players mingled in the middle for photographs, and the crowd roared their appreciation at this display of shared triumph.

The 1–1 draw, in which John Hendry equalized Paul Ince's opener, was enough to lift Spurs into tenth position, a poor outcome given their wonderful start to the season, which had seen them lying third after the early games. But the reality of Tottenham's plight was there for everyone to see at Old Trafford. The question that arose was not whether the team would do well in Europe, but rather, how many of those representing Spurs that night would be around for the European campaign? As the season drew to its close, nothing had been resolved and everyone was left to wonder, what next?

23

London Pride

At the start of the season, there were few signs of the momentous events that were set to overtake football in general and Arsenal and Spurs in particular. That the great old rivals should win the two major domestic competitions in the same season, the first time it has ever happened, would have beggared belief back in August. Arsenal, after a disappointing season in 1989–90, were not widely tipped to win anything, let alone the League Championship, which, by common consent, was reserved once again for Anfield. But by the end of a season dominated as much by events off the pitch as on it, Liverpool looked more vulnerable than they had for thirty years, and no one could be entirely certain how long the 103-year-old Football League would survive in its present form. Despite all this, public interest in the game had significantly increased following the World Cup, attendances at matches and television viewing had continued to rise, and Manchester United's triumph in the Cup-Winners' Cup reminded the rest of Europe that English football was once again on the march.

When the FA deducted two points from Arsenal following the brawl at Old Trafford, even the fans thought that George Graham's side would struggle to make up the lost ground. When they slipped back further and went eight points behind Liverpool in November, it seemed as if the most Arsenal could expect was to consolidate their second position and qualify for the UEFA Cup. Yet here they were in May, basking in the widespread view that Graham was on his way to establishing a dynasty, which, according to Steve Coppell, could see Arsenal dominate English football. 'In terms of coaching, discipline and organization,' he said, 'they are the best team in the First Division.' The way everyone at Highbury reacted to the punishment meted out by the FA was admirable, particularly since after the brawl, other teams attempted to goad the side into further indiscretions.

George Graham claimed that opponents 'were told in their team talks to get us fired up'.

Graeme Souness argued that Liverpool had thrown the title away, that Arsenal had not really won it, but his opinion is not supported by the facts. Arsenal, if the two points had not been deducted, would have been nine points (or three wins) ahead at the finish, and they had beaten Liverpool twice. They had also lost only one League match all season. The truth is that whereas Liverpool were unable to rise above the blows of losing their manager and key players like Whelan and McMahon, the setbacks suffered by Arsenal simply made them more determined to succeed.

George Graham ascribes Arsenal's rise to pre-eminence to their professionalism. He, like many in football, uses the word as if he were a hospital consultant or a senior partner in a solicitors' practice. But football is not a profession. It is not even on the way to becoming one, when a player can be elevated to the status of First Division manager without diploma or experience. In an unprofessional business, it is to Graham's credit that his description of Arsenal as 'professional people' is accepted without query. In fact it is the incorporation of certain key qualities into the system which gives Graham the right to claim that, at Highbury at least, football is a profession.

The first, and perhaps the most important of these qualities is the sense of continuity at Highbury. After the success of 1989, the following season brought no trophies. Instead of tearing the team apart, which is the frequent reaction of a manager in such a situation, Graham, in the main, stuck by what he had got. Those players that did leave went because they did not see eye to eye with him or because they wanted a guarantee of first-team football. Purchases were made to strengthen the squad, like Andy Linighan, to fulfil a specific need, like Anders Limpar, or as direct replacements, like David Seaman for John Lukic. In his pursuit of Seaman, Graham displayed the kind of single-minded approach that should have alerted everyone to his determination to achieve the team he wanted. Moreover, transferred players have not proved him wrong by performing better away from Highbury. Only Lukic appears not to have lowered his standards.

Two of the big successes of the season, Kevin Campbell and David Hillier, are products of the youth policy. The youth team has now become a factory, turning out a staggering number of top-class performers. It is not only a model for other clubs, but could provide important lessons for the whole game. Of the sixteen players who won Championship medals in 1990–91, eight came from the youth team, an achievement unmatched since the days of Matt Busby at Manchester United.

The continuity that George Graham has established has its corollary in the playing strategy, which is designed for consistency. Consistency of performance is the cornerstone of Graham's idea of how his teams should play, and this can be seen throughout the club. Consistency, of course, is also the key to winning Championships. Graham realizes that the English First Division is a marathon that has to be won over thirty-eight games, and strength in depth is paramount. The criterion for greatness at Highbury is the League Championship. George Graham, steeped in the Arsenal tradition, is more aware of this than most, so he has built a squad that can cope with the long haul, rather than one which occasionally reaches the heights.

When looking forward to next season, Graham assessed the opposition his team would face: 'I think the League is going to be fantastic next season. Leeds, Manchester United and Tottenham [could do well] but the biggest question mark over these teams is consistency. Can they do it week in, week out?' Graham takes Liverpool's challenge for granted because he knows that dynasties do not disappear overnight, particularly when entrusted to a manager like Souness, who has been fashioned by his club every bit as much as Graham has been by Arsenal.

Before Arsenal faced Spurs in the Cup semi-final, Graham had said that Spurs could beat anyone 'on their day'. The same could be said for many of the teams in the First Division. This is anathema to Graham, who believes that Arsenal's 'day' should occur every time they play. For Graham, the significance of consistency is that it should be infinite.

'The beauty about being consistent,' he said, 'is that when you've achieved it, the desire for it has still got to be there. There are not many footballers who have achieved that, year in, year out. We've done it over the year. Now we have to do it over the years, plural.'

The third plank in Graham's quest for professionalism is resilience: the desire, in the manager's words, 'to throw off the image of southern softies', so that adversity becomes a launching pad for success. This is true not only in individual games, which Arsenal won when another team might have lost – the away game at Anfield, for instance, when they took a fearful pounding but held out and won with a superb goal on the break from Merson – but in the whole approach to the Championship. After the Manchester United brawl, the points deduction and the crushing defeat by United in the Rumbelows Cup, Arsenal's challenge would have faded away if they had not possessed the necessary toughness. Instead of folding, the team went undefeated for three months.

Paul Merson described how the players put the points loss into perspective: 'We made them up the next week. We won and they [Liverpool] drew.' David O'Leary pointed to the importance of the home game against Liverpool, which came four days after the Manchester United defeat, saying, 'We beat them well and pegged them back three points. I think that gave us a great incentive.' Similarly, when Tony Adams was lost to the side, the defence, if anything, was even more parsimonious, and Steve Bould emerged as a defender of guts and talent.

Stewart Houston saw Adams' absence as the turning-point of the season: 'That time when Tony Adams had his misfortune, a lot of people in the press were looking to say, "Well that's Arsenal going to take a dip". But it was the reverse situation in terms of the team. I must make a big mention of Bouldy. I thought he was exceptional. And Andy Linighan came into the team at that particular time. They maintained the momentum and kept the team together until Tony's return. That, if you are looking for a turning point, was a positive one because sometimes out of a lot of bad comes a lot of good.'

George Graham felt that there wasn't any one turning point: 'I would say that what won us the Championship was just the way we approached it, week in, week out.'

It was resilience also that got Arsenal over a faltering period towards the end of the season, after the semi-final defeat and one or two indifferent League performances. Whereas, in the previous season, Aston Villa had blown up completely when they lost form late in the campaign, Arsenal were able to come back and actually hit their best patch just when it mattered, particularly in awkward encounters against QPR and Sunderland.

In order to first achieve and then sustain the level of performance Graham expects, the club is organized in such a way as to give the manager absolute power over football matters. Most clubs revolve around one dominant individual: it could be the chairman, like Ken Bates at Chelsea or Doug Ellis at Aston Villa, or it could be the manager, like Brian Clough at Nottingham Forest or George Graham at Arsenal. In Graham's case this has resulted in him being given the kind of authority that others would envy. At Tottenham, according to one insider, 'Terry would like to do a Brian Clough but Irving would not let him.' The Spurs chairman admired George Graham because 'he loves Arsenal'. Perhaps Scholar was disappointed that he could not detect similar feelings emanating from his own manager. In fact, being an 'Arsenal man', even one with an undisputed record of success, might not have saved Graham after the Old Trafford incident. As chairman, Peter Hill-Wood recalled on the night the Championship was won: 'I don't think I would have fined George had I not had so much respect for him. I would have done something quite different.'

In turn, the authority exercised by Graham has encouraged a teacher–pupil relationship to develop between the manager and his players. Thus Graham works best with home-grown players or those plucked shrewdly from the lower divisions. Perhaps this is why he got so much pleasure out of coaching when he first started with the youth team at Crystal Palace. As far as 'star' names are concerned, only those who accept Graham as teacher and perform in the way required are acceptable. To Graham, the whole must be greater than the sum of its parts. This is why there have been occasional difficulties with Anders Limpar, the one free-spirit in the Arsenal ranks. When Limpar's goals dried up in the second half of the season, Graham continually exhorted him to shoot more often, and regularly expressed his frustration with the player.

'He's got world-class ability,' the manager said. 'He's easily got the hardest shot in the club, with both feet. When he told me he didn't score many goals, I told him, "It's got nothing to do with your physical make-up, it's your mental make-up. You've got to put yourself in goalscoring positions." It seemed that it took until the last match of the season for Limpar to get the message, and when he did, a hat-trick was the result.

Graham has drawn criticism during his time at Highbury for being too autocratic. However, this does not mean that he does not inspire loyalty from his players. It is not the kind of loyalty that Terry Venables achieves, which comes through a close personal relationship with players, but through the respect which Graham gains from success.

'I am a demanding person,' he said. 'I like people to reach standards I know they can attain, and when they do, I'm delighted for them.' Graham does not seem overtly concerned with his image. 'I think the affection thing is still not there,' he has said of his relationship with the fans. 'That's probably partly my fault, I don't build myself up enough. I'm not a great milker of admiration. The best is to get the respect of your peers. I think the affection could be improved.'

Many of the players at Highbury feel that they owe their success to Graham, who sticks by them whatever the opinions of anyone else. Players who have arrived from lesser clubs, like Perry Groves, Lee Dixon, Steve Bould and Alan Smith, have seen their careers reach levels of success they could only have dreamed about in their lower-division days. Thus any discipline that Graham imposes is accepted by players who understand that whatever the manager does, it is in the interests of the team and has nothing to do with personality clashes and ego problems which beset so many manager–player relationships.

If the Graham method of management, particularly in the area of motivation, is masterly, what of his tactics on the field? Are they innovatory or expedient? In fact, they are a bit of both. The sweeper system is much misunderstood in Britain. It is not just a case of playing an extra defender: the sweeper's game is as much about providing the springboard for attack as it is about defensive duties. Graham's Arsenal do not play a classic sweeper system when the extra defender is included in the side. Rather than the sweeper launching attacks through the middle, the Graham system is designed to lock up the heart of the defence (most English teams, as Doug Livermore said when describing the five-man midfield, like to hit the front two early), which allows the full backs to venture forward and test opponents along the flanks. Although the idea owes something to Alf Ramsey and his 'Wingless Wonders', it has been refined by Graham to the point where it can also be employed while operating with a conventional winger. Limpar, Groves and, later in the season, Merson all filled this role.

While other managers have flirted with five at the back (including Graham Taylor in England's game against the Republic of Ireland), George Graham was able to switch between the five-man defence and the more conventional flat back four with seemless ease. Graham not only changed systems as and when necessary, but was also able to leave players out and bring others in without any disruption to the pattern of play. Late in the season, the introduction of Kevin Campbell and David Hillier made all the difference to the team's push for the title.

Graham explained the reasoning behind these changes: 'There are times in the season – and you can never tell when it's going to be – when some of your better players, or more experienced players, are going to go off form. That's the beauty of having a squad. Whether it be experienced players or young players coming in, it adds impetus, fresh ideas and fresh legs to the team.' The converse was that no player was immune from being dropped, as Paul Davis and Michael Thomas discovered when Hillier made the breakthrough.

In certain games, Graham had no compunction about his team bypassing the midfield. As the season progressed, long punts to the front players, often begun when David Seaman rolled the ball out of his penalty area, became more prevalent. While some teams play little but the long ball, Graham knew that the best sides vary their tactics depending on conditions. To win the Championship, it is necessary to grind out results when performances are below par. This can happen because of loss of form, weather conditions, opposing teams looking to close games down or play an offside game – any number of different reasons.

344

Arsenal came unstuck only three times, twice in Cup games and once in the League. The Manchester United defeat can justly be dismissed as an aberration. The semi-final against Spurs was the only time all season when Arsenal were tactically out-thought, although Graham himself does not accept this view. He puts the defeat down to an exceptional first period by Spurs: 'Who would have imagined that Spurs would attack the way they did in those first twenty minutes? That was pure individual and team desire and drive and we didn't match it.' Thereafter, according to Graham, Arsenal 'were the better team'. This begs the question of what happened to the tactics in the first twenty minutes, during which time Paul Merson's attacking effectiveness was diminished as he played a more withdrawn role, yet Spurs scored twice.

Not having been designed as a team for one-off matches, Arsenal's FA Cup campaign never looked as solid as their assault on the League. They might have been knocked out of the competition by Leeds or even Cambridge before they eventually succumbed to Spurs. The Chelsea defeat appeared almost pre-ordained, the one game when Graham looked to be short of central defenders. The manager's explanation for the defeat – 'the only reason we lost was because of the injury to Steve Bould' – sounds plausible given Bould's heroics during Adams' absence. According to the manager, if the injury had not occurred, 'We could have come through the whole season undefeated, which is absolutely incredible.' (Interestingly, Chelsea intervened in the fortunes of both Arsenal and Spurs at crucial stages during the season. In addition to dishing out Arsenal's only League defeat, they knocked Spurs out of the Rumbelows Cup and assisted Arsenal by beating Liverpool on the penultimate Saturday of the season.)

So while there has been a degree of invention in Graham's tactics, pragmatism, and an understanding of what it takes to win the League, he has always been decisive. Because of this, flair has occasionally been lacking. This is not because Arsenal lack the necessary quality, but because it is secondary to Graham's main aim. He has always been critical of managers and coaches who come into the game to teach entertaining and attractive football: 'I want to do that, but I'm not going to do it to the detriment of winning anything.' Flair teams win cups, but rarely the League. Although flair has not been seen in abundance, there is no question that Arsenal possess their share of it. The 4–1 defeat of Chelsea early in the season, and the last game against Coventry, for instance, saw devastating attacking spells as good as anything seen in the First Division.

Versatility, attention to detail and a flexible approach to tactics have been significant factors in Arsenal's success. These qualities underlie those of continuity, consistency and resilience, which in turn have produced the 'professionalism' to which Graham aspires. All of these attributes will be needed in the 1991–92 season, when teams will be gunning for them as they did following the Championship win in 1989. In football, as Graham knows only too well, you can never stand still.

'Now we're at the top,' he said, 'if we can improve the team by 10 per cent, that would be wonderful. It's a bit difficult to buy a player who is 100 per cent better than who we've got. Players going out, players going in, with a 10 per cent plus – that's an improvement.'

As for the European Cup campaign, it provides Arsenal with the possibility of matching the earning power of the big Continental clubs and gives the fans the chance to see the best players in the world perform at Highbury. David O'Leary believes that the Championship win of 1991 was a greater achievement than 1989 precisely because of the European dimension: 'We've got another prize to go along with our medals and trophy. Most of the lads have never played in Europe and it's a great thing for them.'

For 1991–2, UEFA have revamped the format of the tournament, replacing the quarter-finals and semi-finals with a two-group league system. It may well be that Arsenal, designed for leagues rather than cups, will benefit from this change more than most, or would have done had the Football League not decided to revert to a First Division of twenty-two clubs playing forty-two games. A word of caution, though. The last time the club appeared in the European Cup, in 1971-2, there was an air of optimism about their prospects. After all, the team had just won the double, and to many fans looked invulnerable. Then they ran up against Johan Cruyff's Ajax side in the quarter-final and lost both games. No doubt the lessons of those painful defeats suffered by Graham the player will have been absorbed by Graham the manager. Winning the European Cup is certainly his priority next season and he is looking forward to it. Comforted in the knowledge that 'there are aspects to our game the Continentals would love to have.' Unsurprisingly, he will not be changing his *modus operandi*.

'It's largely a matter,' he says, 'of putting your own house in order. We will go in confidently working very hard as normal and hopefully, we will do well.'

If George Graham can succeed in his quest, and bring the European Cup to Highbury it will confirm his place among the great British managers of all time. In that event the board will surely be looking for a suitable sculptor and will be clearing a place in the marble hall for a new bust to take pride of place alongside that of Herbert Chapman.

While pre-season predictions that Arsenal would win a trophy were few and far between, expectations for Tottenham were high. Following the World Cup, it was thought that the combination of Gazza and Gary Lineker would lift a good team into the realms of greatness. And there was a 1 in the year. When the season started so well, not only in terms of results, but also in the way crowds everywhere flocked to watch the team, it looked as though the early promise was about to be realized.

The reasons for Spurs' failure to make an impact on the League, after such promising beginnings, had everything to do with the club's problems off the pitch. They affected all aspects of life at White Hart Lane, from the plc to the club and the team. In the first place, the financial constraints on Terry Venables, which had been there since the Waddle sale, meant that the manager was unable to add significantly to his squad during the close season, with the result that it lacked depth and was ill equipped to deal with the rigours of a League campaign: those times which George Graham pointed to, when even experienced players lose form. Moreover, with the directors and manager spending ever-increasing amounts of time on takeover talks and the transfer of Gazza, the team was placed on the back-burner.

For a long time the public position was that the financial problems could be kept away from the players, but this was surely nothing more than wishful thinking. Terry Venables admitted just before the Cup Final that it was only in the two weeks leading up to Wembley that he realized exactly how substantial an effect the financial disasters had had on the players. However much they understood that their wages would be paid, they would be less than human if they didn't worry about the situation. Gary Lineker's plea to 'sort this mess out' was a cry from the heart that could have come from anyone in the side.

The euphoria of *Italia 90*, and the exciting nature of the team, carried Spurs though the initial games. During this period the defence was as good as any in the division. But as winter began to take hold, the fun of summer was replaced by the bitter reality that the confidence that was so evident early on was only a mirage.

The turning point on the field was the Liverpool game at White Hart Lane in November. The defeat severely dented the team's self-belief. The manager blamed the loss on some bad decisions on the part of the match officials and said that he still did not know how good his team was in relation to Liverpool, as the result was artificial. Later, Erik Thorstvedt was more illuminating: 'Before, we were rock solid. I think we lost a lot of confidence there and we didn't really pick it up afterwards.'

Not having a squad to last the distance of a thirty-eight-game League season, Tottenham were really up against it when Gazza was injured and Gary Lineker lost his touch not long after the Liverpool match. 'In the early part of the season,' said Erik Thorstvedt, 'it was a war, and we battled and battled.' Against Leeds at Elland Road, for instance, Spurs had taken everything the Yorkshire side threw at them, then played their football, a feat they repeated against Sheffield United. Talking about the Leeds game, Thorstvedt continued: 'We stood up man for man, and then when Leeds tired we started to put passes together . . . If we could stand up to everything in the first half, we knew we had the skills to play and win in the second.'

Somehow, Liverpool knocked the stuffing out of this approach and the disastrous Christmas period followed, which brought dreadful defeats by Coventry and Southampton, and the sending off (and subsequent suspension) of Gazza during the loss to Manchester United.

The players, not to mention the fans, were further undermined when the probability of Gazza's sale to Lazio became public knowledge. Spurs had been built up as a two-man outfit, and perhaps the players themselves had come to believe it to some extent. Erik Thorstvedt told of his reaction when Mel Sterland of Leeds called Spurs a two-man team: 'That really annoyed me. I was just waiting for a chance to give him one when we played them at White Hart Lane, but it was difficult because you have to watch the ball.'

For all Thorstvedt's bravado, however, the fact was that, until the Cup Final, whenever either Lineker or Gascoigne was absent the team's resolve disappeared. Gazza in particular exerted as much of an influence off the pitch as he did on it. Before the semi-final and again at half-time, according to an only half-joking Terry Venables, he was so hyped up he gave the team talk. Steve Sedgley spoke of the Gazza behind the headlines: 'He's such a likeable lad, and he's grown up in the last couple of years. We have got the greatest respect for him, he's a lovely bloke. You have to see him on the training pitch to see how good a footballer he is. You wouldn't believe it, he's in a league of his own.'

Everywhere, the person in demand was Paul Gascoigne. Even Gary Lineker suffered from the national obsession. On the eve of the last League game of the season, Lineker returned to his native Leicester to publicize improvements to a local company's premises. There were any number of things the crowd could have asked him. Tottenham's prospects in the Cup Final perhaps, which was only a week away, or the plight of his home-town club, which needed to win its last game of the season to avoid an unprecedented drop into the Third Division. Older residents had never known the city so keyed up for a game of football, not even in the build up to Cup Finals. But no, what everyone wanted to know was what Gazza was really like.

Behind the scenes, and on occasion in full view of the world, the administration of the club was engaged in internecine strife. It was the rift between Irving Scholar and Terry Venables that probably had the greatest effect on the team. Scholar not only wanted to run the club, he wanted at least some input into the playing side as well. Venables, if money had been made regularly available to purchase players, might just have been able to live with this situation, but once the financial débâcle was revealed for all to see, the two became ever more estranged. Moreover, the fan who had taken over the boardroom with the promise of leading the club into a new era of success both on and off the field had lost his credibility, with his manager and the Spurs supporters. As one supporter succinctly put it: 'I think he is not good enough. If your money isn't on the table you can't do the business, and these days it's a business, not a sport.' When Venables began to believe he could actually take control of the club and oust Scholar as chairman, the differences between them became terminal, and when Scholar spoke of offering his manager a new contract after the Cup Final, Venables' reaction can only be described as one of scorn.

When Venables concentrated on coaching, his tactical know-how gave the players the chance to rise to the occasion of the big match. And when FA Cup ties came around, the team seemed to find that extra degree of commitment. Even then, disaster could have struck, as it almost did against Portsmouth and Notts County, two games in which Spurs went a goal down early on, but Gazza was so determined to succeed that he was always there to rescue them. But Gazza couldn't save Spurs every week, so sights had to be lowered from the League to the competition more readily associated with Tottenham, the FA Cup. Having reached the semi-final, Venables' tactical acumen came into its own. He produced plans that curtailed his opponents' attacking options and provided a platform for his flair players to express themselves. It was the one-off tactical challenge in which he had always revelled. With his plans laid, he could afford to spend more time in smoke-filled rooms, discussing takeovers and transfers, than out at the training ground talking tactics. It still remained for the players to carry out their allotted roles and, at last, rediscover their early-season battling qualities to win the Cup. For this they deserve all the praise that has been heaped upon them. The supporters, too, deserved the Cup win for their forbearance throughout the troubles. The final, when Gazza was lost and Spurs were 1–0 down, should have dispelled for good the idea that they were a one- or two-man team, and it may be, perversely, that the injury to Gazza actually helped the rest of the players concentrate their minds on the mountain they had to climb.

Although the Cup was won, the future of Spurs remained uncertain. Where Gazza would be playing when he returned from his horrific injury was also open to conjecture. As the season closed, the fans were calling for Scholar to leave and Venables to take over. But they should beware. Terry Venables, for all his coaching talent, is a restless individual. In many ways, one club, perhaps even football generally, is not big enough for him. Moreover, his elevation to the boardroom at QPR did not prevent him from taking the job at Barcelona when it was offered. On the other hand, Venables is adored by his players.

Gary Lineker expressed sentiments common to all those who have played for him, when he said, 'I have been fortunate to play under him. I think I've learned a great deal from him. Tactically, he is as astute as anyone. He was the man largely responsible for us beating Arsenal. I don't think he's been given the credit he deserves.'

This loyalty was reinforced when, to a man, the players supported Venables' takeover bid. It could just be that the challenge at Spurs really is of a magnitude that will consume all of his undoubted energy. This Spurs team, like most of its predecessors, came good in the Cup, but was not consistent enough to make a sustained impression on the League. Whoever brings the continuity so evident at Arsenal to White Hart Lane and begins to establish a tradition that goes beyond an attractive team and a reliance on numerology, will be the real saviour of Tottenham Hotspur.

Postscript

A Sweet Finish?

On Saturday 22 June, Terry Venables and the boss of Amstrad Electronics, Alan Sugar, called a press conference to announce that they had reached agreement with the board of Tottenham Hotspur and the Stock Exchange to purchase the shares of Irving Scholar and Paul Bobroff, and were assuming control of the club. If things went well, a rights issue was to follow, which would raise £3.75 million. This would put the total cost of the takeover at £7.5 million. In the new order, Sugar would become non-executive chairman of the plc with the task of 'getting the balance sheet into shape, while Venables would take over the role of managing director. Nat Solomon was to stay on as deputy chairman, Tony Berry would be the new chairman of the football club and, astonishingly, Irving Scholar and Paul Bobroff were to remain as directors of the football club. Sugar was the latest, and most illustrious, of Venables' seemingly endless supply of backers. The manager had finally wrested control from Irving Scholar, in a story that once again went through numerous twists and turns before the final act, including the eleventh hour re-emergence of Robert Maxwell.

After the Cup Final, Gazza's injury threw everything into confusion. Lazio, quite naturally, were not prepared to pay 17 billion lire (over £8 million) for a player who might never play again. Although agreement had been reached between the clubs on the sale at the late-night meeting in Rome on 26 April, that transaction was for a player who could spearhead the club's challenge in the 1991–2 season. Lazio's pursuit of Gascoigne had brought the club worldwide publicity and had propelled them into the elite of big-spending Italian clubs. The Gascoigne factor had worked for Lazio, even though he had never kicked a ball for them. They had not enjoyed such a high profile since the days of Chinaglia, and the fans were eagerly anticipating Gazza's impending arrival. Gian Marco Calleri recognized that to pull out at this stage, when the player was severely injured, might rebound on him and the club. Moreover, Calleri's personal affection for Gazza entailed 'family' commitments that were going to be fulfilled if possible. Nevertheless, the injury was so severe that the world-record transfer fee was out of the question. Calleri was prepared to continue talking, but the context was now completely different.

It had been agreed that Gazza would sign for Lazio prior to the match with Sampdoria on 26 May, provided he passed a medical. 'If I had said no,' Gascoigne said, 'then Spurs could have gone to the wall. I could never have that on my conscience.' After the Cup Final, the boot was on the other foot. From being the reluctant party, Spurs were now desperate to complete the transfer, while Lazio had understandably cooled somewhat. Nat Solomon suggested a new arrangement, under which Lazio paid half the transfer fee immediately, the rest to be forthcoming once the player was fit.

Calleri was interested, but there were a number of unresolved issues. What, for instance, would happen if Spurs were taken over in the interim? Moreover, if Gazza were unfit for a season, Lazio's likely replacement would be another foreign player. In order not to exceed the limit placed on the number of overseas players any one club is allowed in Italy, Gazza would have to remain registered with Spurs. Calleri eventually rejected Solomon's request for a down payment of half the money, but came back with a completely new arrangement. Lazio were prepared to pay a total of £4.8 million for Gascoigne, £750,000 straight away and the rest in instalments as Gazza recovered. If he failed to regain fitness, the money would be repaid to Lazio. This left the Spurs board with something of a dilemma. The Midland Bank had been promised the majority of the original £8 million transfer fee, but some £3 million would have been ploughed back into the club. The reduced amount now on offer would all have to go to the Midland, leaving nothing to strengthen the playing staff, let alone for finding a replacement for Gazza. On the other hand, if the offer were rejected there would be a huge hole in the club's projected cash flow. Caught between the devil and the deep blue sea, the Spurs regime took the least damaging of the alternatives and decided to accept Lazio's offer in principle.

The situation remained confused, however. Stories coming out of England suggested that the deal was complete, and Mel Stein said the transfer had been finalized 'in everything but registration'. Even Gazza confirmed the position when he told readers of his column in the *Sun* that he was on his way to Rome. 'It has been the hardest decision of my life to say goodbye to Terry Venables and the Tottenham players,' he said.

In Italy, the stories were gently denied. According to Lazio officials, negotiations were continuing but nothing had been signed. 'We are aware of Gascoigne's statement that he has signed,' said one. 'But from our point of view we are only offering Tottenham an option which is central on him spending his recovery time in Rome.' What the Italians failed to understand was that the Tottenham board was in no position to barter. The last thing Lazio expected was that Spurs, who had prevaricated throughout the original negotiations, were unconditionally about to accept Calleri's revised offer.

While the talks with Lazio continued, Nat Solomon was attempting to reschedule the debt to the Midland Bank. Having originally set a deadline of Friday 24 May, by which time the 17 billion lire should have been in Tottenham's hands, the bank now decided to give Solomon some breathing space. The decision to accept the reduced Lazio money provided the bank with some reassurance, while a season in Europe would ensure up-front television money, increased gate and advertising receipts, and the prospect of further riches if the later stages of the tournament were reached. Provided that a plan for long-term refinancing was seriously pursued, and the sale of further 'assets' not ruled out, the Midland was prepared to forgo its right to call in the overdraft at any time and give Spurs twelve months to reduce the borrowings.

In the euphoria of the moment, Nat Solomon claimed that the existing board could take its time over any bids for the club: 'No one will be invited to rescue Spurs, because no rescue is required,' he said. 'The whole climate has changed dramatically for us in the last few days. There is no financial crisis here.' David Buchler, a financial consultant and insolvency expert, was taken on as a non-executive director, and it seemed that Solomon was serious in his intention of going it alone.

Meanwhile, Terry Venables had still not given up hope of buying the club. Showing remarkable tenacity, he simply refused to take no for an answer. As backers pulled out, new ones were found and his bid continued with dogged determination. On the night before the Cup Final, Irving Scholar had offered to sell his shares to Venables, but the risk of the Midland refusing to back the deal had been too great for Venables to take. Now, out of the blue, came an approach from a backer of substance, Alan Sugar. Sugar's company, Amstrad, had made a bid to become Spurs' first sponsors back in 1984, but had been rejected because the offer was not high enough. Later, Terry Venables appeared in a testimonial advertisement for Amstrad, extolling the virtues of the company's hi-fi range. Now Sugar, who was reputed to possess a personal fortune of over £100 million, emerged as the front runner in the takeover stakes.

Alan Sugar made it clear that he was not entering into ownership of Tottenham as a philanthropist. In March, he had sold some of his shares in Amstrad for £34 million. When asked what he would be doing with the money, he replied: 'It will be invested in commercial property . . . What I am buying is cheap and unrepeatable.' Whether he was referring to Spurs or not, it signalled his intention to embark on some sort of spending spree. Despite his vast wealth, however, Sugar was only prepared to guarantee the same amount that Venables could raise, which was the £3.75 million the manager had offered for Scholar and Bobroff's shares through his company Edennote in April. Venables found over £1 million himself, but £2 million was borrowed from a finance company called Norfina. This meant that Venables' investment, which was again made through Edennote, had to produce a return in order to service the £2 million loan. The new regime would of necessity be lean and hungry and would be forced to put business considerations before any sentimental attachments.

The Venables–Sugar bid was confirmed to the Stock Exchange on 10 June. It involved an offer to buy the shares of Irving Scholar and Paul Bobroff immediately for 70p each, thereby acquiring a 37 per cent stake in the company. Under Stock Exchange regulations, a similar bid would have to be made to all shareholders. If they all accepted the offer, it would take up all the money available to Venables, and all Sugar was prepared to commit. This would leave nothing for the team, and club income would be siphoned off to repay the Midland. Most importantly, it meant that Gazza, and perhaps others, would have to be sold. The fewer shareholders that sold out, the more money would be available to the club, hopefully enough to underwrite a rights issue, which could raise anything up to £3.75 million.

When the formal offer was sent out to shareholders it emphasized this point. It said, 'Mr Sugar and Edennote intend to underwrite part of the rights issue to the extent that their funds have not been applied in satisfying acceptances under the Offer.'

Sugar himself said, 'We wish to pour most of our money into the club, and we don't want to pour any more money into buying other people's shares.' Tony Berry gave an undertaking not to sell his 7.8 per cent stake, which at a stroke saved Venables and Sugar £500,000. His reward would be the chairmanship of the football club.

The next day, Robert Maxwell was back. Before the AGM in February, Nat Solomon had written to Maxwell to find out if he was still interested in pursuing the deal he had struck with Irving Scholar the previous summer. When Maxwell told him that he was unable to do anything because of the Football League regulations concerning multiple ownership of clubs, Solomon assumed that the deal was inoperative, and announced his conclusion to the AGM. As the season ended with the chairman coming under pressure from the Midland, Solomon, with prompting from Scholar, persuaded the board to contact Maxwell one more time. This time the response was positive.

Harry Harris, the chief football writer of the *Daily Mirror*, was on the other side of the world covering England's tour of Australia, New Zealand and Malaysia. When Maxwell decided to move, Harris was hurriedly recalled to London to cover the story. On 13 June, the *Mirror* ran Harris's piece revealing the details of Maxwell's renewed interest. He was now offering to underwrite a rights offer, but not the one which had been agreed with Irving Scholar the previous summer. The share price then, £1.30, was only a distant memory. Maxwell now valued the shares at 90p each. None the less, it was a considerable increase on the Venables–Sugar bid. Furthermore, Maxwell would not seek a place on the board but would be a 'passive investor'. He also promised that under his patronage, Gazza would stay at Spurs. In a statement, he said: 'I have been re-invited by the Spurs directors to become involved in a new issue of shares, and you can expect me to respond positively.' In a sideswipe at his opposition, Maxwell continued: 'As for Mr Venables, Mr Sugar is the fifth pair of knickers he has tried on. And none of them seem to fit.'

The following day, Maxwell agreed in principle to sell Derby for £4 million, and three days later disposed of his holdings in Manchester United and Reading. The way was now clear for the final battle for control of Tottenham: Sugar (and Venables) v. Maxwell (and Scholar). Before the board could consider the two bids, they were reminded that Venables had other options. Winning the Cup, particularly under such adverse circumstances, had raised Venables' profile once again among the big clubs on the Continent. Juventus, who had failed to qualify for Europe for the first time in twenty-nine years, were trying to tempt back their ex-coach, Gianni Trapattoni, who had brought them so much success in the Platini era. Trapattoni, though, was under contract for another year to Internazionale, so Juventus thought about making a one-season offer to Venables, who immediately expressed interest. Whether it was genuine or designed to bring further pressure on the Tottenham board is impossible to say. Certainly, Venables wanted to coach in Italy – 'For me a one-season contract is no problem. It gives me the chance to be involved in Italian soccer at the top level and maybe win something like I did with Tottenham' – and had been in awe of the £1,000,000-a-year salary Johan Cruyff was being paid by Barcelona. Juventus, however, managed to reach agreement with Inter, and Trapattoni returned to Turin. Meanwhile, it was reported (and later denied) that Venables was approached by Bernard Tapie, president of Marseille. Again Venables said he was interested, and again the pressure was turned up on the Spurs board.

On the day Maxwell announced he had disposed of his shares in Manchester United and Reading, the Tottenham Independent Supporters' Association complained to the Football League that

Maxwell would still be breaking League rules by bidding for Spurs, since his son, Kevin, was in charge at Oxford. 'We urge you,' the letter concluded, 'not to allow Robert Maxwell to have any involvement in Tottenham until he and his family/associates have disposed of their interests in all other clubs.'

The overwhelming public faith in Venables and Sugar was touching, but had little foundation in reality. The Maxwell bid, for instance, would have brought in more money (although his intervention did cause Sugar and Venables to raise their offer to 75p a share); it was also the only offer that stipulated that Gazza would stay.

This cut no ice with TISA. The organization's spokesman, Steve Davies, said, 'If the supporters had a choice, we would rather have Venables and Sugar than Gazza, Maxwell and Scholar. If that's the choice, then it's no contest. One safeguards the future of the club, the other doesn't.'

While the public saw Venables and Sugar as some sort of benefactors, the truth is that their bid was based on business considerations, in Venables' case for the pressing reason of a £2 million loan from the finance company, Norfina. Terry Venables had been careful to take public opinion along with him and had succeeded in projecting himself as someone who really cared for 'this great club', and who was working 'round the clock' to save it. Irving Scholar, on the other hand, who was undoubtedly a real fan (when Spurs were relegated in 1977 he saw forty-one of the forty-two League games and only missed the away match at Hull on a Tuesday evening because he was tricked into attending a dinner party), was seen as the businessman who not only got it disastrously wrong, but was trying to save himself by bringing in someone who was, despite his business acumen, even worse.

Thus the most pressing consideration for TISA, the rest of the fans and, eventually, the board, was that if Maxwell came in, the club would lose Venables as its manager and leave Irving Scholar, one of the architects of the débâcle, in charge. Such a turn of events might be followed by mass disaffection, particularly among season-ticket holders, whose revenue was now desperately needed. Season-ticket prices had already been increased for 1991–2, to widespread protests.

Morris Keston, who has not missed a home match since 1951, was outraged: 'It's a disgrace. For me and many like me, this club has been our lives. But we are kept in the dark while several of the directors fight to look after their own interests. Why should we pay advance money when there is a good chance that we won't even have a club in a few months' time?'

Another fan spoke for many when she said, 'This indecent haste to part the supporters from their cash is just a further demonstration of the current board's contempt for the supporters.'

In the end personality won over price. The dream ticket of Sugar and Venables was preferred because, according to one source: 'Nobody here wanted to work for Maxwell.' It was this antipathy that finally convinced Solomon that the board should accept the Venables–Sugar bid. Irving Scholar was now isolated. When, the next day, the *Daily Mirror* announced that Maxwell was withdrawing his offer, Scholar finally relented and agreed to sell his shares to the Venables–Sugar partnership. The last rites were to take place on Friday 21 June, at the offices of Spurs' merchant bank, Henry Ansbacher. As the meeting would be a formality, the main participants in the drama were not required to attend, and Irving Scholar left for Monaco.

The Friday meeting concluded the sale, but not before another dramatic intervention from Robert Maxwell. He phoned the Ansbacher office as the meeting was under way to announce that he had reached agreement with Irving Scholar and Paul Bobroff to buy their shares. Pandemonium broke out. Nat Solomon, it was reported, went white. Alan Sugar was at Amstrad headquarters in Brentwood, but immediately left for London once he was told of what was going on. Terry Venables also dropped everything and headed for the City. Scholar was contacted in Monaco by phone, while Maxwell sent a team of financial advisers from his merchant bank, Hill Samuel, to Ansbacher's to confirm the new arrangements. It was no use though. Maxwell had reputedly increased the price he was offering for the shares, but Bobroff caved in under pressure from Sugar, and it was explained once more to Scholar that his position really was untenable, that no one would accept either him or Maxwell and that the only course open to him was to sell to Venables and Sugar. At last, just after midnight, Scholar agreed, and Terry Venables and Alan Sugar became Tottenham's major shareholders, but only after accepting Scholar's condition that he keep a token number of shares and remain as a director of the football club.

When asked why he was successful this time, Venables replied: 'It was the situation. The mere fact that Maxwell came in made it a him-or-him decision. They had to make one, and we had popular support.'

When Venables and Sugar announced their takeover on 22 June, their tone was markedly cautious. Whereas Venables had made some very public commitments about keeping Gascoigne – his original Edennote bid contained the clause that 'P. Gascoigne esq.' should not be sold – he now seemed lukewarm, claiming that he did not know whether the club could hang on to Gazza or not. This was an unexpected turnaround. Both Venables and Sugar talked tough, claiming that they would be running Spurs as a business.

The previous day, Venables had pointed to the difference he would make: 'I'm good at football, not property developing or selling pork sausages like some of the other chairmen. Not that there is anything wrong with those trades, but more and more modern-day chairmen seek a degree of involvement in their club for which they are not strictly experienced. I know every job there is to be done. I'd have a coach, someone who looks after the team, and is off home by 1 p.m. and I'd do the rest.'

Venables will certainly need to utilize all this knowledge in his new position. With the mountain of debt still to be tackled and the level of borrowing Venables is now committed to through Edennote, success on the field, and the revenue it brings, is imperative.

The legal status of the Gascoigne transfer was unclear, but Spurs could hardly now withdraw the right of the player to decide, having done everything possible to sell him. When Venables had gone to see Mel Stein before the Cup Final, he had learned of the incredible personal terms Gazza was being offered and was forced to admit privately that the deal was a good one for both the player and Tottenham. The subsequent Lazio offer accepted by the board, however, did not seem so good. But there was little Venables could do beyond seeking to negotiate better terms. The priority now was to raise cash to reduce borrowings and stabilize the overall financial position. If that meant Gascoigne or anyone else had to go, then so be it.

It remains to be seen whether the new owners of Spurs can repay the faith shown in them by the club's supporters. The third regime at White Hart Lane in a decade faces formidable obstacles. For football as a whole, as well as for Spurs, it is to be hoped they succeed.

Statistics

Arsenal 1990–91

by Joe Waters

League Matches

#	DATE		OPPONENTS	H/T	RES	ATT	PSTN	1	2	3	4	5
1	AUG	25	Wimbledon	0–0	3–0	13,733	—	Seaman	Dixon	W'burn	Thomas	Bould
2		29	**Luton**	1–1	2–1	32,723	—	Seaman	Dixon	W'burn	Thomas (1)	Bould
3	SEP	1	**Spurs**	0–0	0–0	40,009	3	Seaman	Dixon	W'burn	Thomas	Bould
4		8	Everton	0–0	1–1	29,919	5	Seaman	Dixon	W'burn	Thomas	Bould
5		15	**Chelsea**	0–0	4–1	41,516	2	Seaman	Dixon (1p)	W'burn	Thomas	Bould†
6		22	Nottm Forest	1–0	2–0	26,013	2	Seaman	Dixon	W'burn	Thomas	Bould
7		29	Leeds	1–1	2–2	30,085	2	Seaman	Dixon	W'burn*	Jonsson	Bould
8	OCT	6	**Norwich**	2–0	2–0	36,048	2	Seaman	Dixon	W'burn	Jonsson	Bould
9		20	Man Utd	1–0	1–0	47,232	2	Seaman	Dixon	W'burn	Thomas	Bould
10		27	**Sunderland**	0–0	1–0	38,539	2	Seaman	Dixon (1p)	W'burn	Thomas	Bould
11	NOV	3	Coventry	0–0	2–0	15,336	2	Seaman	Dixon	W'burn	Thomas	Bould
12		10	Crystal Palace	0–0	0–0	28,181	2	Seaman	Dixon	W'burn	Thomas	Bould
13		17	**Southampton**	3–0	4–0	36,243	2	Seaman	Dixon*	W'burn	Thomas	Bould
14		24	QPR	0–1	3–1	18,555	2	Seaman	Dixon	W'burn	Thomas	Bould
15	DEC	2	**Liverpool**	1–0	3–0	40,419	2	Seaman	Dixon (1p)	W'burn	Thomas	Bould
16		8	Luton	1–0	1–1	12,506	2	Seaman	Dixon	W'burn	Thomas	Bould
17		15	**Wimbledon**	2–1	2–2	30,163	2	Seaman	Dixon	W'burn*	Thomas	Bould
18		23	Aston Villa	0–0	0–0	22,687	2	Seaman	Dixon	W'burn	Thomas	Bould
19		26	**Derby**	2–0	3–0	25,538	2	Seaman	Dixon	W'burn	Thomas	Bould
20		29	**Sheff Utd**	0–1	4–1	37,866	2	Seaman	Dixon (1p)	W'burn†	Thomas (1)	Bould
21	JAN	1	Man City	0–0	1–0	30,579	2	Seaman	Dixon	W'burn	Thomas	Bould
22		12	Spurs	0–0	0–0	34,753	2	Seaman	Dixon	W'burn	Thomas	Bould
23		19	**Everton**	0–0	1–0	35,349	1	Seaman	Dixon	W'burn	Thomas	Bould†
24	FEB	2	Chelsea	0–0	1–2	29,094	1	Seaman	Dixon	W'burn	Thomas	Bould*
25		23	**Crystal Palace**	2–0	4–0	42,512	1	Seaman	Dixon	W'burn	Thomas	Bould
26	MAR	3	Liverpool	0–0	1–0	37,221	1	Seaman	Dixon	W'burn	Thomas	Bould
27		17	**Leeds**	0–0	2–0	26,218	1	Seaman	Dixon	W'burn	Thomas	Bould
28		20	**Nottm Forest**	1–0	1–1	34,152	1	Seaman	Dixon	W'burn	Thomas	Bould
29		23	Norwich	0–0	0–0	20,131	2	Seaman	Dixon	W'burn	Rocastle†	Bould
30		30	Derby	1–0	2–0	18,397	1	Seaman	Dixon	W'burn	Campbell	Bould
31	APR	3	**Aston Villa**	1–0	5–0	41,868	1	Seaman	Dixon	W'burn	Hillier*	Bould
32		6	Sheff Utd	1–0	2–0	26,920	1	Seaman	Dixon	W'burn	Hillier	Bould
33		9	Southampton	0–0	1–1¹	21,200	1	Seaman	Dixon	W'burn	Hillier*	Bould
34		17	**Man City**	2–2	2–2	38,412	1	Seaman	Dixon†	W'burn	Thomas	Bould
35		23	**QPR**	0–0	2–0	42,393	1	Seaman	Dixon (1p)	W'burn	Hillier	Bould
36	MAY	4	Sunderland	0–0	0–0	22,606	1	Seaman	Dixon	W'burn	Hillier	Bould
37		6	**Man Utd**	2–0	3–1	40,229	1	Seaman	Dixon	W'burn	Hillier*	Bould
38		11	**Coventry**	2–1	6–1²	41,039	1	Seaman	Dixon	W'burn	Hillier	Bould

Rumbelows Cup

DATE		OPPONENTS	ROUND	H/T	RES	ATT	1	2	3	4	5
SEP	25	Chester	2 (1st leg)	0–0	1–0	4,135	Seaman	Dixon	W'burn	Hillier	Bould
OCT	9	**Chester**	2 (2nd leg)	3–0	5–0	22,902	Seaman	Dixon	W'burn	Hillier	Bould
	30	Man City	3	0–0	2–1	26,825	Seaman	Dixon	W'burn	Thomas	Bould
NOV	28	**Man Utd**	4	0–3	2–6	40,884	Seaman	Dixon	W'burn	Thomas	Bould

FA Cup

DATE		OPPONENTS	ROUND	H/T	RES	ATT	1	2	3	4	5
JAN	5	**Sunderland**	3	2–0	2–1	35,128	Seaman	Dixon	W'burn	Thomas	Bould
	27	**Leeds**	4	0–0	0–0	30,905	Seaman	Dixon	W'burn	Thomas	Bould
	30	Leeds	4 (rep)	0–0	1–1³	27,753	Seaman	Dixon	W'burn	Thomas	Bould
FEB	13	**Leeds**	4 (2nd rep)	0–0	0–0⁴	30,433	Seaman	Dixon	W'burn	Thomas	Bould
	16	Leeds	4 (3rd rep)	2–0	2–1	27,190	Seaman	Dixon (1)	W'burn	Thomas	Bould
	27	Shrewsbury	5	0–0	1–0	12,356	Seaman	Dixon	W'burn	Thomas (1)	Bould
MAR	9	**Cambridge**	6	1–0	2–1	42,690	Seaman	Dixon	W'burn	Thomas	Bould
APR	14	Spurs⁵	SF	1–2	1–3	77,893	Seaman	Dixon	W'burn	Thomas	Bould

1. Inc. o.g. (M. Adams). 2. Inc. o.g. (Peake). 3. aet; 1–1 after 90 mins. 4. aet. 5. At Wembley.

6	7	8	9	10	11	SUBSTITUTES
Adams	Rocastle	Davis	Smith (1)	Merson (1)	Limpar*	Groves (85*) (1)
Adams	Rocastle	Davis	Smith	Merson (1)	Limpar*	Groves (83*)
Adams	Rocastle	Davis	Smith	Merson*	Limpar	Groves (82*)
Adams	Rocastle	Davis	Smith*	Merson	Limpar	Groves (27*) (1)
Adams	Rocastle (1)	Davis	Groves*	Merson (1)	Limpar (1)	Campbell (75*); Linighan (76†)
Adams	Rocastle* (1)	Davis	Groves	Merson	Limpar (1)	Smith (67*)
Adams	Rocastle	Davis	Smith	Merson†	Limpar (2)	Hillier (68*); Groves (77†)
Adams	Rocastle	Davis (2)	Smith	Merson*	Limpar†	Groves (82*); Hillier (82†)
Adams	Rocastle*	Davis	Smith	Merson	Limpar (1)	Groves (76*)
Adams	Rocastle*	Davis	Smith	Merson	Limpar	Groves (68*)
Adams	Groves†	Davis	Smith*	Merson	Limpar (2)	Campbell (26*); O'Leary (68†)
Adams	O'Leary	Davis	Campbell	Merson*	Limpar†	Groves (83*); Smith (86†)
Adams	Groves†	Davis	Smith (2)	Merson (1)	Limpar (1)	O'Leary (70*); Campbell (77†)
Adams†	Groves*	Davis	Smith (1)	Merson (1)	Limpar	C'pbell (68*)(1); O'Leary (83†)
Adams	O'Leary	Davis	Smith (1)	Merson (1)	Limpar	
Adams	O'Leary	Davis	Smith (1)	Merson	Limpar*	Groves (88*)
Adams (1)	Groves	Davis	Smith	Merson (1)	Limpar	O'Leary (45*)
Linighan	Groves	Davis	Smith	Merson	Limpar*	Rocastle (71*)
Linighan	Rocastle*	Davis	Smith (2)	Merson (1)	Limpar†	Campbell (58*); O'Leary (86†)
Linighan	Groves*	Davis	Smith (2)	Merson	Limpar	Cole (85*); O'Leary (88†)
Linighan	O'Leary*	Davis	Smith (1)	Merson	Limpar†	Hillier (34*); Groves (78†)
Linighan	O'Leary	Davis*	Smith	Merson†	Limpar	Hillier (87*); Groves (87†)
Groves	O'Leary	Davis	Smith	Merson (1)	Limpar*	Campbell (83*); Hillier (87†)
Linighan	Groves	Davis	Smith (1)	Merson	Limpar†	Hillier (45*); Campbell (75†)
Linighan*	O'Leary (1)	Davis	Smith (1)	Merson† (1)	Campbell (1)	Pates (62*); Rocastle (82†)
Adams†	O'Leary	Hillier	Smith	Merson (1)	Campbell*	Rocastle (35*); Davis (86†)
Adams	O'Leary	Hillier	Smith	Merson	Campbell (2)	
Adams	O'Leary	Davis*	Smith	Merson†	Campbell (1)	Groves (74*); Limpar (74†)
Adams	O'Leary	Davis	Smith	Campbell	Limpar*	Groves (65*); Linighan (88†)
Adams	Rocastle†	Davis	Smith (2)	Merson	Limpar*	Groves (69*); Hillier (86†)
Adams	Campbell (2)	Davis (1)	Smith (2)	Merson†	Limpar	Groves (89*); Thomas (89†)
Adams	Campbell (1)	Davis	Smith (1)	Merson*	Limpar†	Groves (71*); Thomas (88†)
Adams	Campbell	Davis	Smith	Groves	Limpar†	Thomas (45*); Merson (69†)
Adams	Campbell (1)	Davis	Smith	Merson* (1)	Groves	Limpar (70*); O'Leary (88†)
Adams	Campbell	Davis	Smith	Merson* (1)	Limpar†	Groves (81*); O'Leary (81†)
Adams	Campbell	Davis	Smith	Merson	Groves*	O'Leary (80*)
Adams	Campbell	Davis	Smith (2 + 1p)	Merson	Limpar†	O'Leary (79*); Thomas (79†)
Adams	Campbell†	Davis	Smith (1)	Merson*	Limpar (3)	Linighan (70*); Groves (80†) (1)

	7	8	9	10	11	SUBSTITUTES
Adams	Rocastle*	Davis	Smith	Merson (1)	Groves	Campbell (75*)
Adams (1)	Rocastle*	Davis	Smith (1)	Merson (1)	Groves (2)	Campbell (74*); O'Leary (77)†
Adams (1)	Groves (1)	Davis	Smith	Merson	Limpar*	Campbell (73*)
Adams	Groves	Davis	Smith (2)	Merson	Limpar*	Campbell (73*)

	7	8	9	10	11	SUBSTITUTES
Linighan	Groves	Davis	Smith (1)	Merson	Limpar* (1)	O'Leary (68*)
Groves	O'Leary*	Davis	Smith	Merson	Limpar†	Hillier (68*); Campbell (88†)
Linighan	Hillier	Davis	Smith	Merson	Limpar (1)	
Groves*	O'Leary	Davis	Smith	Merson	Limpar†	C'pbell (45*); Linighan (112†)
Linighan	O'Leary	Davis	Smith	Merson (1)	Campbell	
Adams	O'Leary	Hillier	Smith	Merson*	Campbell	Rocastle (88*)
Adams (1)	O'Leary	Hillier	Smith	Merson	Campbell (1)	Davis (45*)
Adams	Campbell	Davis	Smith (1)	Merson	Limpar*	Groves (70*)

Arsenal Appearances

LEAGUE		RUMBELOWS CUP		FA CUP	
Seaman	38	Seaman	4	Seaman	8
Dixon	38	Dixon	4	Dixon	8
W'burn	38	W'burn	4	W'burn	8
Bould	38	Bould	4	Thomas	8
Davis	36 + 1s	Adams	4	Bould	8
Merson	36 + 1s	Davis	4	Smith	8
Smith	35 + 2s	Smith	4	Merson	8
Limpar	32 + 2s	Merson	4	Davis	6 + 1s
Adams	30	Groves	4	Limpar	5
Thomas	27 + 3s	Thomas	2	O'Leary	5 + 1s
Campbell	15 + 7s	Rocastle	2	Campbell	4 + 2s
Rocastle	13 + 3s	Limpar	2	Adams	3
Groves	13 + 19s	Hillier	2	Groves	3 + 1s
O'Leary	11 + 10s	Campbell	0 + 4s	Hillier	3 + 1s
Hillier	9 + 7s	O'Leary	0 + 1s	Linighan	3 + 1s
Linighan	7 + 3s				
Jonsson	2				
Cole	0 + 1s				
Pates	0 + 1s				

Arsenal Goalscorers

LEAGUE		RUMBELOWS CUP		FA CUP	
Smith	22	Groves	3	Smith	2
Merson	13	Smith	3	Limpar	2
Limpar	11	Merson	2	Merson	1
Campbell	9	Adams	2	Campbell	1
Dixon	5			Thomas	1
Groves	3			Adams	1
Davis	3			Dixon	1
Thomas	2				
Rocastle	2				
Adams	1				
O'Leary	1				
own goals	2				

Arsenal Statistics

Attendance

	TOTAL	AVERAGE
Home League Attendance	701,236	36,970
Away League Attendance	485,148	25,534
Rumbelows Cup Attendance (home and away)	94,746	23,686
FA Cup Attendance (home and away)	284,348	35,543
Total	1,565,478	31,309

Highest Home Attendance: v. Cambridge United (FA Cup Sixth Round)	42,690
Highest Away Attendance: v. Man United	47,232

League and Cup Record

League Position: Champions

	P	W	D	L	F	A	PTS
Home Record	19	15	4	0	51	10	49
Away Record	19	9	9	1	23	8	34*
Total	38	24	13	1	74	18	83

* Arsenal deducted two points

Rumbelows Cup: Fourth Round
FA Cup: Semi-Final

Statistics

Tottenham Hotspur 1990–91

By Graham Betts

League Matches

#	DATE	OPPONENTS	H/T	RES	ATT	PSTN	1	2	3	4	5
1	AUG 25	**Man City**	1–1	3–1	33,501	—	Thorstvedt	Bergsson	Hauwe	Sedgley	Howells
2	28	Sunderland	0–0	0–0	30,204	—	Thorstvedt	Bergsson	Hauwe	Sedgley	Howells
3 SEP	1	Arsenal	0–0	0–0	40,009	6	Thorstvedt	Bergsson	Hauwe	Sedgley	Howells
4	8	**Derby**	1–0	3–0	29,614	4	Thorstvedt	Bergsson	Hauwe	Sedgley	Howells
5	15	Leeds	0–0	2–0	31,342	3	Thorstvedt	Bergsson	Hauwe	Sedgley	Howells (1
6	22	**Crystal Palace**	1–0	1–1	34,659	3	Thorstvedt	Bergsson	Hauwe	Sedgley	Howells
7	29	**Aston Villa**	1–1	2–1	34,939	3	Thorstvedt	Bergsson*	Hauwe	Sedgley	Howells†
8 OCT	6	QPR	0–0	0–0	21,405	3	Thorstvedt	Walsh	Hauwe	Sedgley	Howells
9	20	**Sheff Utd**	0–0	4–0	34,612	3	Thorstvedt	Thomas	Hauwe	Sedgley	Howells
10	27	Nottm Forest	0–1	2–1	27,347	3	Thorstvedt	Thomas	Hauwe	Sedgley*	Howells (2
11 NOV	4	**Liverpool**	0–1	1–3	35,003	3	Thorstvedt	Bergsson	Hauwe	Sedgley	Howells
12	10	**Wimbledon**	2–2	4–2	28,763	3	Thorstvedt	Thomas	Hauwe*	Sedgley†	Howells
13	18	Everton	1–1	1–1	23,716	3	Thorstvedt	Thomas	Hauwe	Sedgley	Howells (1
14	24	**Norwich**	1–1	2–1	33,942	3	Thorstvedt	Thomas	Hauwe	Sedgley	Howells
15 DEC	1	Chelsea	0–2	2–3	33,478	4	Thorstvedt	Thomas	Hauwe	Tuttle*	Howells
16	8	**Sunderland**	0–2	3–3	30,431	3	Thorstvedt	Thomas	Hauwe	E'burgh*	Howells
17	15	Man City	1–0	1–2	31,236	4	Thorstvedt	Thomas	Hauwe	Sedgley	Howells†
18	22	**Luton**	1–1	2–1	27,007	4	Thorstvedt	Thomas	Hauwe	Sedgley	Howells
19	26	Coventry	0–0	0–2	22,731	5	Thorstvedt	Thomas	Hauwe	Sedgley*	Howells
20	29	Southampton	0–1	0–3	21,405	5	Thorstvedt	Thomas	Hauwe	Sedgley	Howells*
21 JAN	1	**Man Utd**	1–1	1–2	29,399	6	Thorstvedt	Thomas	Hauwe	Sedgley*	Howells
22	12	**Arsenal**	0–0	0–0	34,753	6	Thorstvedt	Thomas	E'burgh	Fenwick	Howells
23	20	Derby	1–0	1–0	17,747	6	Thorstvedt	Fenwick	E'burgh	Sedgley	Howells
24 FEB	2	**Leeds**	0–0	0–0	32,253	6	Thorstvedt	Fenwick	Hauwe	Sedgley	Nayim*
25	23	Wimbledon	0–1	1–5	10,500	8	Thorstvedt	Bergsson (1)	E'burgh	Sedgley	Nayim*
26 MAR	2	**Chelsea**	1–1	1–1	26,168	8	Thorstvedt	E'burgh	Hauwe	Sedgley	Nayim
27	16	Aston Villa	0–2	2–3	32,638	9	Thorstvedt	E'burgh†	Hauwe	Sedgley	Thomas
28	23	**QPR**	0–0	0–0	30,860	8	Thorstvedt	E'burgh	Thomas	Sedgley	Nayim†
29	30	**Coventry**	1–2	2–2	29,033	8	Thorstvedt	E'burgh	Hauwe	Sedgley*	Nayim (2
30 APR	1	Luton	0–0	0–0	11,322	8	Thorstvedt	Thomas	Hauwe	Tuttle	Nayim
31	6	**Southampton**	2–0	2–0	24,291	8	Thorstvedt	E'burgh	Hauwe	Sedgley	Thomas
32	10	Norwich	1–1	1–2	19,014	8	Walker	Howells	Hauwe†	Sedgley	Thomas
33	17	Crystal Palace	0–1	0–1	26,285	8	Thorstvedt	Thomas	Hauwe*	Sedgley	Nayim
34	20	Sheff Utd	0–0	2–2	25,706	8	Thorstvedt	E'burgh (1)	Thomas	Sedgley	Howells
35	24	**Everton**	1–1	3–3	21,675	9	Thorstvedt	E'burgh	Thomas	Nayim (1)	Howells
36 MAY	4	**Nottm Forest**	0–1	1–1	30,891	9	Thorstvedt	E'burgh	Hauwe*	Sedgley	Howells
37	11	Liverpool	0–1	0–2	36,192	11	Thorstvedt	E'burgh	Hauwe	Sedgley	Howells*
38	20	Man Utd	0–1	1–1	46,791	10	Thorstvedt	E'burgh	Fenwick	Sedgley	Howells

Rumbelows Cup

DATE	OPPONENTS	ROUND	H/T	RES	ATT	1	2	3	4	5
SEP 26	**Hartlepool**	2 (1st leg)	2–0	5–0	19,760	Th'stv't	E'burgh*	Hauwe	Sedgley	Howells
OCT 9	Hartlepool	2 (2nd leg)	1–0	2–1	9,700	Dearden	Thomas	E'burgh	Sedgley	Howells
31	**Bradford City**	3	2–1	2–1	25,451	Th'stv't	Thomas	Hauwe	Sedgley	Howells
NOV 27	Sheff Utd	4	0–0	2–0	25,852	Th'stv't	Thomas	E'burgh	Sedgley*	Howells
JAN 16	Chelsea	5	0–0	0–0	34,178	Th'stv't	Thomas*	E'burgh	Fenwick	Howells
23	**Chelsea**	5 (rep)	0–1	0–3	35,861	Th'stv't	Fenwick*	E'burgh	Samways†	Howells

FA Cup

DATE	OPPONENTS	ROUND	H/T	RES	ATT	1	2	3	4	5
JAN 5	Blackpool	3	0–0	1–0	9,563	Th'stv't	Fenwick	E'burgh	Samways	Howells
26	**Oxford Utd**	4	2–1	4–2	31,665	Th'stv't	Fenwick	Hauwe	Nayim*	Howells
FEB 16	Portsmouth	5	0–1	2–1	26,049	Th'stv't	E'burgh	Hauwe	Sedgley	Nayim
MAR 10	**Notts County**	6	0–1	2–1 [1]	29,686	Th'stv't	E'burgh	Hauwe	Sedgley	Nayim*
APR 14	Arsenal [2]	SF	2–1	3–1	77,893	Th'stv't	E'burgh	Hauwe	Sedgley	Howells
MAY 18	Nottm Forest [3]	F	0–1	2–1 [4]	80,000	Th'stv't	E'burgh	Hauwe	Sedgley	Howells

1. Inc. o.g. (Short).   2. At Wembley.   3. At Wembley.   4. aet; 1–1 after 90 mins. Inc. o.g. (Walker).

6	7	8	9	10	11	SUBSTITUTES
Mabbutt	Stewart	Gascoigne (1)	Nayim	Lineker (2)	Allen*	Samways (45*)
Mabbutt	Stewart*	Gascoigne	Nayim†	Lineker	Allen	Walsh (87*); Samways (87†)
Mabbutt	Stewart	Gascoigne*	Nayim	Lineker	Allen	Thomas (88*)
Mabbutt	Stewart*	Gascoigne (3)	Nayim†	Lineker	Allen	Walsh (70*); Samways (70†)
Mabbutt	Stewart	Gascoigne	Nayim	Lineker (1)	Allen	
Mabbutt	Stewart	Gascoigne (1)	Nayim	Lineker	Allen	
Mabbutt	Stewart	Gascoigne	Nayim	Lineker (1)	Allen (1)	Thomas (45*); Walsh (45†)
Mabbutt	Stewart*	Gascoigne	Nayim†	Lineker	Allen	Thomas (81*); Samways (81)†
Mabbutt	Stewart	Gascoigne*	Nayim (1)	Walsh (3)	Allen	Moncur [77*]
Mabbutt	Stewart	Gascoigne	Nayim	Lineker	Allen	Walsh (67*)
Mabbutt	Stewart	Gascoigne	Nayim	Lineker (1p)	Allen	Thomas (45*); Walsh (45†)
Mabbutt (1)	Stewart (1)	Gascoigne	Nayim	Lineker (1)	Allen	E'burgh (45*); Walsh (77†) (1)
Mabbutt	Stewart	Gascoigne	Nayim	Lineker*	Allen	Walsh (86*)
Mabbutt	Stewart	Gascoigne	Nayim	Lineker (2)	Allen	
Mabbutt	Stewart	Gascoigne (1)	Nayim†	Lineker (1)	Allen	E'burgh (45*); Walsh (63†)
Mabbutt	Stewart†	Gascoigne	Nayim	Lineker (1)	Allen	Walsh (45*) (2); Samways (83†)
Mabbutt	Stewart	Gascoigne (1)	Nayim*	Lineker	Walsh	Allen (66*); Samways (85†)
Mabbutt	Stewart (2)	Gascoigne	Nayim	Lineker†	Walsh*	Allen (70*); Samways (85†)
Mabbutt	Stewart	Gascoigne	Allen	Lineker	Walsh†	Samways (59*); Nayim (59†)
Mabbutt	Stewart	Samways	Nayim†	Lineker	Allen	Bergsson (50*); Walsh (58†)
Mabbutt	Stewart	Gascoigne	Nayim	Lineker (1p)	Allen	Moran (68*)
Mabbutt	Stewart	Gascoigne	Walsh	Lineker	Allen	
Nayim*	Stewart	Samways	Walsh	Lineker (1)	Allen†	Thomas (75*); Hauwe (86†)
Mabbutt	Stewart	Thomas	Walsh	Lineker	Allen	Samways (73*)
Mabbutt	Samways	Thomas	Moncur	Lineker	Allen	Gray (60*)
Mabbutt	Stewart	Gascoigne*	Gray†	Lineker (1p)	Allen	Thomas (71*); Moncur (71†)
Mabbutt	Stewart	Samways (1)	Moncur	Lineker*	Allen (1)	Gray (59*); Hendon (75†)
Mabbutt	Stewart	Samways	Gray*	Walsh	Allen	Walsh (60*); Moncur (70†)
Mabbutt	Stewart	Samways	Gray†	Walsh	Allen	Thomas (64*); Moncur (76†)
Mabbutt	Stewart	Samways	Moncur	Walsh	Allen	
Mabbutt	Stewart	Samways	Walsh	Lineker (2)	Allen	
Tuttle	Nayim	Gascoigne*	Walsh	Hendry (1)	Moncur	Garland (62*); Hendon (75†)
Mabbutt	Stewart	Gascoigne†	Samways	Walsh	Allen	Tuttle (35*); Hendry (55†)
Tuttle	Stewart	Nayim	Samways*	Walsh (1)	Allen	Bergsson (89*)
Mabbutt (1)	Stewart	Walsh†	Samways	Lineker*	Allen (1)	Sedgley (73*); Tuttle (76†)
Mabbutt	Nayim (1)	Gascoigne	Samways	Lineker	Allen	Walsh (18*)
Mabbutt	Stewart	Gascoigne	Samways	Lineker†	Allen	Walsh (45*); Hendry (58†)
Mabbutt*	Stewart	Walsh	Samways	Lineker†	Hendry (1)	Bergsson (52*); Thomas (61)†

6	7	8	9	10	11	SUBSTITUTES
Mabbutt	Stewart†	Gascoigne (3 + 1p)	Nayim	Lineker (1)	Allen	Thomas (71*); Walsh (71†)
Mabbutt	Stewart (2)	Moncur	Walsh	Samways	Allen	Gascoigne (60*); Nayim (70†)
Mabbutt	Stewart (1)	Gascoigne (1)	Nayim*	Lineker†	Allen	Moncur (63*); Walsh (63†)
Mabbutt	Stewart	Gascoigne (1)	Samways†	Lineker	Allen	Tuttle (28*); Walsh (70†) (1)
Mabbutt	Stewart	Samways†	Walsh	Lineker	Allen	Sedgley (69*); Nayim (69†)
Mabbutt	Stewart	Gascoigne	Walsh	Lineker	Allen	Sedgley (68*); Nayim (68†)

6	7	8	9	10	11	SUBSTITUTES
Mabbutt	Stewart (1)	Gascoigne	Moran	Lineker	Allen	
Mabbutt (1)	Stewart	Gascoigne (2)	Walsh	Lineker (1)	Allen	Sedgley (52*)
Mabbutt	Samways*	Gascoigne (2)	Thomas	Lineker	Allen	Gray (75*)
Mabbutt	Stewart	Gascoigne (1)	Thomas†	Lineker	Allen	Samways (64*); Walsh (64†)
Mabbutt	Stewart	Gascoigne* (1)	Samways†	Lineker (2)	Allen	Nayim (61*); Walsh (86†)
Mabbutt	Stewart (1)	Gascoigne*	Samways†	Lineker	Allen	Nayim (16*); Walsh (81†)

Tottenham Appearances

LEAGUE		RUMBELOWS CUP		FA CUP	
Thorstvedt	37	Howells	6	Thorstvedt	6
Mabbutt	35	Mabbutt	6	Mabbutt	6
Stewart	35	Stewart	6	Gascoigne	6
Allen	34 + 2s	Allen	6	Lineker	6
Sedgley	33 + 1s	Thorstvedt	5	E'burgh	5
Nayim	32 + 1s	E'burgh	5	Stewart	5
Lineker	32	Lineker	5	Hauwe	5
Hauwe	31 + 1s	Sedgley	4 + 2s	Sedgley	4 + 1s
Howells	29	Gascoigne	4 + 1s	Howells	4
Gascoigne	26	Thomas	4 + 1s	Allen	4
Thomas	23 + 8s	Samways	4	Samways	4 + 1s
Walsh	16 + 13s	Walsh	3 + 3s	Nayim	3 + 2s
E'burgh	14 + 2s	Hauwe	2	Fenwick	2
Samways	14 + 9s	Nayim	2 + 3s	Thomas	2
Bergsson	9 + 3s	Fenwick	2	Moran	1
Tuttle	4 + 2s	Dearden	1	Walsh	1 + 3s
Fenwick	4	Moncur	1 + 1s	Gray	0 + 1s
Moncur	4 + 5s	Tuttle	0 + 1s		
Gray	3 + 3s				
Hendry	2 + 2s				
Walker	1				
Hendon	0 + 2s				
Moran	0 + 1s				
Garland	0 + 1s				

Tottenham Goalscorers

LEAGUE		RUMBELOWS CUP		FA CUP	
Lineker	15	Gascoigne	6	Gascoigne	6
Gascoigne	7	Stewart	3	Lineker	3
Walsh	7	Lineker	1	Stewart	2
Nayim	5	Walsh	1	Mabbutt	1
Howells	4			own goals	2
Allen	3				
Stewart	3				
Hendry	2				
Mabbutt	2				
Bergsson	1				
E'burgh	1				
Samways	1				

Tottenham Statistics

Attendance

	TOTAL	AVERAGE
Home League Attendance	581,704	30,616
Away League Attendance	509,068	26,793
Rumbelows Cup Attendance (home and away)	150,802	25,133
FA Cup Attendance (home and away)	254,856	42,476
Total	1,496,430	29,929

Highest Home Attendance: v. Chelsea
   (Rumbelows Cup Sixth Round)   35,861
Highest Away Attendance: v. Man United   46,791

League and Cup Record

League Position: Tenth

	P	W	D	L	F	A	PTS
Home Record	19	8	9	2	35	22	33
Away Record	19	3	7	9	16	28	16
Total	38	11	16	11	51	50	49

Rumbelows Cup: Fifth Round
FA Cup: Winners

FOR THE BEST IN PAPERBACKS, LOOK FOR THE

In every corner of the world, on every subject under the sun, Penguin represents quality and variety – the very best in publishing today.

For complete information about books available from Penguin – including Puffins, Penguin Classics and Arkana – and how to order them, write to us at the appropriate address below. Please note that for copyright reasons the selection of books varies from country to country.

In the United Kingdom: Please write to *Dept E.P., Penguin Books Ltd, Harmondsworth, Middlesex, UB7 0DA.*

If you have any difficulty in obtaining a title, please send your order with the correct money, plus ten per cent for postage and packaging, to *PO Box No 11, West Drayton, Middlesex*

In the United States: Please write to *Dept BA, Penguin, 299 Murray Hill Parkway, East Rutherford, New Jersey 07073*

In Canada: Please write to *Penguin Books Canada Ltd, 2801 John Street, Markham, Ontario L3R 1B4*

In Australia: Please write to the *Marketing Department, Penguin Books Australia Ltd, P.O. Box 257, Ringwood, Victoria 3134*

In New Zealand: Please write to the *Marketing Department, Penguin Books (NZ) Ltd, Private Bag, Takapuna, Auckland 9*

In India: Please write to *Penguin Overseas Ltd, 706 Eros Apartments, 56 Nehru Place, New Delhi, 110019*

In the Netherlands: Please write to *Penguin Books Netherlands B.V., Postbus 195, NL-1380AD Weesp*

In West Germany: Please write to *Penguin Books Ltd, Friedrichstrasse 10–12, D-6000 Frankfurt/Main 1*

In Spain: Please write to *Alhambra Longman S.A., Fernandez de la Hoz 9, E-28010 Madrid*

In Italy: Please write to *Penguin Italia s.r.l., Via Como 4, I-20096 Pioltello (Milano)*

In France: Please write to *Penguin Books Ltd, 39 Rue de Montmorency, F-75003 Paris*

In Japan: Please write to *Longman Penguin Japan Co Ltd, Yamaguchi Building, 2-12-9 Kanda Jimbocho, Chiyoda-Ku, Tokyo 101*

Brian Epstein: The Man Who Made the Beatles   Ray Coleman

'An excellent biography of Brian Epstein, the lonely, gifted man whose artistic faith and bond with the Beatles never wavered – and whose recognition of genius created a cultural era, even though it destroyed him' – *Mail on Sunday*

A Thief in the Night   John Cornwell

A veil of suspicion and secrecy surrounds the last hours of Pope John Paul I, whose thirty-three day reign ended in a reported heart attack on the night of 28 September 1978. Award-winning crime writer John Cornwell was invited by the Vatican to investigate. 'The best detective story you will ever read' – *Daily Mail*

Among the Russians   Colin Thubron

One man's solitary journey by car across Russia provides an enthralling and revealing account of the habits and idiosyncrasies of a fascinating people. 'He sees things with the freshness of an innocent and the erudition of a scholar' – *Daily Telegraph*

Higher than Hope   Fatima Meer

The authorized biography of Nelson Mandela. 'An astonishing read ... the most complete, authoritative and moving tribute thus far' – *Time Out*

Stones of Aran: Pilgrimage   Tim Robinson

Arainn is the largest of the three Aran Islands, and one of the world's oldest landscapes. This 'wholly irresistible' (*Observer*) and uncategoriz-able book charts a sunwise journey around its coast – and explores an open secret, teasing out the paradoxes of a terrain at once bare and densely inscribed.

Bernard Shaw   Michael Holroyd
Volume I 1856–1898: The Search for Love

'In every sense, a spectacular piece of work ... A feat of style as much as of research, which will surely make it a flamboyant new landmark in modern English life-writing' – Richard Holmes in *The Times*

FOR THE BEST IN PAPERBACKS, LOOK FOR THE

A CHOICE OF PENGUINS

The Russian Album   Michael Ignatieff

Michael Ignatieff movingly comes to terms with the meaning of his own family's memories and histories, in a book that is both an extraordinary account of the search for roots and a dramatic and poignant chronicle of four generations of a Russian family.

Beyond the Blue Horizon   Alexander Frater

The romance and excitement of the legendary Imperial Airways East-bound Empire service – the world's longest and most adventurous scheduled air route – relived fifty years later in one of the most original travel books of the decade. 'The find of the year' – *Today*

Getting to Know the General   Graham Greene

'In August 1981 my bag was packed for my fifth visit to Panama when the news came to me over the telephone of the death of General Omar Torrijos Herrera, my friend and host...' 'Vigorous, deeply felt, at times funny, and for Greene surprisingly frank' – *Sunday Times*

The Time of My Life   Denis Healey

'Denis Healey's memoirs have been rightly hailed for their intelligence, wit and charm ... *The Time of My Life* should be read, certainly for pleasure, but also for profit ... he bestrides the post-war world, a Colossus of a kind' – *Independent*

Arabian Sands   Wilfred Thesiger

'In the tradition of Burton, Doughty, Lawrence, Philby and Thomas, it is, very likely, the book about Arabia to end all books about Arabia' – *Daily Telegraph*

Adieux: A Farewell to Sartre   Simone de Beauvoir

A devastatingly frank account of the last years of Sartre's life, and his death, by the woman who for more than half a century shared that life. 'A true labour of love, there is about it a touching sadness, a mingling of the personal with the impersonal and timeless which Sartre himself would surely have liked and understood' – *Listener*